LEE and GRANT

Also by Gene Smith

Fiction
Where Are My Legions

Nonfiction
High Crimes and Misdemeanors:
The Impeachment and Trial of Andrew Johnson

Maximilian and Carlota:
A Tale of Romance and Tragedy

The Shattered Dream:
Herbert Hoover and the Great Depression

Still Quiet on the Western Front:
Fifty Years Later

When the Cheering Stopped:
The Last Years of Woodrow Wilson

The Life and Death of Serge Rubinstein

Co-Editor (with Jayne Barry Smith)
The Police Gazette

For Young Readers
The Hayburners

The Horns of the Moon:
A Short Biography of Adolf Hitler

The Visitor

The Winner

LEE and GRANT

A Dual Biography

GENE SMITH

McGraw-Hill Book Company

New York   St. Louis   San Francisco
Mexico   Hamburg   Toronto

Copyright © 1984 by Eugene O. Smith

ISBN 0-07-058473-7

LIBRARY OF CONGRESS CATALOGING IN PUBLICATION DATA
Smith, Gene.
    Lee and Grant, a dual biography.
    1. United States—History—Civil War, 1861–1865—
Biography. 2. Lee, Robert E. (Robert Edward), 1807–1870.
3. Grant, Ulysses S. (Ulysses Simpson), 1822–1885.
4. Generals—United States—Biography. 5. Presidents—
United States—Biography. 6. United States. Army—
Biography. 7. Confederate States of America. Army—
Biography. I. Title.
E467.S62   1984   973.7′092′2   [B]   83-25555
ISBN 0-07-058473-7

Book design by Elisabeth Brandfass

Napoleon says: "The personality of the general is indispensable, he is the head, he is the all of an army. The Gauls were not conquered by the Roman legions, but by Caesar. It was not before the Carthaginian soldiers that Rome was made to tremble, but before Hannibal. It was not the Macedonian phalanx which penetrated to India, but Alexander. It was not the French Army which reached the Weser and the Inn, it was Turenne. Prussia was not defended for seven years against the three most formidable European powers by Prussian soldiers, but by Frederick the Great."

To this list, as we shall see, may be added: It was not the valiant soldiers of the South who stood like a wall between Grant and Richmond, but Lee. And it was not the gallant men of the North who drove Lee from the Rapidan to Appomattox, but Grant.

Major General J.F.C. Fuller, British Army

CONTENTS

INTRODUCTION

THERE IS a theory that the United States needed its great war of brothers to weld in a terrible fire what had been and what might be, that the end of one epoch and the birth of another could not be accomplished peacefully; that the irrepressible conflict was preordained. Across a tiny strip of land, not much more than 100 miles in length and 50 in breadth, the rise of the middle class and the modern industrial state was decided. The Industrial Revolution won. Yesterday gave way to Tomorrow. Feudal Europe transported to the New World bowed to modern America. And leading the great armies that decided the issue were two generals who almost too perfectly, almost too precisely, exemplified the meaning of the causes they served. Neither could more exactly represent the South and the North: Lee the Christian soldier, the knight-crusader of ancient lineage at the head of his legions, the image of noblesse oblige whose example reached downward to inspire the men who followed him because he was the representative of all that was best in their doomed society of polished old ways and understood relationships; Grant the great soldier of no roots whose weakness for liquor was known to the least of his followers, who had risen from nowhere, from failure and griminess and physical labor to do heroic and magical things and to hold out to those who followed him the hope that they too—farmers, laborers, craftsmen, new immigrants—could in America attain great heights, rise in the world, lead men, grow rich, grow famous, become President.

One old, one young—as were the societies they represented—they met to end their war in what has been called the finest moment in American history, so perfectly played were the parts, so generous the men in their estimate of one another, so kindly and forgiving their actions and so simple and correct the fashion in which they went about their business. It was said of Lee that he was a born king among men. No one ever said that of plain Sam Grant. It was not his style—not *him*. But when their war was over the divine right of kings was no more. Grant had done away with it through his work and because of what he was. They knew it even thousands of miles from the battle-fields of the War Between the States, sensed it. When Grant came among the Europeans, wearing no gilded uniform and no High Victorian sash or plumed helmet or imperial robes, hundreds of thousands, millions, were proud to cheer him. In Asia other hundreds of thousands and millions came to him. The greatest fellow-soldier of his army, Sherman, said that Grant was of all men the typical American. He called no spirits from the deep, as Lee did. He never said he wanted to, either. Yet he did what the half-dozen generals who preceded him were unable to do: He brought Lee to fight his fight—Grant's fight—and he brought him to surrender, for all that he was, as we shall see, shy, physically unimpressive, quiet and modest. *Character is the first thing*, said the great military theorist Alfred von Schlieffen.

"In war," said Karl von Clausewitz, "everything is simple, but the simple is difficult." An interesting thought. It points to the fact that what we call military genius is far more a matter of temperament than intelligence. By its nature it cannot be tested before it is called into use. One can act the part of a great soldier while serving in junior rank and can be believed to be filled with promise, and believe it oneself, only to show and find out when given responsibility that greatness isn't there. Going to war is like opening the door to an unknown room, said Adolf Hitler, quite correctly. One never can be sure of what's in it. ("You never can tell what makes a general," Grant said. "Our war, and all wars, are surprises in that respect.")

As it is not dependent upon intelligence, so also is military genius not based upon technical knowledge. This is particularly true of the war with which this book largely concerns itself. All of the solders mentioned, both successes and failures, had gone to West Point. There they received the same instruction in the campaigns of Napoleon. That was about the limit of their knowledge. And during 1861–65 there were no secret weapons. The war was a series of duels between commanders. What is such a duel? "War is more of a struggle between two human intelligences than between two masses of armed men," says the military intellectual G.F.R. Henderson, "and the great general does not give his first attention to numbers, to armament, or to position. He looks beyond these." He looks at his enemy opposite number. That is where the answer to any questions he may care to ask will be found.

So it was with the pair of generals studied in this work. They were two men from backgrounds so different they could almost have lived in different countries in different centuries, yet they met in a common opposing effort and together have gone down in history. One thinks of Wellington when one thinks of Napoleon, but each did great things independent of the other, and their meeting at Waterloo was over in a matter of hours. Though it is true Montgomery looked at a portrait of Rommel every night in the desert before retiring, the two names do not come down to us linked with the same firmness. As for other duels, who but the specialist can tell us the name of von Manstein's 1940 opponent, or that of the Japanese who opposed MacArthur? Whom did Marlborough defeat at Blenheim, or von Moltke at Sadowa?

It is the strange marriage of the great general of the South and the great general of the North, a marriage lasting eleven months and involving every kind of warfare, attack, defense, pursuit, evasion, static, parry, thrust, siege, end, and mutual respect also, and personal enmity not at all, in which we find the subject of this book. Two men live sixty-three years each. They meet face to face four times. One is superbly handsome, the finest flower of a civilization now vanished. The other is short and awkward both physically and in manner, the type of fellow (according to H. L. Mencken) who would say to you: "Meet the wife." Yet the society that one symbolizes is narrow and provincial, grooved, rooted, and the world of the other is wide, expanding, youthful, growing.

Both are gentlemen, and gentle men. Both are kind. Each feels most strongly that aggressive action gives one control of an opponent's mind, and each has the self-confidence to pursue such aggression while not demanding certainties, but to go forward dealing with events as they come up. Each knows there is no such thing as utter security and that every possible eventuality cannot be guarded against. Knowing this, each permits himself the taking of enormous, stupendous, chances. Each in the end, when death is near, wonders if he lived the life he should have known. He had wasted life's best years, Lee said. And, "You are not going to be a soldier, are you?" Grant asked a little boy. "I shouldn't. All the soldier can do is kill. He is good for nothing else. It is much nobler to save life than to take it."

Their similarities, differences, the paradoxes, the ironies, the play and point-counterpoint—this is what I have attempted to emphasize in the pages that follow. I have not given undue attention to occurrences in the life of one that do not seem to point to corresponding or contrasting occurrences in the life of the other. But there were not many such. Each of these two soldiers seemed to blend into the other's life. It is hard to take them out of their context and see one, say, as a jump general parachuting down on Normandy, or the other, even less likely, as a Pentagon specialist working the computers for first-strike capabilities; for as well as being born for their time they were born for each other.

Their travels, one in seven-league boots, the other hardly further than down the road a little; their financial fates, each poor, rich, then poor again—but with what divergency of the forms of richness and poorness!—their very *types*, each so true to himself, these are the matters with which I have been concerned. Their postwar presidencies, one of a poverty-stricken college with forty students and four professors, the other of the great reunified America of the Gilded Age; their funerals, one the greatest in the history of this country, the other quiet and lacking even a single flag; their marriages, one destined to be far from happy and entered into at least partially because the bride was an enormously wealthy heiress, the other to a plain girl because of a deep love which lasted always; their children and how they regarded them, one making it most difficult to be a daughter of his, the other making it not only easy for his children but lots of fun—I have tried to describe all this.

Differing in so many fashions, they are alike in that they are unknowable. No one understood Grant, how he functioned, how he *did* the amazing things he did. "I do not understand him and I do not believe he understands himself," General Sherman said. All his life, after he saved the country, Grant was regarded as a mystery beyond solving, and when he was dead the mystery continued. "To the host of biographers and historians who have attempted to account for it, the reasons for this meteoric rise have proved an enigma," said one of those historians, William B. Hesseltine. In the case of Lee, he was, he once said of himself, always looking for something. What that something was, he never explained. Others could not guess. They did not try. "Can anyone say they knew Robert E. Lee?" asked a diarist of the period. "I doubt it!" Perhaps it is in the nature of genius to be beyond perfect analysis. If we knew why Mozart was Mozart, *our* works would be known in every concert hall.

"Men are nothing, the man is everything," Napoleon said. "It is the man who is wanted and not men." An army of sheep led by a lion, says an old military axiom, will defeat an army of lions led by a sheep. For eleven months, in Virginia, in the sixties of the last century, the men of the North and the South were led, each of them, by a man who was a lion. They were two kinds of men, two kinds of lion. No less contrasting than when they met to end their great war, one in magnificent new uniform, shining boots, sword, sash, gold spurs, and the other in private's clothes covered with mud, the words each spoke and left behind were equally unalike. One man was verbal, charming; the other was entirely inarticulate, a clam. Yet the talkative one wrote nothing, and the silent one a book which the greatest writer of his time, Twain, said would last as long as America remembered the roll of the vanished drum and the tread of marching hosts.

Long after they both were gone the magazine writer John W. Emerson talked to an old-time Southern sympathizer about Grant. "Sir," said the man, "he actually hauled cordwood and sold it, sir! A great general! Sir, look at General Lee! Would *he* haul cordwood, or hoe potatoes? *He* was a general, sir! But Grant!"

Yes. To be sure. But that wasn't quite all there was to it. As I trust my readers will see, we are dealing here with that character that Schlieffen puts first of all things, and that difficult simplicity of which Clausewitz tells us. Call it human nature.

LEE and GRANT

1

A Hero Grown Old

HE WAS, they said, born to be a warrior. He had sprung from his mother's womb a soldier, his uncle said, and when the war came he left off his plans to go from Princeton to the Inns of Court in London for law studies, and instead raised a troop of cavalry.

Captain of light dragoons, he outfitted his men in bright-green jacket, high frilled stock, tight lambskin breeches, polished boots to the knee and a leather cap topped by flaring horsehair plume. It was all paid for by his family. From them he had also that Virginia air of command and the horseman gallantry and dash that went with it. "I am wedded to my sword," he said, and went flashing down upon British supply columns with his lightly equipped and fast-moving riders. He bluffed enemy formations, provisioned the troops at Valley Forge. In the long ago, Washington had loved the woman who became his mother; Washington learned to love and esteem the son. He offered an aide-de-campship. But that was too tame for the great gold-epauletted Lieutenant Colonel Henry Lee, who now was always known as "Light Horse Harry." He preferred to go raiding, glory trailing behind.

He was not all thunder and dash and eloquent address to his men. He was a splendid strategist; it was by his plan that Cornwallis was lured from the Carolinas to be cooped up in tidewater Virginia with the French fleet at his rear. Washington and Lafayette listened when he spoke, and Nathanael Greene, who commanded the Continental Army in the South, said he was more in the debt of Lieutenant Colonel Lee than any other man who served under him. At Yorktown, Light Horse Harry could be counted as one of the two or three most outstanding officers who watched as the British laid down their arms. Lord Cornwallis showed poor form, he thought, to send an under-officer to offer his sword instead of doing it personally.

He was twenty-six, impetuous, swashbuckling—and petulant. They had not done enough for him, he said. He should have had more than a lieutenant colonelcy. Nathanael Green tried to mollify him, but, sulking, Lee resigned the army and went back to Virginia to marry a nineteen-year-old cousin so genuinely beautiful that she was known as "the Divine Matilda." She was also the heiress to 6,000 acres planted with tobacco plus additional lands all over northern Virginia, scores of slaves and the great tidewater estate of Stratford Hall in Westmoreland County.

His prospects could not have been more brilliant. As he went to the House of Delegates and then into the Continental Congress, he was spoken of as a coming President of the United States. But the England in whose fashion he lived grandly, after the imperious manner of an English duke or princeling, was cutting back its tobacco imports from Virginia. The great income from his wife's holdings, and his lesser ones, fell off. So he began to speculate in land, which was more exciting than farming. He spoke in expansive terms of canals to connect the tidewater country with the mountains to the west, and of new cities he would found; but the Divine Matilda, noting the carefully worded will in which her father-in-law had diminished Light Horse Harry's capacity to squander his inheritance arranged that most of her own holdings should go directly to their children, of whom soon there were four.

Henry Lee was a close friend to Alexander Hamilton, and James Madison had been his chum since Princeton days. Lee was even free to trade jests with Washington himself—once he made reference to the President's well-known tightness in matters financial and, when Martha Washington's giggle was followed by an imitating cackle from her parrot, Washington said it was obvious Lee was a funny fellow: "See, that bird is laughing at you"—but Lee had no magic touch at making money. His concepts were magnificent, glorious—but when, five years after their marriage, Matilda died, he had made very serious inroads into her wealth. Nothing worked. He bought lands with doubtful titles and then found the titles were spurious. His planned canals and cities came to naught.

He still had the name and the mantle of the past. He was still young, thirty-five. He ran for governor of Virginia and was elected. Two of his children by Matilda survived, the others having died young, and he needed another wife to care for them. Without neglecting his duties as governor, for they were not overwhelming, he was able to pay as much attention to women as to his office. He was "in love with every sweet nymph" he saw, he wrote Alexander Hamilton even as he asked the Secretary of the Treasury to divulge confidential details of government policy—which Hamilton would not do, even for Light Horse Harry. He borrowed money from Washington and repaid it with bonds whose face value was equal to the amount in question, but whose actual value was far below it. Elected governor again, he was bored. There came a possible new beginning in the form of an offer of a major generalcy in the revolutionary armies that had overthrown the King of France. He wrote asking Washington's advice. The President answered that he thought it would be a mistake to accept.

France would have meant uniforms, fife and drums—adventure, glory—but another voice, even more binding than that of Washington, bade him not to go. Charles Carter was perhaps the richest man in Virginia. He had a daughter, Ann, twenty years old, who had noted Governor Lee's unsuccessful pursuit of a cousin. "Maria, you do not know what you are throwing away," Ann had said, and set her cap for the rejected suitor. He responded. But her father would not permit the match unless Lee promised not to take the French commission.

They were married June 30, 1793, at Shirley Plantation on the James River, which was the magnificent center of the miles-long Carter estate serviced by 1,000 slaves. The bride knew nothing of life beyond that of the mansion in which she had been raised amid polished mahogany and old silver and the portraits of her ancestors. She saw the glamorous hero-governor but not the self-indulgent dreamer who had gone through one wife's fortune and would immediately set to work upon that of a second. He had deceived her in respect to finances; now he deceived her in other ways. "Her affections were trampled on by a heartless and depraved profligate," wrote a relative. "I am right as to time. One fortnight was her dream of happiness from which she awoke to a lifetime of misery."

They lived in Stratford Hall when not in the Governor's Mansion in Richmond, but it could be regarded as only a temporary abode, for the Divine Matilda had left it to her son by Henry, who could take it over when he reached his maturity. Governor Lee often went on long trips, his speculations wilder than before, leaving his new wife alone. Eventually Ann became pregnant, gave birth, became pregnant again. He failed in all his money-making schemes, sold her lands, horses, everything. Stratford Hall, with its 30-foot-square Great Hall, 17-foot-high ceilings and double doors opening upon a great staircase leading to the magnificent lawns reaching the Potomac, went into decline. Weeds grew in the walks and formal park after the unpaid overseer packed up and left. Where ocean-going ships had once tied up, wharves sank into the river.

One last moment of glory was left. The farmers of Pennsylvania and the areas surrounding that state rebelled at the imposition of a 7-cents-a-gallon tax on the whiskey that was their main product. Government inspectors were assaulted, and thousands of farmers were in open rebellion. President Washington faced the most serious threat yet presented to the law of the Constitution. He ordered the enlistment of a militia army of 15,000 men from New Jersey, Pennsylvania, Maryland and Virginia. Light Horse Harry was named to command with the rank of major general. Now he was back in his element—in uniform, wearing his saber, on a charger, in front of his men. Before this force the Whiskey Rebellion evaporated, and soon he was back home juggling his debts and stalling creditors as his governorship ended. Years passed and he was reduced to hanging chains across the entrances to his home to keep out sheriffs with writs, and when friends came they found him peeking from behind the curtains to see if it was safe to open the door.

He ran for Congress, and Washington, his constituent, put aside resentment at the matter of the debt paid in questionable bonds, and came to vote for his old comrade. When the Father of His Country died in 1799, Congress asked Light Horse Harry to deliver the eulogy. Lee made a great effort, coining the phrase ever after associated with the first President's name: First in war, first in peace, first in the hearts of his countrymen.

Ann became pregnant again, and still again. Often she went back to Shirley Plantation to live the life she had known and lost, while Lee—so it was said—asked the loan of a pair of horses from a friend. He had to take another of those endless trips in connection with another speculation. The friend sent along a slave to care for the horses. Weeks passed. The horses' owner by chance ran into his slave. He demanded to know where the horses were. "Well, you see," the black man said, "Marse Henry sold those horses." "He did, did he? Why didn't you come back and tell me about it?" "Well, you see, Marse Henry sold me, too."

He made a giant plunge into vast land speculation and tried

to get the financier Robert Morris, who had done so much in the Revolution, to go with him. Morris was short of funds just then, and so by pulling all possible strings, Light Horse Harry raised $40,000, which he lent to Morris to put in. The enterprise, like all his enterprises, failed. And in the end Morris could not pay back the money. Lee was utterly ruined.

From Shirley Plantation his pregnant wife wrote him of her father's death and asked that he come take her back to Stratford where her other children had been born, in a room which saw earlier the births of two signers of the Declaration of Independence. "I trust, my dear Mr. Lee, you will certainly bring a conveyance for me. Do not disappoint me, I conjure you." He did not come. She borrowed an open carriage, in November, and came back to Stratford across the bleak fields and through the winds of the approaching winter of 1806. She caught a cold she could not shake.

Stratford Hall that winter was freezing, and there was coal enough only for one portable brazier. When she moved from room to room she pushed it in front of her. She huddled over it in the Great Hall empty of the sold-off paintings and furniture. One of the house's many dependencies collapsed, but there was no one to put back the bricks that tumbled to the ground, no one to till the fields. Vines engulfed the carriage house from which the horses had long departed. Christmas came, New Year's. She was in the final stages of a pregnancy made very difficult because of the cold which settled in her chest. There was only wood enough to light the fireplace of the room in which she lay desperately ill.

There was no money to pay a doctor. Lee dodged down alleys in fear of creditors when he went to Alexandria or Richmond in attempts to raise money for new harebrained schemes. Ann was in despair at the thought of another mouth to feed, and in January of 1807 wrote a sister-in-law, also pregnant, that she hoped for the sister-in-law the best of luck with her coming baby, but dearly wished that she herself was not in the same fix. Eight days later, January 19, Ann Carter Lee's baby boy came. It was a difficult birth and rumors spread in the neighborhood that the infant had been delivered of a dying woman, but they got through it all right, and she named him for her brothers, Robert and Edward.

Light Horse Harry owed for his hat, some rope, gun flints, powder, and Peter would no longer lend him enough to pay Paul; and what had menaced him for years materialized: debtors' prison. Relatives came to his aid and he was briefly released only to be imprisoned again. For almost an entire year between 1809 and 1810 he was behind bars, still hoping for a windfall as he wrote a history of the military operations he had participated in during the Revolution. It would make a fortune and bring him back, he said. When at last they let him out he had nothing, nothing at all, and his wife had nothing beyond the income from not overly large trust funds willed her by her father and a sister.

Even the decaying roof over their heads was no longer available to shelter them, for the ex-convict's son Henry by the Divine Matilda had come into his maturity and wished to take possession of his property. Ann Carter Lee was ill, suffering from fainting spells and what was called "dropsy," but she got a broken-down carriage and prepared to leave. Three of the children were seated and Nat, a loyal slave they had retained, was on the carriage box when they realized that Robert, three and a half, had wandered away. One of his sisters went past the chestnut tree that Robert had helped their mother to plant, back into the echoing rooms of the empty mansion, and found him in his nursery where he had gone to say good-bye to two cherubs sculpted in metal in the fireplace.

They went to Alexandria to settle in modest lodgings. Her income was less than $25 a week and it had to support a family which now numbered seven, plus Nat and Nat's wife. Light Horse Harry was by then more a guest in his wife's home than the head of the house, but at least he was present and not off on wild money-raising schemes or in pursuit of other women. And he was good with the children, a wonderful storyteller, warm, colorful, gay despite all their troubles. Alexandria looked upon him as a model of a hero who has long outlived his exploits to become a professional ex-soldier turned something of a nuisance. A King Street merchant used to play chess with him occasionally, but the merchant had duties to perform also, and often his clerk was instructed to say he was out. The day came when Light Horse Harry resented it. "You lie, young man, and know he is in, and you are trying to deny me to him!" But the day was gone when people were in awe of Henry Lee. The clerk sprang forward and pointed to the door and said, "Leave this store immediately or I'll find a way to make you." Lee turned, folded his old military cape about himself and walked slowly but majestically out. It hurt.

In 1812 there came a final cruel blow. A friend's newspaper was threatened by political enemies, and Light Horse Harry went to the rescue. The affair turned ugly—more than ugly—and a crowd broke down the door to get at the newspaper editor and his defenders. They were beaten unconscious and thrown out into the street where thugs battered them. A drunk flung hot candle grease into Lee's eyes and then slashed at his face with a knife. From that time he was thin and frail, horribly scarred and never well. White-haired and staring-eyed in his shabby hat and worn clothing, he appealed to President Madison and Secretary of State James Monroe, still friends in spite of all, for aid to go to the islands of the Caribbean where perhaps he might recover his health. They helped him, and always short of money and lonely for the past and for his children he wandered for six years in the sun, never regaining his strength. In Alexandria his wife referred to herself as Widow Lee, and slowly his children forgot him.

Weak and crippled, emaciated, he decided in 1818 to go home. He fell deathly ill on the ship and at his request it docked at Cumberland Island off the Georgia coast. Nathanael Greene, his old commander, was buried there on what had been his estate in life. At the dock there was a fifteen-year-old boy, the nephew of Greene's daughter. "Tell your aunt," Light Horse Harry said, "that General Lee is at the wharf and wishes the carriage sent for him. Tell her I am come purposely to die in the house and in the arms of the daughter of my old friend and compatriot."

She tended to him and he recovered sufficiently to walk at times in the garden, leaning on the nephew's arm. He talked of the old days, of Washington and Lafayette, what Hamilton had said to him and he to Patrick Henry. In March of 1818, sixty-two years of age, he died. General Greene's daughter had the officers of a United States Navy squadron come to give Lee a military funeral in the Greene family plot. The grave was left unmarked for fifteen years until Lee's son Henry sent money for foot and head stones. Forty-four years passed before any of his children visited the grave. Then Robert came. Robert was a general then.

2

Useless

Jesse Root Grant was, people in Ohio said, the essence of Yankeedom—shrewd, cunning, hard and, to top it off, an outstanding know-it-all. That his neighbors found him unlovable did not bother Jesse. He worked deals, got involved in feuds, wrote letters to the newspapers. He was one sharp businessman. You had to get up early in the morning to get the better of him.

He was tough. Had to be. Poverty had driven his people out of Connecticut toward the frontier, where there was land and opportunity. But his father had had no Yankee stick-to-itiveness. He kept heading west, a drifter. He cobbled shoes, raised crops, drank. Jesse was born in Pennsylvania in 1794, 20 miles above the trading post of Pittsburgh. When he was five the family moved, via a flatboat on the Monongahela, out into the Ohio and then downriver, to a rude little log-cabin town where they stayed a while before heading on to Portage County, Ohio. Jesse's mother died there, leaving seven children, far too many for the ne'er-do-well father to take care of. The neighbors took in some of the younger children, and an older brother of Jesse's took in others. Jesse, now eleven, was old enough to earn his keep. He hired out to farmers for his room and board and managed to pick up a total of six months of schooling. At sixteen he apprenticed himself to a brother's tannery and after five years of work could be called a qualified tanner of hides. He got a job and his meals and his bed in a tannery owned by one Owen Brown, whose fifteen-year-old son, John, told Jesse that human slavery was an abomination.

He went into partnership with another tanner in Ravenna, Ohio. The business prospered. At twenty-five, in 1819, Jesse's worth of $1,500 made him perhaps the richest man in town. Then illness struck him down and he lost everything. He moved to Point Pleasant, Ohio, a hamlet of a dozen houses on the Ohio River, 5 miles east of Cincinnati, and started all over scraping cowhides for someone else.

Talkative, harsh, cantankerous, he was tall and thin and wore spectacles. But in basic ways he was a reasonable catch for a twenty-two-year-old girl on the brink of becoming an old maid—which is what Hannah Simpson was. A farmer's daughter, handsome enough, Hannah was accounted as very strange. She rarely said anything beyond yes or no. Her stepmother who raised her (her own mother had died when she was three) said that when Hannah was seven she'd had the deportment of a grown woman. She'd never been known to show the slightest emotion over anything. Her face never changed expression. She never raised her voice.

Jesse married her. They moved into a two-room house 16 feet by 19½ feet in size, which she kept in apple pie order. There was no porch or veranda. She cooked in one room; the other was their bedroom. Ten months after the wedding, on April 27, 1822, their first child was born. It was a boy.

Then and always emotionally unknowable, Hannah Simpson Grant was neither elated nor depressed by motherhood. It did not bother her that for six weeks the infant had no name.

Then the family convened to put their choices on slips of paper to be drawn out of a hat. Hannah's choice was Albert. Other suggestions were Theodore and Hiram. Hannah's stepmother had recently been reading of the Greek hero of antiquity and her name for the baby was Ulysses. Her name was drawn out of the hat by Hannah's young half-sister, but when the grand-father, Mr. Simpson, seemed aggrieved that his "Hiram" was not drawn, they decided to give the baby both names. The child was taught, when he learned his letters, to sign his name Hiram Ulysses Grant, but his mother always called him Ulysses or 'Lyss. She was almost indifferent to him, Point Pleasant's women were soon saying. Once a neighbor rushed in to tell Hannah the toddler was in with some horses, trying to swing on their tails. Hannah paid no attention and made no move to stop him. When he came down with the normal illnesses of childhood she gave him a dose of castor oil, put him to bed and concerned herself no further. Jesse was different, bragging to everybody about how beautiful he thought the baby was, and how intelligent.

A year and a half after the birth, parents and son moved some 25 miles to Georgetown, the seat of Brown County, Ohio. Jesse wanted his own tannery again, and from his wages had saved more than $1,000 to set one up. Georgetown was a new town with only fifteen houses, but it was centrally located along the immigration and trade routes east and west and in the midst of forests, which provided the tree bark needed for converting hides into leather. The tone of the place was slow and southern, more like Kentucky than Ohio, and Jesse's abrasive manner soon made him as unpopular as he had been elsewhere. But his busi-ness did well. He built a small brick home across a narrow alley from his tannery, and the odor of the slaughtered animals joined with the malodorous smell of the rendering vats and their acids and found their way up to Ulysses' room. Unlike his father, the boy hated the smells and the sight of the bloody hides hanging up with bits of animal flesh still adhering to them. It was not the only fashion in which father and son differed, for none of

Jesse's garrulousness found its way into Ulysses. He was far more like his mother, withdrawn, very quiet, emotionless.

He was not outstanding in sports and never hunted, as the other boys did from earliest youth. He said he could not bear to kill things. Small, rather thin, with delicate hands and feet, he was a solitary child. Children did not learn elegant language along the frontier, and Ulysses' refusal to say anything more violent than "doggone it" or "confound it" was considered unusual. It made him seem prim and girlish. In school he was an indifferent student, average or below in everything but math. During recess he usually sat on a stump and watched the others play. Such a boy with such a name could, of course, never hope to be addressed as anything but "Useless" by the other children, and that he seemed slow appeared to the town as a proper punishment for his braggart Yankee father. Adults who disliked Jesse took it out on his son, using the perversion of the name and telling one another that the boy was very dull.

He was less than ordinary in all ways but one: He could handle a horse brilliantly. Grown men paid him to break their young stock. Riding bareback or with a blanket strapped on, he could sit anything. Farmers who wanted a horse to sweat out a fever got him to work the animal in question, knowing that no one could make a horse run faster and longer. When a circus came to town and the ringmaster offered $5 to anyone who could stay on a particular pony, 'Lyss was the winner of the prize. The pony raced and bucked and the ringmaster tossed a monkey on the boy's back, but he kept his seat even though the monkey climbed up on his head and pawed his face.

A great hand with horses, yes, the town said, but still a dullard. Once the boy was sent by his father to bargain for a horse. "Papa says I may offer you twenty dollars for the colt," 'Lyss told the prospective seller, "but if you won't take that, I am to offer twenty-two and a half, and if you won't take that, to give you twenty-five." To a society that prized clever horse trading as much as anything in the world, it was final proof that

sharp Jesse Grant's boy was really Useless. Fifty years and more
later the sometime horse trader still remembered: "This trans-
action caused me great heart-burning. The story got out among
the boys of the village, and it was a long time before I heard the
last of it. Boys enjoy the misery of their companions, at least
village boys in that day did." He was eight.

When his father bought farmland outside town with the
profits from the tannery, 'Lyss was put to work driving teams
of horses to haul wood, furrow and plough. As time went on,
rather than socialize, he spent most of his days with the horses.
He did not esteem animals as pets, and neither then nor later
had any feeling for cats or dogs, but used horses as a means of
expression denied him in all other ways. When groups of boys
and girls went for hayrides he invariably drove, silent and paying
attention to his work while the others frolicked and laughed and
flirted in the back. He did not have any close friends, only a boy
or two he went riding with. Sisters and brothers arrived with
the regularity of families of the time, but he was not particularly
close to any of them.

Jesse sent him away to school for two winters; "I was not
studious in habit, and probably did not make progress enough
to compensate for the outlay for board and tuition." He knew
no ambition but one: to get away from the hated tannery with
its blood and death. He told his father that, if he must, he would
work in the tannery until he was twenty-one, but not a minute
longer. Jesse replied that if 'Lyss felt that way he need not even
start. But if it wasn't going to be the tannery, what did the boy
want? "I would like to be a farmer or a down the river trader,
or get an education."

Some time thereafter a town boy who had been appointed
to the United States Military Academy at West Point flunked
out. His parents, humiliated, forbade him to come home, and
told no one. But Jesse got wind of the boy's failure. That meant
there might be an extra vacancy for an Ohio candidate in the
next class. Jesse wrote to one of the state's senators, who replied
that Jesse should apply to his U.S. representative. That pre-

sented a problem, for Jesse had long since had a violent argument with Congressman Thomas Hamer. When the two met in the street each looked the other way. But the senator's letter had been promising. And Ulysses had said he might want an education. And West Point was free.

"Ulysses," Jesse said, "I believe you are going to receive the appointment."

"What appointment?"

"To West Point; I have applied for it."

"But I won't go."

Jesse replied that he thought Ulysses would go. The letter to Hamer drew an affirmative response—perhaps the congressman thought it might be just as well to turn his enemy into his friend—and the War Department was asked to receive Jesse Grant's son. Hamer knew what the boy was always called, but knew also that he had some sort of middle name. "Hiram" did not present itself at all to the congressman's mind. He decided his nominee's middle name was probably Simpson, his mother's maiden name, and so he requested admission for Ulysses S. Grant of Georgetown, Ohio. In time, an acceptance notification came.

It was the spring of 1839. Ulysses was seventeen, five feet one inch tall, 117 pounds, with very fair skin, delicate coloring and silky, wavy hair. Some of his mother's relatives gave him a trunk with his correct initials hammered on in brass tacks: H.U.G. He had had enough of his longtime Georgetown nickname and saw in his mind's eye the cadets giving him a new and hardly less objectional one, and so he changed the initials to U.H.G. and set out. He stopped a moment to say good-bye to a neighbor, and the man's wife embraced him and shed a tear for his leaving to be so far from home. "Why," he said, astonished, "my own mother did not cry."

He took passage on a steamer for Pittsburgh and then went by canal boat to Harrisburg, enjoying the trip but dreading to reach his destination where, he was certain, he would soon meet the same fate as his hometown predecessor—dismissal or a forced resignation. The people at home shared his opinion. "I'm astonished that Hamer did not appoint someone with intellect enough to do credit to the district," a neighbor told Jesse. Ulysses went on to Philadelphia aboard the first railroad he had ever seen, the train sometimes reaching speeds of 20 miles an hour and making him feel that space itself was being annihilated. In Philadelphia he spent five days with an aunt on his mother's side, who saw him as a plain country lad wearing ill-fitted clothing and coarse shoes with the toes as broad as the heels. He walked like a farmer on newly ploughed land, with a high-stepping clomp. He continued on to New York and stayed two days before going up the Hudson to the Academy to check in.

When he arrived at West Point the adjutant told him there was some mix-up: A place was saved for one Ulysses S. Grant. Hiram U. Grant was unknown to any official paper. The cadet-to-be accepted that and in an instant changed his name, although for a couple of years after he sometimes reverted to Ulysses Hiram when signing things. On the bulletin board the new name was put up with those of the others of the entering class. "U. S. Grant" attracted some attention from a group of upperclassmen, who speculated as to what the initials stood for, one of the upperclassmen being himself sensitive to nicknames and therefore having entered himself as William T. rather than William Tecumseh Sherman out of concern that West Point would call him what they did at home, "Cump" and "Cumpie." Sherman remembered one cadet saying the new man was, obviously, United States Grant. Sherman said no, the new man was Uncle Sam Grant. The Uncle Sam got shortened to Sam, and West Point, and those who had known him there, always called him that— Sam Grant.

Before the commencement of academic studies there was a summer-long military encampment to make the newcomers feel like soldiers. The whole business was out of Grant's line—the drilling and springing to attention, the shined buttons and polished boots and general emphasis on being trimly spic and span. The encampment period took an eternity to pass, Grant felt.

When the school term actually got started he settled into the center of his class, neither close to the top nor at the bottom of a group markedly low in quality, with not a single one of its members destined for appointment upon graduation to the elite of the Army, the Corps of Engineers. His best subject was math, his worst French.

Toward the end of his first year a bill was entered in Congress to disband the Academy as an undemocratic and unneeded drain upon the taxpayers. Cadet Grant followed the debates with great interest, hoping the bill would pass and so give him an easy out from a wearisome existence enlivened only by directionless reading of novels from the library plus his membership in an adolescent secret society of a dozen cadets who called their group the T.I.O—Twelve in One. He was impatient for the end-the-Academy bill to come to a vote, and disappointed when the Washington legislators voted it down.

Out of place in a cadet's world of swallow-tailed coat with high collar, elaborate headgear and white pantaloons, crossed belts and gleaming brass and penalties for sloppiness in dress and the care of muskets and equipment, he was also tone deaf and an absolute stranger to rhythm and so could not learn to march for the life of him. He was constantly out of step. (When he was temporarily made a cadet sergeant before being dropped back to private, where he remained for the rest of his West Point career, the other men said the authorities had promoted him so as not to have to watch him march in column; it was too horrid a sight.) He could not learn to dance and so never went to a ball.

Signally unnoticeable, he made no impression on anyone save for his superb riding. One of the riding hall horses was so unmanageable that only one other cadet was even allowed to approach him; "Sam," said Cadet Charles Hamilton, "that horse will kill you some day." "Well, I can't die but once," Grant replied, and tamed the horse. Cadets had no riding outfits as such, and so used their oldest and most disreputable clothing when in the dusty arena, and that attire suited him worlds better than the uniform.

Halfway through the four years of the course, cadets in good standing were given ten-week furloughs. He went home to be told by his mother that he stood straighter than before. He rode, visited people and mostly enjoyed the freedom from Academy regulations. "Those ten weeks were shorter than one week at West Point."

He returned to continue work that kept him in the middle of his class along with a similar average standing on the Conduct Roll. He had already decided that after serving an obligatory tour following graduation he would resign his commission and try to become a math teacher. Yet once, when with the rest of the corps passing in review he saw the gloriously military chief of the Army, Winfield Scott, he permitted himself to wonder if some day he might not occupy the general's place for a review. But the memory of years of ridicule at home and the certainty that even louder hoots would greet this thought made him keep it to himself, as indeed he kept almost everything to himself. Winfield Scott, nearly six and a half feet tall, festooned in gold lace and plumes, was an unattainable ideal, as was the Commandant of Cadets, C. F. Smith, of whom it was said that no cadet could be in his presence without automatically, almost involuntarily, bracing to rigid attention. The two men were the most to be envied in the nation, Cadet Grant thought, looking at soldiers as close to the *beau sabreur* ideal as he himself was distant from it.

His sole moment of glory came at graduation. With the corps drawn up in the riding hall he was called upon to give a jumping exhibition with York, the horse Cadet Hamilton had thought would kill him. He came cantering in. A soldier held a pole high over his head, with the other end of the pole against the wall. To a first-year cadet, James B. Fry, it seemed as if horse and rider were welded together as they came to the pole; underneath him Cadet Grant felt York gathering himself as they approached the bar and then in a spectacular leap cleared it. "Very well done, sir!" cried the sergeant-instructor.

Grant was graduated number twenty-one in his class of

thirty-nine, with a four-year total of 290 demerits for improper behavior. He hoped for the Dragoons—the Engineers were, of course, out of the question—and got the Infantry. The uniform was not as glorious as that of the Dragoons, but glamorous enough, and when he went through the streets of Cincinnati on a visit he thought to himself that everyone in the city was looking at him with a feeling akin to his when he'd beheld General Scott. He was disabused of the notion when an urchin with ragged and dirty pants screeched, "Soldier! Will you work? 'No, siree; I'll sell my shirt first!' " At home the drunk who did stable chores at the stagecoach tavern similarly estimated him, parading the streets barefoot in a pair of sky-blue pantaloons just the color of uniform trousers with a strip of white cotton sewn down the outside in exact imitation of Infantry kit. "The joke was a huge one in the mind of many of the people, and was much enjoyed by them; but I did not appreciate it so highly."

His orders came down—the Fourth Infantry, Jefferson Barracks, St. Louis. That was the home of his fourth-year West Point roommate, Frederick Tracy Dent. Dent had a sister—Julia.

3

The Junior Officer

EVEN BEFORE her husband found his sad grave by the sea in Georgia, Mrs. Henry Lee, removed from Stratford Hall to Alexandria, had come to regard her youngest son as almost the man of the house. Her oldest son, Carter, was away at Harvard throwing his mother into despair by spending money she did not have. Her middle son, Smith, was away at sea as a midshipman. Robert Edward, six years old when his father went south in a vain attempt to recover his health, and eleven when he died, was of course at school but was no typical schoolboy. He found time to become a capable swimmer, skater and oarsman, and took care of his pet rabbits, but his main concern was to help his mother keep the house going.

The Widow Lee, as she had learned to call herself even while her husband still lived, was not well. Worry and the living conditions of a poverty produced by her husband's wild dissipation of her fortune took their toll. She fought against it, but she was well on her way to complete invalidism. Without Robert she could never have carried on. He did the shopping, going off to market each day with a basket over his arm. He carried the keys to the pantry. At table he apportioned out the food to his sisters. He mixed his mother's medicines and served them to her, and attended to her needs when she could not get out of bed. Her many cousins in the Alexandria area, all in vastly better circumstances than she, saw how willing he was, and predicted great things for so helpful a child. (One little girl, a niece of Mrs. Lee and playmate of Robert's sister Mildred, heard him called a boy of great promise so often that she said she was confused. Exactly what *was* it, the child asked, that Robert had promised to do?)

That she did not have a spare penny to her name did not impair Mrs. Lee's standing in a Virginia which above all things prized tradition and family. She was still a Carter of the family of Robert "King" Carter, and, on her mother's side, a descendant of the colonial governor Alexander Spotswood, who had fought with Marlborough at Blenheim. And she had been married to a Lee of Virginia, who despite his sad end had been a descendant of the Earls of Litchfield and cousin to two signers of the Declaration of Independence, an important soldier of the Revolution, governor and congressman and friend to the founding fathers. By blood and marriage she was kin to every great family of her state, and Randolphs and Fitzhughs and Custises and Harrisons made her welcome. That his mother had no money did not mean that Robert would be barred from the Carter family school for boys of their blood at Eastern View in Fauquier County—the one for girls was at Shirley Plantation—where he was found to be "a most engaging child." He spent two years there before enrolling at Alexandria Academy, which he left each afternoon to walk home to his mother's house on free loan, or the next thing to it, from her remote kinsman and longtime friend and councilor, William Henry Fitzhugh of the great manor house Chatham, near Fredericksburg. When Fitzhugh had used the Alexandria house as his town residence, he had staffed it with twenty slaves. Mrs. Lee made do with Nat and Nat's wife. But it was a splendid brick structure on Oronoco Street, with charming gardens behind.

The boy's vacations were spent with relatives in their country demesnes, Fitzhugh's Chatham, the Shirley Plantation of the Carters, the Arlington House of the Custises. It was out of the question for his mother to buy him a riding horse, and so when none was available that he could borrow he followed the hunt on foot, running in a tireless fashion that helped along the development which was making him an outstanding physical specimen, tall and with broad shoulders. He was often invited for long visits to Stratford Hall, his birthplace, now the home of his half-brother, Henry, who had made an advantageous marriage to an heiress and was engaged in returning the run-down mansion and dependencies and surrounding acreage to former glories.

In Alexandria the family were communicants of Christ Church, where Washington's pew could be seen and where the service was read from a Bible that had belonged to the first President. For its associations with Washington Alexandria was on the schedule for a visit by the aged Marquis de Lafayette when in 1824 he came on a farewell trip to the country whose freedom he had done much to secure. He received visitors at a reception under a war tent of the first president's set up on the grounds of Arlington House, the property of George Washington Parke Custis, a Lee cousin who was the grandson of Martha Washington by her first husband, and who was adopted as a son by her second. A few days later the marquis went down the Potomac to Alexandria where there was a great parade in his honor, Robert acting as one of the marshals. Learning that the widow of his Revolutionary comrade Light Horse Harry Lee lived in the town, Lafayette said he wished to call upon her. With her children she received him in her parlor. Robert was seventeen.

Mrs. Lee's condition by then had deteriorated so that she could hardly walk, and in good weather Robert carried her in his arms to their dilapidated carriage whose windows he stuffed with papers so that there should be no draft to chill her. She must be cheerful, he told her, otherwise the fresh air and drive would do no good. He himself was a notably cheerful young man, with a beaming smile and a sense of fun that sometimes set him to laughing so wildly that he bent over helpless while tears ran down his face from the dark brown eyes under the full brown hair.

That was the gay Light Horse Harry in him. His mother's more somber personality was represented by his attention to the strict rules of conduct she taught him from earliest childhood. Fear produced those teachings, fear and a maturity spent in circumstances so different from those of her youth. Life had disinherited Ann Lee. The reckless and irresponsible husband had destroyed himself, squandering money and moral character. Her oldest son, Carter, away at Harvard, showed similar disquieting tendencies, spending too much money and time at happy collegiate drinking bouts. And there was something else to haunt her and all the Lees, something more terrible than anything Light Horse Harry had ever done.

It was Henry Lee, her husband's son by his first wife, Matilda. His rich wife, Anne McCarty, with whose fortune he had rebuilt Stratford Hall, became pregnant and in time gave birth to a daughter. When the little girl was two she ran past the door to the long, wide flight of stone steps that led from the Great Hall down to the lawns stretching to the Potomac. She tumbled down the stairs to find her death at the bottom. The child's mother was inconsolable and to quiet her sufferings the doctors gave her morphine. They gave her too much too often and soon she was a slave to the drug. She lay in a stupor upstairs and her husband, intelligent, a good writer and phrasemaker like his father, permitted himself the unthinkable: He dallied with his addicted wife's young sister, who lived at Stratford Hall as his ward. She was not yet out of her teen-age years. She became pregnant.

The world in which Virginia families of their type lived was rocked on its foundations at an infamy so complete, and

Light Horse Harry's oldest son became known as "Black Horse Harry," a title he bore to his dishonored grave. Perhaps mercifully the sister's illegitimate child by him was born dead; then the girl shaved her head in imitation of women of ancient times, and went into deepest mourning. To add to the horror, an investigation revealed Henry had improperly diverted funds from the girl's inheritance. Forever disgraced, his wife taken in by relatives, Henry sold Stratford Hall and went west. What he had done hung over the Lees. To Robert's mother it was a final example that showed what the flouting of codes of honor and comportment could bring. She was ill and poor and the name she bore was dishonored, but from these sufferings she found great lessons to teach him with determination even stronger than before: He must learn, a neighbor remembered her drilling into him, to "practice self-denial and self-control" to which must be added "the strictest economy in financial concerns."

He learned. At school he was remarkable for his application. When he did an illustration on the blackboard to demonstrate conic sections, a teacher remembered, he did it as if it were to be engraved on steel instead of being erased at the end of the day. He was extremely careful with money, did not use even the mildest profanities, did not drink. To the day of his death he never mentioned his half-brother's name.

He would turn eighteen in 1825. School days in Alexandria were coming to an end. He thought he might like to be a doctor, but to send him to medical school was impossible. Any college was beyond his mother's means, which were stretched to the limit by Carter's Harvard stay. And his father's greatest moments—his father's only great moments—had been in the Army. And West Point was free. Robert had influential relatives who wrote letters that were given attention, and so it was decided that he would become a soldier.

Five feet ten inches tall but seeming of greater height because of his perfect posture, he had great composure of expression and a poise unusual in one so young. Perhaps it came from his remarkable physical appearance, something noted by all who knew him—not just the young ladies of his circle who uniformly likened him to Adonis. He was economical of motion, never seeming to be in a hurry, but very graceful and efficient in all that he did. His mother's desperate teachings regarding virtue and rectitude might have produced a rebel or, given the circumstances, more likely a prig, but he was neither. He was neither a fault-finder nor holier than thou, noted Joseph E. Johnston, the grandson of Patrick Henry's sister and the son of a Revolutionary War hero who served under Light Horse Harry Lee. He was the only person Johnston knew who could laugh at your vices without making you resent it; rather, he made you want to divest yourself of those vices. He seemed so naturally accomplished, thought Erasmus D. Keyes, a young man who like Johnston would be a fellow-student at West Point, that he seemed without effort to do things better than other people did.

The day came when he had to leave for the Academy. His mother saw him off from Oronoco Street. "You know what I have lost," she said to her cousin Sally Lee when he was gone. "How can I live without Robert? He is son, daughter and everything to me!"

He came to New York and the Hudson and arrived at the Academy, where he began a career never rivaled there. Always at the top of his class in every class, in four years he did not accumulate a single demerit. His buttons gleamed. His sword was spotless. He was never late for formation, never had his bed made up in less than perfect fashion, was never guilty of a sloppy salute, missed no bedchecks, was not cited for abusing a horse or for folding his towel incorrectly. Perhaps equally remarkable, throughout he was enormously popular with his fellow students. He served in higher cadet positions each year, and in his fourth term won the highest post West Point knew: Adjutant of the Corps of Cadets.

The Engineers would take him, of course. That meant membership in the elite corps of the Army. In June of 1829 he was graduated and went back to Virginia on leave. His mother was dying. The Fitzhughs whose Oronoco Street home she had occupied had taken her to one of their country places, Ravensworth, and there he joined her to take up again the dispensation of her medicines and the daily tasks of her nursing. Their cousin Sally Lee, who had stood with the mother when her son left for West Point, noted how she was at ease only when Robert was with her, and how she watched his every move, her eyes lingering on the door when he briefly left her sickroom. In July of 1829, a month after his graduation, he stood by her bed to watch her die. She was fifty-six. Later he would say he owed everything to her.

They buried Ann Lee, and in the fall he got orders for Cockspur Island near Savannah, where a coastal defense installation was under construction. He took with him the aged slave Nat, not to make use of his services, but to nurse him as he had his mother, and in the end to bury him as he had her. As second lieutenant he raised embankments, built a canal, planned a fort. Savannah society during his off-duty hours found him full of life and fun, and he flirted with the sister of a West Point chum, wrote her teasing letters and said he was laying siege to the post office in hopes of getting answers. But in truth he was not free to make serious addresses to her, for he was compromised as a suitor. The whole Black Horse Harry matter had surfaced in the most grinding manner, and was in all the newspapers. After making his wife's sister pregnant, Harry had gone west to Tennessee, where his literary talent got him a job with Andrew Jackson, who had him arrange his military papers. He also wrote political essays praising his employer. When Jackson became President he nominated Henry to the post of United States consul in Morocco. The scandal that had ruined Henry was ten years and more in the past, but when the Senate came to vote on his confirmation it was revived, and he was held unworthy to hold any post within the gift of the government. Every senator who cast a ballot voted against him, and he fled to Europe to die there in poverty. That his half-brother, the young lieutenant of Engineers, bore the name Lee meant that he must expect refusal from the family of any girl of social standing, or that he must seek someone also related to Henry Lee and thus through the binding myriad of Virginia relationships be similarly tarnished.

Such a girl was Mary Anna Randolph Custis, a remote cousin Robert had known all her life. She was the daughter of the George Washington Parke Custis who was Martha Washington's grandson and President Washington's adopted son. Custis and his wife had had four children, but only Mary survived. So she was sole heiress to Arlington House, where Lafayette had stayed during his farewell tour of America, plus White House on the James River peninsula, where Washington had courted his wife, plus another estate, Romancoke. The central seat of the Custis family, Arlington, had some 15,000 acres worked by 250 slaves, and was furnished with memorabilia of the first president. It sat on a bluff overlooking the city named for him, and the view was such that Lafayette had said it was the finest in the world. The main house was massive, with huge rooms.

Mary Custis was blond, slim, intelligent, a great reader. She was also difficult. Most people found her imperious and temperamental, and spoiled not a little by her position in the world. Her father, Mr. Custis, was something of an eccentric. He had been raised as "the Child of Mount Vernon," and liked to be referred to by that title. He was a dreamer, dilettante painter and rather inefficient plantation owner. Mary resembled him in that she hated routine, was unmethodical and forgetful. Her mother, William Henry Fitzhugh's sister, married in the Oronoco Street home, was a gentle person, but there seemed little of her in a daughter generally regarded as far from a pleasant young lady. Lieutenant Lee, notably tolerant of the deficiencies of others, and possessed of a humorous kind of tact that dispelled nastiness, began writing her sufficient letters, and paying sufficient calls, to indicate that his attentions were serious.

A young man possessed of no money who pays court to the daughter of an extremely rich man is of necessity in a questionable position. When such a young man is the son of a Light Horse Harry Lee, who destroyed the fortunes of not one but two wives, it requires an unusual father not to ask himself some probing questions. George Washington Parke Custis was not happy to see his daughter's interest in Robert Edward Lee. Mrs. Custis, however, saw a brilliantly handsome and prepossessing young man, bright, animated, charming, whose concern for his late mother had been extraordinary. She did not oppose the growing closeness of the young people. In the end it was up to Mary. There came a day when Mrs. Custis remarked that Robert had been reading aloud from Sir Walter Scott for quite a time and was perhaps tired and hungry, and that perhaps Mary ought to take him into the dining room where there was some fruitcake on a sideboard. When they came out it was to announce they were engaged.

Their wedding in the drawing room at Arlington House on June 30, 1831, was magnificent. Six bridesmaids came with servants, with horses, dogs, trunks, carriages. The best man was Robert's brother Smith, and the groomsmen fellow-officers or cousins. The Reverend Ruel Keith officiated, soaked from a rainstorm and clothed under his Anglican cassock and surplice in dry things several sizes too small that had been hastily procured from Mr. Custis' wardrobe. The bridegroom found himself less nervous than he imagined. It was rather as if he were back at West Point in front of the blackboard with a difficult problem to solve, he decided. Mary's hands trembled. There followed days and weeks of festivities, hunting, banquets, dancing and flirting between the young ladies and gentlemen. There followed also the first of those very many discussions between the new couple as to the fashion in which they should live. A willful girl brought up with every conceivable luxury had trouble understanding why the son of genteel poverty and rigid concern with matters financial should wish to live in modest manner upon his paltry army wages. In August his leave was up and they went to live in officers' quarters at his new post at Fortress Monroe at the tip of the Virginia peninsula. At his insistence she limited herself to only two servants—people such as they never used the word "slaves."

He was happy in the Army, going to horse races with fellow-officers when he had the chance and following results in the papers, playing some chess. He was fond of the associations army life brings and was a devoted student of the love affairs of his friends. He enjoyed prowling about, as he put it, with his old friend Joe Johnston, also a nondrinker. The enlisted personnel were held to be brutes hardly above the level of horses or mules and the discipline enforced upon them was in keeping with that view, but it was noticeable that Lieutenant Lee achieved his aims by offering commands in the mildest of tones. He had not the bluster or parade-ground manners often found in young officers. The men liked him as did, universally, the members of the officer corps. He was the favorite of the ladies of the post.

Mary Custis Lee elicited different reactions. Someone of her type did not make friends easily, and unlike her husband she had no gift of small talk, so she found no women to whom she could feel close. The officers bored her. She found Fortress Monroe, the place itself and the small quarters allotted to her husband, a dreary fate. Of the social affairs of the post, "Except that we generally get some nice cake and fruit, they would be rather stupid," she wrote her mother. "I suppose it is my fault, but there are not many persons here very interesting."

He catered to her, staying with her at night to read aloud as she knitted, which then and always was a great hobby of hers. But she was unhappy and he knew it. At Christmas he took a leave and they went to visit her parents at Arlington and then, with the difficulties of travel used as a reason, she and Mr. and Mrs. Custis prevailed upon him to return to the post alone, leaving her at home. "I am a wanderer on the face of the earth," she wrote a friend. "I suppose you will remain near your mother? What happiness! I am with mine now—the past and the future disregarded."

In the spring he wrote asking her to leave Arlington and return to him. "I can't consent to your remaining longer than the first of June." But by then she had found she was pregnant, and it seemed better to have the child in her family home. The baby turned out to be a boy and they named him for her father— George Washington Parke Custis Lee. Save for the nicknames the baby's father gave him—"Boo" and "Mr. Boo"—the boy was known in the family as "Custis." The father was ecstatic. It had been his greatest pleasure to play with the children of brother officers. "Master Custis is the most darling boy in the world," he wrote. "I find it rather tiresome to nurse all day such an unsettled brat," his wife said.

Two years later Lieutenant Lee was detailed to service in the Washington headquarters of the Chief of Engineers. He made a token effort to find a house for his little family in the city, but it seemed pointless to take one when a vast mansion was available at Arlington. So each day he rode to his post over the Long Bridge crossing the Potomac and returned each evening. When the weather was very bad or the roads impassable he spent the night in the Washington boardinghouse where Joe Johnston, also on duty in the city, had bachelor quarters.

By now, with his daughter and grandson under his roof, Mr. Custis had forgotten his early qualms about his daughter's choice for a husband. Mrs. Custis had always cared for Robert, and he came to regard her as a second mother. But as the son-in-law in the house where his wife had been raised, the lieutenant found the somewhat disordered life there somewhat trying. Mr. Custis was neglectful and indolent and something of a poseur with his artistic, literary and musical pretensions. His daughter, always somewhat untidy even about her appearance, did not react well to her husband's emphasis upon the right thing in the right place, and eventually he gave up trying to correct her carelessness and perpetual lateness to every engagement. "I don't know that I shall ever overcome my propensity for order and method," he told her, "but I will try."

Even more handsome than he had been when younger, and of course more polished, he was greatly in demand at parties and balls and entertainments. She did not care for such things, so he went alone, or with a sister who once passed him off as her husband before he told the truth to the young ladies present, that he was here on a brotherly duty. "Sweet, innocent things, they concluded I was single and I have not had such soft looks and tender pressure of the hand for many years," he wrote his former commanding officer at Fortress Monroe, Captain Andrew Talcott. As often as he wrote Talcott, he wrote to that officer's wife, always addressing her as "the Beautiful Talcott." She was one of a great number of women with whom he exchanged teasing letters. When those who were single took husbands, he depicted himself as heartbroken: "Oh Mercy. Are you really married Mrs. Stiles? The idea of it is as great a damper to a man's spirit as that of the cholera. But it must feel mighty funny to you. And I suppose you are so busy that you will not have time to read this scrawl."

In 1835 he was sent with a survey party to determine the exact boundary line between Ohio and Michigan; while he was away he became a father for the second time. The infant girl was named Mary for her mother, who had a very difficult delivery. A serious infection took hold and it was months before she could walk. He was promoted to first lieutenant but the small increase in salary did not in any real fashion change a life which found him and his children living off someone else's money. That had been quite satisfactory for Light Horse Harry, but it was different with Light Horse Harry's son. Captain Talcott resigned the Army to find lucrative employment in private life, for it was a time when engineers were in great demand, and Lieutenant Lee wrote him that he was thinking of following his example. "I am waiting, looking and hoping for some good opportunity to bid an affectionate farewell to my dear Uncle Sam." He was past thirty years of age, and the pattern of his life for years into the future was established: He would be away under orders while a wife of pronouncedly different interests would find reasons to remain at Arlington; they would have children he would dearly love and miss but they would be with her, and he would talk about leaving the army.

He went to St. Louis, where the course of the Mississippi River was bearing eastward in such fashion that islands were forming on the Missouri side while the shoreline on the Illinois side was being eaten away. St. Louis was in danger of becoming a stranded inland city. He made a slow careful study, working largely with civilian laborers with whom he shared his rations at the same table, friendly and considerate as always, but showing a reserve which they accepted with no resentment. He built jetties and breakwaters. The job took three years, he going home— Arlington was home beyond discussion now—during the winter months when work was impossible. In the end he saved St. Louis as a port.

Children came regularly and eventually there would be seven; they were his greatest pleasures in a life that did not have many. "Oh, she is a rare one," he wrote of his first daughter. "I would wish myself a cannibal that I might eat her up." His wife, never really well after the birth of their first, went steadily downhill toward an invalidism more complete than that which his mother had known. It did not improve her temper. When her maid had some trouble combing out a snarl in her hair, she took a scissors and impulsively cut out the lock in question. He wrote a friend that he feared to come home and find her bald.

He went to Fort Hamilton in New York harbor to do fortifications work, gun emplacements. In the Narrows he plucked a terrier out of the water, took her home and named her Dart. He trained her to eat from the same bowl as the Maltese cat; they chased rats together. He bred Dart and she produced Spec, who became his inseparable companion, even accompanying him to church. He refused to let Spec's tail and ears be cropped, holding it to be an unnecessary cruelty. Lonely for his children, he wrote them long letters about the dog: "Spec has become so jealous now that he will hardly let me look at the cats. He seems to be afraid that I am going off from him, and never lets me stir without him. Lies down in the office from eight to four without moving, and turns himself before the fire as the side from it becomes cold. I catch him sometimes looking at me so intently that I am for a moment startled."

He knew what children wanted and could tell bright and entertaining stories. He liked to be tickled and a son remembered him saying, "No tickling, no stories!" He was intensely involved in the children's studies, helping them not by revealing the answer to a problem but by showing them step by step how they might find the solution. He offered minute instructions about their horses and explained the purpose of moves a rider must make; he gave them sleds and came to watch the fun as they careened down Arlington's slopes. He bought them skates and, when the ice melted in favor of warmer waters, had them taught how to swim, discussing with them how they were getting along, what strokes they were working on. He competed in jumping contests on the Arlington lawns with young Custis and the second son, William Henry Fitzhugh Lee. Though William was named for his and his wife's kinsman, the kindly donor of the house on Oronoco Street in Alexandria, from earliest childhood the boy was called "Rooney" by his father and eventually the world. When Rooney severely slashed his fingers with a straw cutter and the doctor said there was a possibility he might lose them, Father sat up all night by the boy's bed for weeks to make sure he did not disarrange the bandages in his sleep.

Lee spent years in Fort Hamilton, and on assignments to coastline projects in North Carolina—dikes, jetties, gun emplacements, fortifications and casemates—Fort Lafayette on the Brooklyn side of New York harbor, Battery Hudson and Battery Morton on Staten Island. He obtained his captaincy, and there was a new baby regularly on the way or arriving—"I am sure to be introduced to a new one every Christmas. They are the dearest annuals of the season." But through it all there was a very great, all-pervading loneliness suspended only when he could return home to Virginia: "I felt myself so elated when I again found myself within the confines of the Ancient Dominion that I nodded to all the old trees I passed, chatted with the drivers and stable-boys, shook hands with all the landlords, and in the fulness of my heart—don't tell Mary—wanted to kiss all the pretty girls I met."

He was nearly forty. Then came Mexico.

4

Mexico (I)

THE FIRST TIME little Emma Dent saw her brother's West Point roommate come riding up to their home outside St. Louis, she thought to herself that he was as pretty as a doll with his fair skin, delicate coloring and silky, wavy hair. He was five feet eight and weighed hardly more than the 117 pounds he carried when he entered the military academy four years before.

"How do you do, little girl. Does Mr. Dent live here" asked Sam Grant of the Fourth Infantry. Emma told him yes. White Haven was what her father called their home some 12 miles from St. Louis and 5 from Jefferson Barracks. That was rather an elegant title for what was no mansion but simply a large house surrounded by substantial acreage. It was in keeping with the picture that Frederick Dent had of himself, which was that of the offspring of Southern gentility transported to Missouri's crude environs. Of Maryland birth, a capable merchant although he affected to scorn mere commerce, Dent had gone to Pittsburgh

35

and then St. Louis and made money. Then he settled down to lead the life of what he called a planter—let others term themselves farmers. He kept some twenty slaves, wore a long black coat and high stock, talked about his aristocratic roots and let himself be generally addressed as "Colonel," although he had no military experience of any type. His wife put up with the performance.

The Dents' second son, Fred, had been Sam Grant's roommate and fellow-member of the Twelve in One society at West Point. There were six more children, of whom Emma was the youngest. The oldest daughter was in school at St. Louis and living for the while with relatives there. She was seventeen. Julia.

It was, of course, part of old-time Southern hospitality to make welcome a guest so well recommended as to have been a son's dear friend. Young Lieutenant Grant became a regular visitor at White Haven. His duties at Jefferson Barracks were not so onerous but that he could ride a couple of times a week with the young men of the family, play with little Emma and fifteen-year-old Nellie, and sit at table. Autumn passed. Winter came. In St. Louis the seventeen-year-old Julia Dent finished with school and stayed to partake in the social whirl of the city. Then she came home.

She was a splendid rider, athletic, an outdoors girl. A beauty, no. One eye was strange, it moved involuntarily: strabismus. She was short and plump, with her own slave, Black Julia, named for her. Lieutenant Sam took her to be another playmate and riding companion of the class of Emma and Nellie. Julia took him to be a chum of brother Fred's, along with several other young officers from Jefferson Barracks. She regarded Sam as a family friend somewhat of the level of Lieutenant James Longstreet, always called "Pete," her remote cousin who had been a fellow student of Sam's at West Point. On her Kentucky mare, Missouri Belle, Julia rode with Sam and went fishing for perch. But—strange—when Emma and her troupe of little black slave girls laboriously filled their aprons with grasshoppers for the fishing rod hooks, they often found the place where they had agreed to meet Julia and Sam vacated. Lieutenant Sam had enchanted her, little Emma said to herself, and then he had abandoned her. She had told him he must not toss her up on his shoulders and kiss her, for she was too old for such undertakings; she was getting to be a big girl now. He obeyed her injunction, but he did it in favor of another. It must be the riding, Emma decided. Neither she nor Nellie could ride like Julia. Once when she was on her way to school, Lieutenant Sam came riding along and swept her up and wanted to put her on his lap. She was too big for that, she said. So he put her behind him on the saddle. They came to school. "They're looking at us, Emmy," he said. "They're saying, 'Look at Emmy Dent! She's got her sweetheart with her!' "

But he was making fun of her, she who was seven years old! "No, you're not my sweetheart, you old black nigger fool," she cried with the venom of a young lady of her age. "More like Sister Nell's beau, you mean!" But she had the wrong sister. Lieutenant Grant found himself more and more drawn to White Haven because of Julia. Frequently he stayed so long that he was late for dinners taken at Jefferson Barracks. The rule there was that an officer coming in after the meal had begun was fined a bottle of wine. "Grant, you're late as usual, another bottle of wine," the President of the Mess, Captain Robert Buchanan, snapped at him one evening.

"Mr. President, I've been fined three bottles of wine within the last ten days and if I'm to be fined again, I shall be obliged to repudiate."

"Grant, young people should be seen and not heard!" Neither of them forgot the exchange.

In May of 1844 he took a leave and went home to Ohio. But it was not like before. He found himself wanting to get back to Missouri: "And I understood the reason without explanation from anyone."

He cut short his stay at home and came back to find that the Fourth Infantry had been ordered south to Louisiana as part of the Army of Observation set up along the Mexican border in connection with the threeway problem between the United States, the Republic of Texas and Mexico. He delayed going off to join the regiment long enough to make for White Haven. The little Gravois Creek along the road was swollen from springtime rains, but he put his horse to swimming through the waters and arrived soaked and muddy. One of the Dent brothers lent him dry clothing and Julia came down to say she had dreamt that he would come in citizen's attire. In that moment everything was clear to them both. She understood now the sinking sensation she had felt when she had heard that the Fourth was to go south. He went with the family to a morning wedding in the neighborhood, driving her in a carriage. They came to a bridge over flooding waters and she said, in answer to his assurance that the bridge would hold, that she was going to cling to him no matter what. He asked her to cling to him for life. Then he was off down the Mississippi to join his regiment at Camp Salubrity near Natchitoches, Louisiana. They would see each other only once in the next four years, when he would formally ask for and receive the consent of her parents for their wedding.

Louisiana was troop drill and endless card games of brag with Pete Longstreet and the others, 25 cents being considered a good day's winnings. After six months the Fourth went to Corpus Christi as part of what now in the wake of the American annexation of Texas was termed the Army of Occupation. The glamorous Captain John Magruder, always known as "Prince John," organized a theater company whose director was Pete Longstreet. Pete cast his slim friend Sam Grant as Desdemona and put him in bell-like skirts. The Othello of the piece, Lieutenant Theodoric Porter, declared himself incapable of playing love scenes opposite such a co-star, and a professional actress from New Orleans was sent for.

The purpose of the 3,000-man force under Zachary Taylor was to provoke a fight with the Mexicans, thereby enabling the government in Washington to launch a war that would gain the Mexican provinces lying along the border—Manifest Destiny. To Grant the idea of the planned conquest was unholy, one of the most unjust wars ever fought by a strong nation against a weak one. It was not the position of second lieutenants to sit in judgment upon empire-building, however, and when the Mexicans' perverse refusal to inaugurate hostilities demanded that the Americans provoke them even further, he joined with the others in a march deep enough into Mexico to make the war begin. They went south toward Matamoros through gigantic herds of wild horses. It seemed to Grant that if these horses could be corralled they would have taken up every inch of Rhode Island or Delaware. There were flocks of wild turkey, which the other officers shot for dinner, but Grant stood with gun on shoulder unable to kill a living thing. Perhaps it was the memory of the animals back at his father's tannery.

They reached the Rio Grande and went into camp; and finally the Mexicans fought. He heard the hostile guns and felt sorry that he had ever gone to be a soldier. General Taylor formed up his dragoons and light artillery and went forward. Looking down the lines of the 3,000 men, it came to Lieutenant Grant what a fearful responsibility rested upon Taylor, to command such a host so far from friends. The Mexican lance heads and bayonets glinted in the sun. A cannonball passed through the ranks of the Fourth Infantry and took off the underjaw of a captain and the head of an enlisted man. Blood and bone splinters covered the men nearby.

"You can have but little idea of the influance [sic] you have over me Julia, even while so far away," he had written her. "If I feel tempted to do any thing that I think is not right I am shure [sic] to think, 'Well now if Julia saw me would I do so' and thus it is absent or present I am more or less governed by what I think is your will"; and so he went on in what was now the Army of Invasion. They drove the Mexicans across the Rio Grande and made for Monterrey. He acted as regimental quartermaster. It was not a glamorous position. With the actual American war declaration the tiny regular army of 637 officers and 5,925 enlisted men was swelling enormously, with almost daily arrivals of elaborately garbed militia outfits commanded by lawyers and planters in uniforms Napoleonic in design. Lieutenant Grant was dickering with whoever had mules for sale and was willing to pack kettles and poles and mess chests and ammunition on them. It was a job worthy of a grocery store clerk, made all the more exasperating by the kicking and bucking of the animals and the thievery and unreliability of the men taken on as drivers and loaders. Grant applied for a transfer and was told that the regimental commander would not authorize it. His place was to be back with the mules and wagons while the fighting went on in front.

Taylor reached the outskirts of Monterrey. A rustic-looking frontier soldier wearing homespun jeans and sitting his horse with both feet dangling on one side of the saddle, "Old Rough and Ready" talked about tobacco and crops with his men in leisurely fashion and then opened his guns upon the city. His curiosity getting the best of his judgment, so he said later, Lieutenant Grant disregarded orders and went forward to see the artillery pound the flat-roofed buildings. He was there when an order for a charge came down from Taylor and, so he said, "lacking the moral courage to return to camp where I had been ordered to stay," he went forward with the attackers. Two days later he was deep in the city with the others. Ammunition was running low. The men were pinned down with Mexicans behind them. The brigade commander called for a volunteer to go back and make the situation known, and Grant asked for the job. He put one foot into a stirrup, hung the other over the saddle, clung to the horse's neck and with the horse's body between himself and Mexican riflemen, galloped off for help.

In the end Monterrey capitulated. The garrison filed out and away and the Americans took possession, and Mexico took Grant as it had others before and after: the grandeur of the sky and desert, the magnificent flowers and plants, the sweet smells and the sounds of the tinkling fountains and chiming church bells. But, "Without you *dearest* a Paradice [sic] would become lonesom [sic]."

To take the City of Mexico from the north would mean

crossing miles and miles of difficult country and laying siege to cities and towns. To ship into the port of the capital, Veracruz, take it and follow the route of Mexico's first conquerer, Cortez, appealed to the chief of the Army, Winfield Scott; and so the Fourth was sent down to join his forces. The bombardment of Veracruz and the following of Cortez' trail was primarily an endeavor for the Engineers. They sighted the guns and cut roads through the great mountain chain to flank the Mexican defenders. Scott, in a magnificent uniform of cocked hat, gold, plumes, epaulettes and aiguillettes and saber, sent couriers to order that troops be formed up to receive him when he went up and down the thin column penetrating the heart of Mexico. And so sometimes Lieutenant Grant, bringing up the rear with his quartermaster duties, saw the general ride past with his buglers and trumpeters and richly brilliant turned-out staff. With no line of communications back to Veracruz, for he could not afford the men to guard it, Scott cut loose from the coast and went inland as Cortez had done after burning his boats on the shore.

The column came to Mexico City and Scott vainly negotiated for a surrender before ordering the storming of the outer defenses. Again it was an Engineers performance, and they performed brilliantly. Brevet increases in rank showered down upon them. There were some for infantrymen also, including a first lieutenancy for Julia's brother, Fred Dent. Of the members of the Class of 1843 in uniform, six were captains and nineteen were first lieutenants. Six remained second lieutenants, including Grant. In a report, the regimental commander of the Fourth mentioned every officer, ending with "And Lieutenant Grant, regimental quartermaster, who was usefully employed in his appropriate duties."

The Army waited before the City of Mexico while the adventurer-captain Santa Anna stalled Scott, and then the troops went up the Hill of the Grasshoppers to the great fortress of Chapultepec. The Engineers laid out the way. At three in the morning of September 8, 1846, the Fourth Infantry moved up into support position. The Mexican batteries opened and men dropped. Fred Dent rushed into a fortified mill below the fortress where he took a musket ball in the leg. He dragged himself to a wall and lay there half fainting, to be found a few minutes later by Sam Grant coming up with a squad. Grant tended to him and lifted him up onto the wall, from which a few minutes later Fred tumbled down, breaking bones in the process.

The American batteries played upon Chapultepec and the fortress capitulated, Mexican boy-cadets flinging themselves to their deaths from the high parapets. With the city's main defense position now in their hands, the invaders had all but taken the Mexican capital. The defenders fell back behind low stone walls for a last-ditch effort. Grant saw a church whose belfry, it seemed to him, would command a gate in the walls. He waded through ditches breast deep in water, knocked on the door and explained to the church's priest he must enter, and then with a few men took apart a mountain howitzer and carried it in pieces up to the belfry. Put together again, it opened on the Mexicans sheltered by the walls and drove them from the gate. General William Worth saw, and sent his aide, Lieutenant John Pemberton, to bring the officer in the belfry to him. Grant saluted the general, who complimented him and ordered up another gun for him to take back to the church. Grant knew there would be no room for it up in the belfry but did not think it wise for a second lieutenant to tell a general his business. He departed with the useless weapon.

The City of Mexico surrendered, as was inevitable from the moment Chapultepec fell. The war was won. Grant and the Fourth stayed on. He got his first lieutenancy, went to a bull-fight—"just one"—and left sickened before the performance was over. He went with other officers on an excursion to climb the great mountain of Popocatépetl, the organizer of the trip being Simon Bolivar Buckner, who had been with him in the Twelve in One back at West Point. Snow blindness made the effort a nightmare. He went cave exploring.

The regiment was based in Tacubaya outside the capital, and among the quartermaster's duties was to buy material and find people who could sew it up to resemble regulation uniforms. He also rented a bakery and hired Mexican workers to produce bread. Finally the peace treaty was signed and the American troops departed, the Fourth Infantry to go to Pascagoula, Mississippi. Leaves were issued and Grant made at once for St. Louis and his wedding. Urged by letter to attend, his family declined. Jesse Grant wasn't going to put up with plantation airs, Southern mannerisms and the likelihood of a looking-down-the-nose attitude on the part of old Frederick Dent. So it was Pete Longstreet, not a brother or father, who stood with the bridegroom to see Julia come down the staircase of the Dent city residence, candles lighting her way. Grant was a captain by then, a little heavier than he had been, Emma Dent thought, and clean-shaven in contrast to most other officers.

For years after the war Sam Grant talked about Mexico. Sometimes it seemed to people that he talked of nothing else. All his life he remembered the tropical lushness of the lowlands, the birds, the sunsets. Mexico enchanted him forever. He talked about how even ten-year-olds smoked in Mexico, the strange howling of wolves in the prairie grass, the corralling of mules by lariats, the Bishop's Palace at Monterrey, the Castle of Perote and the Zocala of the City of Mexico. He talked about the time he reported in unkempt uniform on some routine matter to an officer of Winfield Scott's staff. "I feel it my duty, Captain, to call your attention to General Scott's order that an officer reporting at headquarters should be in full uniform," the officer said, tall and immaculately turned out, and the man whose services Scott said were the most brilliant of any of the soldiers who went to Mexico, and without whom in fact there might have been no victory at all—Colonel Robert E. Lee.

5

Mexico (II)

ROBERT LEE went to Mexico a well-enough regarded junior officer and returned an awesome hero. He did not approve of the empire-building war. "We have bullied her," he said of Mexico. "For that I am ashamed." Yet he went at the elbow of his country's first conquistador, Winfield Scott, from off the shores of Veracruz to the Halls of Montezuma, and Scott said of Lee: "The best soldier in Christendom." Trumpets sounded, kettledrums rolled and hands slapped on muskets where Scott went in the City of Mexico when the great audacious conquest as glorious as that of Cortez was completed; and Scott lifted his glass in a toast to Robert E. Lee—"Without whose aid we should not be here now."

Captain Lee, as he was then, first saw Mexican waters while sharing a cabin with his old chum Joseph E. Johnston, who was deathly seasick—"My poor Joe," he wrote home. Engineers had the duty of selecting positions for artillery, and so when after

44

the unopposed landing at Veracruz he waded ashore, he was told to find the correct place for the guns Scott hoped would bring the reduction of the city. With Lieutenant Pierre Gustave Toutant Beauregard he conducted a reconnaissance. "Who comes there" shouted an American voice as they returned to their lines. "Friends," called Lee. "Officers," shouted Beauregard. The sentinel fired his pistol and the ball passed between Captain Lee's arm and his chest. The flames singed his coat. He asked that the man not be punished, and from the positions he had marked out the guns soon brought Veracruz to run up a white flag. He found no pleasure in the spectacle. "It was terrible to think of the women and children," he wrote home.

Scott, in his magnificence, in gold and plumes and all of that—Old Fuss and Feathers—went to church with Lee at his side, and when the Mexicans gave him a taper to carry in their Catholic service, handed it on to the Engineers captain. The Mexicans found a larger one for the general-in-chief. Winfield Scott's immense ego, as gigantic as his six-foot-five frame, 300 pounds, had long ago selected the proper position for him to occupy, President of the United States, and he quailed at the thought of participating in Papist doings. Word might get back home. But Captain Lee carried his candle round the church as if his entire life had been spent in performing the ceremonies of Romanism.

The Army went inland from Veracruz, making for the City of Mexico. All military doctrine taught that the last thing an advancing soldier must do is cut himself loose from his base, but Scott, braver than a lion, was selecting for his men either victory or death. There was no middle ground. He would, he said, throw away his scabbard and advance with the naked blade in his hand. In Europe he was compared to Napoleon moving upon Moscow. "Scott is lost!" declared the aged Duke of Wellington when the British newspapers reported his actions. "He cannot capture the city and he cannot fall back upon his base!" The Americans need only be held for a short time, thought Santa Anna, the Mexican generalissimo, and *el vomito*, the fevers of the lowland, would do the rest for them. To this end Santa Anna emplaced his guns along the National Road that wound its dizzy twisting path up through the great and almost uncrossable mountains between Veracruz and the City of Mexico. With difficulty mules might make it up those heights, but artillery never.

Scott sent Captain Lee to reconnoiter, and clinging to bushes growing from the almost sterile rocks and hovering above heights which would dash to pieces solid steel if it should fall, he heard near a mountain spring the sounds of Spanish. He hid under a log and was there for hours unmoving while bugs bit and Mexican soldiers drank from the waters, smoked, lazed about. They sat on his log. Darkness came and they departed. In the night he found his way back and outlined a path by which the Americans could manhandle their guns up the great ravines by ropes hanging from the cliffs, by their fingernails, their teeth. They outflanked Santa Anna. They shelled his peon soldiers. He fled into the interior, into the great Valley of Mexico where once Montezuma in terrible visions had seen Cortez coming and where now Santa Anna beheld the gringo Scott coming with his men of the Colossus of the North.

Major Lee, "again indefatigable, in reconnaissance as daring as laborious, of the utmost value," Scott said, stood with the general-in-chief gazing down upon the shining great capital of the Aztecs. "That splendid city shall be ours!" Scott said to himself. But first the outer perimeter of the drawn-in Mexican defenders must be pierced. Lee went looking for a weak point, if weak point there was, staying in the saddle for thirty-six hours straight. The approaches all appeared to be covered, but Lee ventured into what the Mexicans called the Pedregal, a vast lava bed resembling a stormy sea frozen in place, and came back to say that he thought he could clear a path sufficient for artillery to be gotten through. Word reached the Mexican general Gabriel Valencia that American guns were coming through the Pedregal, and he roared with laughter. "No! No! You're dreaming, man. The birds couldn't cross that Pedregal." But soon the American artillery was in position.

Back at headquarters Scott dispatched, one after the other, seven officers to find out what was happening. None could find his way through the impenetrable Pedregal. Night came, and with it hurricane-like tropical rains. Lee knew Scott had to be informed and so alone made his way back through the wilderness of volcanic stone. Lightning flashes lit his way. He fell innumerable times but finally found headquarters—only to learn that Scott was elsewhere. He went on, found the general, reported and then recrossed the Pedregal for the third time to rejoin the troops. It was one in the morning when he arrived and his trips were, Scott said, "the greatest feat of physical and moral courage performed by an individual, in my knowledge." When daylight came it took twenty minutes for the guns to drive off the Mexicans.

The Americans poured after them as they fled back in a rout ended only when Santa Anna asked for an armistice. Negotiations went on and then broke down. Lieutenant Colonel Lee sighted the guns and the assault on Chapultepec was ordered. With Lieutenant George B. McClellan as his assistant he worked through the night constructing platforms for the heavy batteries. Afterwards he was in constant motion for forty-eight hours and, ignoring a slight flesh wound, fainted. A friend had given him two bottles of old brandy to take to Mexico for use in just such an emergency, but General Scott himself took out a flask of his own and had it given to Lee, and so months later when Lee went home he took with him the two bottles unopened.

A few hours' rest refreshed him and soon he was back directing advances for the final taking of Chapultepec and the brief forward move to the gates of the City of Mexico. He stood in the Zocalo, the main plaza, as the American flag rose, and then waited as drums rolled and arms were presented and colors lowered for the entrance of Scott on his great horse, wearing his plumed chapeau and gold-knotted saber and pants with two-inch stripes down the sides. "His campaign was unsurpassed in military annals," the Duke of Wellington said of Scott. "He is the greatest living soldier."

Colonel now, the most celebrated soldier of the forces holding rank less than that of general, " 'The' engineer," said Lieutenant Colonel Ethan A. Hitchcock, Lee wept with Joe Johnston for the death in action of Johnston's nephew, whom the childless man had regarded as his heir. No woman could have been more tender, Johnston remembered. For eight months Lee stayed on, making maps and conducting reconnaissances. A Mexican desperado saw him riding alone and took out his lariat; Lee quietly drew his revolver and rested it on the saddle, and the two men passed each other peacefully after exchanging polite greetings. He was often at the general-in-chief's side; that officer had for Lee an "almost idolatrous" regard, said Scott's chief of staff, Erasmus Keyes. If war should ever break out with England, Scott had told Keyes, it would be cheap for the United States to insure Lee's life if it cost $5 million a year—that was what the premiums would be if they accurately reflected his worth. Yet Lee appeared entirely untouched by his sudden elevation to a position so different from the one he had held but a year and a half before. Winfield Scott looked and acted the part of a great soldier; Colonel Lee, by contrast, was always smiling and agreeable and quiet. At Christmas he had in several officers and at each one's plate put a knife or fork once part of George Washington's field equipment. The silver was, of course, from his wife's inheritance. In his letters to her and the children he made almost no mention at all of his exploits, but talked about Joe Johnston; about his brother, Smith Lee of the Navy, smiling through bombardments, and of how he was worried about his dog at home: "Can't you cure poor Spec. Cheer him up—take him to walk with you and tell the children to cheer him up."

It seemed to Lieutenant Raphael Semmes of the Navy that although Lee had great energy, tact, judgment and discretion, there was almost something peculiar about his talent: He seemed to receive impressions intuitively that other men labored to acquire, if indeed they ever did acquire them. "I tell you," Scott said, "that if I were on my death bed tomorrow, and the President of the United States would tell me that a great battle was to be fought for the liberty or slavery of the country, and asked my judgment as to the ability of a commander, I would say with my dying breath, 'Let it be Robert E. Lee!' "

Two years after seeing them last, he came back to his family at Arlington. He took a slow method of getting home out of consideration for his mare, Grace Darling, for, he said, she had suffered enough in his service. A carriage with ribbon-bedecked horses was sent to Washington to meet him, but somehow he missed connections with it, and so came alone up the great hill to his home. Seeking the carriage, the family did not realize that it was he, but Spec did, and went rushing across the lawns to greet him. Colonel Lee came up on Arlington's portico to distribute kisses and caresses; and three-year-old Robert E. Lee, Jr.—his father had at last permitted a son, his third, to be named for him—watched as Lee cried, "Where is my little boy?" and mistakenly swept up in his arms a visiting playmate. But there was a pony brought from Mexico for the boy, soon "Rob" and "Bertus" to his father. And there were to be lifetime memories of a gay and handsome man, the glamorous uniform, "golden epaulettes and all—chiefly the epaulettes," and the jokes and tickling. When the children asked him how it felt to be wounded, he'd pinch them and say, "Just like that."

His family occupied themselves, the colonel wrote, in peering at his gray hair and furrowed face, but that was the grossest exaggeration, for the hair was dark and there were few lines in the face, clean-shaven save for the full dark military mustache on the upper lip. The smaller children were invited to get into bed with him in the mornings. Rob and his youngest sister, Mildred, "Precious Life" and then simply "Life" to their father, always found him to be joyous and with the bright smile that characterized him for them. And yet—"I always knew that it was impossible for me to disobey my father. I felt it in me, I never thought why, but was perfectly sure when he gave an order it had to be obeyed. My mother I could sometimes circumvent, and at times took liberties with her orders, construing them to suit myself; but exact obedience to every mandate of my father was a part of my life and being at that time."

Lee went to Baltimore and some dreary work in the harbor there, the old business of building forts. "I might as well be a pile or a stone myself laid quietly at the bottom of the river," he wrote a cousin. In 1852 came the job of Superintendent of the United States Military Academy at West Point. Twenty-three years had passed since his graduation. The alloted quarters were splendid, and for the first time in many years he was with his family all of the time, having moved them from Arlington to the Academy. Each afternoon he went for a ride with Rob, making the boy hold to a sitting trot for miles at a time. The oldest son, Custis, was a cadet doing splendidly, and in free moments came to dinner bringing his friends, the most intimate of whom, Cadet James Ewell Brown Stuart of Virginia, became a particular pet of Mrs. Lee. It was a time of happiness diminished only by the absence of the older girls, who were away at school. He wrote them often and lovingly. "My precious Annie: I take advantage of your gracious permission to write to you, and there is no telling how far my feelings might carry me were I not limited by the conveyance furnished by Mims' [Mrs. Lee's] letter, which lies before me, and which must, the Mims say so, go in this morning's mail. But my limited time does not diminish my affection for you, Annie, nor prevent my thinking of you and wishing for you. I long to see you through the dilatory nights. At dawn when I rise, and all day, my thoughts revert to you in expressions that you cannot hear or I repeat. I hope you will always appear to me as you are now painted on my heart."

As Superintendent he worked on plans for a new riding hall and for better faculty housing arrangements. He resisted political pressures on behalf of cadets he felt he must discipline, and he tightened that discipline. But it was hard on him, and Secretary of War Jefferson Davis came to feel that the Superintendent's sympathy for young people was more an impediment than a qualification for the job he held. "I wish boys would do what is right, it would be so much easier for all parties," Lee sighed to Rob when they came upon three cadets who were against orders outside the boundaries of the Academy. The three leaped over a wall and vanished. "Did you know those young men" he asked his son, and then immediately said, "But no; if you did, don't say so."

When it became necessary to discharge cadets from West Point, as was not unusual, he tried to do it as gently as possible, saying they must not attach such importance to the matter that it would blight their lives. Or he would give them an opportunity to resign and so save themselves a discharge. One cadet who declined the resignation offer and had to be discharged was Cadet James McNeill Whistler, "Little Jimmy Whistler" to the Superintendent, who remembered him with fond amusement. Told to produce diagrams for a water crossing, Cadet Whistler put in a bridge with two little boys sitting on it. He was informed that the addition of children to the bridge was unnecessary. He erased them and transferred them to shore. He was told to get rid of them. His final drawing showed the bridge and shore empty of living forms. Two little graves were drawn in the distance. Whistler's worst subject was chemistry. "I am required to discuss the subject of silicon," he announced in class. "Silicon is a gas—"

"That will do," said the instructor, and shortly after Colonel Lee ordered Whistler's dismissal. "If silicon had been a gas, I would have been a major general," Whistler loved to say in later years. He left and went on to his great art career, remaining always a fierce partisan of West Point and Colonel Lee, saying the place and man were alike wonderful. He was not alone in his estimate of the Superintendent. "Don't you think," Lee asked a cadet who got involved in a fistfight with one of his fellows, "that it is better for brothers to dwell together in peace and harmony?" "Yes, Colonel, and if we were all like you, it would be an easy thing to do."

The Superintendent's obligations included considerable entertaining—"Pa's delights," the children called them—and Colonel Lee was as always splendid at that, a master of jolly small talk and gossip and jokes. Mrs. Lee joined in with less enthusiasm. Always indifferent to fashion—"Why don't you wear your dresses longer?" he'd ask her; "I look at all the pretty girls in town, and they all wear their dresses longer. If you don't lengthen yours, I shall have to walk with the pretty girls"—age and increasing poor health made her even more dowdy. They went in the summer to the Virginia resort at Hot Springs where a young woman fellow-guest found overwhelming the appearance of a man people often said was the handsomest in the United States. He took her breath away. "Who is *he*?" she whispered to her father. "That is Colonel Lee," was the reply. On the upper porch the girl saw a plain woman in a rocking chair reading a book. She wore a calico dress, low, unfashionable shoes and blue cotton stockings. "*That* is Mrs. Lee," the girl's father whispered.

He was Superintendent three years. By then the United States had accustomed itself to the ownership of the vast territories taken from Mexico as part of the peace settlement, and accustomed itself also to the idea that the army must be enlarged so that the new areas might be policed. Mexican and American bandits, Indians, adventurers and desperados could not be suppressed by artillery nor immigrant trains easily protected by infantry, and so Secretary of War Davis put through a motion to raise two new regiments of cavalry. They would be composed of the cream of American soldiery. In March of 1855 Congress authorized the new troop formations. The brilliant, almost legendary, Albert Sidney Johnston was named to command one regiment. Robert E. Lee was appointed his second-in-command. (General Scott said the positions should be reversed, but the Secretary was feuding with him and chose to disregard his opinion.) The other command went to Edwin V. Sumner, with Lee's old friend Joe Johnston as second soldier of the regiment.

The family, or that part of it not away at school, went to Arlington, and Lee went 1,800 miles west to Camp Cooper, Texas. He arrived in a tiny caravan with escort of eight privates and a corporal, and a coop of seven hens nailed to the tailgate of one wagon. It was his first field command, four companies. The frontier was wind and dust, and the local Comanche chief, Katumse, came to greet Lee in greasy embrace the day after his arrival. He returned the chief's call the following day, going to a village guarded by some twenty wolf-like dogs and consisting of perhaps 100 lodges set irregularly in a barren landscape. The Comanches used buffalo-skin mats for flooring, robes for bedding. Swarms of flies hung on strips of meat drying in the sun. Katumse expected Lee to observe the ceremonial rite of completely disrobing; Lee removed his tie only. Katumse brought forth his six wives for introductions.

Texas was drought, with the almost-dry springs yielding brackish and muddy water that caused violent stomach upsets; it was heat and no vegetables and then sudden rains that made torrents roar through the gullies. Lee's command was 12 officers and 226 enlisted men chasing hostiles past small, mean hovel settlements and then out into the trackless cactus and chaparral deserts, Sweetwater, Laredo, Brownsville, Eagle Pass, San Antonio. "My rattlesnake, my only pet, is dead," he wrote his daughter Mildred back at Arlington. "He grew sick and would not eat his frogs and died one night." He constructed a scaffold to hold his chicken coop three feet off the ground so that the hens would not fall victim to his dead pet's fellows, and tamed one hen so that she was accustomed to hop up on his camp table where she managed to upset his ink. Through the flats and gulches and dry creeks and down into ravine and over mountain he chased plundering Indians who raided the border settlements; he rode escort for the wagon trains filled with pioneers heading west; he sat at court-martial proceedings and read the funeral service for a dead boy whose stay on earth had not exceeded one year. The father, one of his sergeants, asked this favor and though, as he wrote Mrs. Lee, his spirit quailed within him, he went ahead with it before the gathered mourners. "He was as handsome a little boy as I ever saw; I was admiring his appearance the day before he was taken ill." Yet perhaps it was all for the best, for the child had now gone into the presence of the Creator, all unsullied and pure of sin and uncontaminated by the vices of the world.

Northers brought snow and deadly winds, and the water bucket in his tent was frozen solid, mornings; dust storms came that blew into his tent and clogged his pen; he spent a Christmas lying under a blanket raised on sticks to protect him from the blazing sun in the great cloudless sky. The temperature rose well above 110 degrees in the shade. His base was a tent encampment with no stable, just a picket line, and the two men he hired as orderlies quit after seeing that San Antonio at least had something approaching streets, even though they lay under inches of dust most of the time: "My servants have informed me they cannot go back to Camp Cooper. It is too dreary." Stratford, with the Great Hall and winding driveway and rolling lawns, seemed far, far away, and Arlington also, with its high ceilings and polished mahogany and silver and the bed upon which George Washington died, and of course West Point and even Mexico also for its Spanish grace and the inborn delicacy and manners of the Indians there. For a long time he felt Texas a useless and forsaken place, but as the time passed, a year, a year and a half, he began to see it differently—the vastness of the place, the grit of the settlers, the feeling of hope for the future in this the coming American empire. He got new servants, two former soldiers—"Their skill in cooking consists in making coffee, boiling rice and beans and frying ham"—and went to chasing the Mexican bandit Juan Nepomuceno Cortinas, who, with 500 lawless pillagers, was laying waste to the isolated settlements and running off the stock. He never caught Cortinas, though he chased him across hundreds of miles of desert, but he learned to love the West, the sky, the vista, and to esteem the promise.

Orders came calling the regimental commander, Albert Sidney Johnston, to Washington; Lee succeeded to the leadership of the unit with headquarters at San Antonio. It was August of 1857. He was there, in San Antonio, in October when he received news that his wife's father, Mr. Custis, "the Child of Mount Vernon," had died. He knew that Mrs. Lee could never cope with the problems her father's death would bring, and so applied for leave. He reached Arlington in November to receive perhaps the greatest shock he had ever known. His wife was an invalid. Rheumatoid arthritis had taken Mary Lee and she was unable to walk and was in constant pain. One arm was almost useless. "I almost dread him seeing my crippled state," she had written a relative. At forty-nine she was old. She had been a difficult woman, and without alluding to himself or Mary, Lee was to tell young officers that separations for trivial reasons were death to the relationship between a man and woman, and that therefore officers' wives should at all costs join their husbands at duty posts; but the pain and suffering seemed to soften her, and although then and always she could flare up in displays of temperament, she complained very little and made do. Her trial was to last for the remainder of her life, made easier only by the nursing he gave her. What he had learned at his mother's sickbed, he now applied to his wife.

Executor of his father-in-law's estate, he began to make his way through the muddle the dead man had left. Arlington was, upon Mrs. Lee's death, to go to Custis, the White House plantation of 4,000 acres on the Virginia peninsula to Rooney and Romancoke of like acreage to Rob. Ten thousand dollars was to go to each of the girls. Contradictory instructions as to the raising of the money indicated that Mr. Custis, in customary unmethodical fashion, had put together his will without consulting an attorney. He seemed to want the estates to provide the money, but also indicated that other lands in four different counties were to be sold. A final insoluble dilemma was that after the legacies had been paid, but within a period of five years following his death, he said he wanted all his slaves emancipated. There were 196 of them, and under his easy reign they had done virtually nothing for years. Fences were down, the lawns had bushes and weeds and the roof of Arlington House leaked. No hint of how they were to live when freed was contained in Mr. Custis' testament. On top of everything else, the dead man had carelessly run up debts.

Lee knew nothing of business matters beyond his intense desire not to exceed his income—he had learned from Light Horse Harry where that could lead—but he set to work. The first thing was to make Arlington more productive than it had been. In the spring he fixed the main house's roof and repaired the dilapidated stables. He put in a corn crop and rented out mills and unused lands. Slaves not needed for immediate use were hired out to local planters. Each morning he sat in a small room on the mansion's ground floor and went over his accounts. There was no end to matters great and petty in connection with Mr. Custis' will, and he applied to the courts to interpret the document for him. Time went on and his leave ran out. He asked General Scott to extend it and extend it again. He had been away from his regiment for two years when on October 17, 1859, Lieutenant James Ewell Brown Stuart ("Beauty" Stuart then to the other cadets, but more lately "Jeb"), his son Custis' best friend at West Point, appeared at Arlington. Colonel Lee had gone to Alexandria, Stuart was told, and so he followed him there and found him in the apothecary shop making some purchases. Lieutenant Stuart handed him a sealed note from the chief clerk of the War Department. Colonel Lee was to report at once to the Secretary. There was some trouble at Harpers Ferry.

6

Down

THE VOLUNTEER REGIMENTS that had fought in Mexico disbanded and went to their homes while the personnel of the regular army went to where orders sent them. The newlyweds, Captain and Mrs. Ulysses S. Grant of the Fourth Infantry, found themselves at the post of Sackets Harbor, New York, on the eastern shore of Lake Ontario. Then they went to Detroit.

They were a happy couple. His pay was sufficient for him to buy a trotting horse behind which he raced down Jefferson Avenue. She and the wife of another officer gave a costume ball where people came dressed as the Sultana of Turkey, the Veiled Prophet of Khorassan, as flower girls and peasant girls and Little Red Riding Hood, kings, knights and troubadours. She was a tambourine girl. He wore his uniform and stood watching as she danced with more musically talented men.

His work as quartermaster was undemanding, like that of a shipping clerk taking in and then distributing supplies, and much of his duty time was spent in the sutler's store of the post. With the other men he smoked and played checkers—at which he was very good. He did not have much to say. The others regarded him as a pleasantly inoffensive little chap who was awfully good with horses. In due time Julia Dent Grant became pregnant. Detroit was a primitive little western town with board sidewalks to fend off the mud, and it seemed best that she return to her home near St. Louis for the lying-in. He moved into a cottage with Major John Gore. The rent was $250 a year. Their landlord was a teacher who regarded Gore as a man and Grant as a boy. As soon as the two housemates left, the landlord forgot the junior officer's name, what he looked like and what, if anything, he had ever said.

In St. Louis, Frederick Dent Grant, named of course for Julia's father, was born into the world. Orders came for a return to Sackets Harbor, and the little family settled there. The town was dull but they had plenty of friends on the post, and little Fred, the sole baby of the military contingent, was everybody's pet. It was pleasant. She became pregnant again. Meanwhile, the California gold rush was going on and the West was booming. In the spring of 1852 orders came for the regiment to make for the Pacific coast. The route would be by water to Aspinwall* in Panama, then by horse or mule across the narrow neck of land to the ocean. No one could say how long the tour of duty would be.

He thought at once of resigning the Army, for there could be no question of taking along to the coast a pregnant wife with a toddler by her side. But he hesitated to throw away his position without something concrete in hand. So Julia and little Fred went off and, save for letters, out of his life for the while. He missed them more than he had ever missed home when he went to West Point. Family life did not merely suit him; he gloried in it. He could talk to Julia. He could be a father to Fred. The regiment sailed from Governors Island in New York harbor for

*Now Colon.

Panama on the overcrowded side-wheeler *Ohio*, splashing along through a summer sea whose sunsets he watched sitting apart and lonely. At night Delia Sheffield, the wife of a sergeant of the Fourth, saw him pacing the decks silent and solitary.

On July 13, at a time of year when the regimental surgeon had warned it would be "murder" for them to arrive, the regiment came to Panama. It was the rainy season. The port was the hellish offshoot of the California gold rush, built by the financier William Henry Aspinwall as a base for his railroad across the Isthmus. Sudden torrents that turned everything into mud and puddles were in a moment followed by a deadly humid, steaming heat and a murderous glaring sun. It was said that a man died of fever for each tie put into Aspinwall's railroad, which stretched 20 miles inland and then gave out. The Fourth fled the horrible jerry-built falling-apart tropical town filled with rum shops selling liquor and quinine to ward off or cure malaria, and made for the railroad terminus on the Chagres River. The green jungle was terrifying, thick and wet, and with masses of sodden decaying vegetation at the roots of the unfamiliar trees. Rain and sun beat at the soldiers and those dependents who had ventured with them on the trip. At the Chagres, they found dugouts manned by all-but-naked natives, who with poles pushed their crafts across the water to where mule transport hired by the Army was supposed to be waiting. The contractor had said the animals would be on hand in the morning. Meanwhile, nonmilitary travelers, adventurers, escaped convicts, European second sons, prostitutes and bail jumpers flowing toward the western gold fields bought up what mules there were, paying as high as $40 for an animal who could carry them the 25 miles to the Pacific, and who in other days would not have sold for $10.

In the morning the contractor had some story that the mules were on the way. By then cholera was striking people down. One felt cramps, one began to vomit and often in a few hours it was all over. The regimental surgeon speaking about murder was right. Thirty-seven people died in one day. As a quartermaster's duties included transportation of personnel as well as procurement of goods, Captain Grant, amid shivering and moaning soldiers and their dependent wives and children, rounded up native porters and put them to carrying his people in hammocks. They made their way along the thin trails whose paving stones had been laid by the Spaniards centuries before, but whose width was now such that one had to duck the overhanging reaches of the encroaching forest. All of the members of the Fourth who were not yet sick he put to marching toward the Pacific, hustling them on their way with warnings not to drink the water.

Grant himself stayed behind on the banks of the Chagres, seeing people off one by one along the route that might lead to safety. The native porters one step removed from savagery drank, fought with knives and attempted to molest the wives of the soldiers. Grant, in the midst of jungle banks flaming with strange plants and alive with the screaming of strange birds, nursed the sick and the dying and then, throwing away Army regulations, went out into the open market to bid fabulous prices for mules. Shepherding along the last of his Fourth Infantry cavalcade, he pushed on along the trail, burying the dead in the mire where they had breathed their last. Mud-spattered, his caravan staggered into Panama City, one third of their number behind along the jungle trail. He put his people on an old hulk turned into a floating hospital and stood watch to make sure that men made stewards did not slip overboard and desert what they regarded as a deathship. He got bags to load and cannonballs to weight the corpses he lowered into the water, and he bought food and medicines in the city for those who escaped the deadly peril of the disease. A man of iron, so the patients said, he was like a ministering angel, sleeping only two or three hours at a time, if even that.

He played cards with his old Detroit housemate, Major Gore, and during the game Gore dropped his hand suddenly, turned pale and gasped, "My God, I've got the cholera." "No, Major, you've only eaten something that doesn't agree with you," Grant assured his friend, but in a little while Gore was dead. Grant sent a lieutenant with Mrs. Gore on the trail back to

Aspinwall and a ship to home, she in a hammock, her child's nurse in another and her infant son on the shoulders of an Indian porter.

In the end he pulled through those who could be saved and did what he could for the more than 100 who perished, and then the decimated regiment took ship for the north. Those who had been in Panama never forgot what he had been in those days— cool at all times, utterly unrattled. He said nothing of his activities to Julia. "Give my love to all at home Dearest and kiss our dear little one for me. Fred, the little dog, I know talks quite well by this time. Is he not a great pet? You must not let them spoil him Dearest. A thousand kisses for yourself dear Julia. Don't forget to write often and direct, Hd. Qtrs. 4th Inf Columbia Barracks, Fort Vancouver, Oregon."

The post was a primitive fortification built by his old West Point friend and Twelve in One fellow-member, Rufus Ingalls, a tiny settlement in the great forests. Mount Hood towered in the near distance. He lived with Ingalls and another officer in a frame building overlooking the Columbia River half a mile away. Indians and half-breeds and trappers hung around the Hudson's Bay Company trading post. There was virtually nothing to do but keep an eye on the Indians and wait for the widely spaced visits of Army surveying parties or for the immigrant wagon trains that went by from time to time. Mail from the East took ages to arrive. A letter came telling him that Julia was well, and so also was Ulysses S. Grant, Jr. He had dreamt one night that Julia had given birth to a girl; Ulysses, Jr., at that moment was five months old.

Prices on the gold rush West coast were sky high, and he realized that it would be impossible ever to bring out and support his wife and two children there without outside income, so with his housemates he bought 100 tons of ice and sent it down the Columbia to San Francisco where, they were told, it would bring good money. But the ship was delayed in arriving and came into port to find that gigantic shipments of Alaskan ice had completely taken away the market. He bought cattle and hogs and horses to sell to immigrants; it didn't work. He planted potatoes, sowing the seeds from a sheet tied around his neck, only to see them flooded over by the river. It was just as well, for practically everybody else in the area had gotten the idea that potatoes were a ready money crop, and their price wouldn't have made them worth taking out of the ground. He put up money for a merchant to open a store in San Francisco; the man decamped with everything.

In the spring of 1853 Rufus Ingalls was ordered away to Fort Yuma, and Columbia Barracks was lonely without him. The two old comrades had spent hours riding through the forests. Rufus had been a good friend, witty, always making people laugh. Grant asked one of the sergeants to move in with him, bringing his wife, Delia Sheffield, to cook and keep house. The Sheffields remembered always how the captain sat for hours reading and rereading his wife's letters about herself and Fred and Ulysses, Jr. "I want to resign from the Army and live with my family," Grant told Mrs. Sheffield. There were tears in his eyes when he spoke. "He seemed to be always sad," another sergeant remembered.

He did not hunt with the other officers, nor fish, for he retained his horror of killing things, nor did he slake his needs with Indian women. He went about with a letter on which Julia had traced the outline of little Ulysses' hand; and when he showed it to people, his own hand trembled and tears came down his cheeks. A pig-selling operation failed and he lost what he had put into it. At post dances he watched the others waltz with guests from Portland across the river and then went to his room to sit reading Julia's letters. He bought chickens to sell in San Francisco. They died on the trip.

That June, Captain George B. McClellan came to Columbia Barracks. They had known each other at West Point and in Mexico. The gap between the two was painful, for McClellan, second man of his West Point year, was an Engineers luminary sent to survey the route of the proposed Northern Pacific Railroad. Grant's function was to outfit the expedition under McClellan's exacting orders. He stayed in Grant's house for three months and then left for the Cascade Range on his important surveying duties while Grant droned the summer away writing letters and waiting for mail from Julia. "Does Ulys. walk yet? From the progress he appears to be making I suppose he must. Continue dear Julia to write me as you do about the boys. I like to hear of Fred's sayings."

In September of 1853, after a year at Columbia Barracks, he was ordered to Fort Humboldt on Humboldt Bay in California to command a company there. The post was even smaller than Columbia Barracks, a few log troop quarters with cabins for officers. Sawmills of the new California lumber industry were along the waterfront and, behind the barracks, the immense forest. The total complement consisted of about 100 men and 6 officers, Lieutenant Colonel Robert Buchanan commanding. Grant had never liked Buchanan, nor did the lieutenant colonel like him. Neither had forgotten the time back at Jefferson Barracks years before when Buchanan fined Grant the bottles of wine for being late to dinner and told him young people were to be seen but not heard. The work was dullness itself, a dreary killing of time while waiting for boats to bring the irregular mails upriver to Eureka, the wretched little frontier trading-post town.

California and the West were supposed to be the new El Dorado where men became richer than dreams could tell, but Captain Grant had about run out of ways to make money and was stuck making wages less than those paid a cook. Years could pass while he dwindled away his youth thousands of miles from Julia and his sons, and a decade might go by before he went up even a step in the tiny Army. He thought of resigning his commission—but what then? It had been abundantly proved that he was no businessman. "When I get to thinking upon the subject," he wrote Julia, "*poverty, poverty*, begins to stare me in the face."

He had been downcast and sad before, at Columbia Barracks, but in bleak Humboldt, with a hostile commanding officer set above him, he lapsed into a state far worse. "You do not know how forsaken I feel here," he wrote her. "I do nothing but set in my room and read and occasionally take a short ride." He began drifting over to Ryan's, the Indian trader's store, where he sat on the porch and looked out at bleakness, mud, fur-clothed primitive people, flimsy wooden houses and endless lonely forests. If he could have made money, it all would have been different. . . . Julia would have been there with Fred and Ulysses, Jr. . . . But she wasn't there . . . and Ryan's, like all the other trading posts along the frontier had a barrel and tin cup waiting. The barrel was filled with whiskey.

Men on the frontier did not take cocktails before dinner, or sip from a snifter with their evening cigar. They drank—drank. Grant knew that. He knew also that a little went a long way with him. A regular drinker could put the stuff away, laugh, brag, shout, fall down perhaps, but keep on going. But a man whose constitution was such that only a couple of drinks made him stupid could not. Grant was such a man. Back in Sackets Harbor he had joined the national order of the Sons of Temperance and worn its ribbon in his lapel and its emblem of a triangle surrounding the Star of Temperance. "There is no safety from ruin by liquor except by abstaining from it altogether," he had said then. He had been the mainstay of the Sons' Rising Sun Division, No. 210, holding offices in the lodge and keeping it in a flourishing condition. Later in Detroit he had let himself go a few times, and when he sued the rising Michigan dry goods merchant, Zachariah Chandler, for not clearing the sidewalks of his store of snow—Grant had slipped and injured himself— Chandler at the trial had said, "If you soldiers would keep sober, perhaps you would not fall on people's pavements and hurt your legs." (The jury brought in the symbolic 6 cents verdict plus costs in Grant's favor.)

Back at Columbia Barracks during Captain McClellan's stay Grant had irritated that trim and efficient organizer by going off on a brief spree. But it had been a one-time fall from grace. It was different at Humboldt. Melancholy, silent, gloomy, inat-

tentive to what went on around him, solitary, he got the reputation of a souse. He drank in a peculiar way, holding his little
finger even with the bottom of the tumbler and holding his other
three fingers above the little one and then filling in whiskey to
the top of his first finger. He took it without water and he did
it every day and often every day.

Perhaps it gave him courage, for he went on with a final
new business project, a billiard room in Frisco, which did not
pan out. He drank some more. Lieutenant Colonel Buchanan
might have dealt with the problem differently had he liked Grant.
But when Grant showed up drunk for paymaster duty, Buchanan
told him to fill out an unsigned resignation. Another binge and
Grant would sign that resignation, Buchanan said.

For a time he stayed sober. Then at a party an officer's wife
urged him to have a little punch. He took some. The next day
the entire post knew he had become completely done in, and
knew also what must be in prospect as he trudged across the
dismal parade ground to Buchanan's office. A couple of men with
the lieutenant colonel quickly left the room when Grant came
in, unwilling to see what was coming. Buchanan took out the
unsigned resignation and asked Grant what he thought his proper
course was now. Friends had told him to dare Buchanan to bring
him up on charges and put him on trial, that Buchanan could
never make it stick. But Grant replied that he would never stand
trial on charges of drunkenness, that he could not let Julia know
that such a thing had happened to him. He signed. It was April
11, 1854. For fifteen years he had worn cadet gray and Army
blue. Now he was a civilian.

He went to San Francisco. He looked so terrible that one
old friend felt almost ashamed to be seen speaking to him on the
street. He waited for a boat East and talk went around that he
had drunk up his discharge money and accumulated pay and
was completely flat. Major Robert Allen sought him out in a
cheap waterfront hotel where Grant sat dejectedly at a table in
a garret room. When he raised his head, Allen saw that his face
was haggard and despairing.

"Why, Grant, what are you doing here?"

"Nothing. I've resigned from the Army, I'm out of money, and I have no means of getting home."

Major Allen was chief quartermaster of the West coast and had strings to pull, as did his clerk, who remembered the shabby ex-captain asking if he could spend the night on the old sofa in the office. Together they managed a free ticket from the Pacific Mail Steamship Company to New York. He arrived penniless and looked up his old West Point friend, Captain Simon Bolivar Buckner, who went with him to a hotel and told the manager he would guarantee the bill. Buckner also passed the hat around among the officers of the Governors Island garrison and came up with some $50, part of which Grant used for a railroad ticket to Sackets Harbor, where the man who had run off with the San Francisco store money was supposed to be. When he got there he found the man was somewhere else. He went back to New York to receive some money his father had sent to pay his way back to Ohio. Jesse Grant was hoping to get him to stay in the Army. "I never wished him to leave the servis [sic]," Jesse wrote Secretary of War Jefferson Davis. "I think after spending so much time to qualify for the Army & spending so many years in the servis [sic], he will be poorly qualified for the pursuits of private life." Secretary Davis wrote back that the resignation had been accepted and that nothing could be done.

Thirty-two years old, with no money and no trade, with a wife and two children, the ex-captain went to St. Louis. At the time of her wedding, Julia's father had given her sixty acres outside the city. Jesse helped him out with money for seed and implements and animals, and Grant went to farming. He and Julia lived in a house belonging to one of her brothers while, with his father-in-law's promise to put up the money, he planned the building of a home. For ready cash he cut wood on the acreage as he waited for his oats and vegetables to grow. He charged $4 a cord, cut, delivered and stacked in the sheds of St. Louis customers mainly secured because they were friends of Julia's family. It was 12 miles to the city along the Gravois Road and people living along the way saw him almost every day going to or coming from, perched up on the box of his old farm wagon. He worked the land between making his deliveries, using such slaves of the Dents as he could get to help him. But he was a very poor slave driver and so he came to rely upon freed blacks that he hired on a now-and-then basis when he had the money. It was all very unpleasant. "Colonel" Dent was in the best of times a blustering coarse man, and his view of a son-in-law who had to be put to working with slaves in the fields was far from positive. Jesse in Ohio felt, and said, that West Point and the Army had ruined his son, that he'd never be any good for business of any kind.

Sam Grant got the neighbors to come in and help him put up his new house, the timbers for which he had cut and fashioned himself and the cellar of which he had dug alone. The job of raising it took one day. He called it "Hardscrabble," and it was a glorified cabin Julia found crude and ugly, although she did not say so to her husband. She gave birth to their first girl, Nellie, and then with the three children kept house while he worked the fields or delivered his wood to the homes of St. Louisians who had once, but no more, considered her their social equals. For the first time in her life she felt a feeling of despondency. She found herself asking the empty rooms, "Is this my destiny?"

He kept on, a dirt farmer and woodsman who during the entire year of 1856 had less than $50 to spend on clothing for his family. Winter came. He who had once worn gold-laced and braided uniform and been taught at West Point that an officer was not only an officer but a gentleman, stood by his wagon on St. Louis street corners and offered wood to whomever would buy it. When customers gave him the word, he mounted the box, went to where directed, unloaded and stacked the wood and then came to the door to get his money. He wore his old blue Army overcoat with insignia removed.

The approach of the planting season of 1857 found him with no money to buy seeds, and so he had to write to Jesse asking the loan of $500. There was no answer. He wrote again and then again, saying it was his final appeal, that he was not asking charity but a loan. He could pay 10 percent interest, he told his father. There was no one else to whom he could apply, and in the course of two or three years Jesse had to advance him $2,000. Sam had hoped for a crop of 400 or 500 bushels of wheat, but got only 75. He plowed, bound wheat behind the cradles of his father-in-law's slaves, wore rough clothing and delivered wood to Jefferson Barracks where ten years before he had been, in the eyes of his sister-in-law Emma Dent, an officer as pretty as a doll. Now his shoulders were stooped and his pants tucked into muddy old Army boots, and his blue coat was mud-splattered also—a man with the air of an all-pervading bad luck, people said. Under a slouched hat that had a tendency to turn up in front, and down behind, his face was somber. He looked older than he was, and an Army friend coming to his place for a visit was shocked to learn that when he asked a scraggly-bearded shabby laborer where Grant was, he discovered he was in fact talking to the man he sought. "Good God," the man gasped. "What are you doing?" "I am solving the problem of poverty," Grant answered. It was embarrassing for Pete Longstreet and Rufus Ingalls when they ran into him at Jefferson Barracks.

He couldn't make a go of it at Hardscrabble, and so Julia's father told them to come back to White Haven. Sam could manage the 500 acres there for the "Colonel." But his health was not good, for he had picked up what was called ague, a malarial sickness said to occur where decayed swamp vegetation abounded. It brought a sallow complexion, chills and fever. He found it hard to get up and go to work in the fields or woodlots, and his financial situation was desperate. Winter was approaching, the winter of 1857, and there was no money at all for Christmas; and so on December 23 he went to a St. Louis pawnshop and there handed over a watch and gold chain he had hung on to. The broker gave him $22.

It was clear that farming wasn't going to work out. He saw

an Army expedition heading west for New Mexico and approached the commissary officer. They talked and then he went away and another officer inquired who that had been. "Old Ulysses S. Grant of the Fourth Infantry," answered the commissary officer. "He wanted to be employed to drive beef cattle and issue rations while we were crossing the plains. I couldn't employ him."

Along the Gravois Road, in the little shops and stores where he bought things on credit, they noted his shaking from the ague and said he must be drinking again. (The reason for his forced resignation from the Army had long since gotten back to the officers at Jefferson Barracks and through them to everyone who knew him.) Once he was taken violently ill, and when a man told him to lie down in the back of his wagon, he would drive him home, word spread that the captain—that was what people still called him—had been off on a spree. His health did not improve, and in the end he saw that grubbing and hoeing and hauling wood, even if he could keep it up, would soon put him into an invalid's bed or a grave. And there was no money in it anyway, not for him. In late 1858 he put his things up for auction, and while Julia stayed with the children at her father's White Haven, he went to St. Louis.

He had a job there, or rather a partnership in a business. He had been forced on a relative of the Dents, Henry Boggs. Boggs had a real estate and rent collection business. He took Grant with reluctance only after his wife, Louisa, pointed out that old Dent would undoubtedly drum up business for his favorite daughter's husband. But contacts could take a man only so far. And whatever the captain might be, it was immediately apparent that he had neither the salesmanship of a real estate agent nor the dunning ability of a collector of past-due rents. He lived in a back room in the Boggs house that was carpetless and furnished with a bed and washbowl standing on a chair. There was no stove, and on cold nights they let him sit in their parlor before the fire. Louisa Boggs never heard him laugh once.

On weekends, when the office was closed, he trudged the 12 miles to White Haven to be with Julia and the children and then on Sunday evening walked back to St. Louis.

His attempts to get people to buy houses were so fruitless, and defaulting rentors put him off with such ease, that soon he was reduced to sitting limply in the office with a newspaper dangling from his fingers. In the spring Julia and the children came to St. Louis, and he took a shabby house in a wretched neighborhood. The rent was next to nothing but providing it was a great problem to him. It was 2 miles to the office and often he came to work late. It hardly mattered. There was nothing for him to do anyway. Sometimes he talked to people about Mexico.

After a few months it was obvious that the partnership was misconceived. They would have to conclude this, Boggs said. Grant went looking for work. He tried for a job as superintendent of the county roads and had people write letters of recommendation, but the board of commissioners selected someone else for the job. He got work in the custom house, but then the Collector of Customs died and his successor let Grant go. The job had lasted only a couple of months. He walked the streets looking for work of any kind, anything at all, but no offers of employment came. He talked about going west and setting up a hardware store in the Rockies and wrote his father asking if he would stake him; Jesse replied that he would not. Julia's father ridiculed the idea, as he came to ridicule anything connected with this son-in-law who seemed a failure at everything.

In the streets he stopped acquaintances for small loans and soon they took to avoiding him. Louisa Boggs pitied someone who seemed to her "actually the most obscure man in St. Louis." He appeared to be a lost soul who would never get a job, silent and beaten and tired. "Nobody took any notice of him," Mrs. Boggs remembered. Christmas of 1859 and New Year's Day of 1860 found him indescribably sad and at loose ends. In the street one day he saw a face from the past. He and the other man chatted for a few moments, and although they did not go into detail about the situations they found themselves in since last they met, it was evident that neither was doing well. They parted and went their separate ways, Sam Grant and the man who'd given him his nickname, from his initials, back at West Point so long ago. Now the man thought to himself as he walked away that their school hadn't prepared them well for the outside world, not well at all. It was William Tecumseh Sherman.

The first months of 1860 passed and Grant was licked. From earliest childhood he had detested everything that had to do with his father's bloody business of curing the hides of dead animals, but at thirty-seven, with children, debts, no job and no prospects, he borrowed money for a railroad ticket and went to his father to ask to be taken into the family concern. He arrived to find Jesse was not at home, and so he sat for three or four hours in the dining room, not even going through the house to see how things looked, paralyzed at what he had come to in life.

Then Jesse came. Really Jesse had no choice, he told a friend later. "He would have to take U.S. and his family home and make him over again, as he had no business qualifications what-ever—had failed in everything." But at least it wouldn't be the ghastly tannery. Jesse had set up his younger sons, Simpson and Orvil, in a leather goods store in Galena, Illinois. They were doing well. Ulysses could go in with them as a clerk. He would do some selling, some deliveries, make himself generally useful. The salary would be $600 a year.

Simpson, thirty-four years old, nearly four years younger than Ulysses, was a capable man slowly wasting away from consumption. Orvil, twenty-four, the youngest son of the family, was another Jesse, sharp, arrogant, domineering. In April of 1860 Grant and his family came up the Galena River in a steamship. He came down the gangplank wearing his old Army coat and carrying two chairs under his arms, Julia and the children behind him, and they went to live in a little house on Galena's Cemetery Hill. The gravestones began where their back yard ended. The rent was $125 a year.

It was the blue-caped military coat that attracted whatever attention Galena gave to Ulysses S. Grant. No one else in town had anything like it. Little boys admired it. "I suppose people think it strange I should wear this old Army overcoat," the new leather goods clerk said. "It is made of good material, and so I thought I had better wear it out." Wearing his coat—wearing it out—he went about his business. The town was pleasant enough, built on a steep bluff, with 14,000 people. He was not good at remembering the price of things in the store and often charged the wrong amount, often to the customer's benefit ("Nine times out of ten," one said), and so Orvil kept him in the background. Mostly he totaled up the bills; he had been good at math back at West Point. He took no part in town affairs, joined no organization or lodge, but when store hours were over went back to Julia and the children. His house was reached by a long flight of wooden stairs up Cemetery Hill; at the top each evening three-year-old Jesse stood waiting. "Mister, do you want to fight?" he demanded. "I am a man of peace, but I'll not be hectored by a person of your size," Grant would say. They would tussle and battle and then go to the dinner Julia had made.

7

"I Am Willing to Sacrifice Everything but Honour"

JOHN BROWN was a tanner's son who grew up in Ohio. Serving the Lord was the main concern of his life. By the mid-1850s he had come to believe that it was God's enemy, Satan, who had made slaves of the blacks. Brown said that he was God's avenger against evil. A great Hand was guiding him. In Kansas good faced evil, the Lord against Satan, and he must be there doing God's work. So he cut a deadly swath across Bloody Kansas, where the settlers from the North fought a miniature civil war against the settlers from the South. Brown took unarmed Southern sympathizers from their homes to hack them to death in the presence of their families but in the name of his God, and when his own men were slain he took his losses as inducement to do better the next time. The United States Army flailed about trying to keep the peace. It did not succeed.

Brown read in his Bible: *But thus saith the Lord, Even the* *captives of the mighty shall be taken away, And the prey of the terrible shall be delivered; For I will contend with him that contendeth with thee, And I will save thy children. And I will feed them that oppress thee with their own flesh, And they shall be drunken with their own blood, As with sweet wine.** He marked that passage. *For among my people are found wicked men: They lay wait, as he that setteth snares; They set a trap, they catch men. Shall I not visit for these things? saith the Lord: Shall not my soul be avenged on such a nation as this?†* He marked that passage.

Half soldier and half man of God, warrior and priest, Osawatomie Brown of Kansas, called so for one of his massacres in that state, carried his crusade into the heart of the enemy's country. Armed with Sharps rifles purchased with the funds of Northern supporters, and followed by seventeen men, he set out to liberate the slaves of the South. He swept down on Harpers Ferry, Virginia, where the government maintained an armory and arsenal, and took possession. He seized hostages from the leading families of the region and sent out word that the slaves must rally to him. He would lead them south, liberating blacks as he went, storming through Virginia and into Tennessee, an army growing by the hour, burning and shooting, into Alabama and then to the coastal states, Georgia, South Carolina, North Carolina. When he was finished slavery would be dead in America.

But the Harpers Ferry slaves did not rally to him, and he ended up barricaded in the government buildings with every local white man who could carry a gun outside. Telegrams and messages flew to Washington, each one more terrifying than the last, and it seemed to President James Buchanan that a full-scale insurrection, an apocalyptic race war, was at hand. Secretary of War John Floyd did not have a single enlisted man of the Army stationed in Washington, and the only troops at all in the capital consisted of ninety United States Marines of the Navy Yard whose commander was a lieutenant. The Marines were ordered

*Isaiah 49:25–26.
†Jeremiah 5:26, 29.

to entrain at once for Harpers Ferry. But a lieutenant could not be entrusted with putting down what might amount to a revolution. A more seasoned officer by far was needed. Secretary Floyd thought of Colonel Robert E. Lee of the cavalry, on leave from his regiment but still subject to orders. In the antechamber of the Secretary's office a young officer was waiting to demonstrate a mechanism he had invented for attaching a cavalryman's saber to his belt, Lieutenant James Ewell Brown Stuart. He volunteered to ride over to Arlington for Colonel Lee.

He found the colonel and together they passed the District of Columbia policemen who had been told to watch the roads into Washington for allies of Brown's coming with invading armies of slaves, and went to Floyd. He took them to the President, who ordered Lee to follow the Marines to Harpers Ferry and with them put down the insurrection. Jeb Stuart volunteered his services as aide, and a Baltimore & Ohio locomotive fired up to take them to their destination.

The Marines were wired to get off their train a mile from Harpers Ferry and there wait for Lee. He got down from his locomotive wearing a dark civilian suit and was saluted by Lieutenant Israel Green, who was carrying a light dress sword, the weapon he happened to have on when the rush orders about the insurrection reached him. With Green were Maryland and Virginia militia units gathered from nearby areas. Firing could be heard from the complex of government buildings where Brown was barricaded.

It was eleven at night when Lee entered the armory enclosure, October 17, 1859. Brown and his men with thirteen hostages were in the brick building used to house the post fire engines. It had thick walls and heavy oak doors. There was no way of knowing how many men the insurgent party contained or even who their leader was, for Brown had not identified himself, but it was certain that to storm the engine house at night would be dangerous and perhaps futile. The shots of the hundreds of local citizens exchanging fire with Brown had done no damage at all. Lee quieted things down and waited for daylight.

The sky lightened. Mists rose from the river waters. Inside the engine house one of Brown's men looked through a window and saw a dark-mustached man in civilian clothing standing on a little elevation and studying the situation. Brown's follower sighted his rifle. He drew back the hammer. But Brown, at another window, saw the intended victim was unarmed and gave the order not to shoot. A few minutes later Lee sent Jeb Stuart walking up to the engine house door with a white flag. The door opened a crack and Stuart found himself looking down the barrel of a cocked Sharps rifle. In the half-light he saw a face he had seen before during service with the peace-keeping forces in Kansas.

"Why, aren't you old Osawatomie Brown of Kansas, whom I once had there as my prisoner?"

"Yes, but you didn't keep me."

Lieutenant Stuart took a piece of paper Lee had given him and read out: "Colonel Lee, United States Army, commanding the troops sent by the President of the United States to suppress the insurrection at this place, demands the surrender of the persons in the armory buildings. If they will peaceably surrender themselves and restore the pillaged property, they shall be kept in safety to await the orders of the President. Colonel Lee represents to them, in all frankness, that it is impossible for them to escape; that the armory is surrounded on all sides by troops; that if he is compelled to take them by force he cannot answer for their safety."

Brown replied that the terms were unacceptable and demanded safe passage out of Harpers Ferry. Stuart said that was out of the question. They argued the point. Finally Stuart asked for the final time, "Are you ready to surrender and trust to the mercy of the government?"

"No, I prefer to die here."

Stuart stepped back and took off his hat and waved it at Lee. The colonel turned to Lieutenant Green and a squad of Marines. He had expected there would be no choice but to assault

and had individually instructed each of the men that there was
to be no gunfire, that only bayonets were to be used. Lee's
calmness was remarkable in Green's eyes; he seemed to treat the
whole problem as a matter of no moment and easily solved. He
ordered Green to storm the engine house, and the Marines rushed
forward to the cheers of more than 2,000 spectators screaming
for blood and bashed down the door. Lieutenant Green came
running in and saw Brown turn toward him with a rifle. He
struck with his sword and then as Brown staggered, thrust forward. The light dress weapon penetrated Brown's shoulder and
bent double. The man who had drawn a bead on Lee got off a
shot that killed one of the Marines; a comrade of the slain man
drove a bayonet through him and he died pinioned up against
the wall. The others threw up their hands. The entire operation
from the moment Jeb Stuart waved his hat had taken some three
minutes.

The invaders were brought out to the accompaniment of
spectators' shouts that they be lynched. Lee ordered the Marines
to stand in a hollow square around the prisoners and then had
them taken into the post paymaster's office. Outside the people
shrieked for blood. He looked to Brown's injuries and handed
him over to a doctor. The wounds were not serious.

Headlines around the country screamed of insurrection and
riot and revolution, and officials and hordes of newspaper and
magazine reporters descended upon Harpers Ferry. "If you are
uncomfortable, I will bar all visitors," Lee told Brown, but the
prisoner said he would talk to the people, he had nothing to hide,
and so Lee brought them in. In his eyes Brown's act was that
of a madman and a fanatic but still he was glad that his troops
had not had to kill him. "I believe he is an honest, conscientious
old man," he told a friend.

Few Southerners agreed. As Lee stood silently listening,
state officials talked to Brown for hours, telling him he was a
deranged criminal. God, not man, was his judge, Brown replied.
He believed in doing unto others as he wished they might do to

him, and so he had tried to free the slaves. What wages did he
pay his followers, inquired United States Senator James Mason.
"None." "The wages of sin is death," said Jeb Stuart.

"I would not have made such a remark to you, if you had
been a prisoner and wounded in my hands," Brown said.

They took him away for trial and Lee went back to Arlington. John Brown's end came at Charlestown. Thousands of
troops were in formation, including the Richmond Greys, a militia outfit that numbered among its privates the actor John Wilkes
Booth, and the corps of cadets of the Virginia Military Institute
under the command of a West Pointer who had served with Lee
in Mexico and gotten from him a letter of recommendation for
his new job, ex-Major Thomas J. Jackson. As he walked down
the prison steps Brown handed a note to a jailor: *I John Brown
am now quite certain that the crimes of this guilty land will never be
purged away but with Blood. I had as I now think vainly flattered
myself that without very much bloodshed it might be done.* A moment
later he swung at the end of a rope.

Colonel Lee had been away from his regiment for two years
to take care of his father-in-law's estate. The War Department
had been more than generous. It was time for his return to duty,
and so in February of 1860 he went back to Texas. In San
Antonio, weeks from the East coast, he did not at once understand what John Brown's life and death had meant. A South that
almost universally regarded the man as a lunatic murderer was
opposed by a large segment of the North that saw him a saint
made martyr. Memorial meetings were held. Puritan ministers
prayed for his soul. Emerson said that the scaffold was now made
glorious, as once the cross was similarly glorified. The South
was shocked. Was this what the North believed? Did they call
crusader a man who stood for blood and fire and murder? The
Constitution had legalized slavery. Was that even arguable? If
the North saw a John Brown as a voice of truth and an example
to exalt, then perhaps it was time to call it quits to the union of
the states.

In Texas it all came through in the most filtered manner. Across the dusty parade ground the flags and guidons snapped in the wind; and the bugles sounded and drums tapped and the life of the soldier, the life of the officer, went on. There can be things magical in an army. But Lee had been at it a long time. He longed for home and children, for Arlington and green lawns. He was fifty-three. His back was straight, and horses and no drinking or smoking kept him trim and fine. But youth was gone for all of that, and he was lonely. What had he to show for thirty-five years in uniform of cadet gray and then Army blue? Light Horse Harry had swaggered and philandered, it was part of being a soldier to him, but there was none of that in his son. For years he had talked of leaving the Army, ever since he was a lieutenant. Others had left for better or worse—McClellan; Jackson to the Virginia Military Institute; Joe Hooker who served with him in Mexico; "Old Brains" Halleck to be a lawyer; Rosey Rosecrans; Sherman; Jefferson Davis; even Albert Sidney Johnston; Burnside; that little quartermaster captain he'd had to tell to get into proper uniform—Grant. Yet Lee had stayed. Yet what had it not cost him. "But I will not, dear Cousin Anna," he wrote a relative, "impose my sad thoughts upon you, for a man may manifest and communicate his joy, but he should conceal and smother his grief as much as possible. Touching your kind wishes for my speedy return, you know the embarrassment that attends it. A divided heart I have too long had, and a divided life too long led."*

In Texas that spring the sound of the crumbling of the house that had stood for so many years since its erection by the founding fathers came but faintly over the miles of prairie and desert, and he did not hear it. Joe Johnston got a star and Lee wrote to him as "My dear General." He chased bandits and drilled troops. He wrote to his daughters about cats. In the fall Abraham Lincoln was elected President.

To the fire-eaters of the South that meant a sectional party,

---

*The precise meaning of the last sentence can only be speculated upon.

wholly Northern in composition, would now control the government. Four days after the election, South Carolina's legislature voted to call a convention that would take that state out of the Union. To Lee it was madness. The Cotton States were selfish and dictatorial, he wrote his son Custis. Mississippi followed South Carolina out, Florida, Alabama and Georgia. Mrs. Lee sent a newly published life of George Washington out to Texas and her husband read it and wrote her: "How his spirit would be grieved could he see the wreck of his mighty labors! I will not, however, permit myself to believe till all ground of hope is gone that the work of his noble deeds will be destroyed, and that his precious advice and virtuous example will be so soon forgotten by his countrymen. As far as I can judge by the papers, we are between a state of anarchy and civil war. May God avert us from both."

To his son Custis he wrote: "I can anticipate no greater calamity for the country than a dissolution of the Union. I am willing to sacrifice everything but honour for its preservation. Secession is nothing but revolution. The framers of our Constitution never exhausted so much labor, wisdom and forbearance in its formation, and surrounded it with so many guards and securities, if it was intended to be broken at will." To his young relative, Markie Williams, almost another daughter to him: "I am unable to realize that our people will destroy a government inaugurated by the blood and wisdom of our patriot fathers, that has given us peace and prosperity at home, power and security abroad, and under which we have acquired a colossal strength unequalled in the history of mankind. I wish to live under no other government. I wish for no other flag than the 'star spangled banner' and no other air than 'Hail Columbia.' I still hope that the wisdom and patriotism of the nation will yet save it. I see no cause of disunion, strife and civil war and pray it may be averted."

Early in the new year of 1861 Louisiana went out. The Texans met in convention on January 28 to pass an ordinance of secession by a vote of 166 to 7. Officers all around him were sending in their resignations from what, so soon, they would call the Old Army.

But Virginia yet stood by the flag. And what Virginia did would determine what would come to pass. She was the most powerful state of the South, the most powerful of the Union, second only to Texas in size. Virginia was the Mother of Presidents, the birthplace of Washington, Jefferson, Madison, Monroe, Harrison, Tyler, Taylor. The Old Dominion had given to the country Patrick Henry, John Mason, John Marshall. The general-in-chief of the Army was a Virginian. Winfield Scott might have been pompous, flamboyant, a mixture of tinseled show and great soldier, but he was capable of taking a stand. And he took it in front of a group of men from the North who went to him on February 8 to ask what, if anything, he would do to assure that there would be no molestation of the formal counting of the presidential voting results, and the announcement of the results by the electoral college. "Any man," Scott told them in his great rumbling manner, "who attempted by force or unparliamentary disorder to obstruct or interfere with the lawful count of the electoral vote for President and Vice President of the United States should be lashed to the muzzle of a twelve-pounder gun and fired out of a window of the Capitol. I would manure the hills of Arlington with fragments of his body, were he a senator or chief magistrate of my native state! It is my duty to suppress insurrection—*my duty!*"

On the day appointed, Scott had artillery in the street, and soldiers barred from the Capitol all save senators, representatives and those with tickets signed by the Speaker of the House or the outgoing Vice-President. A mob of Southerners beyond the lines of troops screamed imprecations, and when the formal announcement of the election of Abraham Lincoln of Illinois and Hannibal Hamlin of Maine was made, those Southern congressmen who had not yet departed for their homes erupted in shouts of hatred for the general-in-chief. They were echoed by people in the galleries. "Old dotard!" they yelled. "Coward! Free-state pimp!" By then the seven seceded states had elected Jefferson Davis as President of the Confederate States of America.

There remained Virginia. She who had given so much to the country could not see it split apart, and at her call a peace conference aimed at adjusting the differences between the sections was convened in Washington. Virginia also called a state convention to discuss secession, and most of the delegates were judged unfavorable to the idea. In far off Texas, Lee the Virginian could still hope. Hoping still, he received a summons to Washington. He was to report there at once. The call was entirely unexpected. He had been away from the East for only fourteen months. Out in the desert when the orders came, he immediately headed for San Antonio, arriving there on February 16 to find the streets filled with people brandishing firearms. "Who are these men" he asked a friend. They were rebels pledging loyalty to the Confederacy, he was told. The general commanding the Department of Texas, Twiggs of Georgia, had that morning surrendered the state to the rebels, turning over all the arms and equipment the United States had on hand. Tears came into Colonel Lee's eyes and his lips trembled. "Has it come so soon as this?" he asked.

The American flag was gone from every flagstaff in Texas when he left San Antonio and made for home. He went by steamer to New Orleans and then headed for Arlington through what was now a foreign country. As soon as he got home he went to General Scott. In the outer room of the general-in-chief's office was his military secretary, Lee's old friend Lieutenant Colonel Erasmus D. Keyes. They shook hands. "Lee," said Keyes, "it is reported that you concurred in Twiggs' surrender in Texas. How is that?"

"I am here to pay my respects to General Scott; will you be kind enough, Colonel, to show me to his office?"

He was three hours with the chief and mentor who had done so much for him. Afterwards General Scott, normally talkative and willing to discuss everything with Keyes, was strangely silent. A couple of days later Abraham Lincoln, President then for only a few minutes, told the people of the South that in their hands, and not in his, lay the momentous question of civil war. "We are not enemies, but friends," Lincoln said. "We must not be enemies. Though passion may have strained, it must not break our bonds of affection. The mystic chords of memory, stretching from every battlefield and patriot grave, to every living heart and hearthstone, all over this broad land, will yet swell the chorus of the Union, when again touched, as surely they will be, by the better angels of our nature." There was nothing in the President's sentiments that Lee had not voiced over and over again—albeit less eloquently. Yet the Richmond *Enquirer* the next day said: "The question 'Where shall Virginia go?' is answered by Mr. Lincoln. She must go to war."

But there was no war as yet for Virginia to go to. The delegates to the state convention gave every sign that they would vote against secession. Time passed, and in Charleston, South Carolina, the Confederate general P.G.T. Beauregard, who as a lieutenant had been by Captain Lee's side on the Veracruz shore when a sentinel fired and singed Lee's coat, sent a shell arching down into Fort Sumter in the harbor. In Richmond, the Virginia state convention went into secret session. In Washington, a messenger headed toward Arlington with a note from General Scott to Colonel Lee requesting a call at the general-in-chief's office the following day, April 18, 1861.

Scott was working around the clock. Sentries stood guard and orderlies sat in the hall and aides-de-camp were at tables covered with maps, dispatches, calculations. Wrapped in a military cloak he spent nights stretched out on a settee in the office. But he had difficulty rising from it in the mornings, for he was ill and he was seventy-five. He read a report from an officer assigned to survey the defenses of Washington. It pointed out that a single battery on Arlington's high hill overlooking the city could with no trouble level the White House only 2 miles away. The Capitol of the United States was also within easy range.

Scott had some 10,000 troops gathered in Washington, and

he said, "If I could only mount a horse, I—" He checked himself and shook his head and said, "But I am past that. I can only serve my country as I am doing now, in my chair." The new Secretary of State, William H. Seward, always a mollifier, urbane save for when he drank, soothed the old general's feelings by saying that this was a time when experience was more important than youth and strength. Yes, Scott said, but unfortunately most of the officers of higher rank were of Southern birth. He knew it but too well, for in his many years as the head of the Army he had always favored Southerners. They had the air of command. And so now, he told Secretary Seward, the North must have as its leaders men who had never gone beyond major or captain. Of course they would develop with time, there were some splendid people—McClellan, Hancock, Hooker, Sherman, Halleck, others—but none had the training even to handle a brigade, let alone a division, or, higher still, a corps. Or an army. "There is one officer who would make an excellent general," Scott said to Seward. "But I do not know whether we can rely upon him. He lives not far away, and I have sent over to see. If he comes in tomorrow, I shall know."

"I will not ask his name until you hear from him, then, General," Seward said. "Though I think I can guess whom you mean."

Tomorrow came, April 18, 1861, and Robert Lee rode down Arlington's hill on the road to Washington. Spring. Where is the world more beautiful, in the spring, than along the heights that border the Potomac, in Virginia? His first call in the District was not to Scott. Some nights earlier he had dined at the home of his cousin Cassius Lee. His older brother Smith was there, and another cousin of theirs, Samuel Phillips Lee. Both Smith and Samuel Phillips Lee were Navy officers, and when the talk turned, as of course it must, to the desperately troubled situation of the country, Phillips—that was what they called him—said that whatever happened he intended to keep his commission. He was a United States Navy officer. That settled the matter for him. Smith Lee said that if Virginia went out he would go out also. And in case of war, he said, he would place a battery on the Virginia shore and blow Phillips out of the water. Phillips laughed and said Smith would never do that, for he would find himself cagily invited onto Phillips' ship for a drink, and so in no position to open fire. They all laughed and bantered back and forth, thinking and praying, perhaps, that it would never come to that. But Phillips noticed that while all the others declared their views, Robert remained silent.

Phillips was the son-in-law of Francis Preston Blair, Sr., of the Blairs of Blairstown, the most influential political family in the country. Montgomery Blair, Francis Preston Blair's son, was Lincoln's Postmaster General, and his acceptance of the post was more a compliment to Lincoln than a compliment of Lincoln to him. For the Blairs had stood at the elbows of Presidents almost since the Republic was born. Phillips went to his father-in-law and said it appeared that Colonel Lee had not made up his mind about his future course. That information was passed on to Secretary of War Simon Cameron and President Lincoln and, of course, General Scott. And on the day that Scott's summons arrived at Arlington there also arrived a request by Francis Preston Blair, Sr., asking that Colonel Lee pay him a morning call.

He rode up to the Washington seat of the Blair family, Blair House, 1651 Pennsylvania Avenue, just opposite the executive mansion. He sat with Francis Preston Blair, Sr. It was said by Napoleon that every soldier of his army carried in his knapsack the baton of a marshal of France. What did that mean? Did Lee have to be told? He had heard the tapping drums, the bugle calling its sweet notes across the prairie; he had stood a thousand, ten thousand, formations; he had marched and watched march-pasts, the Plain along the Hudson, Georgia, Mexico; he had read morning reports in New York and Texas; had stiffened to attention, his hand rising to the salute—how many times in those thirty-five years he had served? Bayonet drill, battery drill, close-order drill, boots and saddles, squadrons right, draw sabers. . . . But ultimately what is a soldier for? What does an officer desire? Speaking in the name of the Secretary of War, of the President, Blair offered the great answer: command.

Command of 75,000 men, a major generalcy, 100,000 men. An army ten times the size of Scott's, which had amazed the world, an army such as would make Caesar quail, Frederick, Turenne, Lord Wellington, Napoleon, Great Washington. The President—the country—offered it. In later years it was to be said—it seemed like idolatry, but they did not mean it so—that only the offer to Jesus Christ of the three temptations paralleled this. "Since the Son of Man stood on the Mount, and saw all the kingdoms of the world and the glory of them stretched before him, and turned away, to the Cross of Calvary beyond, no follower of the Saviour can have undergone a more trying ordeal."* Fame, power, riches were his at the raising of his hand. Victory.

"I could take no part in an invasion of the southern states," he said to Blair. He went to Scott. "Lee, you have made the greatest mistake of your life, but I feared it would be so," Scott moaned.

He rode from the general-in-chief's headquarters and in the street met a man who had been a cadet during his superintendency of the United States Military Academy at West Point. "Are you not well, Colonel Lee?" asked Ben Hardin Helm of Kentucky.

"Well in body, but not in mind," Lee answered. Helm showed a letter he had been handed by the President, his brother-in-law. He was married to Mary Lincoln's sister. Lee read the letter silently. It offered a commission as paymaster with rank of major. That would mean that Helm would likely never have to fire at Kentucky relatives and friends if there was a war, and if the war was brief. For a longer war no guarantees could be extended.

"My mind is too much disturbed to give you any advice,"

---

*The orator John Daniels at the unveiling of Valentine's monument of the recumbent warrior over Lee's grave, 1883.

Lee said. "Do what your conscience and honor bid." Helm went home and conferred with his fellow-Kentuckian and former West Point instructor, Simon Bolivar Buckner. Then he wrote an answer to Lincoln's offer. No.

Lee headed for Long Bridge over the Potomac. Newsboys of the Washington *Star* were yelling that Virginia had voted to secede from the Union. He bought a paper. The report was unconfirmed, the story said. But the next day in Alexandria he bought a copy of that city's *Gazette*. It confirmed the report. Virginia was going out. The apothecary in whose shop Jeb Stuart had found him with the first news about the Harpers Ferry disturbance asked what the colonel thought about the news. "I must say," Lee answered, "that I am one of those dull creatures that cannot see the good of secession." He went home and silently handed the paper to his wife.

That night Mrs. Lee, sitting in the first-floor drawing room, heard her husband pacing the floor of his bedroom above her. She heard the pacing cease and knew that he had fallen to his knees to pray for guidance from the God to whom he turned more and more in recent years. His dilemma was excruciating. At the base of his being there rested the soldier's belief in obedience, in a code of acceptance of orders—of loyalty. Surrounding him in Arlington's rooms were relics of George Washington. He was married to Martha Washington's great-granddaughter, he was son-in-law to Washington's adopted son. In a sense he was Washington's heir. That was what Francis Preston Blair had pointed out to him. But Washington had served with, and then fought against, the British. Washington had been a British officer and then had turned on Britain. He, Lee, was a United States officer. But to turn on the United States, the country Washington had made? *Traitor*. But if the South was kept in the Union against its will, would not that mean that the war against England had been a mistake and a fraud?

It was written in the Declaration of Independence that all governments derive their just powers from the consent of the governed. And the South no longer wanted to be governed by the United States. But Arlington lay directly in what would be contested land, a battlefield, if the Union and Confederacy came to blows. Virginia would be the battlefield. Could he destroy Virginia's body to save her soul—if that were at stake, her soul?

Downstairs in the wheelchair she used increasingly as disease took her, his wife listened to his pacing. He was a West Pointer. His education had been paid for by the government of the United States. Yet Virginia paid her full share of taxes. She had contributed to the education of her sons at the Academy. Did not she have the right to call upon those sons now? At the moment, in his case, she did not; Lee was still an officer in the United States Army. General Twiggs had been a United States Army officer commanding the Department of Texas when the Texas rebels came to him to demand his surrender. He had turned everything over to them, had not lifted a finger in behalf of the government whose uniform he wore. Was Colonel Lee to do that if the Virginia rebels came to him? That would be dishonor. There was no other way to look at it. But could he fight those who would be rebels—his friends, his relatives, Virginia's people? Yet it might never come to fighting. That was General Scott's hope, and the hope of President Lincoln: The Army would never have to *fight* the South, rather it would simply keep the peace. Yet was that probable? Lee's sons Rooney and Custis did not think so. Rooney felt the people of the South had lost their senses and were making a mistake the consequences of which would be terrible. Custis said that if things were up to him he would fortify Arlington with the guns pointing south.

As for slavery, that was not even a consideration. Old Blair had asked if the possible loss of his slaves had anything to do with Colonel Lee's declining the field command of the United States Army, and Lee had answered that if he owned every one of the 4 million slaves he would gladly free them to avoid a war and save the Union. "Slavery as an institution," he had written long before, "is a moral and political evil in any country. It is useless to expatiate on its disadvantages."

The hours were passing. Soon it would be daylight. He

wrote a letter to Scott, whose favorite he had been, to whom he owed so much, to whom he had been so dear. He thanked the old general for his friendship, for everything. "I shall carry to the grave the most grateful recollections of your kind consideration, and your name and fame will always be dear to me."

To Simon Cameron, the Secretary of War:
Sir:

I have the honor to tender the resignation of my commission as Colonel of the First Regiment of Cavalry.

Very respectfully, Your Obedient Servant

8

"My Heart Resumed Its Place"

WHEN THE NEWS that Southern guns had fired upon the American flag at Fort Sumter reached Galena, Illinois, the town went wild with rage. The national colors were run up on every pole and attached to every building. Bands paraded and placards announcing a mass meeting at the courthouse were stuck up on walls.

At the meeting, the mayor of Galena spoke for peace and accommodation. Let the erring sisters depart in peace. His listeners erupted with shouts and threats and he was chased from the rostrum. Others took his place and spoke instead of the insult to the old flag, of treason and of war. A young and fiery lawyer, John A. Rawlins, spoke for forty-five minutes. "I have been a Democrat all my life," he ended, "but this is no longer a question of politics. It is simply Union or disunion, country or no country. I have favored every compromise, but the day for compromise is past. Only one course is left for us! We will stand by the flag of our country and appeal to the God of Battles!"

The cheering went through the windows and out over the heads of the people outside, and up the hill and beyond. As he walked away with his brother Orvil, the leather goods clerk Ulysses Grant said, "I think I ought to go into the service." "I think so, too," Orvil answered. "I'll stay home and attend to the store."

President Lincoln's call for volunteers allocated to Illinois a quota of some 4,500 men and 225 officers. Galena's share of that consisted of two companies. Men rushed to join, and soon the ranks were filled. In all the town there was only one man who had served in the regular army. He was still wearing the blue overcoat of his time there. Suddenly Grant was no longer trying to remember the prices of bridle reins and saddle pads, but was instead outlining the patterns of Army uniforms to the ladies who wanted to make them for the men of the Joe Daviess County Guards. He got pine laths to substitute for rifles while he taught the volunteers the manual of arms.

The volunteers were authorized to elect officers from among their number. He let it be known that he would not stand for election. Indeed he did not join the Guards, but simply acted as their drillmaster and advisor. Perhaps he was hoping for a higher position than the Guards could offer. And perhaps he knew that Galena men would never make an officer of one who was a clerk looked upon as something of a family charity, had outstanding debts, was said to have had a drinking problem, and was generally regarded as being a far distance from important or a go-getter. He kept to his duties with the troops—if such the men could be called—and the day came when they were ordered to the capital, Springfield, for induction into a state regiment. In their brand-new uniforms the Guards paraded the streets escorted by the fire companies, the civic societies, the officials of the town, including the mayor, who had seen the light. The elected captain of one of the two companies, Augustus L. Chetlain, accepted from Miss Annie Campbell a silk flag made by her according to the dimensions and design given out by Ulysses Grant. The town turned out to cheer and wave handkerchiefs, ministers prayed, and the Joe Daviess County Guards with their new flag went to the Illinois Central Railroad Station to take the train that would start them on the journey to discipline the cursed rebels who had fired on the Banner of Freedom. Behind the men, in shabby clothes, carrying a battered cloth bag, in a slouch hat, at the rear of the column, marched the civilian Ulysses S. Grant.

At Springfield the Guards were mustered into the ranks of the 12th Illinois by Captain John Pope, who had been at West Point for three years with Sam Grant. Chetlain was elected lieutenant colonel. The capital was jammed with lawyers and small-town leaders come to collect on old political debts, payment in their eyes taking the form of a colonel's eagle or at least a major's cluster. There were so many of them to accommodate that the legislature voted to increase the number of Illinois regiments from six to sixteen. Captain Pope himself was angling for a general's star and the command of all of the state's volunteers. Grant took a room with Chetlain; they shared the single bed. Their congressman, Elihu Washburne of Galena, was in town looking after the interests of his constituents, and he was prevailed upon to see what he could do for Grant. He said he would take him to talk to Governor Richard Yates.

A couple of days after the arrival in Springfield, Washburne told Grant to come along to see Governor Yates. But his aid was a questionable blessing, for Yates was not fond of Washburne. In addition, it seemed to Augustus Chetlain that the job applicant did not present a formidable military appearance, dressed as he was in a suit he had been wearing every day for the entire winter in contrast to other men attired either in brilliant uniform or impressive civilian turnout. The governor's assistant, Gustave Koerner, receiving the callers, came to the same conclusion: "He was very indifferently dressed, and did not at all look like a military man." Yates' distaste for Washburne and the impression Grant made combined to cause the governor to say there were at present no openings in the Illinois military formations, but that he would keep Grant in mind. That wasn't much to offer a West Pointer with more than a decade's service, and soon Grant was telling people he'd be going home soon: "The politicians have got everything here, and there is no chance for me." But one day Yates saw him in the lobby of the hotel where he and Chetlain took their meals, and said, "Come to my office tomorrow, Captain Grant, and maybe I can find something for you to do."

The "something" consisted of ruling forms, plus arranging and copying orders. The pay was $2 a day. Chetlain looked in after a couple of days and found Grant in a poorly lit little room working at a table which had three legs and had been shoved up against the wall so that it would not topple over. Grant was not happy. "I am tired of this work," he told Chetlain. "It is no work for me. I'm going back to the store tomorrow." Chetlain said he shouldn't be too hasty but should stay in Springfield. "Something better will undoubtedly turn up." Grant agreed to remain a few days longer. But the get-togethers of former officers back in uniform naturally produced long gossip sessions from which anyone in Springfield who knew Grant got the gist of what the old Army men said about him: "A dead-beat military man—a discharged officer." The plums of the new regiments were being liberally handed out but there was nothing for Sam Grant. He had been in Springfield less than ten days when he wrote his father, "I shall not be here long."

But the next day, May 3, 1861, Yates appointed him to the job of mustering in new regiments. His salary went up to $4.20 a day, and as the work was to be done at cities throughout the state, he was given a railroad pass. One regiment assembled at Belleville, some 18 miles from St. Louis, and during a lull in his work there he went to what had effectively been his hometown to seek a commission in a Missouri regiment. There was none for him. He decided to try to get back into the regular army, which was being held as a separate entity from the volunteers, and wrote the new adjutant general, Lorenzo Thomas, who had replaced the former holder of that position when the latter went south and to the Confederate army. *"Sir: Having served for fifteen years in the Regular Army, including four at West Point, and feeling it the duty of every one who has been educated at the Government expense to offer their services for the support of that Government, I have the honor, very respectfully, to tender my services, until the close of the war, in such capacity as may be offered."* There was never any answer.

He tried for an appointment to the state forces of Ohio, talking with men he had known in Mexico, but nothing came through. By then George B. McClellan, whom he known since West Point days, had resigned his job as chief engineer of the Illinois Central Railroad and, after considering several offers, had accepted a major generalcy commanding all Ohio volunteers. Grant had last seen him in Oregon when McClellan was preparing for vital surveying duties for which Grant as post quartermaster had to outfit his expedition. They had lived together in Grant's log cabin for three months and he had irritated the trim and efficient McClellan by getting drunk one time. McClellan had always been regarded as a top soldier—great presence, quick mind, second in his West Point class, the last word in getting all details right—and it would likely lead to great things if one could get to serve on his staff. Grant went to his headquarters in Cincinnati and was received by several old West Point and Army acquaintances who told him to take a seat and wait for the major general—he had just gone out, would probably be back soon. Then the others went back to work and Grant sat alone for hours. Everything was hustle and bustle. No one had time to say a word to him. They all rushed about with quills behind their ears, he remembered. Finally he told one officer he would stop by the next day; could General McClellan be informed that he had called? The next day he came again to learn that the general had just gone out, might be in at any moment. Grant waited two hours. McClellan never came. He left, and there was never any acknowledgment of his call.

He went around Ohio, tried to get a contract supplying bread for the soldiers, talked about how he ran the bakery back in Mexico long ago in another war. He went to Indianapolis to look up his classmate Joseph J. Reynolds, now a colonel of Indiana volunteers. Nothing resulted. Back in Springfield the brief time the men had enlisted for was running out for some regiments. It was apparent the war wasn't going to be over in ninety days after all, but certain units were highly dissatisfied with the men they had elected as officers. Unless those officers were changed, there was every reason to believe the men would refuse to reenlist. Such a regiment was the 21st Illinois, whose elected colonel turned out to be a buffoon. He went about wrapped in a Napoleon-like cloak telling his men he never slept. He was often intoxicated and sometimes in bursts of good fellowship had his sentries join his carousing in saloons. Under such discipline the regiment had turned into a group familiarly known as "Governor Yates' Hellions," given to robbing hen roosts and staying out all night. They had burned their guardhouse. Yates said they gave him more trouble than any other formation. But he knew the men would be lost to the Army unless he replaced their silly colonel, and so he relieved the man of his duties.

The replacement was Ulysses S. Grant. ("Just appoint him without consulting him at all beforehand," one of the governor's people told him.) With Yates' aide John E. Smith, the new colonel took a horse car out to where his command was encamped. "He was dressed very clumsily in citizen's clothes—an old coat, worn out at the elbows, and a badly dinged plug hat," Smith wrote. "His men, though ragged and barefooted themselves, had formed a high estimate of what a colonel ought to be, and when Grant walked in among them they began making fun of him.

" 'What a colonel! Damn such a colonel!' "

"A few of them, to show off to the others, got behind his back and commenced sparring at him and while one was doing this, another gave him such a push that made him hit Grant a terrible blow between the shoulders." The shabby hat spun off the new colonel's head. Grant picked it up, dusted it off and turned and looked at his troops. Perhaps there was something in that look that they had not expected from him, or perhaps had not seen from other men, for soon they came to explain that it was all in fun. They hoped the new colonel wouldn't be mad about it.

Getting mad was not his way. But the regiment was not being run in anything approaching a correct manner. It took hardly a moment's glance to see that. The camp guard consisted of eighty men with clubs who were supposed to stop the troops from climbing the encampment fence so they could run into town and find women. He disbanded the guard and substituted several roll calls a day, no absences countenanced. A sentry greeted him by saying "How-de-do, Colonel," and he took the man's weapon and snapped it to a present-arms and said, "That is the way to say 'Good morning' to your colonel." The men were rambunctious, certainly, but they were also patriots who wanted to do the right thing. Those who did not yet understand Colonel Grant got a taste of old-time regular army punishment—bucking and gagging, stone-breaking, wooden-horse riding—and in a very short time, a matter of days, the men of the 21st Illinois began to act like soldiers. It was all done unemotionally, with no fuming and shouting. They called him "the Quiet Man" among themselves. Soon they looked more like soldiers than he did, for while he was able to procure them uniforms from state funds, he as an officer was obligated to buy his own pending the payment of allotments, and he had no money. His father had indicated that he had done enough for Ulysses, and old man Dent, the next thing to a professional Southerner, would not lend a cent. The whole idea of entering the Yankee army was a mistake, Dent said. Julia's husband could have, and should have, joined the Confederates. "Don't talk to me about this Federal son-in-law of mine," Dent told people. So Colonel Grant went around in his tattered civilian clothes, his only sign of rank an old saber he found in the state arsenal and tied to his belt. At reviews his lieutenant colonel, who had a proper uniform, gave the orders.

There remained the question of whether the men of the regiment would choose to reenlist. Originally they had gone in for thirty days; that had been extended for ninety more. Now they would be asked to go for three years, or the duration of the war. To inspire them, two Illinois congressmen volunteered to come give speeches. John McClernand spoke first, pouring eloquence and fire upon the soldiers. John A. Logan followed. He ridiculed the idea of men leaving the service in wartime without ever having seen the enemy, without even leaving their home state. "You can't fall out now. If you go home to Mary, she will say, 'Why, Tom, are you home from the war so soon?' " Logan was talking about the defense of the flag and of glory, and of the girl back home. They cheered. He had taken them. They would stay. They would see it through. It was a moment that spoke of hundreds of other outfits all over the North coming to the same decision and combining to form an army. When he knew he had them, Logan called out, "Colonel U. S. Grant!" There were cries from the soldiers of "Speech! Speech!"

He stepped forward. "Men, go to your quarters." That was all. Before weeks were out he was leading them into Missouri and at the rebels. A force under Confederate colonel Thomas Harris was encamped at a little town called Florida. Attired in a new uniform bought with the proceeds of a loan made on an old business associate of his father's, Colonel Grant led his men 25 miles through countryside, the houses of which, formerly occupied by Confederate sympathizers, were uniformly deserted. It came to him that he was frightened. He thought back to combat in Mexico; but that had been different, he was not in command there. Had he been lieutenant colonel, he reflected, with someone else colonel commanding, he would have felt no fear. But he was the colonel.

His 1,000 men went through the unpeopled land, seeing not a soul save two horsemen, who disappeared as soon as the Yankees came into sight. Colonel Harris and his Confederates were said to be in camp near a creek that wound through hills of considerable size. Grant and his men came to the hills. They started going up, and it seemed to him as if his heart were rising into his throat. At any moment he expected to see Southerners and to hear their guns. "I would have given anything then to be back in Illinois."

He kept on. He topped the hill and saw that below him there was nothing. The Confederate camp was empty. The Southerners had fled. "My heart resumed its place. It occurred to me at once that Harris had been as much afraid of me as I had been of him. This was a view of the question I had never taken before; but it was one I never forgot afterwards. I never forgot that he had as much reason to fear my forces as I had his.

"The lesson was valuable."

9

"If Lee Is Not a General ..."

VIRGINIA WAS OUT of the Union and a delegation of Virginians called upon Virginia's Winfield Scott. They were led by Judge John Robertson of Richmond. Fifty-five years earlier he had been at school at William and Mary with Scott. For a moment he spoke of student times they had shared together so many years in the past and then said he was authorized to make in the name of their state certain proposals to the general. Perhaps he felt Virginia's departure from the Union would change Scott's view of his responsibilities as general-in-chief. He was wrong. "Friend Robertson," Scott said, "go no further! It is best that we part here, before you compel me to resent a mortal insult. I have served my country, under the flag of the Union, for more than fifty years, and so long as God permits me to live, I will defend that flag with my sword."

They left. There was another soldier in whom they were

interested. Robertson sent a note to ex-Colonel Robert E. Lee asking an interview for the next day. Lee sent back word they could meet after Sunday services at Christ Church, Alexandria.

Arlington was very quiet that Saturday, the first day of the former officer's civilian life, as still and gloomy as a house in which there has been a death. "My husband has wept tears of blood over this terrible war," Mary Lee wrote a friend. "As I think both parties are wrong in this fratricidal war," she wrote her daughter Mildred, away at school in Winchester, "there is nothing comforting even in the hope that God may prosper the right, for I see no *right* in the matter."

Her husband agreed, writing that day to his sister Ann, whose son was a captain in the United States Army, that he felt secession wrong and many of the South's grievances imaginary. But, "I had to meet the question whether I should take part against my native state. With all my devotion to the Union, and the feeling of loyalty and duty of an American citizen, I have not been able to make up my mind to raise my hand against my relatives, my children, my home." Yet there was still a chance, although slight, that Virginia would not join the Confederacy in favor of remaining independent of North and South. "I am now a private citizen, and have no other ambition than to remain at home," he wrote his brother Smith.

On Sunday a messenger arrived from Judge Robertson. The judge was delayed and was unable to keep the appointment. Would the ex-colonel join him in the morning on a trip to Richmond? Governor John Letcher wanted to see him. Lee sent word he would meet the judge at the Alexandria station. He must have known, had to have known, that Letcher was going to offer him a post in the Virginia forces, which almost surely would soon be joined to those of the Confederacy. One day out of the uniform he had worn for more than three decades, he prepared himself for induction into an army that would fight those wearing that uniform. To his own thinking he had no choice at all. It was loyalty to Virginia that made him take off his blue uniform; it was loyalty to Virginia that would make him put on a gray one.

If the South was wrong in going to war with the North, so be it. They did so, they said, for the principle that the federal government had no right to dictate to them. It was freedom, they said, for which they contended. And, he reasoned, if Virginia rightly or wrongly went with the South, he must go also. Virginia was owed a debt. That debt must be paid whatever it cost, including his life.

In Richmond the next day he took a public hack from the depot at the foot of the Broad Street hill up to the Spotswood Hotel, somber and dressed in black and wearing a silk hat. Homemade versions of the Stars and Bars hung from windows, and for the first time he heard the sound of "Dixie." He tried to find a copy of the music for Mrs. Lee, but none were available. Had he gotten her one, she would have had to take it from Arlington, for soon his letters urged that she depart as soon as possible.

He went to Governor Letcher. They talked for a little while, and two days later Robert Lee, four days earlier a serving officer of the United States Army, stood in the rotunda of the Virginia State Capitol and gazed up at Houdon's statue of George Washington. "I hope we have seen the last of secession," he said. It was a strange wish to voice, for a moment later the doors of the room where the Virginia convention sat were opened for him and a four-man escort. The members of the convention rose. Lee went halfway down the aisle and paused. "In the name of the people of your native state," intoned the president of the convention, John Janney, "I bid you a cordial and heartfelt welcome to this hall, in which we may almost yet hear the echo of the voices of the statesmen, the soldiers and sages of by-gone days who have borne your name and whose blood now flows in your veins."

Here his father had sat as governor, here had spoken his kinsmen Richard Henry Lee and Francis Lightfoot Lee, signers of the Declaration of Independence born in the same bed at Stratford Hall which had seen his first moments.

Here Aaron Burr had been tried for treason.

"Sir," Janney said, "one of the proudest recollections of my life will be the honor that I yesterday had of submitting to this body the confirmation of the nomination by the governor of this state of you as commander in chief of the military and naval forces of this Commonwealth.

"Yesterday, your mother, Virginia, placed her sword in your hand upon the implied condition that we know you will keep to the letter and in spirit, that you will draw it only in her defense, and you will fall with it in your hand rather than the object for which it was placed there shall fail."

Janney finished. Lee realized he must respond. "Mr. President and gentlemen of the convention," he said slowly and distinctly, still standing. "Profoundly impressed with the solemnity of the occasion, for which I may say I was not prepared, I accept the position assigned me by your partiality. I would have much preferred had your choice fallen upon an abler man. Trusting in Almighty God, an approving conscience, and the aid of my fellow citizens, I devote myself to the service of my native state, in whose behalf alone will I ever again draw my sword."

They pressed about him with their congratulations.

He went to processing the volunteer regiments, securing them arms and encampments. The youth of the state poured exultantly into its forces, saying and believing that one Virginian was worth five Yankees. Their commander did not at all concur, saying that if it came to war the war might last five years. His attitude was so much in contrast with the prevailing mood that a Richmond associate of Confederate Secretary of War Leroy Walker decided that Major General Lee's loyalty to the Southern cause was open to question. He sought to repress the enthusiasm of the people, D. G. Duncan wrote Walker. "I believe there is treachery here." A friend of Mrs. James Chesnut, the wife of a prominent South Carolinian, agreed. "At heart Robert E. Lee is against us, that I know," Mrs. Chesnut was told. She herself found him a mystery. She preferred Smith Lee, now an officer in the Confederate navy, whom she knew well. "Can anybody say they know his brother?" she asked her diary. "I doubt it! He looks so cold, quiet and grand."

Behind the façade he was still in pain from what separation from the United States had brought. "What is General Lee going to do to General Scott?" an office visitor asked his carefully coached five-year-old son. "He is going to whip him out of his breeches," answered the child; and Lee said, "My dear little boy, you should not use such expressions. War is a serious matter, and General Scott is a great and good soldier. None of us can tell what the result of the contest will be." Even then, when children told her husband they expected him to whip the man who had been his mentor and guide, Mrs. Lee was writing Scott that she and her husband would gladly have laid down their lives to avoid the war. "Oh, that you could command peace to our distracted country!" She signed her letter "Yours in sadness and sorrow."

As it turned out, he was spared the horror of facing Scott, for when on July 21 the first great battle of the war was fought, Lee was in Richmond acting as advisor to President Jefferson Davis while Scott was in Washington by the side of President Abraham Lincoln. Attired in glorious uniforms and armed with a melange of weapons, some of which belonged in museums, the Southerners and Northerners surged at each other and met by the little stream of Bull Run in northern Virginia. Irvin McDowell, who had been Major General Lee's colleague in Texas and Mexico, had the Union command; Joe Johnston and Beauregard, the hero of Fort Sumter, led the Confederates. The fight was as between two half-trained mobs and looked in the early part like a Yankee victory. Then the Northern troops broke. McDowell had pitched his tent on Arlington's hill—he had written Mrs. Lee he would forbear occupying her house—but by nightfall he and his army were flying into the District of Columbia.

Many in the South thought that this settled the differences between the sections, but no such thought came into Lincoln's mind. Money was voted, troops were enrolled, new campaigns were inaugurated and Robert E. Lee, one of the Confederacy's five full generals, was dispatched to northwest Virginia to co-ordinate the efforts there of three semi-independent Southern forces led by politicians almost as opposed to one another as to the Northern foe. Before Bull Run was fought, Union forces under George McClellan had crossed over from Ohio and de-feated a small Confederate force in the area. McClellan's Na-poleonic addresses to his troops—"Soldiers of the Army of the West: I have heard there was danger here. I have come to place myself at your head and share it with you. I fear but one thing, that you will not find foemen worthy of your steel"—had cata-pulted him into the public eye. After McDowell's defeat Mc-Clellan went as the Young Napoleon to take command of the deposed officer's Army of the Potomac. His replacement in northwest Virginia was Brigadier Joseph J. Reynolds of Indiana, who as a professor of philosophy at West Point had served under Superintendent Lee.

The situation was difficult for the Southern forces far from their main bases of supply—the terrain was mountainous and without railroads, the local citizens were largely anti-Confederate in sentiment and soon would secede from Virginia and, as the new state of West Virginia, choose inclusion in the Union. Lee rode off on his coordinating mission along a road he had last seen when returning from his work on the St. Louis levees of the Mississippi River twenty years earlier. "If anyone had told me that the next time I traveled that road would have been my present errand, I should have supposed him insane," he wrote his wife. He arrived to find his troops tortured with diseases, poorly equipped and worse led. It had been raining for days. Accustomed to the spit and polish and unquestioning obedience of the regular army, he commanded volunteers who acted as though they had already had enough of the war. They had not forseen the lack of glory attendant upon contesting remote moun-tain passes in a landscape perpetually soaking wet. In addition, the leaders of the three semi-independent commands were less than happy over the intrusion of a general assigned to make them work together but given no stipulated and definite instructions by the Richmond authorities.

It was the beginning of a glum and dreary period of trying to coax recalcitrant prima donnas into doing their duty, of fending off controversies and jealousies. President Davis had counted upon Lee's tact to effect reconciliation between the contending Southern leaders; but perhaps his tact was too much utilized. He did not order, but diplomatically suggested. Too much the gentleman asking all to pull together and too little the harsh soldier, he was soon called "Granny" Lee behind his back. A measles epidemic swept through the troops, and many of the men who escaped that became ill with intestinal disorders incurred because they did not choose to listen to Lee's suggestions about hygienic handling of foods. It rained for twenty straight days. Then in mid-August the first mountain frosts came upon troops unequipped with cold-weather clothing.

General Reynolds, on the other hand, had abundant supplies, for he had railroad access to his base. The local inhabitants grew more Unionist in sentiment, the squabbling between Lee's subordinate politician-generals increased. A public that had expected from the son of Light Horse Harry Lee dash and flourish and victory instead got a floundering campaign followed by a withdrawal that brought another nickname: "Evacuating" Lee. The Richmond papers were not kind. Lee was too much the theorist, they said, too circumspect, too much the book-learned soldier and too little the fighter. Too cautious by far.

Three months after Lee had gone from Richmond to the mountains, he returned. He bore no laurels, carried no scalps at his belt. No response to criticism of his campaign was ever offered. He had done what he could, done his best, he told his family. The Ruler of all had decreed the result. There was nothing more to be said. He reported to President Davis, who was sympathetic and understanding. Two weeks after his return, Davis ordered him south to command the defenses of Charleston and Savannah against attack from the sea. He left for a doubtful reception. Unimpressed by his showing in northwest Virginia, certain South Carolina officers protested his appointment over them. Davis replied, "If Lee is not a general, I have none that I can send you."

He spent four months along the Atlantic coast where, a lieutenant then, he had served so many years before. He went to Light Horse Harry's grave. The estate of Nathanael Greene where his father lay had fallen almost into ruins. Accompanied by his aide Armistead Long, he went up a road past oaks and magnolias, olive, orange and lemon trees, past subtropical shrubbery and then into a neglected garden and through it to a dilapidated wall enclosing a falling-down cemetery. He walked to his father's grave. Forty years and more had passed since that tragic man had been placed there. He stood for a few moments in silence and then in silence picked a flower and in silence retraced his steps to the steamer that had brought him and Long to this place. He never mentioned the visit to anyone, save for a letter to Mrs. Lee.

His work on the coastal defense went very well. The exposed points were strengthened, the harbors were fortified, floating batteries and earthworks were constructed where needed. Spring approached, and he wrote his wife that he had done all he could to make secure the work he had been set upon. What resulted would be the will of the Giver of victory. On February 23 he wrote her from Savannah to speak of how they, how the South, must redouble their energies if they would win through. He did not sound overoptimistic when he spoke of the Union victories of earlier in the month in Tennessee. "Not at all cheering," he wrote. "Disasters seem to be thickening around us." Disasters indeed they were for the South, the Tennessee doings of the amazing Yankee general Ulysses S. Grant.

10

Unconditional Surrender Grant

In Missouri, the rebel Thomas Harris and his army having decamped, Colonel Grant drilled his troops. He had never looked at a book on tactics since West Point days and even then he had been no student of the subject. "My standing in that branch of studies had been near the foot of the class." So he got a book on military science and read the first chapter, thinking he would teach the men what was in it and then go on to the second chapter. But his brief reading convinced him that the whole business as applied to actual soldiering in the field was simply a matter of common sense. That concluded his military education as learned from printed information. He never opened a book on the subject again.

His job in northwest Missouri was to show a presence that would help keep the state in the Union. Possession of the border states was regarded as vital in Washington, and Abraham Lincoln the politician knew the value of patronage to their representatives. So when Grant's Galena congressman, Elihu Washburne, asked advancement for his constituent, the capable regimental commander Ulysses Grant, Lincoln gave Grant, along with many others, a star. He was a general. Jesse Grant wrote telling his son now that he had a good job he must make every effort to keep it.

Grant went to St. Louis and out along the Gravois Road to where his failed farm had been, and at every shop where he owed money he stopped and made good his debts with the proceeds of his handsome new salary. He knew them to the last penny and their payment amazed the people less than the sudden rise in the world of someone remembered as a slouching deadbeat and ne'er-do-well. "Who would have dreamed of that man ever being a general?" one former acquaintance asked wonderingly. Grant called upon Mr. and Mrs. Boggs, in whose real estate business he had done so miserably, and Boggs, Southern in sympathy, raved against the Yankees—"cursed and went on like a Madman," the new general wrote his wife. Later Boggs put the matter aside and let Grant stand treat for a theater visit.

He had become a general on the last day of July 1861, ten days after Irvin McDowell broke before Beauregard and Johnston at Bull Run in far-off Virginia; in the first week of September he crossed the Mississippi and went southeastward toward Cairo, Illinois, there to guard the junction of the Ohio and Mississippi rivers. As a general he had a right to a staff, and in Cairo there shortly arrived John A. Rawlins, the Galena lawyer whose eloquence had so taken the town meeting after the rebels first fired on Sumter. He was the only chief of staff Grant was ever to know.

Rawlins was dark, intense, explosive. His profanity was frightful. He feared nobody and screamed as impartially at Grant as he did the lowest lieutenant. He had one sworn enemy: whiskey. He was a fanatic on the subject. He often declared that he would as soon see a friend take a glass of poison as a glass of liquor. People said it was because his father had failed in life through love of drink. Thirty-one years old in 1861, Rawlins was a poor boy who had made good. The worthless father had died leaving him the head of a household of nine children, and he had fed them by cutting wood and firing up pits that produced charcoal. Then he read law and became one of Galena's leading attorneys. He had a wife dying of consumption, and two children, and for them he had not joined Galena's infantry companies. But he held himself in low repute for that, saying he did not fancy himself in the role of a man who said "Go, boys" in place of "Come, boys"; and when Grant wrote asking him to Cairo he put aside all other concerns and came to make sense of the dispatches and letters and orders Grant carelessly filed wherever seemed convenient. (The new general said his method was to put all papers in his pockets until they could hold no more, and then to dump everything into a drawer somewhere.) Together Rawlins and his new chief built up a general's staff. Almost uniformly it consisted of men who, like Rawlins, had known nothing of military matters before the war. Half of their number were young fellows from Galena, who educated themselves in their new profession by spending hours talking about it. The chief of staff led the discussions. Listening silently, as silent as he had always been, in the background, a figure of negligible import in the eyes of anyone who happened by, was Ulysses Grant. The staff argued strategy, moves, sweeps, how to get at the enemy, but Grant said nothing, made no contribution and offered no views. It seemed to those who looked on that he might not have even been listening, that slouched in his chair he was dreaming of other things.

In St. Louis the area commander, John C. Frémont, surrounded himself with a 300-man personal bodyguard while with imported aides in exotic Hungarian and German uniform he plotted strategies which, for complexity and elegance, excelled those of Napoleon. Frémont had run for President only five years before and thought in large terms, and it was quite in character for him to announce, after consulting no one but his wife, that he was liberating Missouri's slaves. (Horrified, Lincoln saw in imagination each and every border state deserting the Union, and instantly countermanded the order.) Years earlier, as "the Pathfinder," Frémont had proved capable of handling columns of a couple of hundred men, but a war was something else, and soon Lincoln would get rid of him. While he stayed, however, local commanders were free to do as they wished.

Without orders, lost in the backwater command of Cairo, Grant listened to his staff talk about how to lick the rebs—and then moved up the Ohio River and took possession of Paducah, Kentucky. No shots were fired. To Lincoln, Kentucky was the most important border state of all: "I think to lose Kentucky is nearly to lose the whole game," he had said, thinking that if Kentucky went, Missouri and then Maryland would follow. "I have come among you, not as an enemy, but as your friend," Grant announced to the people of Paducah, and far away in Washington the President caught the tone of this officer who was obscure enough to qualify, had he been in the East, for the Washington joke that a boy throwing a stone at a dog on Pennsylvania Avenue had missed but instead hit three brigadiers.

Twenty miles south of Cairo, in Columbus, Kentucky, a Confederate army massed; and Grant, in early November, decided they were not going any farther than Columbus. Vaguely ordered by Fremont to make a "demonstration" against the rebels, he loaded 3,000 men on steamers and sailed down the Mississippi to Belmont, which sat across the river from Columbus on the Missouri side. There was a Confederate outpost there. At two in the morning he got his men ashore and moved inland. He made no reconnaissance, and perhaps had no staff officer who would have known how to do it. Feeling his way forward, he came upon the enemy and gave them battle. He felt anxiety when the rebel muskets opened upon him, but not fear. It was not like the moment when he thought he was going to see Colonel Thomas Harris, back on the hill leading to where Harris was supposed to be. He would never be afraid again.

For four hours he fought the Confederates. A horse was shot out from under him. He commandeered another from one of his staff. In the end the rebels turned and ran, and his forces went rampaging through their camp seeking trophies. Officers seized the occasion to make speeches praising the men's efforts— but no speech was made by the commanding general, of course. He did not believe in speeches and never would.

At the height of the celebration loaded steamers were seen coming from the Columbus side of the river. The rebel troops driven from the camp had re-formed and were coming back. Suddenly a Federal disaster seemed in the making. "We are surrounded and will have to surrender!" an officer cried.

"I guess not," Grant replied. "If we are surrounded we must cut our way out just as we cut our way in." Under his leadership the troops fell back toward their boats. Bullets sang around them, and at one point a Confederate detachment came within 50 feet of where Grant was. He looked at them a moment and then turned his borrowed horse and walked the animal away slowly. Only when he was out of their sight did he put the horse into a gallop. At the landings he waited until everyone else was aboard the boats, then turned from the advancing rebels and put his horse down the steep riverbank onto a single gangplank resting on the ship's rail, and from there, with a bound, down onto the deck. It was nicely done. His men raised a cheer. His doggedness, calm, tranquility, a Wellington-like steadiness, had saved the day. The men knew it.

Soldiers see deeply into the mind and soul of their commander, as is not surprising when one considers that it is their lives which are his stock in trade; and while a commander is well advised to fool the enemy, and is sometimes capable of fooling his superiors, he can never hope to persuade his men for very long that he is something that he is not. The men knew what Grant was, and knew also in their western frontier all-men-are-equal fashion that in no way did Grant regard them as Wellington had regarded his troops, whom he termed the scum of the earth, enlisted solely for the hope of loot and drink. Grant was of the men, one of their type, the exact officer suited to them at that time. He was someone they would follow even though, perhaps,

British regulars would not have. But then, Wellington would never have had American volunteers. The raid on Belmont ended rebel plans of moving into Missouri. Grant had killed their impetus, the drive.

A few days later Lincoln appointed a new overall western commander. Henry Wager Halleck was considered the only military theoretician the United States had. His nickname was "Old Brains." Even as a young lieutenant on his way to Mexico he spent his time studying military tomes while other men played cards, and later he had translated Baron Jomini's extensive studies of the campaigns of Napoleon. He had written *Elements of Military Art and Science*, the definitive American work. Leaving the Army, he had gone to build a fortune in California, and then with the war had gotten back into uniform. Halleck was a scholar of war. It held no secrets from him. Cautious, scientific, methodical, reflective, he saw operations as a geometrically exact application of force at correct points—chess on a grand scale. He had known Grant slightly in California: a drunk. He did not care to have direct communication with such a subordinate commander, and anything Grant wanted to say to him had to go through Halleck's assistant adjutant general. When early in the new year of 1862 Grant wrote asking a personal interview with the area commander, the assistant adjutant general replied that the request could not be complied with. Grant went anyway to try to lay before Halleck his plan for a campaign that would take the Confederate fortifications, Fort Henry being the first objective, that lay along the Tennessee River and secured for the rebels the use of railroads through the mid-South. Halleck saw him for a very brief interview. "I had not uttered many sentences before I was cut short as if my plans were preposterous."

Back in Cairo he pushed his scheme with Flag Officer Andrew Hull Foote of the Union navy, who endorsed it. On his say-so Halleck gave his consent, and Foote took Grant's men onto his gunboats, shelled Fort Henry and saw the troops safely ashore and soon in possession of the fort. Washington cabled congratulations and a request that Grant and Foote be thanked for their joint effort; Halleck extended official thanks to the latter only.

The day after Fort Henry fell, Grant went with his staff and a cavalry escort to take a look at the far more important Fort Donelson, 11 miles downstream. Donelson was garrisoned by some 15,000 rebel troops, the same number available to Grant. The textbooks uniformly said a besieging force should outnumber the besieged by five to one, but Grant went ahead anyway. Fort Donelson was the gateway to Nashville and to eastern Kentucky, and if it could be taken the Confederates would be thrown back far to the south, to the boundaries of the cotton states, with vastly important railroad lines and supply points out of their grasp. He cabled Halleck he was off to take Donelson. The area commander expressed neither approval nor disapproval of the information.

On February 14, Foote's gunboats landed Grant's men and then opened on the rebel strongpoint. The emplaced Confederate artillerymen stuck to their guns, however, and soon disabled gunboats were drifting out of control in the river currents. Encouraged by their ability to beat off an initial attack as their comrades at Fort Henry had failed to do, the Southern troops at Fort Donelson came out of their works and attacked the invading Yankee army. Grant was on a gunboat conferring with Foote when the rebels sallied out, and he returned to find his men ready to bolt from the field. A staff officer was white with fear. Men were huddling in groups talking excitedly. Nobody seemed to know what to do. Rebel muskets and guns were sounding. "Gentlemen," Grant said, indicating the highway to Nashville, "that road must be recovered before night." His hand convulsively mashed some dispatches he held.

He rode through his troops saying that the rebels were trying to escape. They must not be allowed to do so. His concept seized the men. They formed up and charged, driving the enemy back into the 100 acres that composed the fort. There the rebels were effectively penned up. There would be no escape. In the night the two highest-ranking Confederate officers stole away, and it fell to General Simon Bolivar Buckner, one of Grant's closest friends before the war—he had guaranteed the ex-captain's hotel bill and raised $50 cash for him when he returned from California eight years before—to write asking what the terms for capitulation would be.

Back came: "No terms except an unconditional and immediate surrender can be accepted. I propose to move immediately upon your works."

Those two sentences electrified the North. Unconditional surrender. U. S. Grant. "Unconditional Surrender" Grant. When Buckner ran up white flags and his 15,000 men laid down their arms, Grant had won the greatest victory of the war so far by either side, the greatest capitulation in the history of the continent. The two old friends held a reunion unstrained by the circumstances they found themselves in—one a prisoner and the other a great victorious chieftain suddenly the toast of his nation, with fireworks set off in his honor, children named for him, golden swords on order for presentation, honorary membership in a hundred organizations and societies.* They talked about old times, West Point and their Twelve in One club, Mexico, the time they tried to climb Popocatépetl and got snow blindness. It was touching, Buckner thought, to see the fashion in which Grant offered the contents of his wallet to his captive, privately and quietly so that no one would see the offer of charity.

One voice failed to join in the chorus of Northern applause. General Halleck could not credit it that a slothful and inarticulate man who knew nothing of military history had won so signal a triumph. Fort Donelson was the work of Grant's subordinate commanders, he telegraphed Washington, asking promotions for

---

*In St. Louis, William Taussig of that city remembered, "People asked each other whether this could be the same Grant, Dent's son-in-law—the same slow, seemingly indolent and apathetic man, whom they had seen drive a team of cordwood near his father-in-law's woods, and whom they had never believed to be much of a man." A railroad executive who had once hired a leather shop clerk to drive his wagon from Galena to Janesville, Wisconsin, would soon say: "I will never doubt the truth of Scriptural miracles hereafter."

them. Meanwhile Grant moved toward Nashville. The streets leading out of the city immediately filled with fleeing rebels, including the Confederate governor of the state and his legislature. Smoke hung over the ordnance works and railroad bridge, and trapped rebel gunboats were set to the torch. The Union troops marched in, bringing with them the newly appointed military governor of Tennessee, ex-Senator Andrew Johnson. But in St. Louis Old Brains Halleck was furious. The whole conquest of the Southwest was going on under an unlettered soldier who not only wasn't doing it by the book, but didn't know what was *in* the book. "I have had no communication with General Grant for more than a week," Halleck wired Washington. "He left his command without my authority and went to Nashville. His army seems to be as much demoralized by the victory of Fort Donelson as was that of the Potomac by the defeat of Bull Run. It is hard to censure a successful general immediately after a victory, but I think he richly deserves it. I can get no returns, no reports, no information of any kind from him. Satisfied with his victory, he sits down and enjoys it without any regard to the future. I am worn out and tired with this neglect and inefficiency."

In Washington, Irvin McDowell's replacement, George B. McClellan, was very much in charge. Remembering the drunken quartermaster of California days and the more recent failed applicant for a post on his Ohio staff, he wired back: "The future success of our cause demands that proceedings such as Grant's should at once be checked. Generals must observe discipline as well as private soldiers. Do not hesitate to arrest him at once if the good of the service requires it."

Halleck had more to add: "A rumor has just reached me that since the taking of Fort Donelson General Grant has resumed his former bad habits. If so, it will account for his neglect of my oft-repeated orders." That explained everything. Once a drunk always a drunk. Save that it was not true. For Rawlins, the fanatical enemy of alcohol, was watching over his chief. When the Galena congressman Elihu Washburne wrote to ask if Grant was staying away from liquor, Rawlins replied that he took a glass of champagne now and then, but that was all. In fact, he had kept away from whiskey ever since returning from the West and getting back to Julia and the children. When he had suffered some minor stomach trouble, Rawlins told Washburne, a doctor had advised him to drink two glasses of ale or beer a day, but he had never exceeded that amount. If, Rawlins ended, Grant ever became intemperate, Washburne would know it by the fact that he, Rawlins, would immediately resign his position on the general's staff.

Perhaps Halleck knew the facts and perhaps he did not. But armed with McClellan's authorization to do what seemed best, he wired Grant: "Your neglect of repeated orders to report the strength of your command has created great dissatisfaction and seriously interfered with military plans. Your going to Nashville without authority was a matter of very serious complaint at Washington, so much so that I was advised to arrest you on your return."

Ten months earlier Grant had been a clerk taken as a charity case into a family business run by younger brothers. Now he led armies. A mention in the newspapers that he liked to smoke had resulted in the dispatch to him of thousands of boxes of cigars from admirers all over the North. But now suddenly Halleck was one with Buchanan, who sent him out of the Army back in California; with Dent, his father-in-law, who regarded him as a nonentity; with Boggs, the real estate agent who told him he had to go; with his father, who said West Point had spoiled his son for business. He wept, and wired Halleck, "If my course is not satisfactory, remove me at once. I do not wish to impede in any way the success of our arms."

In reply, Old Brains sent on an unsigned letter he had recently received. It alleged fraud in Grant's disposal of the rebel property he had taken at Forts Henry and Donelson. "The want of order and discipline and the numerous irregularities in your command since the capture of Fort Donelson are matters of general notoriety," Halleck wrote. That was too much. Even during his worst times back in St. Louis when he stood on street corners trying to sell wood Grant had been meticulous about financial matters. Once in those days he had run into his old friend and best man, Pete Longstreet, still in the Army. He had reminded Pete he owed him $5 from Mexico. Pete saw the shabby clothes and told Grant to forget about it. Grant had replied that he could not live having something in his possession that was not his and that if he had $5 in his pocket it belonged to Pete. The money changed hands. Now Halleck was in effect asking whether he was profiteering on the war. Grant wrote out and sent a request to be relieved of his command.

Word of the situation reached across the miles to Washington and to the ear of the President of the United States. It was a poor moment for Halleck to complain of a general who lacked order, form, background, knowledge. For Lincoln was each day dealing with a general who had these in abundance—and that general seemed to the President to be the biggest problem he had. Of George B. McClellan's brilliance there could be no doubt. From a socially prominent Philadelphia family, he had gone to West Point when only fifteen years and seven months old. For him they waived the age requirements. He was graduated second in his class—into the Engineers, of course—had served with distinction in Mexico, had gotten plum assignments afterwards, being appointed as one of three American officers to act as observers of the Crimean War. He mastered several European languages, including Russian, wrote penetrating reports on the arms and tactics of the contending forces and, using a Cossack model, designed a new saddle which became the standard Army issue. Leaving the service, he rose in the railroad industry, becoming chief engineer of the Illinois Central. With the commencement of the war he took a major generalcy in the Ohio forces, beat the rebels in northwestern Virginia and then went to Washington to replace the loser of Bull Run, Irvin McDowell. The Young Napoleon, Little Mac, the Nation's Hope, he felt no concern about the responsibilities placed upon him: "The people call upon me to save the country. I must save it." He was not yet thirty-five.

McClellan built the Army of the Potomac to colossal size, outfitted it with the most modern equipment, drilled it to perfection. The men loved him. He galloped down their grand-review lines past gleaming bayonets and burnished field pieces, rolled telegraph wires, straight wagon trains, elegantly turned out cavalry horses, trim men and officers in French-style kepis. A splendid force. But as months passed, people began to ask just when he was going to put this host into action against the rebels not a day's march from Washington. McClellan did not care to answer such questions. He had a plan, he told the President, but it was not to be confided to anyone.

Even General Scott was considered an interloper, and so a day came when the old man went off into retirement. His train left in the early hours of a rainy morning for New York, McClellan and a squadron of cavalry coming to see him off. "It may be that at some distant day I, too, shall totter away from Washington, a worn-out soldier," McClellan wrote his wife. "The sight of this morning was a lesson to me which I hope not soon to forget. I saw there the end of a long, active, and ambitious life, the end of the career of the first soldier of his nation; and it was a feeble old man scarce able to walk; hardly any one there to see him off but his successor. Should I ever become vainglorious and ambitious, remind me of that spectacle."

Still he did not move his great army. The autumn of 1861 passed, and the winter, and 1862 came and with it warm weather; but McClellan held reviews and drills and spoke of how he would annihilate the country's enemies. Lincoln continually asked for a date when field operations would commence, and McClellan refused to answer. It was not unknown for him to come home to his Washington mansion, ignore the information that the President was waiting in the parlor and go straight up to bed. He felt no reluctance to lecture Lincoln on the Negro problem and relations with England and France, but he would not say when he would fight the Confederates. European princes and dukes dotted his glittering staff and rode with him on the endless tours of inspection of his more than 150,000 prime soldiers; but he would not fight. "I will hold McClellan's horse if he will only bring us success," Lincoln said, but the Army of the Potomac did not venture out against the enemy.

In the West there was a soldier who occupied towns, made armed raids, took forts, drove rebels scurrying away—and his immediate commander complained of him. "By direction of the President," Halleck found himself reading, "the Secretary of War desires you to ascertain and report whether General Grant left his command at any time without proper authority, and, if so, for how long; whether he has made to you proper reports and returns of his force; whether he has committed any acts which are unauthorized or not in accordance with military subordination, and, if so, what." Halleck realized it was time to retreat. He tamped down the whole business by telegraphing Grant that there was no question of relieving him of his command, that on the contrary, Halleck wished him to continue on to new victories. "The power is in your hands," Halleck told Grant. "Use it, and you will be sustained by all above you."

Grant went to join his troops. They were in two encampments along the Tennessee River some 20 miles from Corinth, Mississippi, which was the junction of the two most important railways in the Mississippi Valley. Those rails supplied troops and supplies for the Confederacy's forces east and west. The enemy was present in force in Corinth.

A major general now, Grant planned his move against Corinth. Albert Sidney Johnston, former head of the Second Regiment of Cavalry, United States Army, was in charge there. His second in command was P.G.T. Beauregard, hero of Fort Sumter and Bull Run. They moved upon the Federal army, and on the morning of April 6 suddenly appeared before one of the camps some 2 miles west of the Tennessee.

At the other Union camp, eating breakfast, Grant heard heavy firing and hurried onto a gunboat. He arrived at Pittsburg Landing to find thousands of terrified men huddling under the river bluffs where they were safe from rebel bullets. He went up to the flatlands and found his army in a panic. Most of the soldiers were farmboys so new to uniform that they hardly knew how to fire their weapons. They had been taken at their morning coffeepots by a sudden onslaught of screaming Southern countrymen, who had driven them from their tents and campfires grouped around a large log meetinghouse called Shiloh, and all the fight appeared knocked out of them. A few regular army officers were trying to restore the lines; one was William T. Sherman. Civilian life following his departure from the Army had not been kind to Sherman, and since returning to uniform at the beginning of the war he had, in the hysterical fashion which characterized all his actions, convinced his superiors that he was mad. For he had said it would take 200,000 men to beat the rebels in the West. Newspapers proclaimed that he was insane, Old Brains Halleck relieved him of his command and Sherman went home to Ohio saying he would kill himself if it were not for the disgrace he would bring on his children. But his brother was a United States senator, and he was restored to his division, to end up on the uplands between Shiloh meetinghouse and Pittsburg Landing as fury itself, taking two bullet wounds as he tried desperately to hold the lines.

The air was filled with panic, and broken regiments ran for the river. But Grant saw something. Albert Sidney Johnston was letting the battle get away from him. His units were mixing together as they pushed forward and were losing their officers— and through that loss the overall guidance they should have had. They were clustering around Union positions that should have been pinched off and isolated while the main Confederate thrust went on. Wasting time, they were hammering at those positions until they eliminated them or wrenched a surrender out of the men who lived through their repeated attacks. But the delays were costing them their forward impulse. It was becoming a soldiers' battle, not a duel between commanders. And war wasn't chess. In chess the pieces are the same whether of wood or ivory; but soldiers have a spirit. The spirit comes from the commander. He had seen the same story at Fort Donelson, Grant told Sherman. Both sides had been about ready to fall down after the rebels sallied forth and panicked the Yankees, but then he had taken hold of his men and told them not to let the Confederates escape, and they had pushed them over. New energies and actions had been proved capable of turning the trend and the meaning of the fighting. He was going to do that right here, he said to Sherman. In the morning he would send the rebels flying.

All day he fell back toward the river, his units using themselves up in receiving routed formations and trying to steady them. He went from officer to officer saying in his unemotional way that it was going to be all right. It looked as if the next rebel push would put the Yankees into the river, but he massed 100 guns to defend the heights and lined up cavalrymen to halt the stragglers from the front. He was asked if he was seeing to his lines of retreat across the river, and replied that before retreating he would sacrifice so great a proportion of his army that there wouldn't be enough men left to worry about.

Across the field of battle, a mile or so away, Albert Sidney Johnston, gallant and brave to be sure, but perhaps not the controlling soldier he was thought to be, involved himself in matters better left to his subordinates and, while trying to rally a brigade, took a wound in the leg. The ball cut an artery, but he ignored it until, faint from loss of blood, he fell from his saddle. Earlier in the fighting General Johnston had picked up a tin cup left by a campfire when the Yankees fled his advance, and all day he had kept it hooked in his pinkie as he directed his men onward. Now it dropped from his grip as he lay on the ground, his staff surgeon away tending others as the commanding general bled to death.

Night came, and a driving rain. The firing died away and Grant took refuge in an improvised hospital set up in a log house a few hundred yards from the river's edge. But he could not stand the blood and the sight and sound of amputations of shattered arms and legs and went out to spend the night sitting under a tree as torrents of rain poured down.

In the morning the battle recommenced. The previous day Grant had committed his last reserves as he fought entirely on the defensive, but now he became the attacker. Everything was reversed. The Confederates sagged back. About three in the afternoon he gathered a body of troops and formed them in line of battle and took them to a clearing in front of the rebel front. He forbade his men to discharge a weapon until they were well within musket range—there must be no premature or long-range firing. Then he stepped aside they charged, and the rebels broke and ran for Corinth. Shiloh was by far the largest and bloodiest battle ever seen on the American continent. By fighting it Albert Sidney Johnston had hoped to drive the Federals across the Tennessee and then carry the war up across the Ohio River. Ulysses Grant had forbidden him that, and now Beauregard bore Johnston's body back along the road on which they had advanced.

But Grant came in for criticism because of Shiloh. He had let himself be surprised by the rebel push and he had taken fearful casualties. Halleck came down from St. Louis to take personal command and conduct an almost comically cautious advance upon Corinth. Poking forward at snail's pace each day and halting at night to construct elaborate fortifications that he abandoned in the morning, Halleck took almost three weeks to cover 18 miles; and when he got to Corinth he found that Beauregard and his army were gone. All the old drinking stories about Grant had surfaced by then: He had been drunk, people said, that was why Johnston surprised him. But all over the country it was repeated that Lincoln had said that if Grant was a drunkard it would be a good idea for the other generals to be sent a barrel of the whiskey Grant favored. Actually Lincoln never said it, and pointed out that the story was a derivative of George I's remark that if a certain one of his generals was mad, he wished the officer in question would bite his other generals.

There was one thing the President did say, however. The Philadelphia editor A. K. McClure expressed reservations about Grant, and Lincoln told him, "I can't spare this man. He fights."

11

The Army of Northern Virginia

GEORGE B. McCLELLAN had commanded the Army of the Potomac for more than half a year and had not fired a shot at the enemy. The members of the Committee on the Conduct of the War called him to Capitol Hill and had at him, and he lectured them on lines of retreat. Lincoln was reduced to saying that if the general did not want to use his army, he himself would like to borrow it. McClellan kept talking about how gigantic the rebel forces were across the river in Virginia.

In March of 1862 the Confederates broke winter quarters and went south. McClellan ventured forth. He moved upon the fortifications that had held him at bay for so long and found the great frowning rebel cannons were "Quaker guns"—wooden logs painted to look like the real thing. McClellan studied them and returned his army to Washington. But the action had been a success, he said, for now his troops had practice in extended marching and had gained new insight into what impediments of their equipment could be discarded. Time passed. Lincoln implored the Young Napoleon to do *something*. "Isn't he a rare bird?" McClellan asked his staff. The Executive and the general-in-chief took to bickering about the number of troops available for service in Virginia. McClellan turned ugly, writing his wife that he was afflicted with rascals set above him, traitorous hounds, fools, dunderheads, colossal asses. Let the President come and break the enemy himself, if he thought he could do it better.

Finally McClellan went into action. The move he made suited him perfectly. He gathered 400 boats, steamers and barges, enough for 120,000 men and 15,000 horses and mules, and transported them and their gear to the foot of the Virginia peninsula. There he spent weeks throwing up entrenchments and erecting batteries preparatory, he said, to moving up the peninsula with his gunboats sailing the James on one side of his force and sailing the York on the other. It was all brilliantly planned by one of the great organizers of military history, and McClellan, the first soldier in the history of the New World to command an army of 100,000 field soldiers, was in his element. Every detail was meticulously attended to. The Young Napoleon appeared supremely confident. Thrusting between his protective gunboats on each side, his sword would go straight up to penetrate Richmond's heart. President Lincoln had been doubtful about transferring gigantic masses of men and material 200 miles by water to fight an army that at their sailing was encamped almost within view of the United States Capitol, saying the act seemed to shift rather than surmount a problem. But he gave his consent. At least after almost a year McClellan was making a move.

Once arrived, working at his fortifications, the Union commander reverted to character. "No one but McClellan would have hesitated to attack," Joe Johnston wrote Robert Lee. Lee by then was back from the deep South and at President Davis' side as military advisor; Johnston was field commander.

When at last the perfectionist chieftain was perfectly satisfied that all was in readiness for the march to Richmond, he charged forward upon the rebel lines—to find them empty. Johnston had consolidated his forces and then ducked the blow. McClellan sent word to Washington that he needed more men and more guns. Lincoln talked about "indefinite procrastination" and desperately asked if anything at all was to be done. "I shall push the enemy to the wall," McClellan said, and wrote his wife of how the men of his army loved him and of the immense responsibility which rested upon his shoulders. Meanwhile he must guard against all eventualities, remove any possibility of failure. Slowly and painstakingly he began to creep up the peninsula toward Richmond, complaining bitterly about the rain as he went. ("He seemed to think, in defiance of Scripture, that Heaven sent its rain only on the just and not the unjust," Lincoln observed.) At the same time, Joe Johnston, seemingly planless, drifted back before him. He had never liked President Davis, nor gotten along with him, and now when Davis and his military advisor Lee came out to confer with him, Johnston made opportunities to avoid them. An unhappy feeling took hold in Richmond. Johnston backed up to within 5 miles of the center of the town, and McClellan was so close that the Union soldiers could hear from their lines the sound of the city's church bells tolling the hours. The Confederate treasury's gold was packed into pine boxes for shipment to Columbia, South Carolina.

On May 14 Davis called an emergency cabinet meeting. His military advisor walked up the stone steps of the Confederate White House, into the parlor and upstairs to where he found grim-faced men. As soon as Lee was seated Davis told him they had convened to discuss the next line of defense after Richmond fell. Lee stared. "But," he said in a loud and passionate voice that no one present had ever heard him use before, "but Richmond *must* be defended!" They were shocked at his tone and the booming sound of his voice. McClellan in front of the city sat still, and then on May 31 the city heard sounds of battle. At last the two armies had opened heavily upon one another.

McClellan's army was split by the Chickahominy River, which ran east from Richmond. There had been torrential rains,

three inches the previous day, and now the southern portion of
the Yankee force was isolated from the northern portion. And
Johnston had attacked it. But like Albert Sidney Johnston (who
was no relation) at Shiloh, he was letting the battle get away
from him. Testy and prideful, he released details of his plans to
no one, including President Davis and the President's military
advisor when they rode out along Nine Mile Road to see what
was happening. His forces were badly snarled with one another,
blocking advances so that units pushing through the watery groves
and soaked underbrush frequently found themselves facing Union
guns alone, with no support on their flanks. Orders got lost or
misunderstood and the situation was chaotic.

Tense-faced and silent, Johnston listened to reports on the
fighting in the oozing and water moccasin-infested wetlands along
the Chickahominy and then equally as unheedful of the duties
of a high commander as Albert Sidney Johnston had been at
Shiloh, rushed forward in front of his lines—partially perhaps
to avoid any questions Lee and Davis might have for him. They
watched him ride forward and then as they sat their horses in
the rising bedlam, musketry and cannons sounding from up ahead,
learned he had been hit. A soldier ran past shouting that the field
commander was likely dead. Dusk was coming on. They saw
litter bearers and went to Johnston. He had been struck by a
musket ball and, a moment later, by a shell fragment which took
him in the chest. Conscious but in great pain, he moaned that
he had lost the weapons his father had carried as a major in the
Revolution under Light Horse Harry Lee. He would give a
fortune to anyone who would retrieve them, he would give, he
said, $10,000. Someone went for the pistols and sword and he
was borne to the rear.

Gustavus Smith came up, Johnston's second-in-command.
Lee and Davis learned from him that he knew next to nothing
of the wounded leader's plans. They learned something else.
Gustavus Smith would not do. Outwardly impressive to the
moment when supreme responsibility came to him, he was suddenly ill—mentally as well as physically—on the verge, it seemed,

of a complete nervous collapse. They told him to hang on and await orders and then together rode back to Richmond along Nine Mile Road past ambulances, walking wounded, coal wagons coming up to seek the injured, hearses, men without officers and officers without men, the backwash and rear-area debris of a fumbling battle of encounter conducted without pattern. McClellan with his enormous army was half an hour away. In the darkness Jefferson Davis talked with Robert E. Lee. In the morning Lee rode out to the front to speak with Gustavus Smith.

During his unhappy stay in northwestern Virginia when it had rained continuously Lee had forgone shaving, and now the beard then begun had reached full growth. It was gray. Gray also was the horse he rode. He had first noticed the animal in northwestern Virginia. Its name was Jeff Davis. Lee asked if he could buy the horse and took it to try out for a week. By then it was called Greenbrier, after the county of its origin. He paid $200 and changed the horse's name. Traveller.

On Traveller, in gray, fifty-five years old, he went to field headquarters, the home of Mrs. Mary Dabbs. There in the home of Widow Dabbs he issued to the troops in front of his country's besieged capital a message announcing that he had taken command; and for the first time the troops heard themselves addressed not as "the Potomac Army," or "the Army of the North" or as "the Army of Richmond," but as the Army of Northern Virginia. They were never from that day to have another title, never to have another commander but the one who signed himself that day: R. E. Lee, General.

McClellan made no serious attempt to continue the fighting, but lay where he was, stretched in an arc bestriding the Chickahominy in front of Richmond. His left had proved secure against the push that Johnston had unleashed; his right stretched out toward the north where, protecting the approaches to Washington, there were tens of thousands of Federal troops. Sending word to Lincoln that his 100,000 men were opposed by more than 200,000 rebels, McClellan demanded the aid of those Washington soldiers. Let them come overland and join his right wing and he would then crush Richmond in his fist. Meanwhile, protected by the enormous collection of heavy artillery he had transported up the peninsula to the gates of the city, he felt himself safe.

Across the lines, the new commander of the Army of Northern Virginia studied McClellan. He saw an engineer with a scientific approach. They had worked together in Mexico and McClellan had been that way then. And his methodical advance by slow stages up the peninsula showed that he had not changed. Such a planner and such a mind works from point to point, thought to thought, line to line, logically. On paper the equation always works out. Lee began to work on McClellan. He put John Magruder, "Prince John" always in the old Army, to making demonstrations. They were not military demonstrations, but theatrical ones. That suited Prince John perfectly. Even on the approach to Mexico long ago he had put on plays, erected theaters, had the slim young Lieutenant Sam Grant attempt the role of Desdemona. Magruder took 10,000 rebel soldiers and paraded them before McClellan's forward posts, led them behind screening woods and led them again in front of the Yankee lines—circling masses of men seemingly countless in number. Fanciful stories in the Richmond papers related the arrival of vast Confederate reinforcements. Soon McClellan was asking himself just how many soldiers were facing him. He increased the intensity of his demands upon Washington for reinforcements.

But soon that was made impossible, for Lee sent Thomas J. Jackson, who had stood like a stone wall at Bull Run, to go rampaging through the Shenandoah Valley. Jackson was an eccentric who as a professor at the Virginia Military Institute had been known to the students as "Mad Tom" and "Tom Fool." He went in for crank diets and water cures and was a religious fanatic. But he was a brilliant marcher of men. Hidden behind the mountains of the valley he flew from place to place so swiftly that his infantry became known as the foot cavalry. Suddenly appearing where least expected, he popped through mountain passes and fell upon Union detachments. "Mystery is the secret of success," Jackson said, and Washington trembled that this magician might suddenly one day appear in its streets. There could be no thought of stripping the city of troops for shipment to McClellan. And McClellan asked himself how Lee could ignore his threat to Richmond and send Jackson away if he did not have vast numbers of men. It had to be even more than 200,000, the Union commander decided.

Atop Richmond's seven hills appeared earthworks, batteries, rifle pits, redoubts, trenches. Southern gentlemen did not like using pickaxes and shovels—nigger work—and derisively dubbed their commander "the King of Spades." Defensively sited, so it seemed, they were performing duties neither Blücher at Ligny, nor Wellington at Waterloo nor the Russian defenders at the Alma had asked of their men. To McClellan it appeared that Lee was preparing to withstand a siege. That suited McClellan. Siege work was scientific, calculable. And in the end his big guns and the North's ammunition factories would win out.

But Lee was not thinking of defense or of a siege. The Confederate artillery officer E. Porter Alexander, riding with a friend who had served in the past with Lee, said, "We are here fortifying our lines, but apparently leaving the enemy all the time he needs to accumulate his superior forces, and then to move on us in the way he thinks best. Has General Lee the audacity that is going to be required for our inferior force to take the aggressive and to run risks and stand chances?" The friend, Colonel Joseph Ives, reined in his horse and said, "Alexander, if there is any man in either army head and shoulders above every other in audacity, it is General Lee! His name might be Audacity. He will take more desperate chances and take them quicker than any other general in this country, north or south; and you will live to see it."

Ives was right. Nothing showed in Lee's face of bloodlust or a warrior's urge to rend an enemy's flesh and cut out his heart; he was not like "Stonewall" Jackson being told that it was a shame to kill the brave men opposite and replying that he did

not want them brave, he wanted them dead. But in Lee the
Christian gentleman there lived also Lee the soldier with a soldier's function. And so after James Ewell Brown Stuart, his
sometime West Point student and sometime Harpers Ferry aide,
conducted an observation tour of McClellan's right wing, his
wing north of the Chickahominy, and found it exposed and
attackable—for the Young Napoleon's equation did not calculate
upon his being attacked—Lee shifted all his forces to mass for
that attack. Disrupt the enemy's prearrangements, Lee said. That
was war. Behind his lines, their movement hidden from the
Yankees, his men rushed north to form up, Prince John Magruder
and a paper-thin screen alone being left between McClellan's
massive south wing and Richmond. Orders went to Jackson to
return from the valley.

By June 25 Lee was almost ready to fight. But suddenly
after weeks of lying supine, McClellan showed signs of life. He
was moving his left wing up against Magruder's handful. Richmond was 4 miles away from his advanced outposts, defenseless.
If McClellan pushed, Magruder's screen would be dissolved in
a moment. Four-fifths of McClellan's army was looking at a
corporal's guard. Earlier a rebel general had explained with math-
ematical precision how McClellan with his great guns and enormous force was unstoppable. The officer got out pencil and paper
to show the Union commander's irresistibility, but Lee had said,
"Stop, stop! If you go on ciphering, we are whipped beforehand."
Now the nightmare of his gamble's failure stared him in the face.
The safety of the Confederate capital, of the Confederacy, hung
on McClellan's not moving. Lee on Traveller cantered south of
the Chickahominy, looked, and decided McClellan was making
only a localized demonstration. The following morning, June 26,
1862, he fell upon McClellan's right wing. Fitz-John Porter commanded there. He held under the Confederate fire. Lee looked
on, giving the appearance that everything going on was routine.
The day wore on. The Federals held. A messenger arrived to
say that things were quiet south of the Chickahominy, that the

Yankees had not realized how thin was Magruder's screen. Lee received the news with no emotion, but the messenger thought he looked a trifle disheveled. His tie was pulled to one side.

His plan called for echelons of rebel troops to rendezvous on the field in front of Fitz-John Porter. From a hilltop Lee heard fifes and drums and through his fieldglasses saw a Confederate flag coming from his left. "Those are A. P. Hill's men," he remarked with no indication of relief. That would mean that Stonewall Jackson would be about arriving from the valley— Hill was his advance guard. Hill's batteries trotted into position, unlimbered, and opened up. Porter did not move and Jackson did not come. For the first and only time in his career the great marcher was slow.

The troops battered at each other. Jefferson Davis and his staff rode out. Shells were bursting around Lee's hilltop. He glared at Davis and his entourage. "Who is all this army and what is it doing here?" Lee asked harshly. He looked, thought one of Davis' people, like the God of War, indignant. "It is not my army, General," Davis said.

"It is certainly not my army, Mr. President, and this is no place for it."

"Well, General, if I withdraw perhaps they will follow me."

Night fell. Jackson did not come. If in the morning McClellan moved his left, he would take Richmond in an hour and go through the city and hit Lee in the rear, using Porter as the steadfast anvil upon which his hammer would beat the Confederacy to death.

Lee slept and awoke in the morning to continue the battle. McClellan did not move. Finally Jackson came. "Ah, General," Lee said, "I am glad to see you. I had hoped to be with you before this." Jackson did not reply to the implied reprimand, but went to work. The opposing forces pounded at each other. Lee went past an artillery section where, under a caisson, an exhausted eighteen-year-old soldier slept. The boy was prodded awake with a gun's sponge-staff and told that someone wanted to see him. Half-awake, smeared with grime, Private Robert E. Lee, Jr., saw who the someone was. He remembered always the loving eyes and smile.

Pounded by Jackson and A. P. Hill and the others, Porter began to fall back. And beyond his retreating army, south of it, across the Chickahominy, the Confederates saw a strange sight. An immense cloud was rising from the ground. It was dust, moving, dust raised by feet and hooves and wagon wheels. The retreat of his right wing under Porter had pried McClellan loose from his positions in front of Richmond.

Jackson came to confer with Lee, stopping at what had been the line of the 17th and 21st Mississippi: The men had been ordered not to fire at the first Yankee elements they met, and so they had lain down and taken the fire of an enemy brigade. They were lying now on their backs with hands crossed over breasts, deadly pale, foreheads shattered. Men passed through the silent rows looking for friends. Stonewall Jackson stared at them for a moment. Not a muscle quivered, noticed the junior officer Robert Stiles, and then Jackson turned a steady gaze to the road down which Lee should be arriving. In a moment the general commanding the Army of Northern Virginia came into sight, his dress and equipment and his horse perfection. A born king among men, Stiles thought to himself. Lee halted Traveller and gracefully dismounted. Jackson jumped off Little Sorrel and the two men stood drawing diagrams on the ground with their boots. Jackson did most of the talking and finished with, "We've got him."

But they did not have McClellan. His telegrams to President Lincoln and Secretary of War Edwin Stanton were such as in a European army would have brought immediate sentence to stand before a firing squad—"I have seen too many dead and wounded comrades to feel otherwise than that the government has not sustained this army. If you do not do so now the game is lost. If I save this army now, I tell you plainly I owe no thanks to you or any person in Washington. You have done your best to sacrifice this army"—but he conducted his retreat brilliantly, even though he did not call it a retreat but rather a change of base. It was the most difficult kind of withdrawal, McClellan unfolding his arc around Richmond and forming it for movement with Lee slashing at his flank as well as his rear and cutting off his way back to his original massing area at the tip of the peninsula. Blocked, McClellan headed due south, the two armies fighting their way for 25 miles through Gaines' Mill, Savage's Station, White Oak Swamp, Malvern Hill, until at last McClellan came to rest under the heavy muzzles of his gunboats docked at Harrison's Landing on the James River. The Seven Days, history would term the series of fights. McClellan had kept his army intact. The beautiful machine was damaged yet still usable. He had lost untold supplies put to the torch at his lost base at the tip of he peninsula, but on a personal basis his opponent, the commander of the Army of Northern Virginia, had lost more.

The fires the Yankees had set to save their trainloads from capture by the rebels had destroyed White House, on the grounds of which McClellan had made his headquarters after sailing from Washington. It was in that mansion, after which the U.S. President's house was said to have been named, that a British Colonial officer fresh from General Braddock's disastrous 1755 defeat at the hands of the French and their Indian allies had courted a certain widow. The house and land had become the property of Mrs. Martha Custis Washington's descendant Mrs. Robert E. Lee. *Northern soldiers who profess to reverence Washington*, she had written on a note pinned to the doorway, *forbear to desecrate the home of his first married life, the property of his wife, now owned by her descendants. A granddaughter of Mrs. Washington.* McClellan, seeing the note, had ordered in his gentlemanly fashion that the house remain inviolate, and only the intercession of a doctor telling Lincoln it was needed for wounded men had forced the opening of its doors. Now it was gone, set on fire by a deserter from a New York regiment who flung a torch into it during the destruction of the vast Army of the Potomac supplies. When

*Great-granddaughter, actually.

next Lee saw it, nothing was left but blackened stones. Its formal gardens and the lawns had been mashed into mud by the wheels of Union army wagons and ambulances.

McClellan had treated Mrs. Lee with the greatest respect, ordering her safe passage through his lines to rebel outposts on two occasions when because of her perpetual tardiness his troops made her a prisoner. But the wanton burning of White House was of a piece with what the war was now becoming. McClellan had written Lincoln that it should be "conducted upon the highest principles known to Christian civilization." Civilian property should be respected. Casualties should be held to an absolute minimum. Pressure would be applied and there would be set-piece battles followed by a dignified and gentlemanly laying down of arms by the enemy. Soldier to soldier. Officers and gentlemen. And the war would be over.

But McClellan was left behind by events. At Shiloh on the Tennessee the Yankees on the first day of battle and the rebels on the second had taken batterings that European regulars, specialists in etiquette, routine, technique, would never have stood. Prior to those displays of ability to take what mercenaries would not, McClellan's old-time California housemate, Ulysses Grant, had felt the rebellion would collapse as soon as the North won a decisive victory of any sort. But at Shiloh in those moments of slaughter so intense, and willingness on both sides to endure that slaughter, Grant saw that only complete Yankee conquest was the answer. Ruthlessness would in the long run be beneficial to both sides, he decided. It was not in McClellan to reach that terrible realization. The suffering of his men haunted him, he wrote his wife. He could not sleep for thinking of the poor fellows dead and wounded. There were generals of his army at Harrison's Landing who said that now the time had come to return to the offensive and roll up the rebels, who had shot their bolt and now could be pushed back to and through Richmond. General Philip Kearny said only cowardice or treason stood against an order to advance. General Joseph Hooker volunteered to go first. But McClellan could not face a fight-to-the-end slugfest.

He could not ask it of the men who loved him. He could not see them do or die. And so he bombarded Washington with demands for reinforcements.

Lincoln understood. If by magic he could suddenly present McClellan with 100,000 more men, he said, McClellan would be ecstatic and promise to be in Richmond the following day. Then he would discover reasons why he could not fight unless Lincoln gave him an additional 400,000. "If I gave McClellan all the men he asks for they could not find room to lie down," the President said. "They'd have to sleep standing up."

So McClellan crouched among his men at Harrison's Landing, intelligent, sensitive, rational, a chartist, a gentleman, and begged for troops that did not exist. He had not the heart of a soldier, that was it. Had he owned a soldier's heart and desire to know and to do, he would have looked over the lines of the magnificent Federal army he clutched to his bosom at Harrison's Landing, and into the eyes of his enemy opposite number and seen that Robert Lee had swept him from the gates of Richmond with not 200,000 rebels, nor 150,000, nor even 100,000. Ninety thousand men of the Army of Northern Virginia had done it—fewer, actually. And even, now having saved Richmond, they were sweeping north to menace Washington.

John Pope was tall, impressive—big beard, big body, piercing eyes, a splendid horseman. At West Point he had once come back from leave wearing pants that buttoned down the middle instead of on the side. The Superintendent's wife was horrified and said that in such garb he would never enter her home. But the style caught on and went from West Point to the Army and then to the nation. He was remembered for that, and for his ready tongue. He told what were called improper stories. When the war came, a captain then, he swore into service the Joe Daviess County Guards of Galena, Illinois, and many other outfits, and then rose quickly to a general's rank. He won some minor engagements against the rebels in the West. He looked like a dazzling soldier and a fighter and talked like one, and they needed that in the East, Secretary Stanton and President Lincoln. They telegraphed him as McClellan fell back from Richmond to Harrison's Landing. They gave him the 40,000 troops that stood in front of Washington.

Pope took command with a barrage of orders of the day and announcements calculated to make him sound as little like McClellan as it was possible for man to be. Their composition may have been aided by a Secretary of War who had had more than his fill of a general whose temperament appeared to resemble that of a uniformed Hamlet. "I have come to you from the West, where we have always seen the backs of our enemies," Pope declaimed. In the West, he said, they believed in attack, not defense. "I presume that I have been called here to pursue the same system and to lead you against the enemy. It is my purpose to do so, and that speedily. I desire you to dismiss from your minds certain phrases which I am sorry to find much in vogue among you. I hear constantly of taking strong positions and holding them; of lines of retreat and bases of supplies. Let us discard such ideas. Let us study the probable line of retreat of our opponents, and leave our own to take care of itself. Let us look before, and not behind. Disaster and shame lurk in the rear." His own headquarters, he said in a not overly well-turned phrase, would be "in the saddle."

Pope represented a new harshness in the war. He ordered his soldiers to live off the Virginia countryside south of Washington. That gave a license to every man who wanted to steal a farmer's chicken. Communities would be assessed for any damage done by rebel guerillas operating against his troops, he said. All Virginians who refused to take an oath of allegiance to the Union would instantly be sent south, and any such who returned would be liable to the death penalty. Anyone who communicated with the rebels in any form—including any mother or wife writing a Confederate soldier—would be treated as a spy for whom the punishment was a firing squad.

To Robert Lee the new general became the "miscreant Pope." He must be "suppressed." But to go north above Richmond to do so would leave the Confederate capital open to a drive from McClellan at Harrison's Landing. For three weeks Lee debated what his course should be. He sent Jackson to feel out Pope. Then his spies reported that Union troops were being taken from McClellan's command to sail north and join Pope. But was it a feint to weaken Lee's defenses against McClellan? With artillery bombardments he tried to annoy McClellan into advancing—if indeed McClellan intended to advance. In early August, a month after the end of The Seven Days, McClellan came out of his sanctuary in force. But the next day he went back into his shell. Lee concluded there was no threat coming from McClellan and ordered masses of his army north to get Pope. The next day he found that McClellan was sending Fitz-John Porter waterborne down the James, heading out into the open water which led to inland rivers, 100 ships rushing him and his troops to Pope. So it would be a race.

Stonewall Jackson commanding, the advance guard of the Army of Northern Virginia rushed at Pope, their leader continually sucking lemons, his main source of sustenance, as he repeated over and over, "Press on, men, press on." Awesomely mad, he halted his horse by the side of the road and sat absolutely motionless, one arm held straight out into the air, his eyes on heaven. John Pope sent cavalry chasing phantoms until the horses could barely stand up, but Jackson raced behind him, burned his supplies, cut his routes to Washington and gave him battle. They met on the old field of Bull Run, where a year earlier the first massed fight of the North and South had its placing. They slugged at each other, Pope and Jackson. Pope never lifted his eyes to the horizon. When at last he did so, it was to behold Robert Lee coming with Pete Longstreet and unstoppable rebel reinforcements. It had been a near-run thing. A day's passage would have seen four-fifths of McClellan's great army arrived on the scene. But that day meant everything. The Federals broke and ran for Washington.

Savior of Richmond, First Captain of the Southern Confederacy, Lee had in two and half months driven from the gateposts of his capital into the forts of the enemy's capital an army vastly better equipped and far larger than his own. He had taken gigantic risks, lowering his hands and holding out his jaw to an opponent whose power could not be doubted. By imposing his will he had caused that opponent not to strike. He had imposed his will on his opposite number across the lines of struggling men, the guns, the patrols, the streams and the fields. He had split his forces in the face of a superior enemy, thus violating the first rule of warfare—Napoleon had specifically warned against doing so. But he had conquered. He had never shown the slightest emotion while he did so. At one point it seemed that Jackson would break before Pope. An officer near Lee could barely sit still on his horse with anxiety, wondering where Pete Longstreet was. "How close?" the officer asked himself. "What was he doing? Why did he not get in the fight?" Other men were quivering, their nerves snapping as they saw the coming rupture of Jackson's line, which would bring defeat, disaster, the ruination of the army. General Lee glanced at some teams with wagons and mildly said to an aide, "I observe that some of those mules are without shoes. I wish you would see to it that all of the animals be shod." When at last volleys of shots announced Longstreet's arrival, the staff could barely restrain themselves from throwing their hats in the air. The officer who had feverishly asked himself about Longstreet's location looked over at Lee. Nothing showed in the calm face. Never during the whole nerve-racking scene of defeat becoming victory did he show apprehension or elation.

Now, the victor, he rode through the men of his army and saw a sergeant of the 16th Mississippi who, barefoot like many of the Southerners whose country had so few manufacturing facilities, had gone into some woods to find a dead Yankee with boots. "What are you doing here, sir,* away from your command?" Lee asked.

"That's none of your business, by God," said the sergeant.

*The word was used in 1861–65 without reference to military rank.

"You are a straggler, sir, and deserve the severest punishment."

"It's a damned lie, sir," said the sergeant. "I only left my regiment a few minutes ago to hunt me a pair of shoes. I went through all the fight yesterday, and that's more than you can say. Where were you yesterday? You were lying back in the pine thickets and couldn't be found; but today, when there's no danger, you come out and charge other men with straggling, damn you!"

One of the staff asked the sergeant if he knew to whom he was speaking. "To a cowardly cavalryman," the sergeant said.

"No, sir, that was General Lee."

"Ho-o-what? General Lee, did you say?"

"Yes."

"I'm a goner!" The sergeant raced down the road as fast as a man could go. Even Lee had to laugh.

He went on, and in Washington the arms at the arsenal and money in the Treasury were ordered shipped to New York. Secretary Stanton had bundles of papers packed for carrying away by men on horseback. McClellan wrote his wife he would have the silver in his Washington mansion shipped out. Even Lincoln gave way to despair, sinking down into a chair and crying, "Chase* says we can't raise any more money, Pope is licked and McClellan has the diarrhoea. What shall I do? The bottom is out of the tub, the bottom is out of the tub!"

Pope would have to go, there was no question of that. "Imbecile" was the kindest term anyone used for him. They sent him off to the Northwest Frontier to fight Indians. It would have to be McClellan who took command of the troops defending the Union capital. "If he can't fight himself, he excels in making others ready to fight," Lincoln said of the engineer-organizer. Taking him back, the President said, was like curing a hangover with a hair of the dog who bit you.

*Secretary of the Treasury Salmon P. Chase.

Meanwhile, Robert E. Lee was moving. On September 5, three days after Second Bull Run, his troops crossed the Potomac into Maryland to carry the war north. On both shores stood Confederate bands playing "Maryland, My Maryland" and "Dixie" over and over again. To the Prussian nobleman Heros von Borcke, a volunteer for Jeb Stuart's cavalry, the sight and sound was magnificent. Evening sun burnished the rifles and bayonets and made them glitter and blaze as the same music repeated and repeated became strangely thrilling. A terrified governor of Pennsylvania wired Lincoln asking for 80,000 troops to defend his state, and the President replied that if he had 80,000 men to spare he would fling them against Lee's rear as he moved north.

Along Antietam Creek at Sharpsburg in Maryland, Lee and McClellan met again, 90,000 Union troops facing half that number of Confederates and sending storms of bullets at one another. "Every stalk of corn in the northern and greater part of the field was cut as closely as could have been done with a knife," said General Joseph Hooker. Each side took casualties of about 12,000. It was a standoff. Lee had barred the enemy from his own country so that the fall harvest could be brought in, but Maryland had not rallied to the South and joined the Confederacy, as had been Richmond's hope. Lee went south. The bands did not play so splendidly any more. "Damn my Maryland," the troops said.

Exhausted, the rebels waited for McClellan to come on. Autumn was the time for campaigning. But McClellan, as always, had what Lincoln called "the slows." The general wrote his wife that the government was trying to force him into a premature advance into Virginia, but he would resist such a move until he was ready. And so he asked for new arms, horses, shoes, bridging equipment. If, said Quartermaster General Rufus Ingalls, a commander waited until everything was entirely perfect and ready, no army would ever move. Eventually, at a snail's pace, McClellan went to the Potomac and crossed it. Having done so, he made no move to attack. November came. McClellan sat. "I said I would remove him if he let Lee's army get away from him," Lincoln finally said, "and I must do so." In a driving snowstorm a messenger went to McClellan with the order of dismissal.

They gave the Army of the Potomac to Ambrose E. Burnside. He took it with tears in his eyes, saying that he was not big enough for the job. "I hate to part with McClellan," Lee said when he learned of the change, "for we always understood each other so well. I fear they may continue to make these changes until they find someone I don't understand."

Burnside was a big, soldierly-looking man with distinctive whiskers.* He did not wish to emulate McClellan's waterborne and then up-the-peninsula move that had led to The Seven Days, but said he would try to take Richmond in an overland campaign. He threw his Army of the Potomac toward the Confederate capital. But first he had to take Fredericksburg on the Rappahannock, which was equidistant between the capitals of two warring nations. Waterways and railroads met there. Quickly he moved to the eastern side of the river opposite the city and waited for pontoon bridges with which to effect a crossing. They did not come. He might have sent his men through shallow fords near the city—but he waited. Meanwhile, Robert Lee came down and took possession of Fredericksburg. It consisted of a few long streets paralleling the river. Behind it was an open plain almost a mile long that ended in gentle ridges. Atop those ridges Lee waited for Burnside.

The new commander had been slow and hesitant in moving his men as McClellan's subordinate at Antietam Creek, and now he seemed to want to show that he could be decisive at Fredericksburg. Looking up at the massed ranks of rebels on their ridges he ordered the throwing of his pontoon bridges, finally arrived, across the river. From the houses along the shoreline advanced Confederate sharpshooters opened fire on the Union engineers. Burnside flung a monstrous artillery barrage onto the city, all but leveling it, and then Federal infantry ferried across

---

*An inversion of his name to describe them has lasted: sideburns.

and chased away those sharpshooters who survived. The bridges were put in position for the troops to cross.

On the morning of December 13, 1862, the Union soldiers went across the river and formed up on the shoreline beyond the range of the rebel gunners on their ridges. A dense fog hung over everything, but the sound of Yankee voices calling commands, the playing of bands and roll of the drums carried to the waiting defenders. As the sun rose, the fog dissipated and those who looked down from the ridges crowned with artillery and bristling with hedges of bayonets saw upon the plains of Fredericksburg a sight few men ever saw duplicated: 100,000 soldiers in perfect alignment, lines dressed and flags flying, slowly, majestically, moving forward to certain destruction. "A chicken cannot live on that field when we open upon it," a Confederate officer said to Pete Longstreet. He was right. Completely sheltered by a stone wall in front of a sunken road where the Union troops directed their advance, rebels stood six deep passing loaded rifles up to the men in front who could not miss hitting the massed battalions of Federals hopelessly struggling up the hills. Over the heads of the Confederate riflemen the Confederate artillery sent round after round crashing down, the blaze of a cannon instantly swallowed in smoke that rose to join great fleecy masses, like summer clouds, hanging over the field. "Oh, great God," gasped General Darius Couch, "see how our men, our poor fellows, are falling!" War had rarely known a more uneven struggle. Losses of 50 percent in Federal units were common. It was not battle, but butchery—murder.

Across the Rappahannock, Burnside went to pieces, crying, "Oh, those men! Those men over there!" There was never a chance of success, but he wildly said that he would go take command of his old corps and lead it himself against the stone wall and sunken road where only death awaited. His officers dissuaded him. Leaving behind a field literally coated with his dead soldiers, he withdrew his army across the frozen mud flats of the river.

The officer commanding the Army of Northern Virginia

had had to do nothing but prepare his positions before the Battle of Fredericksburg. More observer than participant, he gave few orders but simply looked on from a rise thereafter always called "Lee's Hill" while the United States soldiers of what had for thirty and more years been his army spent their strength so fruitlessly. As he watched he murmured to himself—they overheard his soft words, the people of his staff and an English journalist also—"It is well that war is so terrible, else men would learn to love it too much."

12

Vicksburg

THE UNION COMMANDER in the West, "Old Brains" William Halleck, believed in strategy, in the taking and holding of points on the map. The Battle of Shiloh was not strategy as Halleck had described it in his textbooks and lectures, it was blood and death and mutilated men. Ulysses Grant, who had fought that battle, had always been in Halleck's eyes the last thing from a classical soldier—indeed not a soldier at all. So Halleck himself came down from St. Louis to lead the pursuit of the rebels who fled bloody Shiloh.

Goggle-eyed behind his thick glasses, given to encircling himself with his arms while each hand scratched the opposite elbow, Old Brains gathered troops from all over the West. He amassed an army of more than 100,000 men and then set out after the rebels, who had retreated from Shiloh to Corinth, Mississippi. Each day he advanced a mile, and each evening he put the men to building elaborate fortifications that would ward off any rebel attack. It took him four weeks to crawl the less than 20 miles to Corinth. When he got there he did not capture the town, but occupied it. All the Confederates were gone. Halleck built fortifications for Corinth whose expanse was such that tens of thousands of soldiers would have been needed to man them. Then he adopted what was called his "pepper-pot strategy"— detachments of troops maintained at every conceivable point on the map, all connected by long and heavily guarded lines of communication. There was little talk about fighting the rebels.

Throughout all these doings, which certain of his officers regarded as ridiculous, embarrassing and ludicrous, Old Brains made a point of having as little to do with Grant as possible. Given the title of second-in-command, Grant was assigned no duties. When officers came to Halleck for orders, he took them to one side or lowered his voice to a whisper so that Grant would not overhear. When once during the slow-motion advance Grant made a suggestion, he was instantly made aware by Halleck that if his opinion was desired he would be asked for it. He had no more influence, Erasmus Keyes noted, than a lame mule. Entirely a fifth wheel, miserably unhappy, Grant decided to quit. William T. Sherman heard a rumor that Grant was about to leave, and rode to his headquarters. Grant was in a tent sitting on a camp stool and tying letters up into bundles. Sherman asked if the rumor about his leaving was true. Grant said it was. Sherman asked the reason. "Sherman, you know," Grant said. "You know that I am in the way here. I have stood it as long as I can, and can endure it no longer." Sherman asked where he intended to go. "St. Louis," was the reply. He asked if Grant had any business there, and Grant said, "Not a bit."

Sherman was then and always the most enthusiastic and vibrant of speakers, and he began pouring out words. He himself, he said, had only recently been known as "Crazy" Sherman the madman, but then had come Shiloh where he battled the rebels fiercely and from that gained new respect. Now, he said, he was "in high feather." The same thing could happen to Grant. But if Grant went away, things would go along and Grant would be

left out of them. If he stayed, a happy accident could restore
him to favor and to his true place. So he must not go.

Grant stayed. And in Washington President Lincoln, who
had taken to studying books on war borrowed from the Library
of Congress, sent for Halleck to be his military advisor, in effect
the officer commanding the armies of the United States. It did
not take Halleck long to show Lincoln that he knew the history
of every campaign of all the world's wars and that he was alert
to every conceivable danger of any move any Union troops might
make. Grant stayed on in the West guarding lines of communication while the war went on elsewhere. A sluggish, cautious,
campaign was gotten underway in Kentucky, and Grant was
ordered to dispatch troops there but not to go with them. He
stood wistfully on the platform of the Corinth railroad station
and watched the men and horses loaded and talked with Philip
Henry Sheridan, a fiery little man whom he had known in the
old Fourth Infantry days back on the Pacific coast. Sheridan was
a fighter—even with his fists. He had been suspended from West
Point for a year following numerous encounters with other cadets. "What's this, Sheridan?" Grant asked. "Are you going to
Kentucky too?"

"Yes, General, I've been ordered to take these regiments."

"I had not expected to see you go, Sheridan. There will be
active campaigning here soon, and I'd have much use to make
of your ability."

"I'll be more useful in Kentucky, sir. That's where the fighting is going to be." He made it clear, when Grant still urged
him to stay, that he wasn't going to be trapped in the backwash
of the war. Then Sheridan was off for Kentucky. "I felt a little
nettled at his desire to get away," Grant later wrote.

He himself spent his time dealing with people from the
North looking for angles that would make them money, speculators trying to get cotton from the South through the Union
lines, lawyers arranging deals, peddlers and smugglers—including his own father, Jesse Grant, who, always the sharp businessman, saw a good way to turn a dollar. His idea was that his

son should get him an exclusive contract to sell things to the troops. He could make an awful lot of money that way. Grant wrote his father that if he didn't see the utter impropriety of such an arrangement it would be hopeless to explain it to him. Jesse got going anyway in partnership with a Jewish entrepreneur, and Grant blew up. His chief of staff, John Rawlins, was capable of saying that if a relative of his got involved in cotton speculation, he, Rawlins, would see him hung on the highest tree he could find; Grant reacted to Jesse's doings with almost as much violence. He wrote out an order barring all Jews "as a class" from areas under his command. Rawlins and others pointed out that the order was clearly illegal and, among other inconsistencies, would forbid Jewish soldiers on leave from ever rejoining their regiments.* But Grant was adamant. "Well, they can countermand this from Washington if they like, but we will issue it anyhow." He never before and never after offered opinions of any kind on Jews and never seemed to give the subject any thought—but his father's money-making schemes were effectively squelched. (Lincoln, of course, had the order rescinded a few days after its issuance.)

Far away in Virginia and Maryland the war went on, Second Bull Run, Antietam, Fredericksburg, and engagements were fought by other men in the West, but Grant saw no action and heard no shots. He studied his maps. Vicksburg on the Mississippi, he saw, controlled the war. Lincoln in Washington had come to the same conclusion. "See what a lot of land those fellows hold, of which Vicksburg is the key," the President said to Admiral David Dixon Porter. The Confederacy was fed and supplied by the Red River, the Arkansas, the White, all carrying cattle, corn, pork, hominy and cotton and troops to the great Mississippi and the point where the railroads were, Vicksburg. "Let us get Vicksburg and all this country is ours," the President said. "The war can never be brought to a close until that key is in our pocket."

---

*Six thousand Jews served in the Union army. Four thousand were Confederates. The total number of Jews in both countries was 150,000.

But Vicksburg was an American Gibraltar, a fortress on top of a bluff bristling with artillery and manned by tens of thousands of rebel troops. The Mississippi for miles north and south of it wound through soft alluvial soil, wandering to left and right and regularly cutting fresh channels through land characterized by low-lying islands, little peninsulas and stagnant lakes. Over the centuries the river had created a strip of mush 40 miles across, a swampy jungle. With the river itself directly under the rebel artillery, and the land up and down from the city almost impassable, how could Vicksburg and its vital transportation facilities be taken? That was the great problem of the war.

Grant in his rusty and seedy uniform, the gold cord on his hat battered and worn, his coat open and lapels buttoned back, sat with his staff and listened while they talked about Vicksburg. When he got up and paced about, he did so with his hands jammed in his pockets and with the ever-present cigar in his mouth. He looked like a country storekeeper or western farmer, and none of his men—not Rawlins, nor Fred Dent, nor the peacetime writer Adam Badeau, nor the engineer James McPherson, nor Ely Parker, a huge full-blooded Indian Grant had known in Galena—ever decided exactly how their chief's mind worked. They did not know what he was thinking, or even, they said, if he ever thought at all. The volcanic William Sherman, cigar ashes spewing his coat as he gestured and talked—he talked so much that it was said to be easier to describe what he had *not* said than to detail what he *had* said in the course of an evening— certainly did not comprehend the workings of Grant's mind. Grant knew nothing of military history, Sherman said, and was impervious to fear, which was a dangerous way to be, yet somehow he generated faith in his ability. It was a hard thing to understand, Sherman said. He was a hard man to understand, Grant. "He is a mystery to me and I believe also to himself."

Grant in those days of late 1862, studying the way to Vicksburg, was not unhappy. Julia was with him, and the children. Rawlins, ever-alert to the danger that the general would take to the bottle, found he could relax when Julia was around. Grant was safe then. (When she was away Rawlins repeated to every-body that any man who offered the general a drink could expect to be cashiered and hounded out of the service. Grant's black servant was told, in such fashion that he believed it, that if he ever got the general a bottle Rawlins would string him up by the thumbs and burn him to ashes.) And so in a quiet domestic fashion that found Julia sitting at table with the staff officers, Grant presided over his little official family, never, however, making a point of taking the seat at the head of the table. Plain and simple food was served, the meat always well done—almost burned—for the general's plate, because he could not stand the sight of anything resembling blood and was known to leave the table if rare meat was served. He ate no chicken, saying he could not consume something that went about on two legs. There were no sauces for him, no dressings. Sometimes he nibbled fruit. When he got one of the migraine headaches that often plagued him, Julia gave him mustard footbaths and compresses for his eyes. Cheerful and outgoing, she asked the men about their wives and children, and knitted things. They talked about Vicksburg.

In November of 1862, as far away in Virginia, McClellan gave way to Burnside, Grant suddenly went into action. The Illinois politician John McClernand, a major general now, had gotten Lincoln's ear and convinced the President to authorize his raising an army with which he would take Vicksburg. Mc-Clernand was a fiery speaker—he had urged the men of Grant's first regiment to reenlist when their initial short term was over—but he was no trained soldier. That the government now gave him such a commission reflected on the government's faith in Grant. Torpid for forty years before the outbreak of the war, in hibernation almost, Grant had briefly shone before again lapsing into inactivity. Now he awoke again. A mystery and a sphinx, silent, inarticulate, he at once leaped into a campaign the con-clusion of which would find him compared with Hannibal in-vading Italy, with Napoleon at Ulm, the equal of Alexander and Caesar.

From Memphis, 200 miles north of the great river bastion,

he moved an army south. The advance failed. He had expected it to do so. That was part of his plan. He sent troops by water down the river, had them halt north of Vicksburg and then set them to making motions under Sherman. They were repelled by the rebels. It did not surprise him. He put them to digging canals with the aim of rechanneling the Mississippi, never believing the work would succeed, but feeling it good for the men's morale. Rains made the canals overflow, the river acted up and the whole of the area turned into such a morass that when men died of lowland fevers, the only place to bury them was in the levees along the river. Grant appeared to be floundering in the watery bayous, and Vicksburg seemed as safe from him as ever it had been. In Northern newspapers he was called a failure, throwing away time and money and lives on a miserable fool's errand. "Our noble army of the Mississippi is being wasted by the foolish, drunken, stupid Grant," wrote the influential editor Murat Halstead of the Cincinnati *Gazette* to Secretary of the Treasury Chase. "He can't organize or control or fight an army. I have no personal feeling about it; but I know he is an ass." Sherman could fume that all newspapermen were spies bought up by Jefferson Davis, or fools, that they should be hanged to the last man and their presses burned, but Grant said nothing. He performed around the north of Vicksburg so consistently and steadily that all of the rebels' attention was concentrated there.

Then in the spring of 1863 he told his people what he really intended to do. As one man, with the single exception of Rawlins, they objected, saying the plan was far too dangerous. Grant could destroy the North's chances of winning the war. Sherman; John Logan, the North's best political general; McPherson, the engineer; James Harrison Wilson, the cavalry commander—all united in saying that what Grant had in mind was the most hazardous move made in this war or, as Sherman put it, in any other war. But Grant loaded his army on Admiral Porter's gunboats and on the night of April 16, 1863, lights out and the sides of the boats opposite the fortress piled high with bales of hay and cotton, he went downriver under the heights of Vicksburg.

The Confederate artillery opened. A levee battery of a dozen guns—the Twelve Apostles to the Federal troops—poured steel out into the night. The rebels fired houses along the shore to illuminate the targets.

Admiral Porter tried to fire back into the air at the fortress, but the angle was too high. Helpless, the Union boats sustained hit after hit, had their rudders destroyed and their boilers blown up. But the current took them and they staggered down the river and landed on the eastern shore some miles south of Vicksburg. There they disembarked and, with their leader urging them on, rushed inland. Nothing that was not absolutely essential was permitted to be taken ashore to slow their dash at the enemy. General Grant himself took only a comb and a toothbrush— literally. He had no extra clothing, no blanket, not even a horse. He flung his army inland below Vicksburg.

Transfixed by his performances north of the city, hypno- tized, the rebels did not understand the meaning of his landing to the south and his charge upon Jackson, Mississippi, east of the river fortress. Grant fell upon Joe Johnston, recovered from his Virginia wounds, and drove him away. He slept that night in the bed that Johnston had occupied the previous one. The city's railroad station and lines destroyed by his troops, Grant turned west toward Vicksburg to find the rebel commander there finally hastening south of Vicksburg to destroy the Yankee sup- ply lines. But there were no Yankee supply lines. Violating the first axiom of war, that troops on the offensive must operate from a base of supplies always covered, Grant had, like Scott ad- vancing upon Mexico City, thrown away precedent. He would live off the land, he said, and he was doing it, picking up food and horses as he went along, one of the picked-up horses being taken from Jefferson Davis' Brierfield plantation and given to the general commanding. He named the animal Jeff Davis—far away another soldier had changed the name of his horse from just that name to Traveller—and rode him on a saddle tree bare of leather, with only stirrups attached to the wood. He met the rebel com- mander seeking his nonexistent supply lines, John Pemberton—

who long ago as a lieutenant in Mexico had come to bring their mutual general's compliments to Lieutenant Grant for his action in using a church belfry as an artillery post—and sent him reeling back into Vicksburg. A telegram, ten days in the delivery, was handed to Grant. Old Brains Halleck in Washington had learned what he was doing, and ordered him to desist.

He stuffed the telegram away and drove up against Pemberton in the great fortress and extended his right to the north where he could receive supplies from river steamers. So in a great semicircle he held the rebels tight. Behind him Joe Johnston tried to come again, and so Grant formed his lines to face Johnston to the east as well as Pemberton to the west. What he had done was positively Napoleonic in concept. He had split his enemies, routed them, driven them away or into their defensive works, marched and countermarched in their country 1,000 miles from home without a base of supplies. "General Grant, I want to congratulate you on the success of your plan," Sherman cried. "And it's your plan, by heaven, and nobody else's. For nobody else believed in it."

Like the western pioneers whose progeny they were, the soldiers of Grant's army adapted to his plans. They lived very well off the Mississippi countryside. They ate ham, beef, chicken, eggs, and drank wine and whiskey. They made bread from Mississippi's gristmills. They were not professional soldiers schooled in a base-of-supplies mentality any more than their leader was a book-schooled pedant. He flung them up against the landward Vicksburg defenses hardly less powerful than those that faced the river, and stood among them ignoring the shells and bullets while the assault failed of its objective. So it came down to a siege. He dug trenches. Inside the city the defenders hollowed out caves as protection from his artillery. The siege ground on. Julia was far away and the weather turned hot as spring gave way to summer—and Grant got drunk.

On June 6, 1863, on a steamer going upriver from the shore points of his northern wing, Grant went into the boat's barroom once too often. His speech slurred and he staggered. The newspaperman Sylvanus Cadwallader saw what was happening and went to the ship's captain and told him to refuse any more drinks to the general. The captain replied that, after all, this was the department commander and he couldn't do it. Finally Cadwallader got the captain to lock up the barroom and lose the key. Cadwallader escorted Grant to his stateroom—and found bottles of whiskey standing around. The reporter flung them into the river and after much argument got the general into bed. He slept. Then he woke up and ordered the captain to put in to shore. Somehow he had found another bottle. On shore he borrowed a horse and mindlessly roared off through the Federal lines, scattering the guards on the little bayou bridges. Cadwallader rushed after him, caught him, grabbed the bridle of his horse and tied it to his own saddle. Grant was half-falling off his mount. Cadwallader got the horses stopped and got Grant down and laid him out in a thicket with his saddle for a pillow. The general passed out. Cadwallader sat by him with a knife in his hand ready to cut off the two-star shoulder straps if anyone came along. He sent a man for an ambulance. Finally Grant awoke and Cadwallader walked him around while they waited. When the ambulance came they made their way back to camp where Cadwallader told Rawlins what had happened. He could have had a sensational scoop, but did not file a word to his paper.

"Dear General," Rawlins wrote that night. "The great solicitude I feel for the safety of this army leads me to mention what I had hoped never again to do, the subject of your drinking. . . ." And he threatened and raved. What had happened had happened. It did not affect the manner in which his men looked at Grant. He could not hold his liquor. It was weak of him even to take a drop. They understood. He was human. They understood. He laid siege to Vicksburg.

13

The Dignity of Gods

THAT AMBROSE E. BURNSIDE should hever have been given the command of the Army of the Potomac was made clear by his frightful showing at Fredericksburg, and when a little after that deadly slaughter he attempted to flank Lee out of the city and instead got his troops mired down in bottomless Virginia mud, no one in the world, including Burnside, believed he should stay on. He had felt himself inadequate for the job even before he'd fought the disastrous battle that uselessly wasted so many lives.

His successor suffered no similar doubts. Joseph Hooker was a big, blond, florid-faced man so good-looking and dashing that in Mexico the senoritas had titled him "the Handsome Captain." He had gone there as a lieutenant, returned as a lieutenant colonel and then left the Army and went to California where he bought a ranch. When the rebels fired on Fort Sumter he made his way east and was there in time to see the rout of Irvin

McDowell's forces at First Bull Run. He looked around for a commission in the Federal army, but possibly because Winfield Scott had never liked him, was unsuccessful in his quest. Then a friend took him in to see President Lincoln. "I was at Bull Run the other day, Mr. President," Hooker said, "and it is no vanity to me to say I am a damned sight better general than you had on that field." Lincoln gave him a command under McClellan and he did splendidly on the peninsula and at Antietam. Tireless, energetic, an organizer as well as a battler, he disliked his nickname of "Fighting Joe," saying it made him sound like a brainless slugger. Of all the commanders of the Army of the Potomac— McDowell, McClellan, Pope, McClellan again, and Burnside— Hooker seemed the most likely to fight the war through to victory.

Yet there were undertones in Hooker. Secretary of War Stanton said he felt there were two Hookers in the same man: One was an excellent officer, strong, magnetic; the other was rash with a violent tongue. Hooker had spoken so recklessly of Burnside that Burnside had said that if he continued in such fashion he would "swing him before sundown," and Lincoln himself had been described by Hooker as a dullard who should be replaced by a military dictator. "Only those generals who gain success can set up dictators," Lincoln wrote Hooker when he gave him the Army of the Potomac. "What I now ask of you is military success, and I will risk the dictatorship. Beware of rashness, but with energy and sleepless vigilance go forward and give us victories."

Hooker set to work to put together Burnside's shattered army. He divided the troops into distinctive new corps with individual badges; he improved furlough procedures, attended to food and sanitary requirements. Astride his charger, moving in a flurry of brilliantly uniformed aides, surrounded by colonels and brigadiers, accompanied by crashing bands and flaring banners, he simply radiated confidence. He never considered the possibility of failure. "If you get to Richmond, General—" Lincoln once started to say, and Fighting Joe* interrupted, "Excuse me, Mr. President, there is no 'if' in this case."

In the daytime as his army lay in winter quarters waiting for the spring campaign of 1863, Hooker staged magnificent drills and reviews and saw to the outfitting of his troops. "The finest army on the planet," he said, constantly filling his conversation with "When I get to Richmond" and "After I get to Richmond." Seventeen thousand of his horsemen jingled through the snow in a display of the largest body of cavalry that had existed in the history of the world, tens of thousands of infantrymen followed to create what seemed a moving forest of bayonets sticking into the air. There were great rolling concourses of artillery pieces, flags, rattling drums, lancers, orderlies, trumpets and bugles, trains of wagons—all the panoply of a nation in arms, and a vast and rich nation at that. In the evenings Hooker drank and dallied with women, as befitted a dashing soldier who was a bachelor. The headquarters of the Army of the Potomac, said Charles Francis Adams, Jr., son of the United States minister to London, "was a combination of barroom and brothel,"† a place where "no self-respecting man liked to go and no decent woman could go."

Through the winter of 1862–1863 Hooker floated balloons above the rebel lines to spy out their positions, thrust out probes from his side of the Rappahannock, rode among his men on his white horse saying that the damned rebs hadn't made and never would make the bullet that could hit him. His processions through the men of the Army of the Potomac inspired them and fired them up. Anyone could see that. He knew perfectly how to be with soldiers. His was a powerful presence. That he was a leader of troops could never be doubted. "If the rebel army does not run, God help them," Hooker said. "My plans are perfect, and when I start to carry them out, may God have mercy on General Lee, for I will have none."

---

*Now "Mr. F. J. Hooker" in Lee's letters to Mrs. Lee.
†Many people believe that the general lent his name to a term descriptive of a certain type of woman, but the usage predates Hooker's rise to eminence.

In the spring, Hooker moved. Lee had spent the winter trying to feed up his horses and provision his men. He had failed in both attempts. The horses were thin and worn and many of the men were barefoot and suffering from scurvy. The fight between North and South seemed to him a gigantic tragedy. "What a cruel thing is war," he wrote Mrs. Lee on Christmas Day, "to separate and destroy families and friends, and mar the purest joys and happiness God has granted us in this world; to fill our hearts with hatred instead of love for our neighbors, and to devastate the fair face of this beautiful world!" But when before daylight on April 29 he was wakened by distant gunfire only to lapse into sleep again before finally being roused by an officer saying his name, he did not flinch from the war he so hated. But then, cheerfulness in the face of great danger was important. He had always said he could not bear "croakers" who spoke of impending catastrophe. He looked up at the messenger and teasingly asked, "Captain, what do you young men mean by waking a man out of his sleep?" and then, told that Hooker was crossing the Rappahannock in force, said, "I thought I heard firing and was beginning to think it was time some of you young fellows were coming to tell me what it was all about."

He went out to meet Fighting Joe Hooker and nearly 140,000 Yankees magnificently equipped and singing and laughing as they went to war more confident than ever they had been before. Hooker had made them so. In the dark Hooker had stolen a march on Lee. Forty thousand men were safely crossing the river at Fredericksburg where four months previous Burnside had gone to disaster. Lee studied them, conferred with Jackson and his other commanders and decided the true attack would be a few miles to the northeast. He was staking his army on a guess: that Fredericksburg was only a feint. Jackson and the others disagreed. But Lee was the commander. He left a thin screen of 10,000 Confederates to face the 40,000 Federals under the leadership of General John Sedgwick, dear friend of the old days in the old army. (That Lieutenant Sedgwick sent his love was a staple of Lee's letters home in the days when they both wore blue.) He sent the rest of his 60,000 men northeast. And he was right about what Hooker was doing. The main body of the Union army, masked by heavy woods, was crossing the river at the shallow fords off to the northeast, coming hard.

Hooker pushed on, rapidly, secretly, with Lee not knowing for certain where the blow was to fall. Invigorated, Hooker rushed forward, duplicating exactly Alexander the Great's battle at Jhelum. Ten thousand cavalrymen were off to harass Lee's communications with Richmond. And the Union army was across the river in tremendous force. Hooker had Lee pinched between Sedgwick at Fredericksburg and himself at a little farm, the name of whose owner had been given to a tiny crossroads settlement: Chancellorsville.

The area was heavily wooded and with limited visibility to all sides, which made the artillery of the Army of the Potomac, always its best card, nearly useless. So Hooker swiftly pushed on to open land where his guns could have fields of fire. It was the correct move. Never more well-positioned, never up in such strength and style, the Yankee army under Fighting Joe had placed itself in readiness to destroy the Confederacy. For months Hooker had been saying he would take Lee's army in his grasp and crush it like *that*—and he would close his hand firmly. Now he seemed ready to do so. The Army of Northern Virginia, he had often said, was his "meat and drink"; now, he told the newspaper reporters, "The rebel army is the legitimate property of the Army of the Potomac. They may as well pack up their haversacks and make for Richmond." He issued a proclamation to his troops: "The operations of the last three days have determined that our enemy must either ingloriously fly, or come out from behind his defenses and give us battle on our own ground, where certain destruction awaits him."

His advance guards were pushing up against Lee's defenses, his massive main body was poised to swing forward and roll over the rebels, and it was splendid campaigning weather on May 1, 1863—when something happened to Joe Hooker. No one could comprehend it, then or later. It was not that he was drunk, for he had given up liquor as soon as his men crossed the Rappahannock. But something happened to his spirit. Suddenly the soldier who knew what to do and how to do it vanished. It was almost as if, some thought, he had been hypnotized by Robert Lee. Ghastly depression, deepest melancholy, seized him. He was in a trance, helpless. He had been so gallant and fine and inspiring a divisional and corps commander on the peninsula and at Antietam under McClellan and at Fredericksburg under Burnside. Yet now in a moment he was revealed as a leader but not a director. Once his troops were out of his sight, once he was operating on a large scale, he crumbled. He trembled with terror at the sound of distant firing—and, to the horror of his generals, ordered an immediate pull-back from his forward positions in the open, a withdrawal into a turtle-like shell in the wooded recesses near what for centuries had been called The Wilderness.

His order was so unaccountably mad that when General Gouverneur Warren heard of it he said to General Darius Couch that it should be disobeyed. The two men and several others, including General Winfield Scott Hancock—"the Superb," McClellan had dubbed him—sent word to Hooker that they *must* not draw back from the high ground and commanding position, that they were facing only light opposition, that they must push on and join battle and conquer. In half an hour the aide they sent was back with positive orders to fall back. General Couch went to Hooker. "It's all right, Couch," the brooding commander said. "I have got Lee just where I want him." The troops were filing back and one only had to look at their faces to see that the bewilderment of the chief had communicated itself down past the colonels and captains to the corporals and privates. That Hooker permitted himself to believe everything was all right told everything to Couch: "My commanding general was a whipped man."

All that day, lethargic, depressed, frightened, Hooker sat with his head bowed and waited for the blow. It was inexplicable, his officers said. Once he roused himself briefly to rescind his withdrawal order, but by then it was too late; the troops were half into their shell and could not be turned around. It was pitiful. He had made all the right moves in the expectation that Lee would do what Lee logically ought to have done, retreat; but Lee had not played as Hooker had planned, and the entire demoralization of Hooker's soul and mind followed.

Huddled within himself in his stunned disablement, Hooker saw clouds of dust rising from the rebel lines and permitted himself to believe that at last Lee was running. But the despondent and wavering air did not leave him, nor the careworn and anxious look on his face. It didn't seem like Lee, he said. He stayed within his own lines, not venturing to go out and check. At dusk the men of his right wing were sitting by their campfires preparing dinner when a strange procession of animals came running from the woods. Bounding rabbits were followed by racing deer. They were wondering what it meant when the answer burst among them. Facing an enemy more than twice his size, Lee had split his force into three fragments, a screen at Fredericksburg, himself in the center and Jackson rushing on a wide swinging semicircle to Hooker's right flank, saying over and over, "Press on, men, press on" and raising the cloud of dust that Hooker had hoped meant Confederate retreat. Jackson came roaring out of the woods behind the animals fleeing his crammed formations, and almost as one man the right wing of Hooker's army turned and ran. Their muskets, stacked, were left behind, their big guns, pointed the wrong way, also. They fled and their running masses broke into other Federal formations and set them to running also. Half the army was in flight. It was then, for the first time that day, that Joe Hooker came alive. Here was a problem he could see and deal with. At least on a certain scale. He put himself at the head of his old division, wheeled the guns in the direction of the enemy and opened up. The Confederate surge was halted. But the Union position was ruined. The rout of the right wing had unbalanced it. And a complete battle of annihilation might come with the morning.

Darkness fell and through it moved Stonewall Jackson, with a small party of staff officers, prowling and thinking of the morrow. Lee's division of his army and his going on the offensive when Hooker madly gave him the initiative of movement had been possible because of Jackson. The man was at least half insane, a strange mystic and seer. When Jeb Stuart gave him a new uniform to replace the battered one he wore with a decrepit Virginia Military Institute student cap, he was by turns childishly pleased and also acutely concerned that such display was against the tenets of his Presbyterian God. But he was at one and the same time a great soldier. His character repellent to some and unlovable to all, for he had no qualities of pleasant address or of small courtesies, he commanded, nevertheless, the trust of his men. And this day they had given him such a march and such a fight as would resound through history: the Battle of Chancellorsville, one of the world's military masterpieces, achieved against long odds by exploitation of the enemy's weakness and wholesale breakage of all the rules of war. Jackson prowled his front, across which Hooker was cooped up in his entrenchments with the river at his rear; and a volley of musketry sounded.

In the morning Hooker turned and ran for it. Though half or more of his troops had been completely unexposed to rebel fire, and he commanded a force far larger than his fragmented opponent, and Jeb Stuart with the banjo player who always accompanied him was circling about singing, "Old Joe Hooker, won't you come out of The Wilderness, out of The Wilderness?"* Hooker secured his passages back across the Rappahannock and ran. Smoke from rebel rifles clouded the air and the roar of rebel artillery shaking the earth attended his departure, and the Chancellor house that had given the battle its name burst into flames. Robert E. Lee rode Traveller there among masses of smoke- and powder-blackened Confederates firing at the fleeing enemy, and as he did so it seemed to his aide Colonel Charles Marshall that a common impulse suddenly possessed the men: One long unbroken cheer rose high over the roar of battle. It hailed the victorious chief. *He sat in the full realization of all that soldiers dream*

*To the tune of "Old Dan Tucker."

of—triumph; and as I looked upon him in the complete fruition of the
success which his genius, courage, and confidence in his army had won,
I thought that it must have been from such a scene that men in ancient
times rose to the dignity of gods.

As his men cavorted about him near the burning house and
in the burning forests, hailing the great thrilling victory, a courier
rode up. Lee took the note with his gauntleted hands, fumbled
with it, handed it to Marshall. The aide opened it and read out
the message that the rebel volley that had sounded in the night
as Jackson prowled his lines had struck him down. His hopelessly
mangled left arm had been amputated. There were other wounds.
Lee's voice trembled as he dictated a reply: "Could I have directed
events, I would have chosen for the good of the country to be
disabled in your stead. I congratulate you upon the victory,
which is due to your skill and energy." He knew what this wound
meant. Stonewall, he said, had lost his left arm; but he, Lee,
had lost his right.

For a week Jackson lay between light and darkness and then
lapsed into delirium, calling for his corps commander A. P. Hill
to prepare for action. "I must find out whether there is high
ground between Chancellorsville and the river," he said. "Push
up the columns, hasten the columns."

"Surely General Jackson must recover," Lee said. "God will
not take him from us, now that we need him so much." But
Jackson drifted away. "Let us pass over the river, and rest under
the shade of the trees," he said as he took his parting. Lee wept
when he was told.

In the White House the President received a telegram from
General Daniel Butterfield, Hooker's chief of staff. The Army
of the Potomac, it said, had been withdrawn from the south side
of the Rappahannock and was now "safely encamped" in its
former position. That was one way to describe a catastrophic
defeat. Lincoln went with the telegram in his hand to a room
where his friend, the journalist Noah Brooks, sat. Even as the
President approached, Brooks knew the telegram contained news

of a disaster, and it came into his mind that the President's face was gray, gray like the wallpaper of the room. His appearance was piteous, Brooks saw, broken—"and so ghost-like."

"My God!" Lincoln moaned. "My God! It is horrible, horrible; and to think of it, one hundred and thirty thousand magnificent soldiers cut to pieces by less than sixty thousand half-starved ragamuffins!"

Clasping his hands behind his back he walked up and down the room. "My God! What will the country say! What will the country say!" To Brooks, he seemed incapable of uttering any other words. To Secretary Stanton, the President appeared anxious to die, on the verge of suicide. But Lincoln rallied himself and when, a month after Chancellorsville, Lee began to move north and Hooker asked if this were not the moment for a Union advance on Richmond, Lincoln replied that Lee, and not Richmond, was Hooker's objective point. That was not what Hooker wanted to hear. The Army of Northern Virginia stretched itself out into a line 60 miles long, and Lincoln wrote Hooker that this lengthening out must surely offer an opportunity for the Army of the Potomac. "The animal must be very slim somewhere," Lincoln pointed out. "Could you not break him?"

But Hooker pulled away from any possible points of contact and then trailed after Lee, asking as he went for reinforcements. It came to the people of the North that as with the previous year when his troops crossed the Potomac singing "Maryland, My Maryland," Lee was undertaking a major invasion. He had to. His army was starving and in rags, and in the North were supplies of every kind. He did not worry that Hooker would take Richmond, for to do so would entirely uncover Washington. It would be a case of swapping queens, Lee said, and the North could not do that. For if the rebel army took Washington, foreign recognition for the Confederacy would follow, and certain independence.

Lee headed north, the June heat stifling, and Hooker learned that there would be no immediate reinforcements. Around his army swirled Jeb Stuart with his cavalrymen and his banjo player, and the head of the Army of the Potomac saw himself as what he was: a capable organizer, an inspiring divisional commander, a good corps commander, but not an army commander. The waters were rising over Hooker's head. He asked to be relieved of his post. Lee's force poured north, into Pennsylvania this time. They gave the Yankee army to George G. Meade. Long ago he had stood with Robert Lee as Winfield Scott took Veracruz in Mexico, fellow Engineer and good friend. He sent his cavalry out looking for the head of the rebel column, and on July 1, 1863, advance elements of the two forces made contact at a pleasant little Pennsylvania crossroads town—Gettysburg.

To Pete Longstreet, Jackson's replacement, the ground was unfavorable to a Confederate attack. The Yankees held the hills and ridges, and the long open fields would give them too many opportunities to use their superior artillery. Better, he told Lee, to slide to the right toward Washington, get astride the Federal supply and communication lines, take up defensive positions and force the Federals to be the attacking party. But Lee was thinking of how far he was from home and of the difficulty in getting ammunition up. And he was blind to anything going on at a distance. For the eyes of his army, his cavalry under Jeb Stuart, was off on a glorious fun-filled raid far away. Jeb had gotten the bit in his teeth, forgotten his primary function as scout and information-seeker and was off burning depots and tearing up tracks. And there was something else: Lee had before him the finest collection of infantry, he said, that the world had ever known—the Army of Northern Virginia. They were invincible. And Meade was waiting. "If he is there tomorrow I will attack him," Lee said. He slashed his hand through the air. "If he is there tomorrow it will be because he wants you to attack," Longstreet said. It seemed to him that the Confederates faced a Fredericksburg in reverse. But the orders were given and in the moring Lee battered at the Union left wing. It held. "Look at Pharaoh's army going to the Red Sea," a Union woman had cried at Lee as he had moved north; but if he won at Gettysburg then Harrisburg, Baltimore, Washington, Philadelphia, even New York, would be within his grasp. On the next day he swung at the Union right wing.

In the midst of the fighting, fresh from his joyride, Jeb Stuart returned. "General Stuart, where have you been?" Lee demanded. His face was red with rage. He lifted his arm and appeared to be about to strike Stuart. "I have not heard a word from you for days, and you the eyes and ears of my army!" Jeb wilted. "I have brought you one hundred twenty-five wagons and their teams, General," he got out.

"They are an impediment to me now," Lee said. The scene was inexpressibly painful to those who watched and listened. Lee controlled himself. "Let me ask your help now," he said. "We will not discuss this matter longer. Help me fight these people." All his life Jeb regretted his irresponsibility. Perhaps he could have found a more favorable site for the battle. Perhaps his horsemen might have found a weakness in the Yankee line. "He stopped to capture a wagon train," Lee said sadly, "and what was a wagon train compared with the tremendous issues we had at stake?" The Union right wing held.

Dawn came, July 3, 1863. Having tried both sides Lee would now try the center Meade had predicted during the night. He was right. At one o'clock in the afternoon the Confederate artillery opened a prodigious bombardment. For two hours it went on, practically every shell Lee owned flung up onto the Union defenders of Cemetery Ridge. Fifteen thousand rebel infantrymen formed up in long lines, General George Pickett commanding. They looked across the completely open seven-eighths of a mile leading up to Cemetery Ridge. "Take a drink with me; in an hour you'll be in hell or glory," a friend said to Pickett, holding out a flask. He declined. He had promised his fiancée he would not drink. He sat his horse next to Longstreet and handed him a letter to be delivered to the fiancée if he fell on the field leading up to Cemetery Ridge, and waited for the command to advance. To Longstreet's mind it was an impossibility that any assault would be successful, for the Federals were returning fire from the ridge and their heavy guns there seemed

intact. Longstreet looked broodingly into space. It had been
agreed that when the Confederate artillery commander E. Porter
Alexander felt himself running out of ammunition, he would
inform Longstreet; it would then become Longstreet's duty to
order Pickett on.

The bombardment reached its height and slackened. A note
came from Alexander: "For God's sake come quick. Come quick
or my ammunition won't let me support you properly." Pickett
looked at Longstreet. "General, shall I advance" he asked. Longstreet turned his face away. Pickett reached for the note to his
fiancée and wrote on the envelope, "If Old Peter's nod means
death, good-by and God bless you, little one!" He looked at
Longstreet and saw tears on his cheeks and beard. "I am going
to move forward, sir."

What followed was sublime in the eyes of the observer Lieutenant Colonel A. J. Lyon of Her Majesty's Coldstream Guards,
the most magnificent thing he had ever seen: Pickett's Charge.
It began with the 15,000 men in parade-ground formation and
ended with perhaps 100 of them getting past the Yankee infantry
and the Yankee guns and, for a moment, piercing the heart of
the Union center atop Cemetery Ridge and planting there, for
a moment, a Stars and Bars. The Highwater Mark of the Confederacy.

Those who lived staggered back to find the artilleryman
Alexander running his guns out into the open field, those that
had any ammunition at all left. There were not more than a
dozen such. Waiting among them, ready to die in the last-ditch
effort that would meet a Yankee counterattack, was Robert Lee.
"All this has been my fault," he was saying. Then, "All will
come right in the end. We'll talk it over afterwards but in the
mean time all good men must rally. We want all good and true
men just now."

A wild-eyed Pickett came—save for her, he would later
write his fiancée, he would rather, a million times rather, have
fallen with his soldiers—and Lee told him to place his division
to stand against an advance by the enemy.

"General Lee, I have no division now."

"Upon my shoulders rests the blame," Lee said. Across the lines General Alfred Pleasonton rode up to Meade and said, "I will give you an hour and a half to show yourself a great general; order the army to advance while I take the cavalry, get in Lee's rear, and we will finish the campaign in a week." Meade hesitated. Had he moved he would have gone through the rebels as a knife goes through cheese, so Alexander said later. But Meade hesitated. There would follow long days during which Lincoln pleaded with him to attack and crush Lee, and Meade promised to do so and then failed to attack. Then Lincoln pleaded again and Meade submitted his resignation, which was not accepted, and hesitated some more and finally contented himself with letting the shattered Army of Northern Virginia limp back to and across the Potomac River, Lee sitting Traveller for hours in the water until the last man was on the Southern shore.

On the night of the last day at Gettysburg, the cries of the wounded sounding in his ears, Lee had sent word to General John Imboden to come to his headquarters to discuss some details of the coming retreat. Imboden went and learned Lee was with A. P. Hill, sitting on campstools in Hill's tent, a single flickering candle lighting their maps. He was told to wait in the commanding general's tent. He stayed there alone until one in the morning, when Lee came riding back from Hill's entirely unattended, walking Traveller slowly through the soft silvery July moonlight. He halted the horse. There was no sentinel in front of the tent, and no staff officer, and when the effort he made to get off Traveller revealed how exhausted he was, Imboden stepped forward to assist. But Lee got down and then, with his eyes on the ground, threw his arm across the saddle to rest himself a moment. He leaned in silence on Traveller. Both, it seemed to Imboden, were as motionless as statues. He waited for Lee to say something. The silence went on as Lee stood there. "General," Imboden finally said, "this has been a hard day on you."

"Yes, it has been a sad, sad day to us," Lee said. He did not move. Then he straightened up and said tremulously, "I never saw troops behave more magnificently." Then: "Too bad! *Too bad!* Oh, too bad!"

The next day in Washington President Lincoln sat at the bedside of General Daniel Sickles, who had lost a leg in the fighting. They talked about Gettysburg, the President saying that he really didn't think the country could have stood another Fredericksburg or Chancellorsville. And Vicksburg, Sickles asked? What did the President think about the siege? "Oh, I don't know," Lincoln answered. "Grant is still pegging away down there. As we used to say in Illinois, I think he will make a spoon or spoil a horn before he gets through. Some of our folks think him slow and want me to remove him. But, to tell the truth, I kind of like U. S. Grant. He doesn't worry and bother me. He isn't shrieking for reinforcements all the time. He takes what troops we can safely give him considering our big job all around—and we have a pretty big job in this war—and does as best he can with what he's got, and doesn't grumble and scold all the while. Yes, I confess I like General Grant—U. S. Grant—Uncle Sam Grant!"

Even as he spoke a gunboat was speeding up the Mississippi to the telegraph station at Cairo to send him news. On the day that the firing stopped at Gettysburg, the flag of the United States had risen on the flagstaff atop the fortress of Vicksburg.

14

Lieutenant General

FOR TWO MONTHS Grant had held Pemberton in Vicksburg. The city was starving. On July 3 at ten in the morning, three hours before the Confederate artillery opened upon Cemetery Ridge far away, white flags appeared on the breastworks of the fortress. Firing ceased. A courier appeared with a dispatch from Pemberton asking what terms would be demanded for surrender. The following day, the Fourth of July, 1863, Grant rode into Vicksburg past the silent guns to the shell-torn residence where Pemberton had his headquarters. Pemberton was sitting on the veranda and did not rise when Grant mounted the steps. Their days together in the Fourth Infantry in Mexico were long behind them. Pemberton reached into a window and was handed his sword with a belt and revolver attached. Glaring, he thrust it forward. "Retain your side arms, General," Grant said.

More than 31,000 rebels laid down their arms at the feet of the conquerer, 2,000 officers, 15 generals. One hundred and

seventy-two big guns were rolled out. It was by far the greatest
surrender ever seen on the American continent, and it cut the
Confederacy in half and took the Mississippi River from the
South and gave it to the North. "The father of waters again goes
unvexed to the sea," Lincoln said. In every hamlet and city of
the Union fireworks were set off and bands played for the double
victories of the first days of July; and it was not Meade of Gettysburg but Grant of Vicksburg who was the greater hero. He
dawdled away a couple of months, sending for Julia and the
children and visiting New Orleans, and then in reponse to Washington's order went to Indianapolis for a conference with the
Secretary of War. ("General Grant! I knew you at sight!" Stanton
cried, rushing up to the staff doctor.)

They gave him command of all troops between the Allegh-
enies and the Mississippi. ("Grant is the only man that can whip
the rebs every time, and he can do it any time that he tries it,"
Private John Brobst of the 25th Wisconsin wrote home to the
girl he would marry. "We would not give our General Grant for
all the generals that are in the northern army.") He went to
Chattanooga, Tennessee, where the Union general William Rosecrans had gotten himself badly penned up by the Confederate
Braxton Bragg. Besieged with only a thin twisting mountain trail
as a supply line, Rosecrans had completely lost his ability to
think and to act. Like Hooker at Chancellorsville, he sat immobile
and waited for fate to deal him what it would. Grant arrived and
listened as the men on the scene detailed their position. His
apparent inattentiveness disconcerted them, as did his appearance. They had expected a swaggering magnifico, the victor of
Fort Henry, Fort Donelson, Shiloh and Vicksburg, and instead
saw a silent insignificant-looking little man in a soiled, scruffy
uniform with an old wool hat pulled down over his eyes.

Grant listened, asked some questions and then, ignoring
everyone, started writing out orders. Ten thousand of Rosecrans'
horses and mules had starved to death and their carcasses lay
unburied wherever one looked; the men were without cold-weather
clothing to face the approaching winter. With Bragg rated a

brilliant leader, a Union disaster seemed to impend. But the orders Grant wrote one by one and then dropped on the floor prior to gathering them all together set in motion the building of bridges, the opening of rivers, the bringing in of supplies— and a month later an unstoppable Yankee army went roaring up the cliff-like Lookout Mountain and Missionary Ridge at Confederate positions so high that the fighting was said to have taken place above the clouds. "How are *you*, Mr. Bragg?" shouted little Phil Sheridan halfway up as he raised a cup of whiskey; a bullet shattered it and Sheridan cried, "That's damned ungenerous!" and piled forward with the others and sent the rebels flying. Grant watched emotionlessly and then rode up to the heights where the exultant Union soldiers were cheering and cavorting. "All we wanted was a leader!" they yelled at him.

The supreme commander of the hearts of his men and the first soldier of the United States, already acclaimed as "the Great Captain of the Age" in the Northern papers, Grant remained as he had always been. He issued no grand pronouncements, made no show. When asked if he had political ambitions he replied that he did. When the war was over, he said, he would like to go back to Galena and run for mayor. If he was elected he would then be in a position to pave the street which led from the railroad station.

In the East that fall George Meade fought minor engagements with Lee, made a slight movement in force, fired a few shots, withdrew. There was no battle of annihilation in Meade. The armies east and west took to winter quarters. Robert Lee submitted his resignation to Jefferson Davis, saying that he could not do what he himself wanted to accomplish, for, he said, it had taken a dozen errors to lose Gettysburg and he had made most of them, and that he could even less do what others wished of him. Davis replied that if he could find a better man he would appoint him as chief of the Army of Northern Virginia, but that to find a better man was an impossibility.

In Nashville two days before Christmas Grant went to the

theater with Sherman, Rawlins and General Grenville Dodge, his railways engineer. Earlier they had called upon the appointed military governor of Tennessee, Andrew Johnson, a former tailor born penniless who, having gained election to the United States Senate, had been the only Southern member of that body to remain loyal to the Union. Though the South's grandees dubbed him a mudsill, a poor white, Johnson was intensely, fanatically, partial to the people of his origin, endlessly praising the working man as opposed to the aristocrat. A part of his identification with the poor was that he never forgot his early tailoring trade and even as military governor, and later, made his own clothes, which he kept immaculate. He looked with obvious distaste at Grant's tattered apparel, and the general mumbled something about not having had time to change his uniform—which was one of the few untruths anyone ever heard from his lips, for he had no other uniform in Nashville. Johnson launched into his ritual denunciations of the dastardly highborns who had made the war—he would hang them all, he often said; he would make the land sprout gallows—and banged his fist down on a grand piano so loudly that Grant and the others jumped.

They escaped to see a performance of *Hamlet*, which Sherman, an avid theatergoer, ruled execrable. Excitable as always, he raised his voice so that it seemed as if everyone in the theater, which was filled with off-duty soldiers, must soon hear him. "General, don't talk so loud," Grenville Dodge kept saying. "Dodge, that is no way to play Hamlet!" Sherman insisted.

Apparently others agreed and the audience grew restive. (Dodge himself felt the play was simply being butchered.) In the graveyard scene, the frightful actor playing the lead soliloquized over the skull of Yorick, and when he held it up a soldier in the back yowled at the top of his lungs, "Say, pard, what is it, yank or reb?" Of course the house came down, and in the uproar the four officers fled. They went to an oysterhouse where there was only one table large enough for their group. A lone man sat at it. Rawlins asked if the man would move to a smaller table, but he growled, "This table's good enough for me." Sherman said they'd never eat if they had to depend on Rawlins, and asked a policeman where another oysterhouse was. He directed them to a basement restaurant where they sat talking military plans while neglecting their food. At midnight it was still only half eaten, but the woman who ran the place said she was closing and threw them out. In the morning the papers got the story of the ridiculous evening, and the theater manager, the first oysterhouse patron, the woman who ran the second place, the chief of police and others came to apologize. Dodge saw they were afraid Grant was going to close their places or get them fired, but Grant told one and all he had no complaints to make—"in fact had passed an interesting and jolly evening."

There followed invitations, receptions, requests that Grant make speeches (which he uniformly refused), and the bestowal of a diamond-hilted sword of honor with scabbard of gold and a vote of thanks from the Congress to go with a gold medal awarded by that body. Congress did more. A bill was introduced by Representative Elihu Washburne of Galena, Illinois, to revive the lapsed rank of lieutenant general. Only one man in the country's history had held that position in the American Army: George Washington.* The bill passed. In early March of 1864 Grant was ordered to Washington to receive at the President's hands his commission as Lieutenant General Commanding the Armies of the United States. Three years before he had been clerking at the leather goods store. He went with his son, Fred, thirteen years old, who had run away from school several times to be with his father and his father's army and who had gone through the entire Vicksburg campaign with him, sleeping in his tent and scrounging for his own food because, he wrote later, "My father's table at this time was, I must frankly say, the worst I ever saw or partook of." Even when the youngster had been wounded in the leg—"I am killed," he told one of his father's aides—Julia had not objected to his doings. Alexander, she wrote

---

*Winfield Scott had been brevetted lieutenant general—acting in that rank but actually holding only a commission of major general.

her husband, was not older when he accompanied Philip on his campaigns.

Father and son arrived at the station unannounced and un-noticed save for some reporters who had gotten a tip that they were on their way. With the reporters was the great photographer of the war, Mathew Brady. None of the reporters and none of their sources knew just what Grant actually looked like, and Brady had been asked if he perhaps had some photographs of the western general. Brady replied that he had once corresponded with Rawlins and that Rawlins had sent on a picture he identified as being of Grant, but it was of such poor quality that Brady didn't think he could identify anyone from it. When the train pulled in on the evening of March 8, Brady joined the reporters with the hope of asking Grant for a sitting in his studio. A man with a peculiar slouch wearing an Army hat and a linen duster got off accompanied by a young boy, and Brady thought that he bore a slight resemblance to the picture Rawlins had sent. He inquired if this was General Grant. The answer was yes. Brady introduced the reporters and asked where the general would be staying.

"I don't know," Grant said. "I know nothing about the hotels." Brady recommended Willard's, and so Grant and Fred took a cab there. At the desk the soon-to-be Lieutenant General Commanding the Armies of the United States asked for accom-modations and was taken for nobody in particular. The clerk assigned him an upstairs room and glanced at the name on the register only when Grant had turned to go. The clerk read "U. S. Grant and son, Galena, Illinois" and called him back to assign the best suite in the house, Parlor A. Grant and Fred went into the hotel dining room and ordered a meal. The diners at the next table kept looking over and whispering, and finally a man banged the table with a knife and called for silence in the room. When he got it he announced that General Grant was present. People jumped up yelling the name and cheering. Grant had to offer an awkward bow. Men and women crowded up to stare. Grant took Fred and went to their room. A while later ex-Secretary of

War Simon Cameron, now senator from Pennsylvania, arrived to ask Grant to a regularly scheduled Presidential reception.

The White House was jammed as it always was for a weekly reception. They made their way through the people unrecognized and went up to the President in the East Room. From Lincoln's great height—he was a full eight inches taller than Grant—he looked down and took both his hands in his own, saying, "Why, here is General Grant! Well, this is a great pleasure, I assure you."

Word spread who it was with the President, and people started shouting and pushing forward. There were cries for Grant to stand on something so that he could be seen, and Secretary of State Seward suggested that he get up on a crimson sofa. Shrinking, he did so, and everybody saw that he was blushing furiously. Seward commandeered some officers to join White House ushers in clearing the way so that the general could go greet Mrs. Lincoln, who was receiving in another room, and then with her arm in his Grant was forced to make a tour of the East Room, with people jumping up and down or upon the furniture to get a better look at him. "It was the only real mob I ever saw in the White House," recorded the President's friend Noah Brooks, remembering a "little scared-looking man" turned idol of the hour. Sweat poured down Grant's face and the veins on his forehead bulged red.

In a private room he spoke briefly with Lincoln, who told him he would be given his commission the following day at one in the afternoon. "I shall make a very short speech to you, to which I desire you to reply," Lincoln said, discussing what he would say and asking that Grant in return say something which would reduce any jealousy other officers might feel, and something which would put him on as good terms as possible with the Army of the Potomac to which he was a complete stranger.

At the appointed time the next day the Cabinet stood to receive Grant, and Lincoln spoke of the responsibility placed upon him and the trust the country had in the general. In earlier years, during the Mexican War, which as a congressman he had

opposed, Lincoln had spoken of military glory as the rainbow
that rises in showers of blood; but perhaps he had learned to
look at such things differently, for when Senator Benjamin Wade
of Ohio had told him anybody would do to lead the great Union
Army, Lincoln had said, "No, anybody will not do! I must have
Somebody!" Now he had, or hoped he had, Somebody. "I scarcely
need add," he said to Grant, "that with what I here speak for
the nation goes my own hearty personal concurrence." Grant
took out a half-sheet of note paper and in the most embarrassed
and mumbling fashion read out three sentences saying he accepted the task before him and hoped to accomplish it. No mention was made of the two points the President had requested.
Perhaps he did not know how gracefully to phrase the points,
or perhaps with that strange assurance and belief in himself that
had brought him to this position—his faith in himself was, Sherman said, like that of the Christian in his Savior—he did not
wish Lincoln to believe that he could tell his new lieutenant
general what to do.

The previous evening he had promised Mathew Brady he
would come and sit for a portrait after the White House ceremony, but when he and Secretary Stanton arrived at the photographer's studio the late winter afternoon light was rapidly
fading. Grant sat as directed while Brady had his assistant rush
up to the roof of the building and draw some shades so that as
much light as possible might enter. The assistant slipped and
fell against the overhead skylight, shattering it. Sheets of glass
poured down around Grant and it seemed a miracle to Brady
that no sliver hit the general. "And if one had, it would have
been the end of Grant, for that glass was two inches thick! Grant
casually glanced up to see the cause of the crash and there was
a barely perceptible quiver of the nostrils, but that was all! It
was the most remarkable display of nerve I ever witnessed."

The next day Grant went down to Brandy Station, Virginia,
the winter headquarters of the Army of the Potomac, to talk
with its commander. George Meade was a competent enough
soldier, technically skilled and steady. He was a Philadelphia

aristocrat married to a woman whose sister had married Henry Wise, a former governor of Virginia serving as a general in Lee's army. Meade had a ferocious temper and was known as "the Old Snapping Turtle" to his officers. He lacked, however, inspiration, fire, genius. Had he these qualities, he would have flung himself upon Lee and likely destroyed him the day after Pickett's Charge, or perhaps an hour after the charge. Instead, McClellan-like, he had dallied and thought and checked things over; and Lincoln had cried, "The same old story of this Army of the Potomac. Imbecility, inefficiency—don't want to *do*. Oh, it is terrible, terrible, this weakness, this indifference of our Potomac generals." Almost pathologically concerned with the fashion in which history would view him, Meade nevertheless submerged his intensely personal view of events and told the new lieutenant general that if he wished to place an officer more familiar to him in charge of the Army of the Potomac, Sherman perhaps, he should not hesitate to do so. The cause they were engaged in took precedence over any question of careers or feelings. Meade's willingness to give up his high post favorably impressed Grant. He told Meade he would be continued as head of the Army of the Potomac.

Back in Washington Grant mulled over Lincoln's assurances that he, the President, did not know how campaigns should be conducted and had never wanted to interfere at all in military matters but had been forced into doing so by the procrastination of his generals and the pressure from Congress and the people of the North generally. All he had ever wanted was someone who would take responsibility and act. Grant heard from Halleck, now his subordinate, that he should reveal as little as possible to the President or anyone else of his plans; so Grant kept silent and said nothing of the future to either of the two men or to the Secretary of War.

After four days in Washington he told Lincoln that his time there had been rather the warmest campaign he had yet undergone in the war—all that bowing and making graceful remarks. Now he would be leaving for the West—Nashville—that very day. But Mrs. Lincoln was giving a dinner for the lieutenant general that night, the President remonstrated. He couldn't go just yet.

"Mrs. Lincoln must excuse me," Grant said. "I must be in Tennessee."

"But we can't excuse you," the President said. "Mrs. Lincoln's dinner without you would be *Hamlet* with the prince left out."

"I appreciate the honor Mrs. Lincoln would do me, but time is very important now," Grant said, "and really, Mr. Lincoln, I have had enough of this *show* business." He started for the West.

Before he had gone to Washington for those four days it had been Grant's intention to stay in the West and lead a campaign against Atlanta, the hub of the lower South, while loosely and from afar overseeing the drive of the Army of the Potomac against Richmond. He returned with an entirely different conception. Washington and the eastern officer corps, he saw, were hypnotized by the enemy general whom they referred to, perhaps in imitation of the President's example, as "Bobby Lee." (To Lincoln, the President of the Confederate States of America was always "Jeffy D.") All they could talk about in the East, Grant told Sherman, was of how brilliant and unbeatable Bobby Lee was. There could be no question of overseeing the eastern fight from a distant western perspective, not when the eastern army had such attitudes. So, he said, Sherman would lead the campaign against Atlanta. And Grant himself would in days return to the East where, with George Meade acting in effect as his executive officer, he would put the Army of the Potomac into the field against its ancient enemy, the Army of Northern Virginia, and its leader—Bobby Lee.

One word appears on
Philadelphia's statue:
GRANT.

Richmond's statue
bears one word: LEE.
*(Metropolitan Richmond
Convention & Visitors
Bureau)*

Light Horse Harry.

Stratford Hall. *(Robert E. Lee Memorial Association)*

Lieutenant Lee, Corps
of Engineers.

Lieutenant Grant,
Fourth Infantry.

Superintendent Lee, United States Military Academy.

Arlington. "Fifteen thousand acres, two hundred and fifty slaves." *(National Parks Service)*

The Grant log cabin outside St. Louis, Hardscrabble. " 'Is this my destiny?' "

Mary Custis Lee.

Julia Dent Grant with Fred and Nellie.

The Lieutenant General Commanding the Armies of the
United States smokes a cigar, seated in front of the smaller
tree, while others look at maps of the route to the siege
of Petersburg: Massaponax Church, Virginia.

The former commander
of the Army of North-
ern Virginia is sketched
as he rides from the
McLean house in
Appomattox.

The McLean house,
photographed a few
days later.

Robert E. Lee a week after the surrender, in uniform for
the last time.

The Lee children. From left, top, Mary, Agnes, Mildred; bottom, Robert, Rooney, Custis. No picture of Annie is known to exist. *(Confederate Museum, Richmond)*

The eighteenth President of the United States. "A man faced with a problem the terms of which he did not understand."

"Grantism."

The last days of Robert E. Lee.

At Mount McGregor, with from left, standing, Jesse, Julia, Jesse's wife, and Fred; seated are Nellie, Fred's two children, Jesse's daughter, and Fred's wife.

The last days of U. S. Grant.

The dedication of Grant's tomb in 1897.

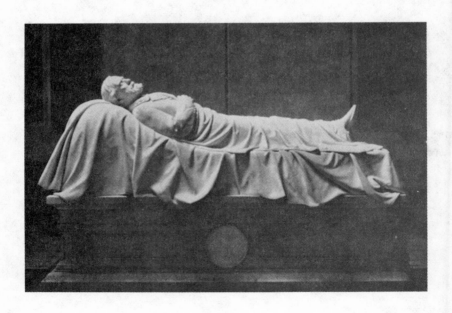

The Recumbent Warrior above Lee's tomb.
(Washington and Lee University)

15

The Opponents

.

COULD ANYONE SAY they knew Robert E. Lee? wrote the diarist Mrs. Chesnut. "I doubt it!" "The Marble Model," the cadets called him when he was superintendent of West Point. *Duty is the most sublime word in the language*, a widely publicized and perceptive—although fraudulently concocted—letter had him saying. "Marse Robert," the men of the Army of Northern Virginia called him, Marse Robert the gentle, the forgiving, the man who never put himself above other men, who got down from Traveller and knelt before corporals when they read divine service, who made room at his table for a hungry private. He had risen above victory at Chancellorsville by giving all the praise for that great battle to Jackson; he had risen above defeat at Gettysburg by taking all the blame unto himself.

Yet the unruffled man so rooted in an old society rounded and smooth could coldly order the immediate hanging of one of his men who had gone pillaging and stolen a pig from a farmer.

(Turned over to Stonewall for execution, the soldier instead found himself put in the front lines, where he performed splendidly. He had lost the pig, said an officer, but he brought home the bacon.) The strong neck had a way of turning beet-red and the temple veins would swell, the massive head jerking in a certain fashion, and the staff officers would know their general was in a fury. They loved him, but they feared him too. "You wait and see," Major A.R.H. Ranson was told when he reported to head-quarters and an assignment on Lee's staff. "You have known the general socially. You have now to make his acquaintance as your commanding general." Soon, Ranson was assured, he would be terrified of Lee. Ranson laughed at the idea. But they were right. Soon he *was* scared of Lee. There was something about him of the tiger, thought one little boy looking up into his face. It was not safe to breathe normally about him, the child decided.*

Aided by a tiny group of half a dozen young men, none of whom were professional soldiers, clerks more than staff officers, Lee *was* his army. "Well, Captain," he had a way of saying, "what shall we do now?"; or, "What should our move be now, Major?"—but they understood no answer was expected. Pete Longstreet took himself to be the equal of General Lee—or *almost* the equal—and interpreted orders as he thought best, but no one else did. Longstreet in later years came to believe that the doomed sending of Pickett to certain destruction at Gettysburg, the battle where Lee did everything an hour late, where he had lost his magician's wand, was made to satisfy a bloodlust on Lee's part. Bloodlust? But on the march to Gettysburg he issued the strictest orders that the Pennsylvania farmers and townspeople were to be left undisturbed and all goods were to be paid for. Approaching the battlefield the men passed two Confederate soldiers swinging from a tree by the road. Lee had put them there. They'd robbed and killed a farmer. (Philip Sheridan said in an official report to his War Department that by his orders 2,000 Virginia barns had been put to the torch in a matter of days and that a crow flying

*It was Woodrow Wilson.

over the area in question would have to carry its own rations. William T. Sherman on his march to the sea burned even more barns, and private residences too.) When in Pennsylvania a defiant woman sang "The Star-Spangled Banner" as Lee rode by, he took off his hat.

A man who by his heredity would in Europe have been called the son of a hundred earls, Lee commanded the souls of his men as no other commander in history ever did. Napoleon after Waterloo was one lone soldier fleeing with thousands of others, none of whom cared a fig for him; but Lee after Gettysburg was among men who by the thousands would have laid down their lives for him. Yet who were the men? Only 10 percent owned slaves and thus could even tenuously lay claim to belonging to the aristocracy of what came to be called "the Old South." The others were farmers, mountaineers, men of very limited means, the spear carriers of history. What did they know about, what could they *care* about, states' rights? What was the cause of the Confederacy to them? One Confederate officer thought he understood: He heard some of the men discussing Darwin's *Origin of Species*, published just before the war. It was entirely possible, they agreed, that the likes of them could be descended from monkeys, but it took God to make a man like Marse Robert. That ended the discussion. The moral to the physical in war, Napoleon said, is as three to one. In the case of Lee's forces, the ratio was higher. The Lord of Hosts is with us, with Lee's army, they said. The annual Yankee defeats proved it. God marches in the ranks of the Army of Northern Virginia. He could not do otherwise when the leader was Marse Robert.

"How much depends in military matters upon one mastermind!" cried Abraham Lincoln when time after time he found that the men he had put at the head of the Army of the Potomac were anything but. Lee was that, but he was something above that, thought a future commander of the British Army, Victoria's finest soldier, perhaps—Lord Wolseley. In his life he met the great of the world, Wolseley wrote, but Lee was in a different category. Lee stood on a different level from all others. What he owned was above mere soldiers' genius, Wolseley said. It could not be defined.

Can anyone say they know Robert E. Lee? I doubt it! wrote Mrs. Chesnut, but when in 1864 Ulysses Grant visited his parents and his silent unquestioning mother bestirred herself to ask her son if he was not worried about going off to face Lee, he replied, "Not at all. I know Lee as well as he knows himself. I know all his strong points, and all his weak ones. I intend to attack his weak points, and flank his strong ones."

He knew Lee? But how could that have possibly come about? This rootless son of the western frontier, indolent, passive, quiet all his life, militarily inactive for years before the war, forty years of failure behind him, they said, claiming that he knew and understood the Sir Galahad of the Old South, of Old Virginia? Saying that he would conquer one whose strength was the strength of ten because his heart was pure? He, Grant, who became sodden and stupid whenever he had two drinks? Who slumped about, read nothing and knew nothing of military history, whose entire definition of Napoleon was that he was a great soldier but very unkind in his treatment of Josephine? Lee was the flower of the civilization that produced him, complete unto himself, the Chevalier Bayard of America, a knight without fear and without reproach. Who was Grant of Galena, Illinois, to understand *him?* McClellan, the brilliant student of men and affairs, proficient, schooled, certainly did not know Lee. Hooker, the critic, inspiring, exciting, the Fighting Joe who could do everything, as it turned out, but fight—*he* certainly did not know Lee. Once an ignorant peasant girl in the backwaters of her time saw visions, put on armor, took command and executed historically documented complex maneuvers and became her country's hope— and it was all so baffling that only the direct intervention of God in Heaven can explain it. As with Joan of Arc, so it seemed to be in the case of Ulysses S. Grant. The nineteenth century did not believe that it was within itself to throw up saints and so those who watched Grant put it in scientific terms: When the body is threatened by an invasion, an attack, the body throws up defenses from its bloodstream or glands, and the body fights the invasion and the attack. So with the United States in the spring of 1864. The last, best, hope of mankind—so Lincoln called his country—was threatened by an attack almost unearthly in its mystery. For how could a little band of half-starved ragamuffins, as Lincoln defined Lee's army, menace so successfully the mighty North? And in response the Union found within itself what it hoped would be the antidote—the Lieutenant General Commanding the Armies of the United States—and sent him forth to face Robert E. Lee.

16

Battle

IN THAT SPRING of 1864, the Army of Northern Virginia lay in its camps around Orange Court House and from mountaintop observation posts looked down upon the great white-tented city that was the Army of the Potomac. All was hustle and bustle there as new men drilled. The Yankees had drained not only the slums of the North for new soldiers, the Southerners said, but with their cash bounties they had hired mercenaries from the mean streets of every European town. Whole regiments of men who could not speak English were to go forth in the name of the United States.

Washington was filled with the North's officers back from winter leave. They dressed in the old tradition of the Army of the Potomac's bravos in uniforms with sashes, bullioned cuffs, double rows of buttons, elaborate belts with glittering buckles from which hung sabers adorned with golden sword knots, elegant lined capes, long riding whips, gleaming boots. Among them moved their new commander, a stranger among strange troops. The author Richard Henry Dana in late April saw a short round-shouldered man in a tarnished uniform at the center of a staring crowd at Willard's. "There was nothing marked in his appearance. He had no gait, no *station*, no manner, rough, light-brown whiskers, a blue eye, and rather scrubby look withal." Dana joined the starers. Some officers were being introduced. Grant had his usual cigar in his mouth. "I saw that the ordinary, scrubby-looking man, with the slightly seedy look, as if he was out of office and on half-pay, had an entire indifference to the crowd around him. To see him talking and smoking in the lower entry of Willard's in that crowd, in such times—the generalissimo of our Army, on whom the destiny of the empire seems to hang! How war, how all great crises bring us to the one-man power!"

What did the officers being introduced think? "There is a habit," Rawlins wrote home, "anything but praiseworthy. Namely, of saying of western successes, 'Well, you never met Bobby Lee and his boys; it would be quite different if you had.' And in speaking of the probabilities of our success in the coming campaign: 'Well, that may be, but mind you Bobby Lee is just over the Rapidan.' "

Beyond the Rapidan and beyond Lee lay Richmond. For three years the cry in the North had been "On to Richmond"—but Grant did not care about Richmond. He never had and never would. Taking cities was an eighteenth-century concept. "Lee's army will be your objective point," he told Meade. "Where Lee goes, you will go also."

April came, May. The leaves were out on the trees of that battered Virginia which, in the years since 1861, had come to resemble a medieval landscape where for years warring armies and roving bands had done combat. The houses unburned looked hardly better than those whose foundations alone stood. The window sashes had been used for firewood, the fences were down and weeds and vines grew in the gardens. The women were coarsened by the years of hard work that men once performed.

The roads were rutted by army wagons and filled with furrows. Desolation reigned, stumps were all that remained of forests cut down for fuel, and the skeletons of horses and mules lay about, fragments of rifles and bayonets, the drainage trenches of old camps. Lee waited for Grant. It was personal now, a duel between the two commanders.

To get at Lee, Grant had to feint at Richmond and, more importantly, at Lee's lines of supply south. He looked at his map. To head down toward Richmond by an easterly route would mean having to get across a series of rivers. To go by a westerly route would mean cutting himself off from any waterborne supplies, which meant every bit of food, forage and ammunition would need to be wagon-carried. He thought of a central route. But in the very center of that path was the 20-mile-square morass of The Wilderness, near where Joe Hooker had just a year earlier come to grief. There were no real roads there, only a few trails penetrating a tangle of laurel bushes and brambles and low stunted thickets of bristly scrub oak. There were sluggish streams spreading out into marshland in that lonely and dense undergrowth through which a man had to turn sideways as he picked his way along. Long before, The Wilderness had been an area where iron ore had been smelted, and its forests, cut for the fuel for that purpose, had given way to this dismal impenetrable tangle. Cavalry would be unusable there and artillery also, for the gunners would never be able to get their pieces forward, and if they did they would not be able to see a target in a place where visibility was never more than 100 feet. A natural fortress.

On the evening of May 3, 1864, the 127,000 men of the Army of the Potomac fell in for dress parade. In their masses regiment after regiment and battery after battery lined up. Bugles sounded, trumpets, distant drums. Then in a silence most profound they listened to the reading of a march order for the next morning. That night thousands of fires burned as the old veterans destroyed things they did not intend to carry south. Some of the new men spoke of burning the huts they had constructed to keep out the winter chill, but the veterans knew better. They had seen six other generals one after the other set out with great plans and optimism only to come hurtling back in retreat. "Leave things as they are," an old hand said to the newly enlisted Private Frank Wilkeson. "We may want them before snow flies."

From atop Clark's Mountain with its long views over the Rapidan, General Lee stood dismounted with his officers and with a gauntleted hand pointed off to the distance. Grant would come by way of the Ely and Germanna Fords, he said. That meant The Wilderness. That meant difficulties for the Army of the Potomac. But Grant, he reasoned, came wearing the laurels gained at Donelson, Shiloh, Vicksburg, Missionary Ridge. His confidence would send him on a direct nonmaneuvering route. It would be The Wilderness. Perhaps there those western laurels would wither in Virginia's climate.

Seventeen miles away, Grant said to Meade, "I never maneuver." Lee had read him rightly. "Colonel," Lee said to his aide Walter Taylor, "we have got to whip them; we must whip them, and it has already made me feel better to think of it." The general, Taylor wrote his fiancée, seemed exceedingly anxious to battle "the present idol of the North." Now with the Yankee army on the move, Lee, on the morning of May 4, 1864, seemed gay and cheery. At breakfast he said grace and then told his staff that even now Grant was crossing the Rapidan. He had sent Phil Sheridan's cavalry to drive away the Confederate guards at the fords so that Union engineers could throw pontoon bridges across. With three corps of about eighty regiments each, with cavalry and artillery, with more than 50,000 horses and mules, 4,000 wagons and ambulances, Grant was coming. "We might have him to breakfast with us."

At the crossings Grant waited for a Confederate strike. None came. His men were getting across the river with no opposition. In front of them, dogwood blossoms, white against the new green of the springtime woods, was The Wilderness. Once through it he would be in open ground where his artillery and cavalry and heavier battalions could make themselves felt. Even as Meade's men went into The Wilderness darkness, Grant had sent Sherman driving on Atlanta, the political general Benjamin Butler to probe the way to Richmond along the James River and the German immigrant Franz Sigel to try the rebels in the Shenandoah Valley. Other Federal forces were on the move in West Virginia under Nathaniel P. Banks. He expected no great results from anybody save Sherman, for the other commanders were known incompetents given their posts by Lincoln solely to help keep discordant Northern elements in the fight. Their nicknames splendidly described them: Butler was known as "Beast" and, for the silver he was said to have stolen in New Orleans, "Spoons"; N. P. Banks was "Nothing Positive" and the timorous German, Sigel, was "the Flying Dutchman." But they could hold a leg while others skinned, as Lincoln put it.

That Lee did not contest the river crossings surprised Grant. He made camp a few hundred yards on the southern side of the Germanna Ford and telegraphed Washington: "Crossing of the Rapidan effected. Forty-eight hours now will demonstrate if the enemy intends giving battle this side of Richmond." A moment's walk away was Meade's tent, with an immense, gorgeous headquarters flag of magenta, swallow-tailed, with a wreath enclosing a golden eagle. "Is Imperial Caesar about here?" Grant asked.

All night the troops and equipment passed over the pontoons and down the wretched thin little roads—dirt tracks, really—that led south through the woods, 30 miles of marching infantry followed by 60 miles of wagons. A reporter asked how long it would take to get to Richmond and Grant deadpanned, "I will agree to be there in about four days—that is, if General Lee becomes a party to the agreement. If he objects, the trip will undoubtably be prolonged."

The troops kept on, Major General Gouverneur Warren leading with the V Corps. He had done brilliantly at Gettysburg. But Warren's nature was to concern himself not only with what was his own direct responsibility, but with other matters. It was not timidity, although perhaps Phil Sheridan thought so. (Tough little Sheridan found all the eastern officers' concern about Lee almost humorous. He himself feared nothing, and never had.) Warren thought about what was in front of him and what might be forming behind, and moved slowly and cautiously. Too slowly and too cautiously. Evening came and the head of his column had not passed through The Wilderness. Behind him the following VI Corps was bottled up in the narrow roads.

Robert Lee had always used the enemy to get his ideas. He was a reactor, a counterpuncher. He saw Grant plow into The Wilderness, saw his intent—and moved. For 1,800 years it had been an accepted rule that armies did not attack in dense forests. Turenne had adhered to that rule, Saxe, Gustavus Adolphus, Marlborough, Frederick the Great and Napoleon. Lee went back to Roman times and the destruction of Varus' legions in the teutonic forests by Arminius,* and sent the Army of Northern Virginia to hit the Army of the Potomac on a right angle. He sat Traveller, both as motionless as though made of stone, and his men quick-timed by him from their winter quarters in a column of fours, the gathered country people cheering them on. It was a lovely spring morning, and he was going in to hit Grant's strung-out and bottled-up army.

A couple of shots sounded, the Union private Luther Hopkins remembered, little pop-pops in the dawn, and then the rebels were on the Yankee flank. An eighteen-year-old farm boy of Company I, 18th Massachussetts, went down, the first casualty of the first meeting between Ulysses Grant and Robert Lee.

At General Warren's headquarters an officer arrived to bring word that the rebels were advancing in force. To the watching Lieutenant Morris Schaff it seemed as if Warren had never had a greater surprise in his life, and Grant's surprise when he found out could not have been less. Never before had he been taken unaware by an enemy commander, not Buckner, not Pemberton, not Bragg, not anybody, and he had made no provisions for being attacked in flank, had kept only token guarding pickets out. Perhaps Warren of the V Corps thought to himself that his

---

*Hermann the Conquerer, to Germans.

early concerns had been correct. Perhaps he was not the same soldier he had been before at Gettysburg. He sent word to Meade that a line of enemy infantry was advancing; he would see how strong the line was.

That morning in his camp by the Germanna Ford, Grant had breakfasted off a cucumber, which he sliced and dipped into vinegar, plus a cup of coffee. Then he had called for cigars, and his servant, Bill, brought him twenty. He put on a sash and sword and pulled on a pair of brown thread gloves. None of his staff had seen him bedecked in such fashion before. They decided that either the general on this first full day of the campaign was going to try to live up to the standards of dress of the Army of the Potomac or that Julia Grant had told her husband to spruce himself up. When the word came that his troops were exchanging fire with rebels, Grant sat down on the ground with his back against a small pine, picked up a piece of wood and started whittling. He was there whittling while Meade went off to confer with Warren, and was there when Meade sent word that the attack felt heavy. The Northern army, or that part of it not bottled up behind Warren, got off the trails and tried to change front and form up in order of battle. But it was murderously difficult in the tangled underbrush, for the lines could not be dressed, and men only a stone's throw away were invisible. The rebel fire poured into the soldiers.

Warren's men tried to push forward but gaps developed in their lines. They lost their sense of direction. The enemy's positions were identifiable only by smoke from his guns; one saw gray filmy clouds rising toward the treetops and fired in that direction. It was next to impossible for officers to keep in touch with their men. Major General Alexander Hayes must have been happy to meet up with a recognizable unit, his old regiment, the 63rd Pennsylvania, but when he stopped to say a few words, a bullet of the rapidly increasing storm of steel hit him squarely above the gold cord in his hat. Grant was told as he worked at his whittling. He sat still for a long moment and then talked about Hayes, how they had been at West Point together and then had gone together to Mexico long ago. It was like him to die at the head of his troops, Grant said.

Swells of musket fire roared through the thickets of The Wilderness below a sun that seemed a deep poppy scarlet through the clouds of smoke. Both Grant and Lee had in the past moved both the red pieces and the black pieces on the chessboard, the enemy's formations as well as their own, but on this day neither could budge the other. Lee tried with cavalry and infantry to cut Grant off from his water crossings behind him; it didn't work. Grant tried to push forward out of the maddening thickets but couldn't make it.

Their men intertangled as they wormed along trying to get forward, shot at sounds, blundered into little disasters and little victories. It was almost a battle between two armed mobs, with no rear and no flanks. Officers maneuvered by compass in the blind fighting. North of the two struggling armies the countryside filled up with rebel cavalry and irregular formations of detached Confederate marauders, and Army of the Potomac communication with Washington was entirely lost. Lincoln came and came again to the War Department where the military telegraph system had fallen silent. There was a drawer where yellow tissue copies of incoming telegrams were placed, but save for Grant's first announcement that he was across the Rapidan and waiting to see what the next forty-eight hours would bring, the drawer was empty. Horrible rumors spread in Washington. "Another twenty-four hours and Lee will be here!" was heard on all sides, and clerks in the government buildings stared through windows facing south, expecting to see gray swarms coming at them. A steady stream of officials, congressmen and senators came to the White House seeking news but getting none. Grant had disappeared through a hole, Lincoln said, and then pulled the hole in behind him: the lost army. In Richmond, the ladies of the city sat in their parlors with jewelry on, ready to flee if some catastrophe struck.

Evening in The Wilderness brought a slow dropping of the rate of fire followed by a complete halt when darkness fell. The casualties on both sides had been appalling, the Union forces suffering greater losses. Grant met with Meade and said he wanted an all-out attack aimed at getting the army freed up and out in the open, away from the stifling spider's web they were caught in. It should begin at 4:30 in the morning, he said. Meade protested that dawn was not until 4:48 and that it would be impossible to form up the troops in complete darkness. Six o'clock was the time he suggested. They compromised the matter at 5:00. Across the lines, perhaps a mile away, Lee ordered a rebel assault at exactly the same hour.

In the smoking woods made frightful by the cries and moans of the wounded, and frightful also for the shattered forms everywhere who would never rise again, the exhausted men of both sides fell into stuporous sleep. Young Lieutenant Morris Schaff, West Point '62, his first day in combat completed, thought back to a conversation he had had some months earlier, before he saw the flash of an enemy gun and heard the crashing report and strode over and among bodies. He had been discussing General Burnside with some older officers. Why, Schaff had asked, had Burnside been reluctant to take the command of the Army of the Potomac when McClellan was dismissed, just before Fredericksburg? After all, Schaff had said, Burnside was a West Pointer educated for this kind of business and this kind of emergency. Why the hesitation? Schaff and his friends had been drinking, but were far from drunk. He was quite rational, he remembered, when he had said that if *he* had been offered the command, he would certainly have taken it. The others flung back in their chairs and offered something between a howl and a roar of laughter. But Schaff had stuck to it: He would take command of the Army of the Potomac if asked. Now, in the smoldering Wilderness, he said to himself that if General Grant sent for him and said, "I'm thinking of assigning you to the independent command of one of the ambulances and want you to get it safely out of this," he would reply, "I'm not very experienced in handling ambulances, and if you can get anybody else I'll not object."

In the darkness a young reporter for the New York *Tribune*, Henry Wing, went to Grant and asked him how things were going. Shot down ten minutes after Burnside had launched his disastrous advance at Fredericksburg, Wing had been invalided out of the Army. But he was young and strong, although his wound made him walk with a limp, and he told Grant he intended to get through the rebel bands to the north and to a telegraph station where he could send his paper details of the fight in The Wilderness. "Yes, you may tell the people things are going swimmingly down here," Grant said blandly. The remark was so pointless that Wing smiled as he wrote it down, thanked the general, and turned to go. Grant walked along with him and said, "You expect to get through to Washington?" Wing assured him of his intent. "Well," Grant said, "if you see the President, tell him from me that whatever happens there will be no turning back." With his horse freshly fed and with his saddlebags filled with oats, Wing headed north. Washington was 70 miles away.

In the morning the two simultaneous attacks hit one another all along the line. Each commander had expected to attack, not be attacked. Each had underestimated the other. Now the carnage of the previous day was repeated and excelled. But the Yankee strength was beginning to tell. Hancock The Superb charged forward. Lee's center began to give. But he had yet another card to play. Pete Longstreet's corps was coming from its winter quarters. Messages went out urging Longstreet to hurry. The Confederate center sagged back. If Grant got through he would split the rebel army and make a path through which his forces could rush to open ground. There it could form and destroy the split segments at leisure.

The sun was up, and red above the tremendous clouds of smoke. Grant shoved his units forward. Lee had never felt such pressure, never sensed such determination. Months earlier, when Grant had been named to his high command, some rebel officers had derided him, but Pete Longstreet had known better the friend whose best man he had been. "That man will fight us every day and every hour," he had said. He had been right, and now the rebel line was crumbling. "My God, General Mc-Gowan," Lee cried to a South Carolina officer, "is this splendid brigade of yours running like a flock of geese?" He looked around desperately. There were no reserves. Up ahead a blue skirmish line came worming its way out of the woods. Couriers came to say Longstreet was a mile and a half away, his men double-timing toward the battle. The Yankee line formed up, thickened. Lee was in the front line of his forces now among artillery pieces almost unsupported by infantry, wreathed in smoke. Northern bullets spun past him. His artillery thundered. The Yankees came on.

Behind him there were shouts. He turned and saw Long-street's advance guard. "Who are you, my boys?" he yelled at the top of his lungs.

"Texas boys," they yelled back.

"Hurrah for Texas!" Lee shouted. He took off his hat and waved it in circles above his head. "Hurrah for Texas!"

They raced panting into formation, the First and Fourth Infantries of Texas, some 800 men. "Charge them!" he called, and they started forward with a slight gap showing between the two regiments. And into the gap, in line with the moving men, went Robert Lee on Traveller, red in the face and with the light of battle in his eyes—there was no other way to put it. The tiger had come out of the man. The line of foot soldiers and the one horseman moved forward toward the Union infantry, and one of the men looked over and hesitated, and then another, and suddenly the 800 men, half of whom were to fall that day, realized that their general intended to go at the Federals with them. "Go back, General Lee," someone yelled, and immediately the cry was taken up by a dozen others—Go back, General Lee.

But he was sending Traveller straight at the enemy. A swarthy sergeant leaped, and grabbed the reins. Lee was urging the horse forward and the sergeant was hanging on the reins, to be joined by others who spread their arms out to stop Traveller, a living barrier. "Lee to the rear," someone yelled; but Lee was trying to put the horse through the men to get at the Yankees who never before had fought him with such determination—to be at close quarters with them and ultimately their commander. "Go back, General Lee, this is no place for you; we'll settle this," the swarthy sergeant yelled. "Charge! Charge, boys!" Lee was shouting as he tried to get Traveller freed up; but someone yelled, "Go back, General Lee! Go back! We won't go on unless you go back!" They took up that cry, shouting up at him that nothing would be done until he went to safety. He came out of his trance then, slowly, and when his aide Colonel Charles Venable told him that Longstreet himself was just arriving and should be conferred with, he turned Traveller away, said, "Charge them, then," and watched as the Texans went up and drove the Yankees away.

Longstreet coolly fed his incoming men into the line. The firing was so great that a constant rain of branches cut by the bullets came down on the soldiers' heads. The Confederates pushed forward and by noon the Union left began coming apart. Lee shifted men to strengthen Longstreet's drive and Grant tried to counter. But to the terribly difficult task of getting troops through The Wilderness was added the additional deterrent of having to move them over wounded and slain comrades. It was difficult also for the massed Confederates to advance. In the past, the troops of both sides had been reluctant to throw up breastworks, but in The Wilderness they learned how to fight from cover. And so when Longstreet advanced he had to send his men against Union soldiers firing from behind logs and shoveled-up mounds of dirt. The rate of casualties exceeded anything ever experienced in any other battle of history, far overshadowing any losses of any fight of Caesar, Alexander, Frederick or Napoleon. Pete Longstreet, so reluctant to order Pickett forward at Gettysburg, was in The Wilderness lavish with his men's lives. The Union left was in disarray. "Steady, men, steady, steady, steady," officers kept repeating as the Confederates came on, but the Yankees wavered back, the rain of bullets so intense that it seemed to Private Frank Wilkeson of upstate New York that if he could hold up an iron pot on a pole like a butterfly net, the pot would be full in an instant. Behind the Union troops the provost guard with capped and cocked rifles halted anyone who could not show blood from a wound. If a would-be deserter got past the foot guards he found provost horsemen swinging sabers.

Longstreet's philosophy of battle had always been that it was best to take up a position and force the enemy to assault it, but now on the attack he was magnificent, urging his men on, ready to roll up the entire left wing of Grant's army. If he did that, he would be astride the fords to the north, and the Union cause would have suffered a blow that would leave it in a condition not unlike that which Great Britain had faced when it threw in its hand and allowed the colonies to go free. And the Union would let the Confederacy go. Longstreet went forward to reconnoiter, like Jackson at Chancellorsville one year and four days earlier, and like Jackson he went down, hit by a volley from his own men. Blood bubbled from Old Pete's mouth as he gasped that the attack must continue, that victory depended upon one more push. They took him to the rear, and without him his attack stalled.

As evening came on, General John B. Gordon of Georgia said to Lee that he wanted to try the Union right. He went in with a rush, and at Army of the Potomac headquarters a series of terrifying reports came one after the other. Two Union generals were prisoners, and the VI Corps under John Sedgwick was said to be in flight for the Rapidan River. Grant sat whittling under his tree. The brown gloves were in tatters. Word came that two New Jersey cavalry regiments guarding the river had been thrown into such a milling-around panic that they seemed likely to saber off the heads of their own horses. A high officer rushed to Grant and cried, "This is a crisis that cannot be looked upon too seriously. I know Lee's methods well by past experience; he will throw his whole army between us and the Rapidan, and cut us off completely from our communications!"

Grant took his cigar out of his mouth, and those who had

known him in the West saw him almost for the first time in their lives show a flash of temper: "Oh, I am heartily tired of hearing about what Lee is going to do," he said. "Some of you always seem to think he is suddenly going to turn a double somersault and land in our rear and on both of our flanks at the same time. Go back to your command, and try to think what we are going to do ourselves, instead of what Lee is going to do!" Word spread in the ranks—Frank Wilkeson wrote that he heard it fifty times that night—that the frightened general who had rushed to Grant had been Meade himself, that Meade had lost his nerve and urged that the army be withdrawn across the river out of fear of Lee.

Night was coming on. Reports of disaster to the right wing under Sedgwick kept coming in. "I don't believe it," Grant said; but then he got up and went into his tent and flung himself on his cot; and two officers of his staff, outside, heard the sound of muffled sobs. Sedgwick held. At eight o'clock Hancock came to headquarters and Grant asked if he'd like a cigar. Hancock said he would. Grant reached in his pack and found a single one. He had begun that day with more than twenty.

From the right came word that Sedgwick had blunted and then held Gordon's attack. The firing all along the line slowly died away. Flames lighted up the horizon, and wounded men lying untended loaded their weapons so as to have one shot left for themselves if the fire should reach them. The Wilderness burned, steam and gases and a ghastly odor arising from what burned with it. In front of Grant's tent the reporter Sylvanus Cadwallader, who had ministered to the drunken commander back at Vicksburg, sat by the campfire distressingly awake. "Unpleasant thoughts ran riot in my mind. We had waged two days of murderous battle, and had but little to show for it. We had been compelled by General Lee to fight on a field of his own choosing. We had scarcely gained a rod of the battlefield at the close of a two days' contest. And now had come the crowning stroke of rebel audacity in furiously storming our line." For the first time Cadwallader asked himself if he had followed Grant from Vicksburg to Chattanooga and Missionary Ridge to here only to "record his defeat and overthrow, as had been recorded of every commander of the Army of the Potomac."

Cadwallader looked to his right. There in an army chair by the slowly dying embers of the campfire sat the subject of his thoughts, high collar of blue overcoat turned up over one ear, one leg crossed over the other knee. Grant shifted his legs. He was not asleep. He saw that Cadwallader was looking at him, and commenced a pleasant chat on indifferent matters. There was no allusion to the battle in the half hour's conversation. Then Cadwallader said that if they were going to have any sleep they had better get at it and that in Grant's case it was a duty to get all the rest he could. Grant smilingly agreed. "Sharp work General Lee has been giving us," he remarked as he entered his tent.

Across the lines a mile away Lee was thinking of Grant and of the battle. If he had had the dead Jackson, Lee thought, he might have been able to crush Grant, or if Longstreet had not been wounded at the moment of his great drive on the Union right. General Gordon came and said he thought that after two days of such battle Grant, like every other previous Union commander, would retreat. "Grant is not a retreating man," Lee answered. From that day on he would himself always be afraid to attack, afraid of what a Grant counterattack might do. "Gentlemen," he said to his aides, "the Army of the Potomac has a head."

In Washington nothing at all was known of the battle—indeed it was not known if there had been a battle at all. "In deep suspense," General Ethan Allen Hitchcock wrote in his diary. "War Department silent all day. I cannot sleep. I cannot read. What news shall I hear in the morning? I saw the Secretary about eleven yesterday morning, and I noticed that, when reaching for a piece of paper, his fingers showed a nervous tremor which I never observed before. Has he received some sign of failure on the part of Grant?"

Stanton knew nothing. Nor did the President. No one knew anything until a filthy young man in old clothes and heavy brogans, with his pants tied around his ankles with cords, walked into the Union army telegraph station at Manassas Junction in the middle of the night, identified himself as Henry Wing of the New York *Tribune* and asked the use of the wire to telegraph a friend in the War Department: "I am just in from the front. Left Grant at four o'clock this morning."*

Back came a message from Secretary Stanton. "Where did you leave General Grant?"

Wing replied that he would say nothing until given permission to send 100 words to his paper. Stanton telegraphed that he would be arrested as a spy unless he spoke to government officials first. But young Wing stuck to his guns. He had not ducked rebel patrols, lied left and right, been shot at and chased only to lose his opportunity for a great scoop. He demanded his 100 words. Back came a telegram from the President saying he could send his story if he would then come immediately to the White House. Wing agreed, and a locomotive appeared to carry him to Washington. He found the President with several Cabinet members. For half an hour he stood in front of a wall map and showed the positions of the two contending armies across the Rapidan. The sky was almost light outside. He finished and then said, "Mr. President, I have a personal word for you." The others withdrew and he was alone with Lincoln.

"You wanted to speak to me?" Lincoln asked.

"Yes, Mr. President, I have a message for you—a message from General Grant. He told me I was to give it to you when you were alone."

"Something from Grant to me?" Lincoln advanced upon Wing. He had never realized before how tall the President was. He looked up into his face. Lincoln stooped down, brought his eyes level with Wing's and asked in an intense tone, "What is it?"

The reporter found himself deeply moved and found himself beginning to stammer. "General Grant told me to tell you, from

*Wing slept for several hours after his talk with Grant and before setting out on his journey.

him, that, whatever happens, there is to be no turning back."

What happened next formed the title of a little book Wing wrote: *When Lincoln Kissed Me.*

Two days. Eighteen thousand men lost from his force of 127,000. The Lieutenant General Commanding the Armies of the United States rested his soldiers. There was no firing along the ragged line. His opponent, the commander of the Army of Northern Virginia, removed all marauders from the roads leading back across the Rapidan. A Union retreat would thus be uncontested. All the past Union leaders would have welcomed such an invitation to depart, for each had retreated or rested for months after such a fight. In the ranks of the Yankee army all the talk was of going back across the river.

That talk reached General John B. Gordon of Georgia through spies, Union deserters and prisoners. There were rumors, he said to Robert Lee, that Grant would soon be heading north. Yes, Lee said, scouts had reported that. But the talk had made not the "slightest impression" on his mind. "General Grant is not going to retreat," he said. "He will move his army to Spotsylvania." That meant Grant would be going forward and to the left. Gordon wondered how Lee could be so sure it would be Spotsylvania and not some other place. Had Lee information of such a move? Was there special evidence of such a purpose? "Not at all, not at all," Lee told him. "But that is the next point at which the armies will meet."

In the Union camp Grant sat under a pine. "Tonight Lee will be retreating south," he said; and Colonel Theodore Lyman of Meade's staff thought to himself, Ah, General, Robert Lee is not Pemberton; he will retreat south, but only far enough to get across your path, and then he will retreat no more, if he can help it. Night came. Neither army appeared to be doing anything. But behind a screen of stationary men and impenetrable trees Grant put forces into motion. In the darkness Union soldiers marched through raised dust as fine as flour. They did not know where they were headed. The word in the ranks was that they would be going north. Once they heard from the Confederate lines the sound of cheering. The rebs had discovered that the Yankees were fleeing, the men muttered to each other.

They came to a crossroads in the track out of the eastern reaches of The Wilderness. If they turned left it would mean they were heading north. They turned right—south. And from their throats burst a tremendous shout of exultation. It was in the darkness and dust that they had what they later remembered as a rebirth of themselves as men and as an army. Through their ranks came Ulysses S. Grant, and they shouted for him and waved their hats in the air for him. The night march had become a triumphal procession, his aide Horace Porter thought. Behind the soldiers was The Wilderness of charred woods, of hasty-dug graves, abandoned knapsacks and the shattered rifles of men who would use them no more, turned-over wagons and lost bayonets, shoes, cartridge boxes—The Wilderness of death in which they had dueled the enemy. No other general in the world would still have been on the southern side of the Rapidan, Lincoln said to his secretary, John Hay. But Grant was, and his troops were, and heading south they sang for him and for themselves: John Brown's body is a-mouldering in his grave. We'll hang Jeff Davis to a sour apple tree. It was, William Sherman came to feel, the supreme moment in the life of Ulysses Grant. To have turned back would have destroyed the country.

They marched in the night for hours out into the open country past The Wilderness, unable a single one of them to say if they had won or lost the two-day fight whose field they were leaving, if they were marching on or escaping. They had been deflected from their straight path to Richmond, they knew that, and were sliding off to the left; but it was only a detour, they said, and they had stolen a march on the rebs, left them behind. They were half-asleep in the dark as they marched, and seemed to see the faces of dead comrades staring out at them from the roadside. A clump of trees came to resemble the enemy, a runaway horse a cavalry charge. The correspondent George Alfred Townsend thought to himself as he went along that, like Dante, he was now to pass through greater and greater horrors; such would be this campaign where the clouds would rain blood.

So they marched. And came to Spotsylvania and found Lee waiting for them.

He had studied Grant like a detective who seeks clues. There would be no Union retreat, he had been sure of that. The Army of the Potomac might have taken a direct easterly course before heading south, he reasoned, but that would be too blatant a detour. It would not appeal to a man of Grant's type. And so, Lee reasoned, the Federals would slide left and try to get behind him. That he could not allow. And so at a tiny crossroads village he would throw up entrenchments and breastworks and parry the thrust. His aides Walter Taylor and Charles Venable could not comprehend how their general dared move his men from their Wilderness positions, for Grant's movement had gone entirely undetected and the Army of the Potomac appeared present in force along the quiet line. It must be intuition, they decided, mind reading. John Gordon reasoned that "the brains of the two foemen had been working at the same problem: Grant stood in his own place and calculated from his own standpoint; Lee put himself in Grant's place and calculated from the same standpoint; and both found the same answer: Spotsylvania." When the head of the Union column arrived at its destination it found Jeb Stuart's cavalry waiting. Behind the horsemen the rebel infantry was coming in the smoky night. Lee rode among them speaking in a friendly way of the necessity that they go as fast as possible, and from the ranks a voice growled, "Well may you order us to move on, move on, when you are mounted on a horse." Lee ignored the remark and then they recognized who it was and there were cries of "Marse Robert! Yes, Marse Robert, we'll move on and go anywhere you say, even to hell!" Once an officer had asked Charles Venable how the general reacted to all this. "It awes him," Venable said.

He came to Spotsylvania. His guides had been two young

soldiers from the area. He found they had no food and told them that after getting provisions for their horses from the quartermaster they should go to his tent for something for themselves. There they were given all that the general's orderly had, two awful biscuits each and a cup of something awful that the orderly called coffee. The general couldn't do much for them, the two soldiers told each other, but he did all that he could. They understood.

The rebel cavalry that had blocked the Union infantry fell back, and the rebel infantry moved forward. As the horsemen withdrew, the word was passed up and down the line not to cheer for the footmen, as was customary. Perhaps thus they could surprise the Yankees. So in silence the horsemen vanished and the infantry men, who had been lying down, rose suddenly to their feet and blazed away. The Battle of Spotsylvania began. It was the eighth of May. Five days had passed since Grant crossed the Rapidan.

As the heads of the columns began to collide, Lee's men moving by the chord and in their own country got up more quickly than Grant's, who moved by the arc and had to guard against flank attacks and to clear trees cut down in their path by Lee's scouts. To the sound of rapidly rising fire Lee laid out the lines he would defend, a d breastworks of logs and dirt rose magically atop the hills and slopes. The armies slugged at one another for two days. "Pooh, men, they can't hit an elephant at that distance," the commander of the VI Corps said to some Federals ducking from distant rebel shooting, and then fell with a bullet in his brain. "Is he really dead? Is he really dead?" Grant asked when they told him. He had been with John Sedgwick less than five minutes earlier. Steady and dependable, Sedgwick had been the perfect complement to the impetuous and driving Winfield Scott Hancock, Hancock the Superb, and an aid in propping up the third corps commander, Gouverneur Warren. Lee the soldier could not mourn an enemy, but Lee the man could mourn a dear old friend. In the war he always referred to

him by the highest rank he had held when both wore blue, in
the old army. He would miss not ever seeing Major Sedgwick
again.

The armies battered at each other from behind their entrenchments. The level of noise was far greater than that generated in The Wilderness, for in the open spaces around
Spotsylvania artillery could be used. The losses of a campaign
without parallel in history rose, and when they got the figures
the European newspapers asked how it was possible to get men
to fight on in such circumstances and amid such carnage. From
the battlefields of The Wilderness and Spotsylvania went a steady
stream of wagons taking away the wounded—in the Southern
case to Richmond, where Chimborazo Hospital became the largest medical facility that had ever existed, and in the Northern
case to boats headed for Washington's Sixth Street Wharf. There
ambulances waited to carry them to hospitals around the capital,
including the one established at Arlington House, now the property of the United States government because of a tax delin-
quency in the amount of $140. (A relative had offered to pay,
but was told that the owner of the house must tender payment
in person.) There was, remembered the Washington correspondent Emily Edson Briggs, a strange quality to the noise those
ambulances made. "We shall never forget that peculiar sound,
unlike that produced by any other vehicle. Perhaps it was the
zig-zag course the drivers took to avoid any little obstruction in
the street." The ambulances seemed long in coming when first
heard. "The movements were always slower than a funeral march."
That was what many of the Northern newspapers opposed to
the war would call the move over the Rapidan, that spring, when
their columns recorded for page after page the 18,000 names of
The Wilderness' casualties, and the like number for Spotsylvania:
Grant's Funeral March.

It was different for the vehicles carrying the men who had
been alive when loaded on the transports coming up to the Sixth
Street Wharf but who arrived with faces covered. The wagons

marked U.S. HEARSE, Emily Edson Briggs remembered, could not be distinguished in their movements from grocery carts.

They fought at Spotsylvania, and in the Union camp George Meade had a raging argument with Phil Sheridan, saying that Sheridan's cavalry had blocked the march of the infantry in the race to get the better positions before the rebels took them. Sheridan replied that Meade knew nothing about cavalry anyway, that it should not be used for guard and picket duty, but for large-scale fighting. If it was up to him, he snarled, he would take every last one of his horsemen and go south and duel Jeb Stuart and cut the railroad and supply lines behind Lee. Meade went to Grant fuming about Sheridan's disinclination to do anything but go out to cut lines and destroy Jeb Stuart. "Did he say that?" Grant asked. "Well, he generally knows what he is talking about. Let him start right out and do it."

So little Phil left, 10,000 horsemen with him, a column of riders four abreast 13 miles long carrying guidon after guidon behind his headquarters flag of red with the two stars of a major general. He was thirty-three, short and squat and so ungracefully formed that his men referred to him as "the Jack of Clubs." He had dark hair cut short and looking almost like a coat of paint roughly painted onto his skull. He wore a squashed little porkpie hat two sizes small. He looked like a hard-bitten little sergeant and had no illusions of the glory of men at war on horses, but said a cavalryman was just a soldier with four detachable legs. Opposed to him, taking up his challenge and rushing to meet him, was handsome Jeb Stuart, all plumes and red-lined cloak, of the dashing chivalry of Virginia and with his banjo player accompanying him as sang, "Jine the cavalry, if you want a good time, jine the cavalry." A hardheaded and practical Irishman, representative of his chief, was going off to do battle with what the South would call the last cavalier, representative of his chief. To Grant, Sheridan was the greatest soldier the war produced, a captain never surpassed. To Lee, Stuart was almost like a son ever since West Point days, his aide at Harpers Ferry and his eyes in the war; and when, a week later at Yellow Tavern, 7 miles from Richmond, the duel ended, Lee cried. A thousand bullets had missed Jeb in the war, but one hit him. He was carried to Richmond to lie on a bed of pain and ask his friends to sing "Rock of Ages" with him before he passed on. He was thirty-one. "I can scarcely think of him without weeping," Lee said.

Riding his lines at Spotsylvania Grant saw a weak point. There was a jutting semicircle protruding from the Confederate positions. The Mule Shoe, the rebels called it, an upside-down U-shaped salient nearly a mile deep and half a mile wide. It could be hit from both sides and the front at the same time. It was at the center of the rebel line, and if it could be taken the rebel army would be pierced. And then, like a wedge forced through a log, the Army of the Potomac could split its enemy and conquer each segment.

Lee saw the danger and ordered construction of a second defense line to the rear, which would flatten out the bulge. But Grant feinted an attack to the Confederate right, and, tricked into thinking a push would come there, Lee removed the emplaced heavy guns from the salient, twenty-two of them, and sent them to repel the expected thrust. That night, the night of May 11th, it rained constantly as Winfield Scott Hancock moved his corps to within 1,200 yards of the Mule Shoe. The sound of his progress through the mud reached rebel ears, and Lee sent word to return the guns. It was too late. In a misty, dripping dawn Hancock hit the salient from three sides. His men got over the breastworks in a rush. Over their heads their artillery poured down fire to isolate the defenders from reinforcements. Boxed in and outnumbered, the men in the Mule Shoe died at their posts or surrendered.

At Grant's headquarters couriers rode up to say the first line of works had been captured, and the staff broke into cheers. The lieutenant general sat in a camp chair before a fire, ignoring the smoke that blew into his face as he did a wind that now and then tossed the cape of his greatcoat around his head. An officer galloped up to announce that 3,000 rebels had been taken prisoner, and Grant said, "That's the kind of news I like to hear." A little while later one of the prisoners rode up on a horse Hancock had lent him, dismounted and saluted. Meade stared, stepped forward and shook hands with a West Point fellow-cadet and old friend. "General Grant," Meade said, "this is General Johnson—Edward Johnson."

"How do you do?" Grant said. They had known each other in Mexico. "It is a long time since we last met."

"Yes," Johnson said, "it is a great many years, and I had not expected to meet you under such circumstances." He kept coughing, Colonel Theodore Lyman noticed, and it seemed to Lyman that he did it to conceal his emotion.

"It is one of the many sad fortunes of war," Grant said. He offered a cigar and pulled up a chair and put it near the fire. "Be seated."

"Thank you, General, thank you; you are very kind." Usually Grant read the courier dispatches aloud, but from then on, out of consideration for the prisoner who was also his guest, he passed them around to his officers. Across the line, Robert Lee poured men into the salient regardless of loss as the fighting built up to an intensity that dwarfed anything that had come before. Wild with anxiety for his army and his cause in deadly danger, Lee as at The Wilderness tried to join with the men going forward, and General John Gordon blocked Traveller with his own horse and cried out, "General Lee, you shall not lead my men in a charge! No man can do that, sir. Another is here for that purpose. These men behind you are Georgians, Virginians and Carolinians. They have never failed you on any field. They will not fail you here. Will you, boys?"

Men were yelling that they would not fail. "You must go to the rear!" Gordon shouted. Soldiers blocked Traveller, some clutching at the bridle, some pulling at the stirrups. Those standing at the horse's hips seemed ready to shove him around to face the rear, and it seemed to Gordon that if necessary they would have picked up and carried horse and rider on their shoulders.

Finally Lee turned Traveller and was gone, and Gordon went forward and pushed the Yankees back. But the Northerners did not go back beyond the outer line of works, only to its far side, and so they crouched there on one side while the Southerners stayed on the other, and through the crevices they jabbed at each other with bayonets. Men leaped up on top of the logs and fired downward at the enemy, were shot, fell back, and alive or dead served as steps that their comrades mounted to get at the opponent. "Lee and Grant began to hurl their columns against that portion of the works held by both," Gordon remembered. "Thus was inaugurated that roll of musketry which is likely to remain without a parallel."

Soon the disputed breastworks were formed more of bodies than of logs, men lying seven deep while their comrades fought on. Hell's Half Acre, they called it. The Bloody Angle. For twenty hours, in the rain, in the mud, in daylight and darkness and daylight again, they fought there, men clambering up the ghastly embankment and clubbing or shooting or stabbing each other and then falling to be clambered upon. Bullets were fired in sheets, like a pelting hail. The standing timber fell, including a hickory tree with a 2-foot diameter cut down by bullets to crash on the men of the 1st South Carolina.

The previous day Grant's original sponsor, Congressman Washburne, who had accompanied his constituent on the move south, had said he felt he ought to get back to Washington. (The soldiers who saw his black suit had told each other he was the general's private undertaker, or a parson brought along to read the funeral service over the Confederacy.) "Hadn't you better send Stanton just a scratch of the pen?" Washburne had asked.

"Perhaps so," Grant had said, and wrote out a brief note ending with, "I intend to fight it out on this line if it takes all summer." He owned a strange ability to say things that caught at people, Grant. *Unconditional surrender. I propose to move immediately upon your works.* And now he proposed to fight it out on that line if it took all summer. The words sounded as written with compressed lips, and people read them with clenched teeth.

Repeated and repeated, the phrase helped the 20 million of the North bear the losses that reached into every home and that for three straight days and nights saw the wagons leave the Sixth Street Wharf in a steady stream for the hospitals, deposit their loads and then return empty down another street to pick up new loads. The loss of blood by the wounded, it was said, produced a terrible thirst, and people stood for hours handing out water. It touched those who saw that the ones who did it most faithfully were the black men and women of Washington. When the rains falling on the battling soldiers of the Bloody Angle fell also in Washington, a strange and eerie sight was seen: From the wagons protruded thousands of bandaged arms and legs, held out for the moisture by men who knew the water would loosen wrappings whose removal when dry and encrusted with blood would be agonizing. White limbs and arms held out under the gray sky— it was not a sight one soon forgot.

At the Bloody Angle the rebels worked on the breastworks across the base of the salient and then fell back upon them, giving up the area that had seen such horror. Hancock followed them and threw himself upon the new defense position. Lee came to the rebels there and rode slowly past them. He held his hat in his hand. He did not say a word, but they understood his appeal. "It was," remembered a man who was there, "the most eloquent address ever delivered." They held.

There followed days of Federal tapping at the Confederate front and investigations of the flanks as Grant tried to find a weak point. Lee also probed, saying he must strike Grant a blow. He did not seem to understand how much the modern rifle, which twirled a bullet through the barrel and gave it tremendous range and hitting power, had changed war. In the past the effective range of a musket was 50 yards, and so only one shot could be gotten off before the attacker was upon the defender. But the rifle bullet had ended the days of the cavalry charge and the sword duel. The best defense was no longer a good offense.*

---

*A truth not understood until the lessons of 1914–18 were absorbed. Then what had been true became untrue, as 1940 proved.

A line of entrenched men could hold off the world. But Lee, thinking of the elegant and stylized minuets of the eighteenth century, sought to launch a broad and sweeping offensive that would roll up the Yankees and send them flying. *His name might be Audacity* had been said of him back at the moment of his assumption of the command of the Army of Northern Virginia. Trying to join his soldiers in close-quarter combat at both The Wilderness and Spotsylvania, that was audacity. And wrong. But he was a warrior.

Something else had escaped him. (He was not alone in failing to understand what was happening. In Europe, the Continent's greatest military authority, Helmuth von Moltke, perhaps the most brilliant German-speaking officer who ever lived, dismissed the American Civil War as a matter of two armed mobs chasing each other around the countryside.) European history from Cannae to Waterloo indicated that single battles decided campaigns and the fate of nations. But the railroad and steamship, the telegraph and the industrial power of modern nations, the new ability to mass enormous armies and equip them—the Industrial Revolution—made the single battle no longer so telling. The former chiefs of the Army of the Potomac had not known that, and had tended to fight a duel-like sword-point to sword-point engagement and then suspend operations for months. But Grant knew it. He sensed it. He knew, as Lee did not, that they were in a war between societies, not armies. Such a war could end only when a society was conquered, and only conquest could do that, conquest at the end of pressure so intense that it was unendurable. He did not fight battles, but a war. And so he abandoned Spotsylvania as he had The Wilderness and again, as he had before, slipped off to his left, the Grand Flanker executing his Jug-Handled movement, so the men said, and again heading east and south.

He detached Hancock's corps, sending it off alone and hoping to lure Lee into attacking the isolated corps and thus getting involved in an open-field battle where there would be no entrenchments and where the Union strength could tell. But Lee resisted the bait and moved in the same direction as Hancock, on an interior, parallel line. So Grant moved his other two corps after Hancock.

The nature of a countryside, its geography, sometimes pulls armies to where they must logically go, and, Lee said to his staff, the armies would next meet along the little North Anna River. It was not a matter of mental telepathy, John Gordon decided, but again that ability Lee had "to spot almost at the very instant the movement was taking shape in Grant's brain" what his opposite number was planning, "to reason out his antagonist's mental processes, to trace with accuracy the lines of his marches and to mark on the map the points of future conflicts."

So they came to the North Anna. Meanwhile, the Union political general Sigel in the Shenandoah Valley had well demonstrated the meaning of his nickname, the Flying Dutchman, and the Union political general Butler had completely mishandled his forces along the James River below Richmond. He was, Grant remarked, as securely bottled up as the wine is by the cork, and as unable to flow in any direction. N. P. Banks was achieving nothing in the West, and Sherman's drive on Atlanta was bogged down in the face of the particularly skillful action conducted by a Joe Johnston at least strong enough to fend off if he could not attack. So the entire course of the war devolved upon the two forces separated by the North Anna.

The Federal batteries on the north bank opened fire and a round arched over the water and crashed into the doorframe of a house where Robert Lee stood on the porch drinking buttermilk. He held the glass steady and finished his drink. "I wish they were all dead," General Jubal Early had said of the Yankees the day they left Spotsylvania. "How can you say so, General?" Lee had answered. "Now, I wish they were all at home, attending to their own business, leaving us to do the same." In such calm manner did he receive the near miss, but then fearing that the enemy knew he was in the house and would therefore make it a prime target and destroy it, he mounted Traveller and hurried his people away. (Jubal Early also said, "I would not say so before General Lee, but I wish they were not only all dead, but in hell." Lee laughed when he was told of Early's amendment to his wish. Early was the only man who regularly swore in front of his commander. "My bad old man," Lee called him.) But he had been wrong in thinking the Federals knew he was personally present on the North Anna. To a man, the Union generals had been of the opinion that the main body of the Army of Northern Virginia had fallen back much farther to the south, perhaps to the gates of Richmond. They thought they were up against a thin rear guard, but when Hancock attacked on a limited front he realized something far greater was in front of him. So the Army of the Potomac spread out along the river's northern side and the Army of Northern Virginia did the same on the southern side.

Still desperate to attack, the Yankees coming on, Lee ordered A. P. Hill to push them with the Confederate left wing. Hill's response was uninspired, and Lee flared up. "Why did you not do as Jackson would have done, thrown your whole force upon those people and driven them back?" It was an unkind question to ask of a fine soldier who in fact had been in Jackson's mind at the moment of his death—"Order A. P. Hill to prepare for action," he had said. But Lee was not well. He was suffering from ptomaine poisoning, and as the day went on his condition worsened. Struggling with the pain and associated discomfort of a violent stomach upset, he had to face the fact that Grant's two wings of army were now on his side of the river and coming on. So in a flash of tactical inspiration he made his danger a trap for the enemy. Holding a single crossing of the river, he made it the apex of a triangle, and bent his flanks back in a sharp upside-down V upon both of whose faces he emplaced his artillery. Unable to ride Traveller and forced to travel in an ambulance, he had so arranged things that either of his two wings could reinforce the other while standing on the defensive, while Grant's army was badly split, with neither wing nor the center able to bring up reinforcements without making river crossings and passing for long distances under rebel artillery fire. Presenting an open umbrella, Lee had suddenly closed it, leaving Grant to strike the air or face an extended division of his army into three components.

They stared at each other. No real fire was exchanged. Lee had thrown down the gage of battle, and Grant declined it. Checkmate. For the moment. But it was not good enough for Lee. Tossing on his bed or weakly making his way to a latrine, his fever rising, finally confined entirely to his bed, he murmured over and over, "We must strike them a blow. We must not let them pass us again. We must strike them a blow." He could whip Grant if given one more chance, he told his doctor. Grant sat. For two days Lee writhed on his bed saying he must attack. But to do so would have been impossible, for Longstreet was down from his Wilderness wound, and Richard Ewell, another corps commander, was turning sickly in body and perhaps in mind, and Jackson was dead and Stuart also. If he didn't strike the chance for an offense would be gone forever, he moaned, and finally Charles Venable came out of the improvised sickroom and said to the other aides that he had just told the general to his face that they had better send to Richmond for Beauregard. Once before, ill after Gettysburg, Lee had said he was not fit to command his army. In worse shape now, he tossed on his bed. Across the lines Grant sat still.

"We must not let them pass us again," Lee said, and to Mrs. Lee he wrote, "I begrudge every step he takes toward Richmond." Grant again slid off to his left, his marching columns stretched out for miles. "Wherever Lee goes you will go also," he had said to George Meade, but now Lee was going to Meade, moving inside Grant's leftward sweep across the lonely countryside and the series of little rivers that led to the little town of Cold Harbor, where immediately he built breastworks to greet the Federals.

At Spotsylvania, once, Grant had seen from his horse a grievously wounded soldier. He had been shot through the chest. He halted his mount, and when his aide Horace Porter saw that the lieutenant general was about to get down to minister to the boy, Porter did it himself while Grant watched intently. The soldier's eyes were wandering sightlessly and then freezing into a stare, and there was redness in the froth about his mouth, and soon they heard the death rattle. "The poor fellow is dead," Porter told his chief. A staff officer went by, the hooves of his horse throwing mud into the dead man's face. Porter wiped it off. He remembered the sad look on Grant's face. "Well, General, we can't do these little tricks without losses," Meade had said to him, but even as at Shiloh where he could not bear to be in a hospital and see the blood, it was hard for Ulysses Grant, very hard, to deal with what war brought. Greater acquaintance with wounds and death did not make him better able to bear them, but he was thinking of the malarial horrors a prolonged siege in the lowland swamps before Richmond would bring to his un-acclimated north country troops. An attack of annihilation was on his mind. The hard way would be the easy way. He made for Cold Harbor.

Along the way he took time to sit on the porch of a house in the countryside turned into lost desolation by the rampaging troops—by the war—and an old woman with a nose so sharp that it looked like it had been caught in the crack of a door (Porter thought) and a voice squeaking like the high notes of an E-flat clarinet came strolling up. "I'm poerful [sic] glad General Lee has been lickin' you-all from the Rapidan cl'ah down h'yah and that now he's got you jes wh'ah he wants you," she cheerfully told Grant. She drew up a camp chair alongside, seated herself and went on, "Yes, and afo' long he'll be a-chasin' you-all up through Pennsylvany ag'in. Was you up thah in Pennsylvany when he was aftah you-all last summer?"

"Well, no, I wasn't there myself," said the conquerer of Vicksburg as he tried to keep his face straight. "I had some business in another direction." She told him some of the rebels had brought her back fine draft horses from Gettysburg. She hoped the rebels would head north soon again. A few more horses were always welcome. They parted very pleasantly. But she was back soon to say a horse of hers had been stolen by Yankee soldiers. Perhaps. Grant suggested, it was one of those fine Pennsylvania draft horses. The boys must have made up their minds to take him home. She demanded the horse. He pointed out that the troops were on the move and that what she wanted was impossible to give her. Had the army been in camp he would have tried. She shook her fist and went off muttering, "I'm sart'in of one thing, anyhow; General Lee'll just dust you-all out of this place afo' you can say scat."

He went on toward Cold Harbor, and on the first day of June saw an army teamster whose wagon was stalled in mud cruelly hitting his horses in the face with the butt end of a whip. "What does this conduct mean, you scoundrel?" Grant demanded. "Stop beating those horses!"

"Well," said the teamster, coolly giving a slap to the face of the wheel horse, "who's driving this team anyhow—you or me?"

"I'll show you, you infernal villain!" Grant cried. He called an officer of the escort and said, "Take this man in charge, and have him tied up to a tree for six hours as a punishment for his brutality." Twice that day he referred to the incident in vehement language. Horace Porter had never before seen him so angry and asked Theodore Bowers, another staff officer who had been with Grant longer, if there was any precedent for the general's rage. Bowers replied there was only one, to his knowledge. In the West, Grant had leaped from his horse, seized a rifle and hit over the head with it a soldier who had raped a woman. That night at dinner Grant was still discussing the cruel teamster and saying how kindness to horses paid. In the future, he said, "when I get too feeble to move about," he would train horses from an armchair in the center of a ring while holding a lead line as the horses went through their paces. All the men must come and see him do it. He wolfed down oysters as he spoke, a supply having been brought in from the tidal waters. Usually he ate hardly more than enough to keep a bird alive, his staff had seen, but oysters were a weakness. Prior to the feast, ever since the campaign had begun, he had pretty much been living on hard bread and roast beef—well done, of course.

At Cold Harbor the next day he looked at Lee's earthworks and trenches. To assault them would mean a lot more boys brought to the pass of the one whose death rattle Horace Porter had heard and from whose face he had wiped mud. On the way down from the North Anna, Private Frank Wilkeson, crossing the Pamunkey River, had looked at the lieutenant general. "The Army of the Potomac has always longed for a fighting general," one of the old veterans had told Wilkeson, "one who would fight, and fight, and fight, and now it has got him." Passing that fighting general, Wilkeson saw a tired look in the sallow face. There was a dead cigar in Grant's teeth. "His face was as expressionless as a pine board. He gazed steadily at the enlisted men as they marched by, as though trying to read their thoughts, and they gazed intently at him. He had the power to send us to our deaths, and we were curious to see him. But the men did not evince the slightest enthusiasm. None cheered him, none saluted him. Grant stood silently looking at his troops and listening to Hancock, who was talking and gesticulating earnestly."

By then he had stripped Washington of its defenders, including the heavy artillerymen manning the scores of forts ringing the capital against an invasion by Robert Lee. They were needed to replace the 50,000 casualties whose fingers, feet, arms, legs or hands were in horrible piles outside the hospitals, or those who lay with flesh frightfully and unnaturally swollen, either emitting ghastly convulsed cries, or, unconscious, already entering into the valley. Sometimes it seemed as if Grant would put his entire army into the line of wagons leaving the Sixth Street Wharf. He had "provided either a cripple or a corpse for half the homes of the North," said the New York *Daily News*. Grant seemed, people said, almost a Moloch, a God who could be propitiated only by human sacrifice. The less than one month he had spent with the Army of the Potomac in the field was bidding to fill Washington's sole military cemetery, the one at the Soldiers' Home, and when on the afternoon of May 13, after the Bloody Angle, President Lincoln visited the wounded at that Arlington House now turned into a hospital, he found by the side garden gate dead men in their coffins. Word had just come, that day, from the Soldiers' Home that there was not space enough left for a single additional grave. Standing by what had been Robert E. Lee's home for all of his married life, since he was a lieutenant—thirty-three years—Lincoln said the dead soldiers should be buried at once, near the place where they had breathed their last. From that day on, the men of Grant's army who died fighting Lee came up the Potomac and went to their final rest where Lee had lived.

And the breastworks of Cold Harbor, which would produce many such, awaited. If he could break Lee there, Grant reasoned, the war would be over. If he let the chance go, Lee would retire into the enormously strong fortifications that ringed Richmond's seven hills. That would mean a siege in summertime swamps. He ordered an assault for the morning of June 2, but the troops were slow in getting into position, and he postponed it until the following day. In the evening, Horace Porter saw a strange sight. Men by the dozens and hundreds appeared to be sewing up rips in the backs of their jackets. "This exhibition of tailoring seemed rather peculiar at such a moment." He looked more carefully. The men were pinning their names and addresses on, so that when their bodies were found their people could be told.

At 4:30 A.M the lieutenant general sent masses of stiff and compact Union columns at the rebel works. There was no attempt at deception and no prior feinting nor any attempt to flank the enemy, but instead an all-out straight-ahead attempt to rip Lee's lines. The rebels stood in rows behind their works passing loaded rifles up to the men in front, who simply could not miss hitting blue uniforms. It was Fredericksburg all over again. For twenty minutes the Federals kept trying. Richmond came awake to the loudest sounds of battle it had ever heard. The Confederate postmaster general, John H. Reagan, stood by Lee, gazed at Grant's massive columns, and said, "General, if he breaks your line, what reserve have you?"

"Not a regiment," Lee answered, "If I shorten my lines to provide a reserve, he will turn me. If I weaken my lines to provide

a reserve, he will break them." What the Union troops later
called the butchering in the slaughter pen went on. The boys
who sewed identifications on their uniforms had known. Ten
thousand casualties, 500 men a minute, 10 a second. The rebel
losses were one-tenth that number. Then the attackers went to
ground. In the afternoon Grant intimated to Hancock that if he
thought it wise he could try again. The second attack was never
launched, and word spread all through the North that it had
been ordered and that the order had been refused by the troops,
who had suffered 55,000 casualties in the one month that had
elapsed since they crossed the Rapidan River,* a count not far
from the number that Lee had been able to put in the field against
them. From that day on, Army of the Potomac headquarters
ceased to ask morning reports from its company rank officers.
The people of the North would not stand it if the figures were
to become known among them.

The assault on Cold Harbor was almost the only thing he
regretted doing in the war, Grant came to feel. It had accomplished nothing. Perhaps he attacked entrenched Confederates
with his smashing Missionary Ridge and Lookout Mountain victory in mind. There his men had swept the rebels out of their
trenches and from behind their breastworks and sent them flying.
This was different. ("I think Grant has had his eyes opened, and
is willing to admit now that Virginia and Lee's army is not
Tennessee and Bragg's army," Meade wrote.) The ground in
front of the rebel line was filled with mutilated men, and when
the brief fighting ended Grant sent a note to Lee under a white
flag: "I would propose that either party be authorized to send to
any point between the pickets or skirmish lines unarmed men
bearing litters to pick up their dead or wounded, without being
fired upon by the other party. Any other method equally fair to
both parties you may propose for meeting the end desired will
be accepted by me." Lee replied that such an arrangement might

*Comparable losses to the Northern states of the present would mean that the one
month of fighting produced losses of around 600,000.

lead to "misunderstanding and difficulty," and that when a commander desired to recover the victims of a battle it was usual for him to ask for a suspension of hostilities, a truce. "It will always give me pleasure to comply with such a request." The words implied a demand that Grant ask for an armistice—the act of a soldier who has lost a battle. Lee was thinking of what the reaction in the North would be if Moloch admitted he had lost. Terrible cries of "Water, for God's sake, water," could clearly be heard from men lying under a blazing sun and literally dying of thirst, but Grant could not bring himself to ask for a truce. He repeated that both armies should contract to allow rescue parties to go into the field of battle for a period of three hours. Lee answered that he could not consent to such an arrangement without a formal truce. The wounded soldiers, untended, died— all save two. "Regretting that all my efforts for alleviating the sufferings of wounded men left on the battlefield have been rendered nugatory, I remain, &c.," Grant concluded the correspondence.

For a week the armies lay in their positions, pulling reinforcements to themselves from whatever source. They had gone 70 miles together from the Rapidan and Grant was repeating the exact same positions, was in the same place, that McClellan had held two years earlier when Joe Johnston went down and Robert Lee took his post. "Grant is beating his head against a wall," Lee's aide Walter Taylor wrote his fiancée. "Old U.S. Grant is pretty tired of it—at least it appears so." But Taylor's chief was in a corner. The fencer had lost the room in which to maneuver. He was backed up upon Richmond and facing position war, a static defense. And if the Federals took another step south? "We must destroy this army of Grant's before he gets to the James River," Lee said to Jubal Early. "If he gets there, it will become a siege, and then it will be a mere question of time." The very last thing he wanted was to wait upon any move of Grant's, yet he had been afraid ever since The Wilderness to launch an attack. His precise and agonizing dilemma appeared insoluble. He stayed at his field headquarters foregoing the short run to Richmond where Mrs. Lee and the girls were—all three sons were in the army, Custis a military aide to Jefferson Davis, Rooney a cavalry officer and Rob an artilleryman—and tried to figure a method of getting at Grant.

Across the lines the morale of the Army of the Potomac was down, the offensive spirit drained. "My troops do not charge as they did a month ago," an officer wrote home. The best men of the North, many of them, were gone to their graves or invalided home, squandered by the Popes and the Burnsides or lost in the drive down from the Rapidan. The price of a United States dollar in gold dropped steadily. Summer with its fevers was coming. If Grant was in the slightest discouraged, or afraid, he did not show it. On the night of June 12, nine days after the catastrophe of Cold Harbor, he began withdrawing troops from his positions opposite the rebel entrenchments. In the morning, not a soldier was in the Union lines. He was hurrying on a lengthy trip south to attack Petersburg, 25 miles below Richmond, and thus cut the supply lines from the rest of the Confederacy to its capital and Lee's army in front of it. Old Brains Halleck advised against the move, fearing that with Grant's army off to the south Lee might drive north. Always able to see problems but never solutions, ready with maxims and opinions but never orders, unable to take responsibility, the pedant sublime, Halleck had the idea that it was unsafe for Grant's army to be anywhere away from that of Lee. "We can defend Washington best," Grant said, "by keeping Lee so occupied that he cannot detach enough troops to capture it"; and he threw pontoon bridges across the James River. Three schooners laden with stones were sunk above the crossing points to prevent the rebel gunboats at Richmond from coming down to make trouble. The Yankees went across the bridges, which swayed in the water from their marching feet, saying to one another when they got over that the end of the war was really at hand now, that they would take Petersburg first and then rush up to Richmond. Twenty-four hours should decide the matter.

To Lee, the empty Union trenches at Cold Harbor seemed

indicative of another of Grant's short slides to the left. He had got in the habit of thinking of Grant only as a fighting general, not as a moving one, and had forgotten the speed with which his opponent had moved once he was over the Mississippi at Vicksburg. Even as Grant's men massed before Petersburg in such number that they held an eight-to-one advantage over the defenders, Lee did not realize what had happened. Sheridan's cavalry by Grant's order was off raiding to the west, and Lee in response had been forced to send Wade Hampton, Jeb Stuart's replacement, chasing after. So he had no horsemen's picture of what the Federal dispositions were. "Until I can get more definite information of Grant's movements, I do not think it prudent to draw more troops," he said.

Poised with his fellows before Petersburg, Frank Wilkeson heard men saying, "The city is ours! We have outmarched them!" He heard, "Put us into it, we'll end this damned rebellion to-night!" The moon was shining, opposite were earthworks entirely empty of enemy troops. Only a few pickets opposed a force that was hourly increasing as the pontoon bridges swayed. A push anything like that undertaken at Cold Harbor would in minutes completely rip the rebel lines. But the memory of Cold Harbor and its fruitless slaughter was all too dominant in the mind of the commander of the 15,000 Yankee troops gathered before Petersburg. General William F. Smith—always "Baldy" Smith to those who knew him—hesitated, probed, conducted an hours-long personal reconnaissance. Grant was back on the line of march and Hancock was coming, but Smith was the man on the scene. He ordered up artillery, but the horses to pull it were being watered. Time passed. One of his subordinates said to him that they could *walk* into Petersburg, and from there to Richmond; and finally Smith pushed at the Confederate line. It broke at once. The city with its many railroad lines to Richmond lay before him. "Petersburg at that hour was clearly at the mercy of the Federal commander," wrote the city's defender, Pierre Beauregard, who was down to mustering up boys and old men, handing them weapons and sticking them into the trenches be-

hind the captured main line. Smith, having captured those forward trenches, settled down.

Hancock's forward elements arrived, but Smith simply used
them to relieve the men who had taken the foremost trenches,
those men including one of the new divisions composed of blacks.
When the arriving veterans saw that inexperienced, largely ex-
slave, soldiers had been able to take rebel trenches with no trouble, they immediately knew that Lee's soldiery were not opposite. They begged to attack before the Army of Northern Virginia
men got into place. But Smith held back. The end of the war,
triumph and home, were in their hands, the men realized, and
they weren't being given the chance to do what they wanted to
do. "Baldy" Smith was another Joe Hooker, a splendid commander on a limited scale but a helpless one when the scale
enlarged. Stiff, an Army-regulations West Pointer, he had served
with Grant in the West. "What are you thinking about, Baldy?"
General Montgomery Meigs had asked him once at Nashville.
Pacing up and down, Smith had not replied. "Baldy is studying
strategy," Meigs had said to Grant with a laugh, and Grant had
remarked, "I don't believe in strategy in the popular understanding of the term. I use it to get just as close to the enemy as
practicable with as little loss as possible."

"And what then?" Meigs inquired.

"Then? 'Up, Guards, and at 'em!' "*

That was exactly what was called for at Petersburg, but
through the night the Federal troops sat in front of the empty
Confederate lines. "The rage of the enlisted men was devilish,"
one of them wrote. "The most blood-curdling blasphemy I ever
listened to I heard that night." In the morning the rebel trenches
were no longer empty. Finally realizing the situation, Lee had
rushed men down. The great chance was lost, and when the
Union troops attacked they did not show the vigor and force
they had displayed in The Wilderness and at Spotsylvania and
Cold Harbor. "Now we will rest the men and use the spade for

---

*The words attributed to Wellington in ordering the final charge that broke the
French at Waterloo.

their protection until a new vein can be struck," Grant said, and his army stretched itself out in a line 35 miles long to cover both Richmond and Petersburg. Trenches were dug, redoubts, strongpoints, and artillery pieces were emplaced in fortified places atop every hill. Opposite, the rebels followed suit. Two long and twisting lines of men faced each other under the Virginia sun. A siege, and then it will be a mere question of time, Lee had said. In the first days of July he thinned out his lines and gave Jubal Early 20,000 men with whom to slip behind the sheltering mountains of the Shenandoah Valley and go north. If there was anything that would draw the Federals from the gates of Richmond, it would be the appearance of a rebel army at the gates of Washington.

On July 11, Early arrived at the outskirts of the Union capital. He took Silver Spring and the country home of the Blairs—who speaking at Lincoln's behest, had long ago, it seemed, offered the command of the United States Army to Colonel Robert E. Lee of the First Cavalry—looted the family's houses and burned them. The Seventh Street Road to the heart of Washington was open. Old Brains Halleck was the ranking officer in the capital, but as usual he was unable to decide what to do. Given an army, said Senator Benjamin Wade of Ohio, Halleck would be still unable to "scare three sitting geese from their nests." Panicky telegrams went out to Grant in front of Petersburg to return at once. Early appeared to be the parallel of Britain's Admiral Cockburn of the War of 1812, who had burned all of Washington that he could, and driven President James Madison away.

For a moment Grant considered going north. It was startling, to say the least, that at that point in the war Lee was able to deploy his forces so that the capture or destruction of the Union capital seemed at hand. But Rawlins violently opposed any move. "I told the general that his place was here," he wrote home from before Petersburg, "that he had started out to defeat Lee, that his appearance in Washington would be heralded all over the country as an abandonment of his campaign, a faltering at least in his purpose." Grant saw that Rawlins was right. Going to Washington, that would be "just what Lee wants me to do." He ordered General Horatio Wright, the slain John Sedgwick's replacement, to take the VI Corps upriver to the capital.

A hastily mustered force of government clerks from their offices and wounded soldiers from the hospitals were sent out to hold off Early while the VI Corps came on. Abraham Lincoln went out to hear bullets sing by for the first time in his life and to hear, also, young Oliver Wendell Holmes, son of the celebrated writer, shout, "Get down, you God-damned fool!" Another officer was more politic: "Mr. President, you are standing within range of five hundred rebel rifles. Please come down to a safer place. If you do not, it will be my duty to call a file of men and make you."

"And you would be quite right, my boy," Lincoln said. Up the road from the Potomac River landings came the VI Corps to drive Early away. Had he pushed forward with a little more resolve, sabered down everyone found in the streets of Washington, burned the Capitol, freed all Confederate prisoners held in the city, looted the Treasury—who can say what might have resulted? But he was slow and hesitant. The late Mr. Early. Yet he went away unpursued and unmolested while Washington's chairborne soldiers bickered over their lines of authority. Without Grant, the President said, nothing got done right.

In coming and going Early exacted levies from towns he burned or threatened to burn. The staunchest of Unionists before the war, he had in the years of fighting turned ruthless. To permit him the Shenandoah Valley was dangerous, and so Grant sent Sheridan to rout and destroy him, which little Phil did, in the process leveling every barn that could supply Lee's army. In the long lines winding down from above Richmond to below Petersburg, nothing of moment took place. A siege is, technically, a situation in which a point is completely cut off from the outside world; and that was not the case, for roads and railroad tracks ran into both Richmond and Petersburg, but that is what they called it: the Siege. The value of the U.S. dollar dropped to its lowest point of the war: $2.88 in paper was needed to purchase $1.00 in gold.

On the red clay plains they built forts that connected with one another by zigzag trenches in front of which were sandbags intersected with loopholes through which sharpshooters fired. Mines were laid, and pointed wooden stakes that would stop horses. They diverted streams to form ponds that would slow down infantry. Sometimes as close to each other as 100 yards, they brought mortars to fire shells that soared upward and then downward in graceful arcs. At City Point,* where the Appomattox River met the James, near where Pocahontas saved John Smith, Grant pitched his camp, and around his tent there sprang up a city—hospitals, warehouses, sutlers' huts, telegraph offices, drinking places, a depot for the steamboat-landing railroad going 7 miles up to the trenches—all the things needed for the use of the army that had crossed the Rapidan and fought down through The Wilderness and Spotsylvania, across the North Anna and to Cold Harbor, and now lay draped in a great quarter circle before Petersburg and Richmond. Yet it all seemed so terribly futile. The Army of the Potomac was back in the exact positions it had held in the days of McClellan's peninsula campaign of two years before, with summer coming on, a lowland summer of malaria and poor water and swamp fever. "This army is nearly demoralized," Provost Marshal General Marsena Patrick wrote in his diary, and to Lincoln's friend Noah Brooks it seemed that the darkest days of the war had arrived, the more difficult to endure because they had come so unexpectedly to shatter the high hopes with which the North had greeted the opening of the spring campaign: "A deadly calm prevailed where so lately resounded the shouts."

The value of the dollar in gold stayed down as it became apparent that Richmond was not to fall, and the damage to the Union's financial stability was such that the brokers in New

*Now Hopewell, Virginia.

York's Gold Room became known as the left wing of Lee's army. In Washington, Secretary Stanton wondered if everything was being carried on correctly, and the President said, "Now Mr. Secretary, you know we have been trying to manage this army for nearly three years and you know we haven't done much with it. We sent over the mountains and brought Mr. Grant, as Mrs. Grant calls him, to manage it for us, and now I guess we'd better let Mr. Grant have his way." "He is a butcher and is not fit to be at the head of an army," Mary Lincoln told her husband, and when he pointed out that Grant could not be called wholly unsuccessful she said, "Yes, he generally manages to claim a victory, but such a victory! He loses two men to the enemy's one. He has no management, no regard for life." She went on to aver that he would depopulate the North. "I could fight an army as well myself. Grant, I repeat, is an obstinate fool and a butcher." "Well, Mother, supposing that we give you command of the army. No doubt you would do better than any general that has been tried."

In the lines, the musketry sounded like popcorn going off and men died; artillery salvos sought the enemy in his bomb-proofs. It was hot and deadly dusty. Boredom was the great foe. In late June, Lieutenant Colonel Henry Pleasants of the 48th Pennsylvania heard one of his men mutter of the rebel position opposite, "We could blow that damned fort out of existence if we could run a mine shaft under it." The regiment was composed mainly of coal miners, and Pleasants himself was a mining engineer. He went back to his tent and said to one of his company commanders, "That God-damned fort is the only thing between us and Petersburg, and I have an idea we can blow it up." The idea went through division and corps and up to Meade and Grant, who approved. For weeks the miners dug to produce a tunnel more than 500 feet long, with a cross gallery at the end just under the Confederate position. Eight thousand pounds of gunpowder was put into place, enough to blow up a mountain. For several days troops north of the James were secretly sent south at night, over the swaying pontoon bridges, the wooden planks covered with hay so that the men would make no noise. During the day, bands blaring, they marched from south to north, the idea being to fool Lee into thinking massive troops transfers were being made away from Petersburg. Artillery off to the north boomed out in a feint to make him believe an attack was imminent there.

In the early morning hours of July 30, the fuse to the tunnel was lit. The resulting explosion, as terrifying as a volcano, greater than anything ever heard or seen before, instantly created a gigantic crater 200 feet long and 30 feet deep. Hundred of rebels perished, and field pieces were flung city blocks away. Lee's line was pierced, and the way to Petersburg was open. But the Yankee troops, their divisional commander drunk and hiding behind their advance, rushed into the crater and milled about there. Delay was fatal. The rebels hurried up reinforcements and stood on the lips of the vast hole firing downward. They fixed bayonets on muskets and flung them down on the trapped Yankees. What had begun as the war of knightly idealism three years before had come to this: men burrowing like moles into the earth to blow up other men, and then being in turn harpooned as they groveled in the hole they had made. "A stupendous failure," Grant said of what became known as "the Battle of the Crater." It cost him 4,000 casualties. It also ended any hope for an immediate and swift end to the war.

It seemed to the correspondent Sylvanus Cadwallader that Grant was saying to Lee, "If you are the general you claim to be, come out and fight me," and that Lee was replying, "If you are the general you are represented to be, compel me to come out and fight you." Neither could do what he wished to do to the other, and so their conflict settled down into a monotonous series of little raids at the northern and southern terminuses of the long twisting lines. A stalemate, said the newspapers. And what was the whole point? "Nine-tenths of our bleeding, bankrupt, almost dying country shudders at the prospect of fresh conscription and new rivers of blood," said the New York *World*. "Who shall revive the withered hopes that blossomed at the opening of Grant's campaign?"

In Washington, General Halleck foresaw forcible resistance to the draft, and on August 11 wrote Grant asking for troops with which to press-gang recruits into service. Grant replied he could spare no troops; to do so would weaken his lines. The governors of the Northern states would have to take care of the matter with the Home guards. Back came a telegram: "I have seen your dispatch expressing your unwillingness to break your hold where you are. Neither am I willing. Hold on with a bulldog grip, and chew and choke as much as possible. A. Lincoln." Grant burst out laughing.

But twelve days later the President had his cabinet witness a statement he had written out: "This morning, as for some days past, it seems exceedingly probable that this Administration will not be re-elected. Then it will be my duty to so co-operate with the President-elect so as to save the Union between the election and the inauguration; as he will have secured his election on such ground that he cannot possibly save it afterwards." The Democratic nominee was to be the former commander of Army of the Potomac, George B. McClellan, and the party platform would call for a negotiated end to the war. That their former leader had in effect turned against them hardly decreased the feeling of hopelessness mixed with nastiness that took hold of the army. The corps commander Gouverneur Warren looked at the army's leader and saw, he thought, a man who seemed to be unconcerned with anything as he sat whittling and smoking. Warren decided that if Grant deserved admiration, "then Nero fiddling over burning Rome is sublime." Meade, always testy and ready to see insults to his dignity, exploded when Edward Crapsey of the Philadelphia *Inquirer* wrote that the rumor that Meade had wanted to return over the Rapidan after the first day's fighting at The Wilderness was correct. He seized the reporter, had him mounted facing backwards on a sorry mule, hung a placard LIBELER OF THE PRESS around his neck and, preceded by a drum corps beating "The Rogue's March," had him paraded for hours behind the lines.

City Point was thronged with six-mule teams to haul ammunition and food, and the docks were jammed with transports from the North. Sight-seers wandered past the guards. It all had the appearance of permanance. "Does General Grant smoke?" Sylvanus Cadwallader heard asked. "Where does he sleep and eat? Does he drink? Are you sure he is not a drinking man? Where's his wife? What became of his son that was with him at Vicksburg? Which is General Grant? What? Not that little man!"

Across the lines Lee wrote Mrs. Lee in Richmond, "We must suffer patiently to the end, when all things will be made right." His men ate thin rations, sweltered in the summer heat and called themselves "Lee's Miserables" or in imitation of the book's first section, "Fantine," "Lee's Miserables Faintin'." The dull hammering at the ends of the long fortifications north and south went on, Grant timing his raids like a pendulum back and forth as he sought to extend the lines and so thin Lee's defenses that the day might come when the Yankees could pierce the rebel screen. ("If Grant once breaks through our lines," the Southern novelist-in-uniform, John Esten Cooke, heard a general say, "we might as well go back to Father Abraham and say, 'Father, we have sinned!' ") Every day there were casualties. At Burgess' Mill 8 miles southwest of Petersburg, Preston Wade, son of Jeb Stuart's successor, went down, and when his brother, Wade Hampton, Jr., went to his aid, he too was hit. Their father came up, saw Preston's wound and said to a surgeon coming to help, "Too late, Doctor." Lee wrote: "I grieve with you at the death of your gallant son, so young, so brave, so true. I know how much you must suffer. Yet think of the great gain to him, how changed his condition, how bright his future. We must labor on the course before us, but for him I trust is rest and peace, for I believe our Merciful God takes us when it is best for us to go. He is now safe from all harm and all evil and nobly died in the defense of the rights of his country. May God support you under your great affliction, and give you strength to bear the trials He may impose upon you. Truly your friend." It was one of many, many such letters that he had to write, yet never then or ever he did voice a word of bitterness for those everyone around him

called "the enemy" or "the Yankees." He did not call them that.
It was always "those people" or "General Grant's people." He
prayed each night for those people, General Grant's people.

Yet Lee's determination to beat them was as it had always
been—stronger, even. All about him was death and hungry soldiers in rags, but when riding with one of his officers he saw
some Federal pickets had pushed up close to his lines, he said,
"Who are those people out there? What are they doing there?
We are in the habit of believing this country belongs to us. Drive
them away, sir. Drive them away!" A surgeon of his army wrote,
"I have never looked into such eyes as his. There was a deep
meaning in his steady gaze that I have never seen in any other
eyes." What was that meaning? It was, perhaps, that when he
prayed that God would give him this day what God would give
him, he meant *this day*. For he did not discuss the future, did
not repine that Sheridan had completely ousted Early from the
Shenandoah Valley, or that Sherman had taken Atlanta, that Joe
Johnston's replacement, John B. Hood, had in the most reckless
fashion destroyed the chief rebel army to the south by flinging
it at George Thomas in Tennessee, that the ports of Savannah
and Wilmington were soon to be lost. Lee stood alone in his little
strip of land, William Sherman said, his back to the wall, par-
rying every thrust, fighting like "a gallant knight, as he was."
But, Sherman said, "he never rose to the grand problem which
involved a continent and future generations. His Virginia was
to him the world. He stood like a stone wall to defend Virginia,
stood at the front porch battling with the flames whilst the kitchen
and house were burning."

Lee did not look at it that way. The Almighty had placed
him there in the lines before Petersburg and Richmond and there
he would do his best. Long ago at the beginning of the war he
had been asked what he thought the prospects were and had
replied that the question did not concern him. He would do his
best and be content to let God decide the outcome. He held to
that view when Jackson died, Stuart, all the other tens of thousands of unknowns, through good times and bad: It was not his

to judge or to predict. That belonged to God above, Who if He did not choose to make His view clear at the moment when things occurred would give an explanation when the time was right. Wearing an old coat with a colonel's insignia—that was really as high as he ought to have gotten, he said; that or perhaps, given good subordinates, a brigadier of cavalry's star—he went about his work, his duty, saying to Constance Cary, the spokeswoman of a group of Richmond belles asking if it was proper in such times to give dances, "Why, of course, my dear child. My boys need to be heartened up when they get their furloughs. Go on, look your prettiest, and be just as nice to them as ever you can be."

Across the lines Ulysses Grant received the gift of a fine new coat of wonderful material and great workmanship, tried it on and, after some moments of silence, said, thinking perhaps of the old Army garment that had been his sole distinction back in Galena in the leather goods store, "There have been times in my life when the gift of an overcoat would have been an act of charity. Now when I am able to pay for all I need, such gifts are continually thrust upon me."

The siege ground on and on. "Ingalls," he said to the quartermaster of the Army of the Potomac, who was once his old Twelve in One fellow club member back at West Point, "do you expect to take that yellow dog of yours into Richmond with you?" "Oh, yes, General," Ingalls answered, "he belongs to a long-life breed." Those who heard almost burst their sides with suppressed laughter. The leaves of those trees not cut down for breastworks and embankments on the plains before the embattled cities began to turn color, and November's election time came. To Private Theodore Gerrish of Maine it was sublime, heroic, that the men of his regiment gave 137 of their votes to Lincoln, who would continue the war, and but 13 to McClellan, who would end it. They were at one with the country and Lincoln swept the balloting.

Christmas Eve arrived. Sylvanus Cadwallader came upon Grant's aide Colonel Theodore Bowers stretched out in a camp chair in his quarters. A doleful look was on his face as he thought of his mother and his home, of happier Christmases. Rawlins walked in and asked if the two men had not heard the bugle sounding Taps and Lights Out and demanded to know if he had to put them under arrest for such flagrant violations of army regulations. They turned the tables by asking what he was doing wandering around the camp at such an hour of the night. He gave the same explanation as Bowers, that he was gloomy and lonesome. Within five minutes the lieutenant general came in, equally unhappy to be away from his family on this night. They sat and talked and ran out of cigars. Grant told everybody to wait, he had an unopened box in his quarters. They smoked a while and decided to go to sleep, Grant insisting each man should take a cigar with him. Cadwallader put his in his pocket and said he would smoke it next Christmas Eve in memory of this one before Petersburg. (A year later in Grant's home he showed it and Grant told him to save it another year. Cadwallader put it into a glass container and saved it into old age after Bowers, Rawlins and Grant had gone on.)

That day General Lee ate the scantiest of Christmas dinners. A large box filled with dressed turkeys had been sent, and the staff laid the contents out in the snow. The biggest one was marked for the commanding general. He touched it with the scabbard of an unslung and undrawn sword he happened to have in his hand. "This, then, is my turkey?" he asked. "I don't know, gentlemen, what you are going to do with your turkeys, but I wish mine sent to the hospital in Petersburg, so that some of the convalescents may have a good Christmas dinner." He walked away. The staff members packed up all the turkeys for the wounded. There was also a saddle of mutton someone had sent; it vanished. "If the soldiers get it, I shall be content," Lee wrote his wife. "We can do very well without it. In fact, I should rather they have it." "General Lee, I'm hungry," men called to him when he went down the line. He saw bloody footprints in the snow. By then his army was supporting the country, not the other way round. And the country with Sherman's march to the sea was effectively a little strip of Virginia and North Carolina. He was the Confederacy, thought his aide Colonel Charles Marshall; the men fought only for him. "To them he represented cause, country, and all."

But it was hard. They were ragged, covered with lice, unpaid, starving. They were cold, for the trees of the area, never too abundant, were gone for campfires and there was no additional fuel. They lived on corn bread and, when they could get it, bacon. Bit by bit, man by man, they began to fall away. In the past Lee had exerted only the mildest of disciplines, but in that winter he said that desertions must be stopped. Confederate bullets sang into the bodies of Confederate soldiers. Behind the lines in Richmond and Petersburg it was unwritten law that the future not be spoken of nor distress shown, and what were called "Starvation Parties" were held, meaning that host or hostess had little or nothing to offer for consumption. At such affairs women appeared in tableaux or playlets wearing dresses made of old curtains or carpets. At dawn they walked home through the snowy streets, for there were no horses or carriages. There was great tomorrow-we-die gaiety, and romances sprang up between Petersburg and Richmond girls and men who for years had been away in the field but now were available during their leaves from the front. Soldiers went, it was said, from a dance with their lady love back to the dance of death in the trenches. The wolf of hunger was no longer at the door. He had taken up residence in the house. So depreciated was the Confederate dollar that it was said you took your money in a basket to the market and brought back your purchases in your pocketbook. "You should have seen Uncle Robert's dinner today," said a visiting member of the British Parliament. "He had two biscuits and he gave me one!" Another day he said, "What a glorious dinner today! Someone sent Uncle Robert a box of sardines!"

Lee remained cheerful, even gay. "Last night," he said to Mrs. Roger Pryor, "when I reached my headquarters, I found a card on my table with a hyacinth, and these words: 'For General Lee, with a kiss.' Now, I have my hyacinth and my card—and

I mean to find my kiss!" When he called upon people he would say, "I don't want to see you, you are too gloomy and despondent; where is—?" and he would name the little girl of the family. Entirely crippled, Mrs. Lee in her wheel chair knitted socks for the soldiers. "I know He will order all things for our good, and we must be content," her husband wrote her.

At City Point, in the huts that replaced the tents of summer and fall, the lieutenant general Grant had a room with an open fireplace, which served as living room–dining room and office. Behind it were two small bedrooms. Julia and the children came down to crowd in with him, and he lived an informal family life, tusseling on the floor with the boys and rising to dust himself off and say to Colonel Horace Porter, "Ah, you know my weaknesses—my children and my horses." The younger children turned everything into a toy; he did not reprove them but simply appealed to their affections when he desired better behavior. His companion since Vicksburg days, Fred, the oldest boy, fourteen, went fishing in the James; a gunboat pulled alongside and Fred spent an uncomfortable few hours trying to convince the arresting officers that he was not a rebel spy. Grant permitted his usual reticence and modesty to fall away when he discussed his children, causing the eyes of his people to open wide when he seriously spoke of Fred's having immense military ability. (By the time Fred turned twenty-one, Grant opined that he was the superior of Helmuth von Moltke, the conquerer in three successive wars of Denmark, Austria and France.) Sometimes the lieutenant general would sit holding Julia's hand in a quiet corner and when found so by one of his officers would look bashful. He was never the imperious generalissimo with them, going himself across the room to get a paper he wanted, and walking down to the post office to pick up his own mail. So far as his three stars went, he said, he received satisfaction from ranking only one soldier in the United States Army: Robert Buchanan, who had driven him out of the service back at Fort Humboldt in California ten years before. (Once Buchanan, raised to brigadier general from his lieutenant colonelcy of California days, made his way to Grant and said to his erstwhile subordinate whose position had so dramatically changed that he hoped they could let bygones by bygones.)

A few of the men he had known for years called him "Grant" when alone with him; in front of other people they called him "General." Julia referred to him as "Mr. Grant" in the presence of most people, or when he was absent; among intimates she addressed him as "Ulyss" or "Dudy" or, as she had since Vicksburg, "Victor." Sometimes in mock imperiousness she demanded to know details of the coming spring campaign, and he made up impossible numbers and confused the geography, outlining ridiculous moves in a fashion that made his men laugh. She always acted as if there was no doubt of his eventual triumph, telling people that Mr. Grant had always been a most determined man. When she was there the officers of his staff felt themselves able to relax. There was never a question of his falling off the wagon when Julia was about.

He remained, as always, the most private of people, the most guarded as to his emotions. Most officers bathed nude in front of their tents in barrels cut in half and filled with water, or showered by having their orderlies fling water on them, but it was notable that the lieutenant general never did so. When he bathed, it was inside his tent, alone, his orderly forbidden to come past the lowered and tied flap. It was the same when he changed his clothes. Years later, decades later, he remarked that nobody had seen him naked since he was a boy.

Mild, unhurried, almost never known to raise his voice, never known to say anything stronger than "confound it" or "doggone it," he yet conveyed the sense of a great and terrible reserve power. Lee's old friend Erasmus Darwin Keyes, who had shown him in to speak with General Scott when he returned from Texas to give up his commission in the United States Army, felt a ruthlessness in Grant equal to that of Tamerlane or the Duke of Alva. He held Lee in an iron vise, Keyes thought, whose tightening was such that the impression was always present that he possessed a reserve of force not yet brought into play. So in the end it was futile to oppose him. He always had something left—always kept something back. That the war had gone on as long as it had was due "almost wholly to the genius and energy of this one man"—Lee—yet Keyes concluded that Lee stood in the second rank as a general. Ulysses Grant stood in the first. The suggestion of power held back impressed itself also upon the lieutenant general's youngest son, Jesse. Even his quiet physical movements seemed more forceful than the violent actions of another man, Jesse thought, remembering that only once had his father spanked him—when he'd misbehaved at an official dinner. With Julia and Rufus Ingalls the lieutenant general went up the line, and, across, George Pickett looked through field glasses and pointed the trio out to the girl he had sent greetings to just before his doomed charge at Gettysburg. "Yes, that's Rufus: see him laugh, the old rascal," Pickett said to Mrs. Pickett. He had married her after Gettysburg and their child was born in the first days of the siege. When Grant and Ingalls, old friends from West Point, found out, they dispatched a message marked UNOFFICIAL across the front: "We are sending congratulations to you, to the young mother and the young recruit." She was a good cook, and gathered together chicken, pork, corn, tomato, lima beans, with bay leaf and onion seasonings, and made a Brunswick stew that Lee pronounced the most delicious thing he had ever tasted. "But, you know," he told Mrs. Pickett, "I never eat anything without thinking of the soldiers—the poor fellows who have always been used to good things at home." She listened to the sound of his horse as he went away after talking of how people in the South did not realize how few resources were left, how many lives had been lost. "Hear the horses' hooves saying, 'Blood-blood, blood-blood,' " she said to her husband. "So they do, little one," Pickett said. "Strange—strange. I had not thought of that before."

February came. Grant reached out his extreme left to come behind Petersburg and cut off Lee's supply line south, and at Hatcher's Run, near where Wade Hampton's son had died, the

Confederate general John Pegram went down. Not a month had passed since his romance with the reigning belle of Richmond culminated in their wedding at St. Paul's. Hetty Cary Pegram had auburn hair, superb features and a perfect figure. "Look well at her," the New Orleans *Crescent* said, "for you have never seen, and will probably never see again, so beautiful a woman! It is worth a king's ransom, a lifetime of trouble, to look at one such woman." With her sister and her cousin Constance Cary, who had asked Lee if it was proper to hold dances in such times, she had made the first three battle flags of the Confederacy, assigned the honor by a Congressional committee. During their brief marriage Hetty and John Pegram had lived in a little cottage located near the scene of his death, he the "prizewinner of the invincible beauty of her day." None of his men could bear to tell her what happened. In an ambulance she sat carding lint for bandages. They heard her gay laughter. They let her sleep that night but in the morning she came down to find his body in the house. She took from his pocket the watch she had wound for him when he went out the previous morning, and a miniature of herself. Both were drenched in blood. She seemed to her cousin Constance like a flower broken in its stalk. For her wedding she had worn a snowy robe, orange wreath and misty veil, and three weeks to the day later she knelt in the same spot in the chancel, now swathed in black. By her side was his coffin with a victor's palm beside his soldier's accoutrements, his cap, sword, gloves. Outside was the hearse and, behind, his horse with empty boots reversed in the stirrups, the ancient mark of a fallen warrior. The mourners went to Richmond's Hollywood Cemetery. "The wailing of the band that went with us on the slow pilgrimage will never die out of memory," Constance wrote. Snow covered the hillsides. Custis Lee stood by the widow's side as the minister who had married Hetty consigned her husband's remains to the earth. "The warmest instincts of every man's soul declare the glory of the soldier's death," Robert Lee wrote in a series of notes to himself that he placed in a little satchel. "It is more appropriate to the Christian than to the Greek to sing, *Glorious his fate, and*

envied is his lot, Who for his country fights and for it dies." Union
shells screamed down into Petersburg and trains could no longer
safely approach the city, and one passed deserted and half-
destroyed buildings. There was a little half-starved child who
sang there, in Petersburg, the young soldier John S. Wise
remembered. He saw a few dirty, haggard, Confederates
listening as she sang of one who was dead: "Gone where the
roses are faded, Gone where the meadows are bare, To a land
by orange-blossoms shaded, Where summer ever lingers in the
air." THERE IS A TRUE GLORY AND A TRUE HONOR,
Robert Lee wrote in a note for his satchel, THE GLORY
OF DUTY DONE, THE HONOR OF THE INTEGRITY
OF PRINCIPLE.

Over the heads of the soldiers, the political leaders sought
peace. President Lincoln of the United States met with Vice-
President Alexander Stephens of the Confederate States of America, and found their differences were irreconcilable. But something of their intent penetrated downward, and when General
Edward O. C. Ord met Pete Longstreet between the lines for a
discussion of political prisoners and allied subjects, including the
bartering of Southern tobacco for Northern coffee between the
opposing troops, Ord said to Longstreet that the war had gone
on long enough. Perhaps Lee ought to ask Grant for a meeting
so that "old friends of the military service could get together and
seek out ways to stop the flow of blood."

Longstreet told Lee what Ord had said, and Lee went to
Richmond and the Confederate White House to sit with Jefferson
Davis in a little downstairs study. Davis said the matter should
be pursued, so Lee wrote Grant that perhaps a military agreement might arrive at "a satisfactory adjustment of the present
unhappy difficulties." He asked for a meeting. During the conversation between Ord and Longstreet the possibility had been
raised that Mrs. Longstreet should visit her old friend Julia Grant
at City Point and that Julia should then repay the visit in Richmond. This demonstration of goodwill between the ladies might

lead the way to a general peace. "How enchanting, how thrill-ing!" Julia cried. "Oh, Ulys, I may go, may I not?"

"No, I think not."

"Yes, I must. Do say yes. I so much wish to go. Do let me go." He telegraphed the contents of Lee's note to Washington. It was March 3, 1865. The following day Lincoln would be sworn in for his second term. If he intended to let two generals settle the issues of the war, Secretary Stanton told him, he had better not take the oath at all, and then at Lincoln's dictation sent a message to Grant saying he could meet with Lee only on purely military matters, or to accept his surrender. "Meanwhile you are to press to the utmost your military advantages." Grant sent across the lines: "In regard to meeting you, I would state that I have no authority to accede to your proposition of the subject proposed. Such authority is vested in the President of the United States alone. General Ord could only have meant that I would not refuse an interview on any subject on which I have a right to act." The reply did not surprise Lee. He had expected it. He stood alone at two in the morning, his arm on the mantle of the fireplace of the house in which he was staying,* his head on his arm as he gazed into the coal fire, and when General John Gordon entered the room he saw for the first time in his life a look of painful depression on his leader's face. Lee showed Gordon re-ports from the different commands spread out in their long trenches. They told of shivering men emaciated and unable to do physical labor for more than half an hour before becoming faint. Of his 50,000 men, Lee said, perhaps 35,000 were even marginally fit for duty. Grant must have 150,000. What, he asked Gordon, did duty to the army and the people demand now? Peace negotiations, Gordon answered. It was something Gordon had never permitted himself to think of before. He had not realized things were as bad as they were. One did not discuss such things in Richmond and Petersburg, that winter.

Lee went to President Davis. He explained everything. They

---

*Previously he had almost always lived in his tent, which explains the dearth of "Lee Slept Here" residences in Virginia and elsewhere.

must continue to fight, Davis replied. A man "tenacious" in his views, Davis, Lee remarked to John Gordon. But he was the President. Richmond, Lee had often said, was a millstone around his neck. Protecting it deprived him of the ability to maneuver. Now Davis said that if necessary they would abandon the capital. But that was not the main question. The main question was whether they would continue their war. And the answer was yes. Let Lee unite his army with the force under Joe Johnston, returned to command in North Carolina. Fight on. Better to die in the last ditch than accept defeat.

"I am a soldier," Lee said. A soldier obeys orders. There was only one thing to do, he told John Gordon: "Fight to the last."

In City Point, Grant received a delegation led by his congressman, Washburne. They had come to present him with a medal struck by order of Washburne's colleagues. There followed square dancing, and Julia got him to clump through one round, an unusual performance for a man whose sense of music was such as to lead him to say that he could recognize only two tunes: One, he said, was "Yankee Doodle"; the other wasn't. (Some people said he only *thought* he recognized "Yankee Doodle.") A few days later he telegraphed Lincoln, "Can you not visit City Point for a day or two? I would like very much to see you and I think the rest would do you good." It was a kind act on Grant's part, and perceptive also, for Lincoln had wanted to come but was hesitant about asking. The previous commanders of his main army had not bestirred themselves to make him welcome.

He came with his family for the first holiday of his Presidency, to ride around on Grant's horse, Jeff Davis, giving the appearance, the soldiers thought, of a praying mantis whose long legs were in danger of becoming entangled with those of his steed. He took carriage rides with his wife. They paused once by a quiet Virginia graveyard along the James. "Mary," the President said, "you are younger than I. You will survive me. When I am gone, lay my remains in some quiet place like this." Half-mad and terribly hurt by the unjust but widespread stories that she was a rebel spy whose sympathies were entirely with the Confederacy in whose service her family had lost several members,* she was ferociously jealous of her husband. At a City Point review of the Army of the Potomac she sat in an ambulance with Julia Grant and heard Grant's aide Adam Badeau say something about the President's having given the wife of General Charles Griffin permission to visit the front.

"What do you mean by that, sir?" Mrs. Lincoln demanded of Badeau. "Do you know that I never allow the President to see any woman alone?" Badeau tried to offer a reassuring grin. It had the opposite effect. "That's a very equivocal smile, sir!" Julia tried to calm the President's lady, but Mrs. Lincoln demanded that the ambulance be halted. "Let me out of this carriage at once. I will ask the President if he saw that woman alone!" She reached past Julia and clutched at the driver. Julia managed to quiet her, but the scene was so mortifying that Julia and Badeau agreed they must speak of it to nobody.

At another review Mary Lincoln's incipient insanity boiled to the surface again. Traveling with Julia, Badeau and Horace Porter in an ambulance, she saw General Ord's wife riding near the President. "What does that woman mean by riding by the side of the President?" she raved. "Does she suppose that *he* wants *her* by the side of *him*?" The ambulance was standing in a sea of mud, but she demanded to be allowed to get out. "There come Mrs. Lincoln and Mrs. Grant," said the unsuspecting Mrs. Ord to the people she was with. "I think I had better join them." She rode to the ambulance and was greeted with a flood of horrifying insults pouring out of the mouth of the President's lady. Porter and Badeau were actually afraid that Mrs. Lincoln would get out of the ambulance and attack Mrs. Ord in front of the lined-up troops. Julia tried to calm the frenzied woman, and Mary Lincoln turned on her and burst out, "I suppose you think you'll get to the White House yourself, don't you?" Julia said

---

*Including Ben Helm, who on Robert Lee's last day in Washington talked with him about taking a Union commission, decided to take a Confederate one instead, and went to his death at the battle of Chickamauga.

she was quite satisfied with her present position, that it was a better one than she had ever expected to attain. "Oh, you had better take it if you can get it," Mrs. Lincoln rasped. "Tis very nice." She profanely abused Mrs. Ord, who burst into tears and asked what in the world she had done. It was inexpressibly painful for Badeau and Porter and most of all for Julia, who lapsed into an embarrassed silence. At dinner with the Grants, Mrs. Lincoln denounced Ord, saying he should be removed from his command.

After dinner, after Captain John Barnes of a navy boat that had escorted the President's *River Queen* down from Washington had gone to bed, he was awakened and told the President wanted him. With Mrs. Lincoln grimly looking on, the President had to ask Barnes, who had been at the review, if Mrs. Ord had done anything wrong. Barnes replied that she had not. From then on Mrs. Lincoln treated him abominably. Captain Barnes appealed to Julia Grant for aid, and she advised him to try to mollify the distraught woman by kind attentions. It didn't work. A day or so later, Mrs. Lincoln beckoned Julia to her, an animated discussion took place and Julia had to go to Barnes and tell him that his presence on the *River Queen* was unwelcome. He departed. All through the visit to the army the subject of the doings of Mrs. Griffin and Mrs. Ord was brought up by Mrs. Lincoln, who took out much of her sadly disjointed rage upon Julia. "How dare you be seated until I invite you?" she demanded, also indicating that Julia was to back out of her presence in the fashion of persons leaving a European royalty.

Lincoln bore it martyr-like and when away from his wife and with his officers was easy of approach and filled with apposite story. Grant told him of various suggestions received from the North as to how to end the siege. An engineer had suggested that Richmond be walled in and the James River diverted into it so that the rebels would all be drowned; another writer wanted shells filled with snuff fired into the city so that the constantly sneezing rebels would soon become exhausted. A "sorcerer in Rochester" sent Grant's horoscope in order to aid him in his work. Someone else recommended that bayonets of remarkable length be manufactured; then the Union soldiers could easily stick the rebels with no danger to themselves. This appealed to the President's ever-ready sense of humor. "Well, there is a good deal of terror in cold steel," he told Grant. "I had a chance to test it once myself. When I was a young man, I was walking along a back street in Louisville one night about twelve o'clock, when a very tough-looking citizen sprang out of an alleyway, reached up to the back of his neck, pulled out a Bowie knife that seemed to my stimulated imagination about three feet long, and planted himself squarely across my path. For two or three minutes he flourished his weapon in front of my face, appearing to try and see just how near he could come to cutting my nose off without quite doing it. He could see in the moonlight that I was taking a good deal of interest in the proceedings, and finally he yelled out, as he steadied the knife close to my throat: 'Stranger, kin you lend me five dollars on that?' I never reached in my pocket and got out money so fast in my life. I handed him a bank-note and said: 'There's ten, neighbor; now put up your scythe.' "

Sherman came up from North Carolina for a quick visit and sat with Grant while the President asked if it would be possible to end the war without too much additional bloodshed. There had been so much already. They told him there would have to be more fighting, Sherman doing most of the talking while Grant sat silently listening. He was terribly worried that Lee would slip away into interior Virginia when the spring days dissolved the last of winter's mud: "I was afraid, every morning, that I would awake from my sleep to hear that Lee had gone. If he got the start, he would leave me behind so that we would have the same army to fight again further south—and the war might be prolonged another year."

A mile away Lee's thoughts ran in the exact same direction but with a different hope: that at the end of the additional year of war the North would finally give up the fight. On March 24, Grant wrote out orders for a movement around Lee's right. On that night Lee prepared for a morning assault on Fort Steadman opposite Petersburg. Later those who had been there would reflect that it was remarkable that so late in the day he was still able to strike. But then, it had been remarkable earlier that, even then so late in the day, he had been able to send Jubal Early to menace the Yankee capital. To attack was his forte. In the early morning hours of March 25, General Gordon at Lee's order threw thousands of rebels at Fort Steadman. They overwhelmed the defenders and spread out right and left so that soon they held a mile of Federal works. The Yankee army was split. If it could be kept split, Lee reasoned, Grant would pull back his left half and run it around his rear to join his right. Then the way south would be open for Lee and he could rush to join Joe Johnston in North Carolina, crush Sherman and return with Johnston to handle Grant. But Grant mustered artillery and opened upon the captured fort as Lincoln watched. The storm was too much for the rebels and the torn line was mended.

Four days later Grant and his staff parted from City Point to join the massive lines of Union infantry and cavalry heading southwest to assault the extreme right end of the Confederate line. The spring campaign of 1865 was about to begin. Meade was worried about shifting the center of gravity of the Union army to the south, away from Richmond, but Grant told him that Richmond was only a collection of houses "while Lee was an active force injuring the country." He cared nothing for Richmond, everything for Lee. Julia Grant stood in the front door of the lieutenant general's headquarters and he kissed her again and again. Then the men walked to the little railroad station. Their horses were already on board. Colonel Porter thought President Lincoln wore a look more serious than ever he had shown before on his visit. He shook hands with his officers. "I hope we shall have better luck now than we have had," Rawlins said to him, and Lincoln replied, "Well, your luck is my luck, and the country's—the luck of all of us—except the poor fellows who are killed." He stood by the train looking up at them. When it began to move they took off their hats.

They went southwest. It began to rain. Lee saw to his defenses. He rode through the land adjoining the home of Mrs. Roger Pryor and she said, "You, only, General, can tell me if it is worth my while to put the ploughshare into these fields."

"Plant your seeds, Madam," he said. Then a moment later, "The doing it will be some reward."

The rain went on and it seemed to Rawlins that Grant had moved too soon. Forewarned, Lee would now have time to take measures that would forestall Union success. Phil Sheridan did not agree. The troops were making jokes about sending for gunboats to navigate the flooded fields, but Sheridan said that if necessary he would put every man of the command to cutting down trees with which he would pave the roads. "I tell you, I'm ready to strike out tomorrow and go to smashing things!" He begged Grant for the VI Corps under Horatio Wright to support his cavalry but was told he would have to use Gouverneur Warren's V Corps; Wright was too far distant. Staff officers went ploughing through the mud to tell Warren to hurry on.

On the first day of the new month of April, Sheridan with 10,000 cavalrymen broke upon the Confederate defenders of the little crossroads dot on the map called Five Forks. Robert Lee's nephew, Fitzhugh Lee, the son of his older brother, Smith, was in command of the rebel horsemen there, and George Pickett in charge of the infantry, but neither was present on the field. The first shad of the season had been plucked from the Virginia rivers, and they were at a shadbake.

Phil Sheridan in action was Mars himself, plunging his horse, Rienzi, among the men as he waved a flag, shook his fist, entreated, encouraged, threatened. He pushed the rebels back upon the Southside Railroad, the last link of Petersburg and Richmond to what was left of the Confederacy. "I want you men to understand we have a record to make, before that sun goes down, that will make hell tremble!" Sheridan roared, standing up in his stirrups. "You understand?" he demanded of General George A. Custer. "I want you to *give* it to them!" "Yes, yes," Custer cried, "I'll give it to them!" Another officer came up saying he had captured three rebel guns and Sheridan roared, "I don't care a damn for their guns, or you either! Go back to your business, where you belong! What I want is that Southside Road!"

The position that was the buttress of the left wing of Lee's army was being overrun. "Hold Five Forks at all hazards," he had telegraphed Pickett, but the rebel formations began to disintegrate. They fled away, dropped their rifles, surrendered. Sheridan spurred Rienzi up to the breastworks, cleared it with a bound and landed in the midst of a huddle of Confederates. "Go right over there," he cried, pointing to his own lines. "Get right along, now. Oh, drop your guns; you'll never need them any more." Yankee cavalrymen right and left were going over the works with a hurrah. But Warren of the V Corps was dilatory. Sheridan raved at him and he answered, "Bobby Lee is always getting people into trouble." Sheridan relieved him of his command. He had Grant's authorization to do so. Warren had never been quite right since that first day in The Wilderness. When Warren asked Sheridan to reconsider, "Reconsider hell!" was Sheridan's answer.

A blue tide flowed over what had been the southwest base of the rebel line. "Well, Captain, what shall we do?" Lee asked the courier who brought the disastrous news. It was a rhetorical question, of course, for the answer was plainly that he must pull away from the lines he had held so long. And flee. The route south was no longer open to him, for Sheridan was there and coming on. So it would have to be to the west. The Yankee artillery roared as he sat with his adjutant general, Walter Taylor, and laid out plans for his withdrawal from the clutches of his adversary. He had held the 40 miles of line north of Richmond and south of Petersburg for nine months.

Through the mud Grant's aide Horace Porter galloped to get the word to headquarters that Five Forks was in Union hands, his orderly behind him shouting the news to everybody he saw. "April fool!" men yelled back. Porter had forgotten what day it was until he heard that response to the glorious news. At Grant's headquarters in a formerly deserted field now so churned up that

officers stood by the campfire on felled trees so as to be out of
the mud, Porter flung himself off his horse and ran to Grant to
seize his hand and clap him on the back. The first impression of
the staff was that Porter was drunk, but when they understood,
they began dancing about and throwing their hats in the air.
Grant asked how many prisoners had been taken. About 5,000
was the answer. The lieutenant general smiled.

Night came. Partially disrobed, Lee lay down for a little
sleep, to waken in the early hours to the news that formations
of men were coming up to his headquarters, the home of a family
named Turnbull. He sprang up and saw shadowy forms advancing. Officers were leaping on their horses to see if the approaching troops were retreating Confederates or advancing
Yankees, and A. P. Hill, for whom Stonewall Jackson had called
in his last moments, dashed off with a sergeant-courier. In the
dim light Lee saw that the moving men wore blue. The house
was in the direct line of their advance. Seven of his big guns,
Napoleons, came rattling up, and he stood in their midst and
heard the artillerists shouting, "Let 'em come on! We'll give 'em
hell!" Through the mist and smoke came the sergeant who had
gone with Hill. He was riding the general's horse, and Hill was
lying in a patch of woods nearby with a Union bullet in his heart.
Tears came into Lee's eyes. "He is at rest now," he murmured,
"and we who are left are the ones to suffer." Wagons and ambulances pounded by, running for Petersburg less than 3 miles
away.

The Yankee skirmishers held up. Inside the house Colonel
Taylor sat with a telegrapher sending out Lee's complex orders
dictating where pontoon bridges would be placed, and the routes
of the wagon trains. The main flight of the Confederate army
from its lines would begin at eight that night, some twelve hours
in the future, the artillery to go first, then the infantry save for
pickets who would not be withdrawn until three in the morning
of the following day.

Among the telegrams was one for the Confederate Secretary
of War: "I advise that all preparations be made for leaving Rich-

mond tonight." Lee dictated the message, Taylor remembered, in an utterly noncomittal tone, as if giving a routine communication. The message got to Richmond and was taken in a sealed envelope to Jefferson Davis, who sat at Sunday services in St. Paul's. It was a beautiful spring morning. Davis read the telegram, his lips tightened and he rose and slowly walked up the aisle out of the church, passing the Lee daughters as he went. The minister, Charles Minnigerode, read from the 44th and following psalms: *Thou hast broken us in the place of dragons, and covered us with the shadow of death.* The dull boom of heavy guns outside the city sounded. People whispered to each other that President Davis must have received news of the rupture of the lines. *He maketh wars to cease unto the end of the earth; he breaketh the bow and cutteth the spear in sunder; he burneth the chariot in the fire.* The Lee girls returned to the family's rented house at 707 Franklin Street and reported the rumor. Their mother said she didn't believe it.

In front of the Turnbull house outside Petersburg the rate of Federal fire increased. Shells were hitting the grounds, and the telegraph operator told Colonel Taylor he could no longer use his instrument. The two men left the house. Lee was outside, wearing a sword. He almost never did that, and soldiers wondered if it was because he expected to die fighting. A Yankee shell crashed into the house, starting a fire that soon enveloped it. Another shell came down and took off the legs of the telegraph operator's horse. Lee was on Traveller, pointed in the direction of Petersburg. He turned in his saddle and looked at the Federals and his neck turned red and a look of rage came onto his face. His eyes were gleaming. They were almost upon him, shooting at the artillerists limbering up and preparing to rush away. His savagery spent itself. He put Traveller into a walk.

In Richmond, Jefferson Davis dictated a telegram pointing out that the government was not being given much time to pick up its records and supplies. Lee read the message, tore it into bits and stamped it into the mud. Panic seized Richmond. Wagons roared through the streets loaded with valuables, and people ran about offering any amount of money for transportation out of the city. In the afternoon banks opened so that people could empty their safe deposit vaults. The trains were jammed, and the canal boats. Smoke rose from bonfires where government clerks burned documents.

The evening light faded as the last defenders of the Petersburg end of the Confederate line filed past their commander, who stood on a bridge over the Appomattox River with Traveller's bridle in his hand. Walter Taylor came and asked for a brief leave. He wanted to go to Richmond and marry his fiancée. Lee looked surprised for a moment and then gave his consent, and Taylor galloped off to find that the last train out of Petersburg had just left. He commandeered a locomotive, chased the train, caught it, got on board and made his way to Miss Elizabeth Seldon's house through the rush and tumult of a city that knew the Yankees would be there the next day. At midnight St. Paul's minister, Dr. Minnigerode, performed the ceremony while outside the streets were filled with shouts and the sound of hurrying footsteps. By then Richmond was jammed with the men from the trenches. At Petersburg the ammunition magazines were exploded. The earth shook and the skies lit up. Lee rode at a slow pace through the dark, the men plodding by his side walking skeletons after the long and terrible winter.

In the emptying trenches bands played to drown the sound of men moving away, and little squads of soldiers lit bonfires here and there to make the Yankees think the defenders were still present. Every light in every home in Richmond burned as people went through valuables to be buried, or selected those to be carried along as they made their run for safety. Soldiers loaded nine gunboats at the riverfront with kegs of powder, and preparations were made to fire the railroad trestle and bridge after the last of the troops had gone. All night long the soldiers from the trenches poured through and headed west. In the early morning hours of April 3, as the Federals got ready to attack along the entire length of the now deserted lines, the last Confederate soldiers crossed the James. When the last available wagon had followed them, departing quartermaster officers spread word that all remaining government stores were to be had for the taking. Crowds rushed to help themselves to meat, cereals, sugar, coffee, flour—everything the Confederacy owned in its capital save for $500,000 in gold, which was sent away under the guard of a detachment of navy cadets. The City Council had ordered that all stocks of liquor be destroyed, and from the government warehouses came a stream of whiskey from kegs bashed open and poured out of windows. Men and women caught it in pots as it came down, or cupped their hands to scoop it up from the gutter. In the state penitentiary a convict forced the door of his cell, ran and got an axe and freed his fellows. They poured out into the city to join other men lying in the street and lapping at the whiskey.

Just before first light, the fuses in the gunboats ignited the powder kegs one by one and the boats vanished in a roar of spray and noise that rattled houses and shattered windows as far as 2 miles from the river. Fired by government order, the immense tobacco warehouses sent flames hundreds of feet into the air. Cinders came drifting down to light new fires—fires that would destroy a third of Richmond. Engineers of the rear guard of the departing Army of Northern Virginia lit piles of turpentine-drenched wood stacked on the bridges, and when Walter Taylor left his new bride and paused for a moment in Manchester across the river, he saw behind him Mayo's Bridge blazing, a long string of flame spanning the James and reflected in the waters below. Richmond burned, and through the streets ran drunken looters breaking into shops and homes. A hellish mass, they pushed carts and wheelbarrows and carried tubs and pots to take what they might. The army went on its way; and behind it the capital of its country endured a fate no other American city ever knew.

In Petersburg, a procession of old men bearing a flag of truce that appeared to have been a linen table cloth came down the principal street toward the advancing Yankee troops. They walked as if attending a funeral. They saw a man riding a horse adorned with staff officer equipment and said to him that they were the town councilmen come to offer the formal surrender of Petersburg. The horseman they addressed was the reporter Sylvanus Cadwallader. Ever after he felt this to have been the most ridiculous moment of his life. He told them he would have been happy to have received the surrender at any time for months past, but that now the moment was too late, for the Union Army was already in possession. Cavalry and infantry swirled past him as he spoke. Soon Ulysses Grant received Abraham Lincoln coming up from City Point. They sat together on the Petersburg Court House steps.

At that hour the United States flag was flying atop what had been the Capitol of the Confederacy. Up Richmond's Main Street, through smoke, past the horror of the night's death and looting, had come unopposed Federal troops, including a mass of black cavalry, sabers bared, singing. From what had been Jefferson Davis' Confederate White House a proclamation was issued: "Major General Godfrey Weitzel, commanding detachment of the Army of the James, announces the occupation of the City of Richmond by the Armies of the United States under the command of Lieutenant General Grant." The first duty was to fight the fires. The men began pumping water as best they could—some mad impulse had driven vandals to cut the hoses of the city fire department as Richmond underwent its torture. They blew up smoldering buildings and organized bucket brigades. A vast cloud of smoke that hid the sun hung in the sky, and half-burned bits of government documents swirled through the streets in front of the charred houses and the bashed-in windows of stores that the mob had sacked.

"I have got my army safe out of its breastworks, and in order to follow me, my enemy must abandon his lines and can derive no further benefit from his railroads or the James River," Lee said. My enemy. He had never said that before.

In Washington, salutes of 300 guns for the capture of Petersburg and 500 for the capture of Richmond went on for hours. In a little boat rowed by twelve sailors a tall civilian came to the wharves of captured Richmond and, holding the hand of his young son, went ashore. "Do you know that man?" a Northern newspaperman asked a group of blacks who had been put to work by Union officers to clean up some debris.

"Who *is* that man, master?"

"Call no man master. That man set you free. That is Abraham Lincoln. Now is your time to shout. Can't you sing 'God bless you, Father Abraham'?" At once they broke into a stumbling rush to the landing party. "Saviour! My Jesus! There is the great Messiah!"

One old man fell on his knees in the dust and took the President's hand and covered it with kisses; and Abraham Lincoln took off his hat.

Julia Grant also went to Richmond. She saw the wreckage, the dead horses floating in the James, and the empty streets, for the people kept to their silent houses, coming out only at night for fresh air, the women heavily veiled. She went back to her cabin on the dispatch boat of the Lieutenant General Commanding the Armies of the United States docked at City Point. She heard the twitter of the little river frogs in the water. A fit of weeping took her, and she sat alone crying for the city, and for the war. Off to the west her husband tracked Robert Lee. He did not want to trail directly after the fleeing rebel army, for that would mean getting entangled in rear-guard engagements. And so, south of Lee's path, he pushed his men on a parallel course, the artillery horses shouldering the infantry off the roads, the wagon trains rocking in the rear, the whole a mass of rushing men and horses running a race in the Virginia springtime.

The dogwood was beginning to bloom, the grass was showing its first green of the season, the willows were yellowing and swelling. Lee sped on, heading for Amelia Courthouse some 40 miles away, where trainloads of supplies had been directed. He was arrow-straight in the saddle, his men noted, his face as calm as though he were watching the dress parade of a victorious army instead of a fleeing horde of smashed formation and broken regiments diminishing by the hour as exhausted men fell out and

dispirited ones slipped away. He saw his cavalry officer son
Rooney, and said, "Keep your command together and in good
spirits. I will get you out of this." He saw a junior staff officer
who had skirmished with Sheridan's cavalry and asked, "Did
those people surprise your command this morning?" The officer,
puzzled, said they had not. Then what was it, Lee asked, that
had prevented the young man from completing his toilette? Judging from appearances he had been unable to do so. He pointed
to the officer's boots. One leg of his trousers had been stuffed
in. The other was out. The man took the rebuke in silence,
saluted, turned to go. Lee called him back and explained that on
a retreat those who served near commanders must not permit
anything in their dress or conduct to imply a tone of demoralization.

He came to Amelia Courthouse with 30,000 hungry men
and found boxes of ammunition and harnesses for the artillery
horses—but nothing to eat. The trainloads of food, mistakenly
sent on to Richmond, were now in Federal hands. He took the
news with no show of emotion, but from then on there was a
haggard look in his face. He signed an appeal to the country
people asking them to feed his men—"the brave soldiers who
have battled for your liberty for four years."

Twenty-five miles south, at Wilson's Station, Grant heard
from a railroad engineer the details of how Jefferson Davis' train
had passed through the previous day, headed for Danville on the
North Carolina border. He had taken with him a trunk, four
pistols, a case of ammunition and a picture of himself and his
wife and a picture of Lee—that was all. Grant went on to Not-
taway Courthouse where a dispatch from Sheridan arrived saying
he had intercepted the route Lee would have to take west out of
Amelia Courthouse. The news was read to the troops, who wildly
cheered it.

Another message came from Sheridan, wrapped in chewing
tobacco tinfoil and carried by a scout masquerading as a Confederate soldier. "I wish you were here yourself," Sheridan had
written. Grant had been in the saddle all day, but now he had

a fresh horse saddled and set out to ride the more than 15 miles to Sheridan. There was no nearby cavalry for an escort, so he gathered a dozen officers as a guard. As they traveled they saw rebel campfires off to the north. The scout appeared to have lost his way, and it came into Horace Porter's mind that they were being betrayed. He took out a revolver, cocked it and rode directly at the scout's back. Late at night they struck Sheridan's pickets and were directed to a log cabin in a tobacco patch in whose loft the cavalry commander was sleeping. He came down to offer a meal of beef, cold chicken and coffee. "Lee *is* in a bad fix," Grant said after talking with Sheridan. "It will be difficult for him to get away."

"Damn him," Sheridan said, "he *can't* get away. We'll have his whole army: we'll have every ——— of them."

"That's a little too much to expect," Grant said. "I think if I were Lee I could escape at least with some of my men." The subject of their talk would, Grant predicted, leave Amelia Courthouse that night. He set his own troops into motion to get ahead of Lee and try to cut him off, whatever direction he took. The Yankees marched on and saw that their commander's prediction had been correct, for off to the right they heard the sound of Confederate columns on the move.

In the morning Sheridan struck at those columns, his horse artillery flinging shells at the men, his cavalry flashing in to shoot the animals that pulled the wagons. Famished, the Confederates staggered on, men's minds wandering from lack of sleep. "Tomatoes are very good," said General Richard Ewell as the Union artillery opened up on him. "I wish I had some." At Sayler's Creek the rear-guard rebel infantry took one road and the wagon train another, and the Yankees swooped down shooting and burning, capturing 3,000 rebels including General Ewell and Custis Lee. A little to the west of the route Robert Lee heard the firing, went to a rise, got off Traveller and took out his binoculars. "Are those sheep or not?" he asked.

"No, General," a captain said. "They are Yankee wagons."

Lee looked again. "You are right," he said slowly. "But what

are they doing there?" The Federal wagons followed the Federal
infantry. That meant enemy foot soldiers were right on him—
and he had received no notice from Ewell or General Richard
Anderson. He stood with General William Mahone, and his aide
Charles Venable rode up and asked if the general commanding
had received his message. He had not, and Venable had to tell
him that the wagon train at Sayler's Creek had been captured.
"Where is Anderson?" Lee asked. "Where is Ewell? It is strange
I can't hear from them." He turned to Mahone. "General, I have
no other troops. Will you take your division to Sayler's Creek?"
He rode ahead with Mahone, the shrunken division following,
and came to a high ridge overlooking the creek. He halted Traveller and straightened himself and stared down. Running up the
ridge toward him were teamsters who had lost their wagons,
soldiers who had thrown away their rifles, wrecked regiments,
a routed mob, not a military formation.

"My God!" he cried. "Has the army been dissolved?" He
went forward and seized a battle flag and, alone, on Traveller,
held it up. Some of the men kept running, but others halted and
formed with Mahone's division. The bunting blew itself around
his motionless figure. "Our cause is gone," General Ewell would
say that night to the Union officers who held him prisoner. "Lee
should surrender now, before more lives are wasted." Sheridan's
dispatch to Grant from Sayler's Creek said, "If the thing is pressed
I think Lee will surrender." ("Let the thing be pressed," Lincoln
telegraphed back when Grant sent on Sheridan's words.)

But holding his flag Lee said, "I wish to fight here."

"General Lee! Uncle Robert! Where's the man who won't
follow Uncle Robert?" his soldiers shouted back; and they fought.

The Yankees paused and then came again, columns of blue
thrusting at the disheveled Confederates struggling on. There
was no thought of burying the dead, and motionless forms marked
the line of retreat into Farmville and then beyond it, the bridges
over the creeks put to the torch so that the Federals would be
delayed. Artillery shells crashed down on the rebels as they fled,
and there were panicked shouts of "The Yankees!" as Sheridan's

raiders swooped in and out. That night John S. Wise, the eighteen-year-old son of the former governor of Virginia, came to
Lee as he stood by a campfire of burning fence rails in an open
field near Rice's Station. Young Wise had been on duty along
the railroad line over which the last train from Richmond had
passed. All had been rush and urgency and then the last train
was gone and the rumblings had stopped, to be replaced by an
unbroken silence that seemed to Wise like that of death following
violent convulsions. He kept to his post in the strange quiet until
the telegraph from the south clicked off a message from Jefferson
Davis asking that an officer find Lee and get a report on his
situation.

"General Lee?"

"Yes." One foot was on a log. His hand rested on the high
wheel of a wagon where his aide Charles Marshall sat with lantern
and lap desk taking the quiet-voiced dictation of orders. Wise
explained his mission.

"I hardly think it is necessary to prepare written dispatches
in reply," Lee said. "They may be captured. The enemy's cavalry
is already flanking us to the south and west. You seem capable
of bearing a verbal response." He told Wise to tell Davis that
the army would retire in the direction of Lynchburg.

"Have you any objective point, General—any point where
you contemplate making a stand?"

"No. No, I shall have to be governed by each day's devel-
opments. A few more Sayler's Creeks and it will all be over—
ended just as I have expected it would end from the first." The
remark amazed Wise. It showed, he thought to himself, that Lee
had knowingly sacrificed his home, his rank in the old army,
everything, to serve faithfully to the last as a duty—even when
it was against his judgment from the start.

It was past midnight. "You must be very tired, my son,"
Lee said. "You have had an exciting day. Go rest yourself and
report to me at sunrise. I may determine to send a written dispatch." Decades later, in old age, Wise still remembered how

that "my son" made him feel as if he would have gladly died for Robert E. Lee.

Behind them, to the east of the rebels sleeping the sleep of the long retreat, Ulysses Grant had walked up the steps of Farmville's Prince Edward Hotel. He wrote:

> *Headquarters, Armies of the United States*
> *April 7, 1865—5 P.M.*
>
> *General R. E. Lee*
> *Commanding C. S. Army*
> *General:*
> *The results of the last week must convince you of the hopelessness of further resistance on the part of the Army of Northern Virginia in this struggle. I feel that it is so, and regard it as my duty to shift from myself the responsibility of any further effusion of blood, by asking of you the surrender of that portion of the C. S. Army known as the Army of Northern Virginia.*
>
> *Very respectfully, your obedient servant,*
> *U. S. Grant*
> *Lieutenant General,*
> *Commanding Armies of the United States.*

Under a white flag the note began its journey to Lee's hands. Spring evening was coming on. Grant sat on the porch of the hotel and watched endless columns of his troops march by. Dark came, and the men lit torches. Carrying them, a long waving line of dancing flames, they cheered their commander sitting on the porch. A band broke into "John Brown's Body" and by the regiment and division they sang it. The night march became a grand review with a silent slouched figure on the porch as the reviewing officer. At City Point that night the Lincolns prepared to return to Washington—Secretary of State Seward had been injured in a carriage accident and the President wanted to visit him. A reception on the *River Queen* was planned. There was no invitation for Julia Grant. So she ordered her husband's dispatch boat to take her on a cruise during the hours of the Lincolns' party. She took with her the headquarters band. Alone, she sailed up the James River. When she returned, the *River Queen* was all alight and filled with guests. But there was no music there. To Mrs. Lincoln's great discomfiture Julia had taken with her the only band available. She had the dispatch boat pass the *River Queen*, make a U-turn and pass it again, and when the band leader asked if there were a particular tune she wished played, she coolly said, "Yes, play 'Now You'll Remember Me.'"

Grant's note reached Lee. He read it and silently handed it to Pete Longstreet.

"Not yet," Longstreet said.

Lee wrote back that "though not entertaining the opinion you express of the hopelessness of further resistance on the part of the Army of Northern Virginia I reciprocate your desire to avoid useless effusion of blood, and therefore before considering your proposition, ask the terms you will offer on condition of its surrender." In his mind, and in those of his officers, there arose the specter of a Roman Empire-like chaining of captives together, felons and traitors taken in shackles in the train of a triumphant conquerer and delivered by him to rows of gibbets. Grant replied that the only condition he would insist on would be that the men who laid down their arms would pledge not to take them up again. The rebels kept their westward course, the hardest lashing hardly able to raise their exhausted horses to a walk, mules falling into the mud to gasp and pant before their eyes glazed, the famished men eating wild onions, grass, last year's rotted potatoes and turnips from the fields, anything.

In the morning John S. Wise went to Lee as ordered. He had spent the night sleeping in a thicket. On his way to the commander he passed fleeing wagons, caissons and limber chests floating by without officers on a tide of disorganization. He met his father, ex-governor, now general, Henry Wise, George Meade's brother-in-law. The senior Wise had that morning washed in the red clay water of a Virginia creek and it had left streaks on his face. He looked, he told his son, like a Comanche Indian and Lee seeing him had smiled and said that he saw he had his war paint on. It seemed to father and son that panic and demoralization and abandonment of hope surrounded them. "This is the end," the ex-governor said. They found Lee on the rear portico of the house he was using as headquarters. "General Lee," the elder Wise said, "my poor, brave men are lying on yonder hill more dead than alive. For more than a week they have been fighting day and night without food, and, by God, sir, they shall not move another step until somebody gives them something to eat."

"Come in, General," Lee said soothingly. "They deserve something to eat and shall have it, and meanwhile you shall share my breakfast." Wise took to denouncing another general whose conduct he considered reprehensible and Lee put on an air of mock severity and joked, "Are you aware that you are liable to court martial and execution for insubordination and disrespect?"

"You can't afford to shoot the men who fight for cursing those who run away," Wise said. "I wish you would shoot me. If you don't, some Yankee probably will within the next twenty-four hours." Lee turned serious and asked General Wise's opinion of the situation they faced. "Situation!" Wise exploded. "There is no situation! Nothing remains, General Lee, but to put your poor men on your poor mules and send them home in time for spring ploughing. This army is hopelessly whipped and is fast becoming demoralized. These men have already endured more than I believed flesh and blood could stand, and I say to you, sir, emphatically, that to prolong the struggle is murder, and the blood of every man who is killed from this time forth is on your head, General Lee."

"Oh, General, do not talk so wildly. My burdens are heavy enough. What would the country think of me, if I did what you suggest?"

"Country be damned! There is no country. There has been no country, General, for a year or more. You are the country to these men. They have fought for you. They have shivered through a long winter for you. Without pay or clothes, or care of any sort, their devotion to and faith in you have been the only

thing which has held this army together. If you demand the
sacrifice, there are still thousands of us who will die for you.
You know the game is desperate beyond redemption, and that,
if you so announce, no man or government or people will gainsay
your decision. That is why I repeat that the blood of any man
killed hereafter is upon your head."

Lee said nothing but stood for some time at an open window
studying the crowd of men fleeing west through the roads and
fields. He turned to the younger Wise and wrote out a few words
indicating he was to make a verbal report to Jefferson Davis. He
told the older Wise to come to breakfast and turned away. The
father and son embraced, and John Wise offered his father his
horse. "What?" asked Henry Wise with a laugh. "A dispatch
bearer giving away his horse! No, sir. That is too pretty a little
animal to make a present to a Yankee. I know they will bag us
all, horse, foot and dragoons, before long. No, I can walk as well
as anybody. Have you any chewing tobacco?"

That request was the announcement, John Wise thought,
that his father now considered him a man, not a boy. He went
away through the wreckage of an army he had considered invincible. He heard a cock grouse among the laurels drumming
to its mate, and the gobbling of the wild turkey. A redbird gave
the soft wooing call of springtime. Behind was the sound of
artillery. It was all a nightmare, he thought—"In blood and flame
and torture the temples of our lives were tumbling about our
heads."

Half an hour's slow ride away the Federal columns were on
the move. A detachment under General Nelson Miles had hardly
slept for laughing. Among the wagons taken at Sayler's Creek
they found one loaded with freshly minted Confederate money,
all crisp and new and of enormous denominations. Men filled
their hats and arms with it, spread a blanket by the bivouac fire
and got going at poker. Ten thousand dollars was the usual ante.
"Be prudent, stranger; don't go beyond your means," men told
each other as they competed for pots of $1 million or more.
Shouts from the gamblers punctuated the air: "Freedom forever!"

"Rally round the flag, boys!" "We are coming, Father Abraham!" The pursued and the pursuers rushed on. Private Theodore Gerrish of the 20th Maine had never seen such marching as his unit did that day. They went 35 miles after the fleeing rebels, their artillery horses thundering and crashing along, men dropping out to collapse semiconscious among the debris the rebels had left—wagons, dead horses, canteens, knapsacks, guns—and wounded men and dead ones. The Reverend William N. Pendleton, serving as chief of artillery for the Army of Northern Virginia, went to Lee and said that he and several other high officers had agreed that the situation was hopeless and that they wanted Lee to know that they thought he ought to stop the fighting. They wanted Lee to understand, Pendleton said, that they made their opinions known to their commander in order to relieve him of having to take the full responsibility for an offer to surrender.

"I trust it has not come to that!" Lee said. "We certainly have too many brave men to think of laying down our arms." Sooner than accede to a demand by General Grant for unconditional surrender, Lee said, he would die. "Indeed, we must all determine to die at our posts." Pendleton withdrew.

Grant's letter saying he asked only that the men lay down their arms was delivered. Lee read it and inquired of Colonel Venable how he would answer it.

"I would answer no such letter," Venable replied.

"Ah, but it must be answered." He wrote: "In mine of yesterday I did not intend to propose the surrender of the Army of Northern Virginia, but to ask the terms of your proposition. To be frank, I do not think the emergency has arisen to call for the surrender of this army." He went on to say he could not surrender, but would be glad to meet Grant for a discussion of how peace could be restored. He asked for a meeting at ten the next morning along a certain road.

His note reached Grant just after midnight in the very early morning hours of April 9, Palm Sunday, via a courier who brought it to the house he was staying in, the property of a man named

Chilton. To the sound of jingling spurs and clanking saber the courier woke up the staff by calling, "Dispatches for General Grant."

Grant and Rawlins had possession of the one bed in the house, upstairs, while the other men had thrown themselves on the parlor floor. The reporter Sylvanus Cadwallader used his field glasses as a pillow in a corner where he had the least likelihood of being stepped on by those coming or going. The note went upstairs to Grant and downstairs the men heard him discussing it with Rawlins. "He did not propose to surrender!" Rawlins said angrily. "He did propose, in his heart, to surrender. Now he wants to arrange for peace, something beyond and above the surrender of his army. No, sir. No, sir. He don't think the emergency has arisen! That's cool, but another falsehood. That emergency has been staring him in the face for forty-eight hours. If he hasn't seen it yet, we will soon bring it to his comprehension! He has to surrender. He shall surrender. By the eternal, it shall be surrender, and nothing else!"

Grant's voice, the men below heard, was soft and persuasive. "Some allowance must be made for the trying position in which General Lee is placed," he said. "He is compelled to defer somewhat to the wishes of his government and his military associates. But it all means precisely the same thing. If I meet Lee, he will surrender before I leave." Rawlins reminded him that President Lincoln had specifically said Grant could meet with Lee only on minor matters or to accept his surrender. Nothing else would do. Grant wrote, "As I have no authority to treat on the subject of peace the meeting proposed for 10 A.M. today could lead to no good. I will state, however, General, that I am equally anxious for peace with yourself, and the whole North entertain the same feeling. By the South laying down their arms they will hasten that most desirable event."

At that moment Lee lay sleeping in the open. "I will strike that man a blow in the morning," he had said that evening to Longstreet in the loudest tones Major A.R.H. Ranson had ever heard him use. Longstreet had earlier rejected a plea that he tell the general commanding that it was time to quit, saying that if Lee didn't know when to surrender without being told, then he would never know. Now Longstreet spoke realistically of the strength and condition of the army but said it was, of course, up to Lee. The commander's voice was almost fierce, Ranson remembered, as he answered. "I tell you, General Longstreet, I will strike that man a blow in the morning!"

Sleeping near Lee was his aide Charles Marshall, using his saddle for a pillow, his coat over his face. The sound of passing troops awakened Marshall, and it came into his mind that they were Yankees, for there was no front and no rear now, only burning campfires off in the distance on all sides. Then a voice sang out, "The race is not to them that's got, The longest legs to run, Nor the battle to that people, That shoots the biggest gun!" John Gordon's men were moving to attack Yankees across the last direction of Confederate retreat. Lee and his staff arose. If the blocking forces were only cavalry, they could be pushed aside. If there was infantry behind the cavalry, the problem would be different. Quite different. They made their toilette, Marshall remembered, by putting on their caps. Breakfast consisted of a little cornmeal mixed in a can normally used to hold hot water for shaving. The commanding general refused even that. Off to the south the Union infantry rushed through the darkness, heading toward the position of their blocking cavalry, the marching men assured that rations would be handed out at nine.

At the Chilton house Colonel Horace Porter got up at four and looked into Grant's room. The general was not there. Porter found him walking up and down in the yard, both hands holding his head. He had a frightful headache, he told Porter. He had bathed his feet in hot water and mustard and applied mustard plasters to his wrists and the back of his neck, but it hadn't helped. Porter said he had never known the general to feel ill but that good news had followed. He was really superstitious about it, Porter said. Grant smiled and said, "The best thing that could happen to me today would be to get rid of the pain."

The other men came down and they went off to Meade's nearby headquarters, took breakfast with him and then set out to join Sheridan at the head of the Union advance away to the west. Grant was urged to travel in an ambulance, but he had Cincinnati saddled and, head throbbing, pounded along over fields, farms, hills, through muddy streams. At eleven o'clock they stopped to rest by some burning logs from which they lighted their cigars. They heard a man shouting from where they had come, and turned to see Lieutenant Charles Pease of Meade's staff on a coal-black stallion white with foam. Pease was waving his hat. He jumped off his mount, saluted, and handed over a sealed envelope.

Earlier, John Gordon's rebel infantry at the farthest point of the fleeing army pushed at the Yankee cavalry blocking the way. The blue horsemen fell back. It was around nine in the morning. True to the promise that rations would be given out at that hour, the hurrying Union infantry had been halted a short ways to the east and told to fall out for breakfast. Private Theodore Gerrish, like all the men, was famished after marching all night. With the others he stacked his rifle and then rushed off to find something with which to make a fire for coffee. He grabbed a fence rail and dragged it to where his friends were, just in time to hear the bugle sound the call to get back in ranks. There would be rations later. Everyone laughed at Gerrish's wooden burden, and people suggested that he carry it along on the march. Up ahead they heard heavy firing. It was Gordon pushing at the Union cavalry. The blue infantry was put into doubletime march and panting and sweating they went through woods and out into a field and up a ridge where there was a house and barn and outbuildings. Sheridan and Charles Griffin, the dismissed Gouverneur Warren's replacement, were sitting their horses and talking excitedly, Sheridan pounding his right fist on the palm of his left hand.

The upcoming Federal infantry formed in two lines. Their cavalry, which had been struggling against Gordon's push, was falling back. The rebels were over the hill. They heard the rebel artillery fire, and a shell crashed into the barn on the ridge. It burst into flames. A swarm of chickens came pouring out and officers screamed at the men to keep in ranks, but nothing could hold them and there was a wild chase of men choking with laughter as they scrambled after the future dinners. Then as the cavalry retired, they went forward and the laughter died away. Three quarters of a mile away was another ridge at the foot of which was the Confederate skirmish line. The rifle pits were clearly visible. Private Gerrish thought of his friends who had fallen out of the march back at the brief stop where he'd found his fence rail. They were probably sleeping back there in the woods. He himself had gone on because of the promise that soon rations would be handed out.

The rebel infantry had not opened, but their artillery was firing rapidly. It did seem hard, Gerrish thought, to serve three years, to see his regiment reduced to 100 men, and now to be put into this scrape for the hope of rations. He pulled his hat down and went forward into what seemed to him to be the gates of death. Up behind the rebel lines a white object appeared. A signal flag for the rebel infantry to open, someone said. They waited for the rebel line to be mantled in fire and smoke, but nothing happened. Then they saw that the white object was changing position—it was advancing. It came at them, three men carrying it, a white flag.

Like a curtain in a theater, the Confederates had thought, the Yankee cavalry had drawn back to reveal what was behind them: Private Gerrish and the others, increasing in number every minute. Yankee infantry. "Tell General Lee," Gordon had said, "I have fought my corps to a frazzle and I fear I can do nothing unless I am heavily supported by Longstreet's corps." But Longstreet's corps was holding off thousands of Federals in the rear. The Army of Northern Virginia was caught, surrounded, enclosed. Lee heard Gordon's message without a word. Four years less three days had elapsed since the first shells screamed down on Fort Sumter.

He spoke as to himself. "There is nothing left me to do but to go and see General Grant, and I would rather die a thousand deaths."

He ordered a flag of truce, the one that Private Gerrish saw, sent forward.

General Rawlins took the sealed envelope from Lieutenant Pease and, standing by the smoldering logs, opened one end slowly, took out the enclosed note, read it deliberately to himself and handed it to Grant. Nobody said anything. Rawlins' lips compressed. He was very pale. Grant read the message mechanically, handed it back to Rawlins and said in his usual voice, "You had better read it aloud."

There was no more expression in his countenance, Sylvanus Cadwallader thought, then in last year's bird's nest.

Rawlins took a deep breath and in a sepulchral voice, a little tremulous, read, "I received your note of this morning with reference to the surrender of this army. I now request an interview in accordance with that purpose.'"

There was a blank silence for a moment. No one looked at anyone else. Then Colonel William Duff of the artillery jumped on a log, waved his hat and proposed three cheers. A feeble hurrah came from a few throats and ended brokenly as men began to cry. Again there was silence. "How will that do, Rawlins?" Grant asked. His headache had vanished the moment he read Lee's note. "I think *that* will do," Rawlins said.

"Oh, General, what will history say of the surrender of the army in the field?"

"Yes, I know they will say hard things of us. They will not understand how we were overwhelmed by numbers. But that is not the question, Colonel. The question is, Is it right to surrender this army? If it is right, then I will take all the responsibility."

All along the lines stretching back from the west to the east of the long retreat, white flags were turning out as word spread that the two commanders would be meeting. Yet shots sounded here and there. "How easily I could be rid of this, and be at rest!" Lee said. "I have only to ride along the line and all will be over!" He stopped and took hold of himself. "But it is our duty to live." There is a true glory and a true honor; the glory of duty done, the honor of the integrity of principle.

He lay on fence rails covered with blankets under an apple tree, wearing a new uniform with embroidered belt and new gauntlets, high boots with red silk stitchings on their tops and gold spurs at the heels, a sash and a gilded presentation sword whose hilt was formed in the head of a lion. "I have probably to be Grant's prisoner, and I thought I must make my best appearance," he said to General Pendleton. The firing had died and to the Confederate officer John Esten Cooke the calm that followed had something of a magical quiet about it, a mysterious quality of great silence. All along the heights appeared noiseless dark blue columns, a great host that looked below on white flags. A little after midday a Confederate staff officer came riding to the fence rails under the apple tree. By his side was a Union colonel. "General Lee," said the rebel officer, "allow me to introduce you to Colonel Babcock."

Grant's aide Orville E. Babcock saluted. He was engaged to the Galena girl who, under Sam Grant's instructions, made the flag that the Jo Daviess County Guards had carried off to the war, so long ago. Robert E. Lee stood up. Never, thought at least two men who saw him at that moment, had he looked grander. He bowed. Gentle-eyed and kindly voiced, Babcock handed over a letter from his chief. Lee fumbled in his pocket to find a pencil with which to endorse receipt as to day, hour and minute, failed to find it and accepted one from a member of his staff. When he finished with it, he mechanically handed the pencil back over his shoulder to the officer who had furnished it, but Babcock reached out and took it to bear away and parade as, he said, his only valuable trophy of the war. Under the apple tree Lee read Grant's acceptance of his offer to meet to arrange the surrender. "Notice sent on this road where you wish the interview to take place will meet me."

He ordered Traveller saddled and asked Walter Taylor to go with him on this last mission. Taylor begged off, and so Lee asked Charles Marshall, who, ragged and disheveled, borrowed a clean collar and a respectable sword to wear, and some decent gloves. They set out with Babcock and Sergeant George Tucker, the dead A. P. Hill's orderly still riding Hill's horse. Tucker waved a white handkerchief as they rode along, a sign that the truce was still in effect. Through silent lines of men they went up a hill. Traveller drank at a stream. They went on, word flying to Grant that they would meet in the little hamlet of Appomattox Courthouse, two dozen houses, two dirt streets. It was Palm Sunday afternoon, April 9, 1865.

Some rebels broke into cheers as they passed; Lee waved his hand to silence them in fear that any excitement might bring a shattering of the truce. They came to the outskirts of the town, a little county courthouse, the tavern, a jail. In front of them was a Yankee skirmish line. They halted and waited there. Marshall and Tucker detached themselves and went on to find a suitable place where the two commanders could meet.

The first townsman Marshall saw was named Wilmer McLean. Four years before he had owned a house located in peaceful countryside which became the site of the first battle of the war, Bull Run. Cannon shots had crashed through his house. He sold out and went to a remote backwater where, he thought, he and his family would be safe from the fighting. Marshall asked him for a place where General Lee could meet General Grant. McLean led him to a dilapidated house with no furniture. That wouldn't do, Marshall said. "Maybe my house will do," McLean said. Marshall saw a substantial dwelling with a well-furnished front parlor just to the left of the entrance door. He sent Tucker back to tell Lee. With Babcock by his side, Lee started forward. Seated in the village, the Union general Joshua L. Chamberlain seemed to feel a strange sense of some presence invisible but powerful, something, he thought, like those unearthly visitations told of in ancient legends. He turned and saw coming at him a man in whose face deep depression was overmastered by deeper strength. It was Robert E. Lee, riding, General Chamberlain thought, in splendor and sadness. Awe competed with admiration in Chamberlain. He sat immobile.

Lee, Marshall and Babcock dismounted and went up the stairs onto McLean's porch and into his front parlor. Little Lulu McLean had been playing there. Her cotton and straw doll sat on a chair. The men took seats. Outside, the street filled up with Union officers. Through their number, half an hour later, came Ulysses S. Grant. He was riding with one hand in his pocket. "He seemed greater than ever I had seen him—a look as of another world about him," Chamberlain remembered. He did not salute the commanding officer. "Anything like that would have been too little."

"How are you, Sheridan?" Grant asked his cavalry leader.

"First-rate, thank you; how are you?"

"Is Lee over there?"

"Yes, he is in that brick house, waiting to surrender to you."

"Well, then, we'll go over." He had ridden more than 35 miles that day over Virginia's muddy springtime roads. He wore the uniform of a private with lieutenant general's stars sewn on. The straps were dingy, Sheridan noticed.

Grant got off Cincinnati, who went to munching the spring grass by Traveller's side, and mounted the steps of the McLean house, alone, dirty, no sword, no sash, one coat button buttoned in the wrong hole. Mexico came into his mind, he told people later, Mexico and a colonel telling him that General Scott wanted officers to come to headquarters in full uniform. Embarrassment and a strange depression seized him, embarrassment that that colonel might now, almost twenty years later, think he had come covered with mud and in a private's crude clothing to rub salt into a wound, depression because of the mission he was on, to demand surrender of a man who had fought so long and hard, so nobly.

"General Lee."

"General Grant."

"I met you once before, General Lee, while we were serving in Mexico, when you came over from Scott's headquarters to visit Garland's brigade, to which I then belonged. I have always remembered your appearance, and I think I should have recognized you anywhere."

"Yes, I know I met you on that occasion, and I have often thought of it, and tried to recollect how you looked, but I have never been able to recall a single feature."

They began talking about Mexico and then the weather in Virginia. Marshall and Babcock listened silently until Grant signaled his aide and told him to invite in the other gentlemen. Babcock stepped out on the porch, waved his hat and called, "The general says come in." Some one dozen Union officers filed in, acting in the fashion of persons entering a sickroom where someone lies dangerously ill. Seated at small tables some 10 feet apart, Lee and Grant chatted while the other men listened. The talk went on aimlessly for a few minutes, and then Lee said, "I suppose, General Grant, that the object of our present meeting is fully understood. I asked to see you to ascertain upon what terms you would receive the surrender of my army."

It must have been a relief for Grant to have Lee bring up the subject. He had been reluctant, his officers saw, to mention it himself. His deference to Lee had been so marked that one officer whispered to another, "Who's surrendering here, anyhow?" Now the matter was on the table. "The terms I propose," he said, "are those stated substantially in my letter of yesterday—that is, the officers and men surrendered to be paroled and disqualified from taking up arms again until properly exchanged, and all arms, ammunition and supplies to be delivered up as captured property."

"Those are about the conditions I expected would be proposed," Lee said. There would be no triumphal march with prisoners in tow, no hangings. "I would suggest that you commit to writing the terms you have proposed, so that they may be formally acted upon."

"Very well, I will write them out." Grant took an order book and started writing in pencil. In the midst of his work he paused and looked at Lee's elegant saber hanging from a gold-braid sword belt. When he was finished he rose, crossed the room to Lee and handed him the draft, a younger man performing a duty rather than waiting for the older one to do it. It struck the watching Federal officers how deliberate and slow Lee's actions were as he placed the order book on the table in front of him, pushed away two candle holders, took out a handkerchief, wiped a pair of glasses, put them on his nose carefully, crossed his legs and began to read. The room was entirely quiet. "After the words 'until properly' the word 'exchanged' seems to be omitted," Lee said. "You doubtless intended to use that word."

"Why, yes, I thought I had put in the word."

"I presumed it had been omitted inadvertently, and with your permission I will mark where it should be inserted." He felt for a pencil, as he had once before that day, and again found none. Horace Porter handed him one, and he put in a caret. When he had finished with the pencil he began twirling it in his fingers and occasionally tapping the table with it. He came to Grant's final sentences: "The arms, artillery and private property to be parked and stacked and turned over to the officers appointed by me to receive them. This will not embrace the side arms of the officers. This done, each officer and man will be allowed to return to their homes not to be disturbed by United States authority so long as they observe their paroles and the laws in force where they may reside."

He looked up at Grant. "This will have a very happy effect on my army," he said. The elegant sword would not have to be handed over in days-of-chivalry display.

"Unless you have some suggestions to make in regard to the form in which I have stated the terms, I will have a copy of the letter made and sign it."

There was a long pause. "There is one thing I should like to mention," Lee said at last. "The cavalrymen and artillerists own their own horses in our army. Its organization in this respect differs from that of the United States." All present noted the expression. "I should like to understand whether these men will be permitted to retain their horses."

"You will find that the terms as written do not allow this. Only the officers are allowed to take their private property."

Lee read over the two pages of the note. "No, I see the terms do not allow it; that is clear."

"Well, the subject is quite new to me," Grant said. "Of course I did not know that any private soldiers owned their animals; but I think we have fought the last battle of the war— I sincerely hope so—and that the surrender of this army will be followed soon by that of all the others; and I take it that most of the men in the ranks are small farmers, and as the country has been so raided by the two armies, it is doubtful whether they will be able to put in a crop to carry themselves and their families through the next winter without the aid of the horses they are now riding, and I will arrange it this way: I will not change the terms as now written, but I will instruct the officers I shall appoint to receive the paroles to let all the men who claim to own a horse or mule take the animals home with them to work their little farms."

"This will have the best possible effect upon the men. It will be very gratifying and will do much toward conciliating our people."

The letter was given over for copying to Colonel Theodore Bowers. He began it, made a mistake, began again, made another mistake. Meanwhile Grant asked leave to introduce the officers in the room. Lee shook the hands of those men who extended them. He bowed to the others. He did not say a single word.

General Seth Williams came up. He had been Lee's adjutant at West Point and very close to him. They exchanged a few sentences and Williams essayed a mild joke about something in the past. There was no response beyond Lee's silent nod to acknowledge the reference.

Colonel Ely Parker, the Indian, was presented, and it seemed to the viewers that a look of surprise came into Lee's face. They surmised that he took Parker for a Negro. At a table Bowers was finding himself too nervous to perform the work Grant had put him to. "Parker," he said, "you will have to write this, I can't do it." Long ago, four months before his birth at the Tonawanda reservation near Buffalo, Parker's mother had had a strange dream. She had gone to the council house and consulted there the dream interpreter. He told her that a son would be born to her who would become a warrior for the white man and that one day he would be distinguished among his nation as a peacemaker. Parker picked up the table Bowers had tried to work at, carried it to a corner of the room, borrowed a pen and a boxwood inkstand that Lee's aide Charles Marshall always carried and went to copying the words that would bring peace.

"I have a thousand or more of your men as prisoners, General Grant," Lee said. "I shall be glad to send them into your lines as soon as it can be arranged, for I have no provisions for them. I have, indeed, nothing for my own men. They have been living for the last few days principally upon parched corn." He added that he had ordered rations sent to him from Lynchburg and that when they arrived he would be able to feed his men. There was a stir among the Union officers and they all looked at Sheridan, for the previous night he had captured the trains that bore those provisions. "Sheridan," Grant asked, "how many rations have you?"

"How many do you want?"

"How many can you send?"

"Twenty-five thousand."

That the rations were originally Lee's was not mentioned. "Suppose that I send over twenty-five thousand rations," Grant asked, "do you think that will be a sufficient supply?"

"I think it will be ample. And it will be a great relief, I assure you."

Parker finished and gave the copied document to Grant, who signed it. Parker sealed it. Lee told Marshall how to reply. Marshall did an acceptance draft and his chief made one correction. "Don't say, 'I have the honor to acknowledge the receipt of your letter'; he is here. Just say, 'I accept these terms.'" Marshall wrote:

> *Headquarters, Army of Northern Virginia*
> *April 9, 1865*
> *Lieut-Gen U. S. Grant,*
> *Commanding Armies of the United States*
> *General:*
> *I have received your letter of this date containing the terms of surrender of the Army of Northern Virginia as proposed by you. As they are substantially the same as those expressed in your letter of the 8th instant, they are accepted. I will proceed to designate the proper officers to carry the stipulations into effect.*
> *Very respectfully, your obedient servant.*

Lee signed, Marshall sealed the envelope and handed it to Parker, who handed him Grant's letter in return. It was over. "I started out from my camp several days ago without my sword," Grant said, "and I have not seen my headquarters baggage since." He was still worried that Lee might think his sloppy dress implied an insult. "I have generally worn a sword as little as possible," Grant went on. "I was about four miles from the wagons where my arms and uniforms were, and I thought you would rather receive me as I was, than be detained."

"I'm much obliged to you. I'm very glad you did it in that way."

It was getting on to four o'clock. Lee stood up, shook hands with Grant, bowed to the other men. He went through the door carrying his hat and gloves. Some Federal officers sitting on the porch sprang up and saluted. He mechanically returned the honor. His brow, thought General George Forsythe, was remarkably clear and white where it had been shielded by his hat from the weather. He gazed out over the yard, past the village and to the little valley where his army was. He drew on his gloves slowly and then absently banged his fists together several times. There is a true glory. He seemed completely oblivious to his surroundings. Traveller and Sergeant Tucker were out of sight. He roused himself, and in a voice Forsythe thought choked and hoarse, cried, "Orderly! Orderly!" And a true honor. "Here, General, here!" Tucker cried from around the corner. He tried to put the bit into Traveller's mouth. The horse pushed down for a few more bites of grass. Tucker worked on buckling the throatlatch. The glory of duty done. Lee took Traveller's forelock from under the browband, arranged and smoothed it. Inside, the Union officers were shaking hands with one another. "This will live in history," Lieutenant Colonel Adam Badeau said to Grant. There was no reply. "I am sure that the idea had not occurred to him until I uttered it," Badeau wrote. "The effect upon his fame, upon history, was not what he was considering."

Tucker stepped aside and Lee mounted. A long sigh came from him. "Almost a groan in its intensity," Forsythe wrote. Marshall came down the steps and got on his horse. Behind him was Ulysses Grant, followed by the other Union officers.

Grant stopped and took off his hat. His men followed his example.

Lee looked at them, raised his hat in silence, turned Traveller and rode to his men. The honor of the integrity of principle.

Wilmer McLean rushed about his room fending off the rampaging Yankee officers thrusting bills at him for his furniture. He flung their money on the floor, but they seized souvenirs anyway. Cane-bottom chairs were ruthlessly cut to pieces, haircloth upholstery was sliced from chairs and sofas and into patches and strips for carrying away. Sheridan forced two $10 gold pieces on McLean. (He had carried them through the war thinking they might come in handy if he were ever taken prisoner.) He took the table Grant had used for writing his draft, handed it to Custer and told him to give it to Mrs. Custer. Custer jumped on his horse, balanced the table on his head and raced away.* General Ord paid $40 for the table where Lee had sat.† Lulu McLean's doll was tossed back and forth over the heads of the men until Lieutenant Colonel Thomas Moore of Meade's staff caught it and took it home for his own children.

Lee rode back to what had been his army. A cheer from the troops along the road greeted him, but it died off very suddenly when they saw his face. The road was packed with men. His eyes were on a line between Traveller's ears. More men came running, hats off, to pack themselves about him as he slowly made his way. They came cheering, but their shouts died in their throats. He tried to go on but the press of bodies halted the horse.

"General, are we surrendered?" a man asked. Lee took off his hat.

"Men," he said, "we have fought the war together, and I have done the best I could for you." His voice was ragged. "You will all be paroled and go to your homes." Tears came into his eyes. His lips moved and formed a soundless broken attempt at "Good-bye."

He pressed Traveller through them, they weeping and touching the horse, and his boots. A confused mass of men sobbing, some babbling and cursing, surrounded the single horse and rider slowly moving toward the apple tree where, three hours before, Colonel Babcock had found him, commander then of what had been but was no more the Army of Northern Virginia.

Grant rode away to where his camp would be that night. Someone remarked that perhaps he ought to inform Washington of the day's event, and he dismounted and sat down on a large stone by the road and wrote out a telegram. *General Lee surrendered*

---

*The table is now in the Smithsonian Institution.
†Now in the Chicago Historical Society.

the Army of Northern Virginia this afternoon on terms proposed by myself. The accompanying additional correspondence will show the conditions fully. U. S. Grant, Lieutenant General. He heard the sound of gun salutes from his lines. "Stop the firing," he said. "The rebels are our countrymen again." He got to the camp and sat in front of his tent despite a slight shower coming down. Bands played. "Ingalls," he said, "do you remember that old white mule—" and he talked about someone's mount back in Mexico.

He paced back and forth under his apple tree. Rage seized him. There was a savage look on his face. He walked, turned, walked. To Captain W. W. Blackford he looked the very image of a caged lion. For the rest of the day he stalked up and down. The men of his staff knew better than to approach him, and a picket line was put in place to keep back any well-wishers of what had been his army. But it was hard to turn away Federal officers, old friends or men simply curious. They came generally in groups of four or five to be received by Walter Taylor and escorted into Lee's presence. It was amusing, Captain Blackford thought, to see the deference with which the former enemy treated the defeated leader. When Lee would see Taylor coming with a new group he would halt his pacing, stand at attention and glare at the visitors. "They would remove their hats entirely and stand bareheaded during the interview while General Lee gave a scant touch to his hat in return and sometimes did not even do that." He shook hands with none of the men.

When evening approached, he mounted Traveller and headed for his tent, a mile in the rear. By then word of the surrender had reached every Southerner at Appomattox, and thousands of them lined the way. He went through two solid walls of men cheering and sobbing at the same time. "Good-bye, General, God bless you," he heard over and over. Men kissed Traveller. Hat in hand, tears running down his face, he said farewell over and over again and in broken phrases told his veterans to go home, plant a crop and obey the law. Victorious generals are always cheered by their men, but history knew no such precedent for a commander defeated. Through their masses he made his way in the rain to his tent and dismounted and went in, alone.

In the morning, by prearrangement, they met again. Surrounded by Yankee officers they sat their horses, Traveller and Cincinnati, just outside the village. Grant had been halted by Southern pickets as he rode to the rendezvous—force of habit keeping him out of Lee's lines, thought Horace Porter—and when Lee was informed he put Traveller into a gallop to join his former opposite number. They talked for nearly an hour in a drizzling rain, Grant suggesting that Lee meet with Lincoln. "I want you to meet him. Whatever you and he agree on will be satisfactory to the reasonable people of the North and South. If you and Mr. Lincoln will agree on terms, your influence in the South will make the Southern people accept what you accept, and Mr. Lincoln's influence in the North will make reasonable people accept what he accepts."

"General Grant, you know that I am a soldier of the Confederate Army, and I cannot meet Mr. Lincoln. I do not know what Mr. Davis is going to do, and I cannot undertake to make any terms." They saluted each other and Grant rode back to his tent to pack up and make for City Point. Lee returned to his tent to work with Charles Marshall on a last message to his men. As he rode he met a Union officer who took off his cap and offered a cheery good morning. Lee did not recognize him at once and the officer said, "Don't you know me? I'm George Meade."

"Oh, is that you, Meade? But what are you doing with all that gray in your beard?"

"You have to answer for most of it!"

Old friends from long ago, they rode along together. It seemed to Theodore Lyman of Meade's staff that Lee was entirely overwhelmed by his fate, but determined to keep up his pride to the last. At times, it seemed to Lyman, his mind wandered. They passed some rebel veterans who raised a cheer. Meade's color bearer unfurled his flag, and a Southern voice yelled, "Damn your old rag! We are cheering General Lee!"

After lunch he worked with Marshall on his final words to the men.

After four years of arduous service marked by unsurpassed courage and fortitude, the Army of Northern Virginia has been compelled to yield to overwhelming numbers and resources.

I need not tell the brave survivors of so many hard fought battles who have remained steadfast to the last that I have consented to this result from no distrust of them: but feeling that valor and devotion could accomplish nothing that could compensate for the loss that must have attended the continuance of the contest, I determined to avoid the useless sacrifice of those whose past services have endeared them to their country-men.

By the terms of the agreement, officers and men can return to their homes and remain until exchanged. You will take with you the satisfaction that proceeds from a consciousness of duty faithfully performed; and I earnestly pray that a Merciful God will extend to you His blessings and protection.

With an unceasing admiration of your constancy and devotion to your Country, and a grateful remembrance of your kind and generous consideration for myself, I bid you all an affectionate farewell.

R. E. Lee
Genl.

Grant went to City Point, his train going off the tracks several times. He had telegraphed Julia he would arrive in time for dinner and she had it prepared in the dispatch boat galley. Then dressed to the nines, she sat with Mrs. Rawlins* and the wife of General Michael Morgan and waited. The men did not come and the ladies killed time by playing the piano in the boat's salon and singing. Then one would play while the others waltzed. A telegram arrived saying the general's party was delayed. At four in the morning Julia lay down in her berth fully dressed,

*His second wife, a woman he had met at Vicksburg.

to awaken in broad daylight with her husband standing over her. Last night's dinner was eaten as breakfast and when it was over, Julia asked if he would be going to that Richmond whose possession had been fought over for four years, Grant said, "I would not distress these people. They are feeling their defeat bitterly, and you would not add to it by my witnessing their despair, would you?"

Instead they went to Washington. The city was wildly celebrating the great victory, the buildings illuminated, bands playing, and, across the Potomac, 1,000 freed slaves gathering together on the grounds of what had been Robert E. Lee's estate to sing "The Year of Jubilee." Rockets shot off into the air from the lawn in front of Arlington House. "U.S. Army, U.S. Navy, U.S. Grant," read signs in the city, "Glory to God Who to US GRANTED the victory." Grant sat in at a Cabinet meeting and the President asked if anything had been heard from Sherman in North Carolina, where it was expected that following Lee's example Joe Johnston would shortly surrender his forces. Grant replied he was hourly expecting news, and Lincoln said he had reason to believe it likely. There was a dream he had had several times, the President explained; it preceded every great and important event of the war, Fort Sumter, Bull Run, Antietam, Gettysburg, Vicksburg and other battles. He seemed in his dream to be in some singular, indescribable vessel that was moving rapidly toward an indefinite shore. "I had," Lincoln said, "this strange dream again last night, and we shall, judging from the past, have great news shortly." The men chatted about what the President had said, one saying it was merely a coincidence that great events followed the President's dream, another saying that at the times when the dream came to Lincoln there were possibilities of great change or disaster and that the President's feeling of uncertainty might have led to the dim vision in sleep. "Perhaps," said Lincoln, "perhaps that is the explanation."

After the meeting he asked Grant if the general and his wife would join the President and First Lady in a visit to the theater that night. Grant tentatively accepted, and the afternoon papers reported that Lieutenant General and Mrs. Grant would be joining the Lincolns, but Julia Grant told her husband she would not spend an evening in the company of the woman whose maniac behavior had been so upsetting back at City Point when she had raved about Mrs. Griffin and insulted Mrs. Ord. The President would have to be told that the Grants were going off to visit their children, all of whom were in school in New Jersey. Grant complied with her wish. Ever after he wondered what would have happened had he been in Ford's Theater that evening.

The following morning, April 15, word spread in Richmond that General Lee was coming home. He had stayed in Appomattox until the last parole was made out for the last Confederate, and the last flag surrendered and the last musket stacked for the conquerer to take home. General John B. Gordon commanded the Southerners at the final ceremonies. The big guns were towed to a designated spot and then, between a double line of Federal infantry, Gordon came at the head of an endless line of marching men. There were no trumpet calls nor roll of drums. Joshua Chamberlain commanded the Union forces, two blue walls at shoulder arms. He ordered the rifles shifted to carry arms: a last salute. Gordon's head had been drooping, but he lifted his eyes and lowered his sword in salute and ordered his own men to the carry arms: honor answering honor. Then the muskets were stacked and the flags laid down. It went on for six hours, 20,000 men, some weeping, some kissing the old banners. Now and then a word passed between those who had so recently been combatants, but never an unpleasant word. "Well, old fellows, we have met again," a Southern soldier said to the members of the 20th Maine, a unit directly opposed on many a field. As he marched to the last moment of his career as a soldier, Robert Bingham of North Carolina thought back to how once the Yankees had overrun his unit's position. They had cheered then, the Yankees. If they cheered now, Bingham thought, he didn't see how he could stand it. He began to cry as he marched. Others wept also. He looked at the Union soldiers. Tears were coming down their faces.

It was over. Six hundred and twenty thousand men were dead, more than a quarter million Southern, more than 350,000 Northern.* Robert E. Lee went home, on Traveller, followed by his old headquarters wagon and an ambulance carrying an ill member of his staff. A detachment of Union cavalry escorted him for about a mile from his camp on the road to Richmond and then turned back. He went on, declining to stay in private homes along the way, but pitching his tent as he had during the war. He took breakfast with one family and played with the ten-year-old daughter of the house, who kept all her life the memory of a white-haired and white-bearded man saying, "Polly, come with me to Richmond and I will get you a beau."

In some fashion news of his last journey in uniform ran ahead of him. When he got to Manchester, on the western side of the James, a great throng was waiting along the route he would have to take from the Richmond end of the pontoon bridge set up to replace the one burned on the night his army left what had then been the Confederate capital. It was by some strange intuition that the city knew of his coming, wrote T. C. deLeon, who had spent the war there. The people were silent, with hats off. "There was no excitement, no hurrahing; but, as the great chief passed, a deep, loving murmur, greater than these, arose from the very hearts of the crowd. Taking off his hat and simply bowing his head, the man great in adversity passed silently to his own door; it closed upon him, and his people had seen him for the last time in his battle harness."

---

*Losses which on a percentage scale in the America of today would mean some 5 million dead.

17

Afterwards

THROUGH RECEPTIONS, balls, dinners, crowds, moved the Lieutenant General Commanding the Armies of the United States.
Abraham Lincoln who had saved the Union was dead, but the
great soldier who had been his right arm lived to receive the
thanks of the nation. A group of Philadelphians in the first month
of peace tendered a splendid house equipped with everything
down to the linen, with larder and coal bin filled and fine silver
on the dining-room table. (There was also a well-stocked wine
cellar, the immediate sale of which was recommended to Julia
by John Rawlins.) The merchants of New York City presented
a purse of $100,000.

In June, two months after the surrender, Grant went to
West Point, which he had never seen since leaving it, to attend
the graduation ceremonies and also to go to the nearby residence
of Winfield Scott and be greeted as "from the oldest general to

the greatest general." To his former Academy instructors he appeared shy and deferential.

He went to Boston. A magnificent collection of leather-bound and gilt-paged books was presented, the works of every author of note included. (The man assigned to plumb the depths of the general's existing library so as to avoid duplications found to his astonishment that Grant did not have a single book dealing with military matters.) Serenaders came to his hotels, crowds lined the streets of his movements. He traveled in the private railway car of William Henry Vanderbilt. Honorary degrees were presented. "See that hand," shouted Governor Yates of Illinois to a great Chicago throng, "that very hand signed the commission of Ulysses S. Grant as a colonel, and it was the best day's work it ever did!" He returned to the Galena he had left in the wake of the Jo Daviess County Guards. Thousands of people were in the streets to see him pass under triumphant arches of bowers and greenery and a great sign referring to what he had once said he would do if he were mayor of the town: GENERAL, THE SIDEWALK IS BUILT. Frock-coated and in tall black hats, a committee of citizens presented a house with plush furniture, heavy chairs, gilt clock, ornate Bible on marble-topped table. He went to his parents' place near Cincinnati and Hannah Grant in her apron said, "Well, Ulysses, you've become a great man, haven't you?" and went back to her household tasks. (Once, and only once, did she appear at a public rally in her capacity as mother of the country's savior; "Since then she can't be got out to any public place," her husband explained. "She says she don't want to make a show of herself.")

A total of fourteen horses were presented to the general. For all gifts he murmured thanks, reiterating a hundred times that he would not make a speech. (In Detroit as they stood on a hotel balcony looking out over flowers, flags, bunting, waving men and women, his little son Jesse said, "Papa, the people want you to make a speech. Do try." "No, I will not," Grant answered. "I will make you a speech," the boy cried as the crowd cheered, and called out, ' "The boy stood on the burning deck—' "). He consulted with the great financier of the war, Jay Cooke, on the proper investments for his new money, and took possession of yet another home, this one at 205 "I" Street N.W. in Washington. With it came $75,000 from people canvassed for contributions by General Daniel Butterfield, they uniformly being rich men who had done well, and better than well, in the war. In fact, Grant was constantly in the company of rich men. He seemed to like them, and of course they were a novelty in his life. Often in civilian clothing but surrounded by a glittering staff of officers whose association with him had raised them all to high rank— General Fred Dent, General Horace Porter, General Ely Parker, General Orville Babcock, General Adam Badeau, General Rufus Ingalls—he stayed in mansions and journeyed on yachts. He himself, the year after the war, became the first full four-star general the American army had ever known. He ranked George Washington.

With politicians he had as little truck as possible. The long struggle between President Andrew Johnson and the Radical Republicans had begun. The only Southern senator who had stayed with the North, Johnson of Tennessee had reviled the Confederates for years. Those who met him during the war came away with no impression of him save for his burning hatred of the men who made the rebellion, particularly the aristocrats who had led them. "One would have thought that if this man ever came into power," wrote the officer-politician Carl Schurz, "the face of the country would soon bristle with gibbets, and foreign lands swarm with fugitives from the avenging sword." But within two months after succeeding Lincoln, Johnson turned what the Radicals thought was an entire somersault. He began issuing pardons to ex-rebels wholesale, by the thousands.

Perhaps responsibility sobered Johnson. Perhaps, as the Radicals trumpeted to the world, this poor white mudsill had been seduced by the Southern highborns who once spurned him but who now came asking for pardon and office—including Pete Longstreet. That such a man even *dared* walk into the White House was outrageous, the Radicals said. The guns had hardly cooled before Johnson was allowing the former Confederate states to elect senators and representatives who, in full armed rebellion against the United States government at the last sitting of Congress, expected to be honored members of the next. In such a situation the Radicals looked for support against "His Accidency" Johnson. They did not get it from the country's four-star general. "As quick as I'd talk politics, he'd talk horses," said Senator Benjamin Wade of Ohio. "Well, in these times a man may be all right on horses and all wrong on politics." No one knew where the general stood on the all-consuming question of how the South should be treated, on the question of Negro suffrage, on anything. "General Grant, the man who dwells behind a mask," the Washington correspondent Emily Edson Briggs defined him. Ready to speak openly with old friends, although remarkably free from using the word "I" when speaking of the war, he turned entirely silent when strangers were brought forth. An unknown person would seal his tongue.

His relations with President Johnson would never be close. They were exact opposites. Often somber and brooding when in the company of a single person or small group, Johnson's passions immediately burst into flame when a crowd was at hand to be addressed. His ghastly and never-to-be-forgotten speech upon the occasion of his inauguration as Vice-President was the most outstanding example of his recklessness on the stump. Ill, he had taken three glasses of whiskey to steady himself and then launched into a shouted stream of gibberish largely dealing with his humble origins. Many of his other speeches were almost equally indiscreet. Told by his advisors to tone down his public remarks, he was capable of agreeing before telling a crowd that Congressional opponents of his policies were more evil than Jefferson Davis.

In the late summer of 1866, at open war with the Radicals led by Senator Charles Sumner and Representative Thaddeus Stevens, Johnson decided to take what he called a "swing around the circle" by which he would bring his views to the voters casting their ballots in the fall elections. Abraham Lincoln would have conciliated, compromised, talked enemies around. Johnson could only bludgeon, and it was obvious that the tour would be one long display of invective. If there was anything that Grant did not want to do, it was to accompany what the Radicals would shortly characterize as a traveling circus. Johnson could not order Grant to go, but when immediately after promoting a number of the general's friends he pointedly invited him, Grant had to accept. (The General of the Army's acceptance lessened Secretary of State Seward's fears for the safety of the Presidential train heading north and then west, for by then the dispute between Johnson and the Radicals was so bitter that Seward thought there was a good chance someone would fire on the President's party or try to dynamite the special off the tracks. The inclusion of Grant would be a deterrent to violence.)

The trip was a nightmare. The Southern states had never been out of the Union, Johnson cried. "They are our brethren. They are part of ourselves. They are bone of our bone, and flesh of our flesh." Back came shouts from Radicals in the audiences: "Traitor! Liar!" Any applause that greeted the train was for Grant and Admiral David Farragut, similarly dragooned into attendance, decided John Rawlins. Shouts of, "Shut up!" greeted what the President said, or "It's a lie!"; and, at St. Louis, a voice from the dark outside the hotel shouting, "Judas, Judas!" It became a drawn-out chant, "Judaas, Judaas, Judaas," and Johnson shouted back, "If I am a Judas, who is the Jesus Christ? Is he Thaddeus Stevens? Is he Charles Sumner?"

The crowd screamed and hooted and he, lost to all restraint and logic, yelled into the darkness, "These are the men who compare themselves with the Savior! And anybody who differs with them is denounced as a Judas!"

"Impeach him!" someone cried out, and the President demanded to know what offenses he had committed. "Plenty, here, tonight!" was the shrieked rejoinder. Often at brief way-station stops the President was told to sit down and shut up, the people wanted to see Grant. Back in the baggage car the general smoked endlessly, and, undone by the turmoil, took to the bottle despite

Rawlins. Finally he said he had enough, he did not care to see a man dig his own grave, and using a trumped-up story that he wanted to see his father, he fled. An intoxicated Surgeon General Joseph Barnes said he would take his pulse before he left, and ended up by falling over the equally intoxicated patient. The frightful tour went on, people still calling for the departed Grant so loudly that the President was often unable to make himself heard. Charles Sumner in Washington said that Johnson had done more evil than anyone in history and was "the author of incalculable woe to his country."

Grant was almost inclined to agree. He decided that Johnson was planning some sort of a revolution, and wrote Phil Sheridan that no one loyal during the war retained any influence with the President "unless they join in a crusade against Congress, and declare the body itself illegal, unconstitutional and revolutionary." When Johnson asked him to travel to Mexico to look into the affairs of the Austrian archduke Maximilian of Hapsburg made Mexican Emperor, Grant said he would prefer not to do so. Later, sitting in on a Cabinet meeting he was startled to hear the President say that he, Grant, would soon be departing on the mission.

"You know I told you that it would not be convenient for me to go to Mexico," Grant said. It was in his mind that the President wanted him away so that a coup d'etat might be carried out more easily.

Johnson stood up at the head of the Cabinet table and slammed his hand down. "I would like to know if there is an officer of the Army who will not obey my orders!" he snapped. Perhaps he was thinking of a possible Radical coup and that Grant wanted to be in on it.

Grant took his hat and stood up. "I am an officer of the Army," he said, "but I am a citizen also. The service you ask me to perform is a civil service, and as a citizen I may accept or decline it, and I decline it." Sherman was sent in his stead. Made the Lieutenant General of the Army when Grant got his fourth star, Sherman often told Grant (and everyone else) that Washington with its politics and politicians was a cesspool of corruption to be gotten as far from as possible.*

The long and fevered battle over what form Reconstruction should take went on, with speeches and charges in the White House and on the floors of Congress. But the country's attention turned to other matters. The war was over. The South was down and out. The Negroes were free. Let region and freedmen make their way as best they could. Out west was a whole new land to be peopled and developed, its plains to be broken by the Deere steel-rimmed moldboard plow and its crops to be harvested by the McCormick reaper. Interest in men and causes and issues gave way to excitement over the money to be made by giant corporations set up to build textile mills on New England's streams, to bring oil, coal and iron out of Pennsylvania's hills and, most dramatic and important of all, to throw endless railroad tracks across the western prairies. It was on the financial pages of the daily paper, not the front page, that the history of the times was being written, there and in the Society section, stories of great stock booms and great money. John D. Rockefeller and Andrew Carnegie, castle-like residences coming up on New York's Fifth Avenue, the invasion of European spas by the wives and daughters of new millionaires, the Gilded Age, the sudden colossal fortunes to which a man could aspire—suddenly Charles Sumner speaking of the rights of the blacks was an obsolete footnote from an earlier, now-distant, day. The victorious North's new men in Congress, pure of ideology and interested only in industrial expansion and political spoils and power, laughed at him.

The United States Army shrank to a twentieth of its wartime size, its duties confined to policing indifferently the occupied South and, more excitingly, to driving away the Indians who stood in the way of the expansion west. Grant's duties as general-in-chief were not onerous. He went on trips. Julia and he gave brilliant parties at the new Washington residence. The city was

*Sherman differed from Grant in his views of honorariums for military services performed. When General Butterfield offered to lead a fund-raising drive to buy Sherman a house, as he had done for Grant, his offer was refused.

booming, new houses going up everywhere as the new rich set up homes from which they could keep an eye on the political technicians sent to the capital to pass laws favorable for ever more glorious business expansion. The last moment for enactment of Reconstruction measures for race equality was at hand: soon the old Abolitionist idealogues still fighting the dead battle of North against South would be gone. Johnson fought on, holding that the former rebel states must be eased back into the Union with as few restrictions upon local mores as possible. It was the Constitution, he said, that told him that the federal government could not do what the Radicals wished, which was to treat the states of the former Confederacy as conquered provinces or military zones of occupation. The Radicals fought back, passing bills over the President's veto, including the Tenure of Office Act, which held that the President could not dismiss certain appointed officials without the advice and consent of the Senate. The act had been passed specifically to protect the Radical Secretary of War, Edwin Stanton, but in the summer of 1867 Johnson sent Stanton an order of dismissal. Stanton refused to accept it. Johnson asked Grant to take up the post on an ad interim basis. He hesitated, but took the job, retaining at the same time his command of the Army.

The Senate met early in the new year and prepared to vote on whether it would give its consent to the firing of Stanton. On January 11, Grant talked with the President for more than an hour and said he could not say what his response would be if the Senate ordered Stanton returned to the War Office. He reminded Johnson that the Tenure of Office Act carried a $10,000 fine and a jail term for anyone who violated it. It was like Johnson to declare to Grant that he, the President, would pay the fine and take the jail term if the act were held constitutional by the Supreme Court, which he was certain it would not. All he asked was that the office not be surrendered to Stanton until the Court ruled.

Not entirely reassured, Grant agreed to talk with the President again on Monday, two days in the future. Perhaps he thought he had made his position clear; more likely he did not have a position.

On Monday the Senate voted that it did not accept the President's discharge of Stanton. Grant sat down and wrote out his resignation as Secretary of War ad interim. That evening at a White House reception the President asked him why he hadn't come to their agreed-upon morning conference. Grant made some excuse and did not mention that he carried his resignation in his pocket. The next morning at nine Grant locked the Secretary's office on the second floor of the War Department building. "I am to be found over at my office at Army headquarters," he told Assistant Adjutant General E. D. Townsend, and walked over to Seventeenth Street south of Pennsylvania Avenue, diagonally opposite the War Department. From there he sent a messenger with his resignation to the President.

An hour later Edwin Stanton, smiling, entered the War Department to find the Secretary's door locked. Told that Grant had the key, he sent Townsend to get it. In a few minutes Townsend was back to perform a mock present arms with the key. Stanton unlocked the door.

There followed a terrible scene in the White House between the President and the general, Johnson charging that Grant had broken his word to hold the War Office, Grant maintaining that he had made no promises. Washington rumor had it, incorrectly, that Johnson kicked over chairs and cursed Grant and that the two had narrowly escaped coming to blows. The upshot was that Grant told Johnson that in the future he would accept no orders unless they were written and that he would at the same time consider himself under the authority of the Secretary of War. Johnson replied with an outline of what he called the general's apostasy as a man who gave his word and then broke it. Grant wrote a denial, ending, "When my honor as a soldier and my integrity as a man have been so violently assailed, pardon me for saying that I can but regard this whole matter, from beginning to end, as an attempt to involve me in the resistance of law, for which you hesitated to assume the responsibility in

orders, and thus to destroy my character before the country."
Johnson sent General Lorenzo Thomas to oust the Secretary.
Stanton refused to give up his office. Rumors of coup and coun-
tercoup filled the air, stories of troop movements, blood and
terror, a new civil war. On February 25, 1868, Thad Stevens
went before the Senate to say that he, in the name of the House
of Representatives and all the people of the United States, impeached Andrew Johnson for high crimes and misdemeanors.

Entirely innocent of and impervious to all politics for the
whole of his prior life—he had voted only once, halting his wood-
delivery wagon at a polling place to cast a ballot in 1856 for James
Buchanan, solely on the basis that he had known but not respected John Frémont in the Army—Grant flung himself into
lobbying for the conviction of the impeached President. He was
almost irrational in his detestation of Johnson. Only the President's lack of courage had prevented total "riotousness" in the
White House, Grant said, and a not guilty verdict would give
the man courage. Perhaps it was a reaction to the interior belief
that he had not played the most noble role in relation to his
commander-in-chief, perhaps it was rage at finding himself in a
questionable situation regarding the value of his word, perhaps
it was that after years of adulation something else was coming
his way, but suddenly he hated Johnson more than he had ever
hated any Confederate. On a Washington streetcar he saw Senator John Henderson of Missouri, who was known to lean toward
a not guilty verdict, and sat down and asked Henderson if he
had changed his mind about the impeachment.

"No, General, I am of the same mind about it."

"Do you think you can defeat it?"

"Well, I can't warrant that. We have friends enough against
it to defeat it, but I cannot give a pledge that we shall actually
defeat it."

"Well, I hope you won't."

"Why, General, you wouldn't impeach Johnson?"

"Yes, I would impeach him if for nothing else than because
he is such an infernal liar!"

The trial began. It lasted until mid-May when, by one vote, that of Edmund Ross of Kansas, Andrew Johnson was found by the Senate to be not guilty. It was, in a sense, the last battle involving the North versus the South, Abolitionism and the rights of the freed slaves against the Black Codes that made them hardly better than serfs, the end of all the questions that had dominated national thinking for so long. All that was obsolete. As much a part of the past as the influence of the once lordly planter aristocracy of the South, the strivings of idealist and Radical, strict constitutionalist and soft-peace exponent, became a page in history. The trial itself was largely symbolic. Even as the senators rose to record their votes, the delegates to the Republican National Convention were gathering in Chicago. They represented the future of industrialism and great expansion and wealth and but one name was presented to them for nomination as their candidate, that of the General of the Army, Ulysses S. Grant.

18

President

IN THE FIRST DAYS OF PEACE Robert Lee sat stunned and silent in his Richmond home. Most of the time he spent in bed. Part of each day he was in the rear parlor staring out into the walled garden. Looking worn and aged, he spoke almost not at all. The front shutters of the house were closed at all times. Godfrey Weitzel, the commander of the Union troops in the city, was a prewar friend of Lee's nephew Fitzhugh, and when he sent an aide to offer a purse full of money, the aide saw how gentle Fitz Lee was with his uncle, kneeling by his chair with his hand on his knee to speak softly to him. Then Fitz came to tell the aide that money was not needed, but that if General Weitzel could do so, it would be appreciated if passes were issued to some distant women of the family so that they could come through the Union lines to Richmond. If General Weitzel in his official capacity could not do so without embarrassment, Fitz stressed, then the request should be regarded as not having been made. Weitzel issued the passes.

A block and a half away, past smoking ruins and solitary chimneys, at the Capitol, there was noise and hubbub and the sound of Yankee bands blaring. Freedmen lined up for rations from the soldiers. Past them went returning Confederate veterans, thin, hollow-faced, shoeless. Often they paused to join the crowd that always stood silently in front of 707 Franklin Street. Lee never showed himself outside, but sometimes they asked to be admitted. One tall ex-soldier in dusty homespun came in and said, "General Lee, I followed you for four years and done the best I knowed how. Me and my wife live on a little farm away up on Blue Ridge Mountains. If you will come up thar we will take care of you the best we know how as long as we live."

Lee took both of the man's hands in his own. Tears ran down his cheeks, his daughter Mildred saw. "I don't need a thing," Lee said. "My friends all over the country have been very kind and have sent me more clothes that I can possibly use, so I want to thank you for coming and give you this new suit." It was in a box, unopened. The man snatched his hands away, crossed them over his chest and said, "General Lee, I can't take nothing offen you." Then he said, "Yes, I will, General, I will carry them back home, put them away, and when I die the boys will put them on me."

Sometimes the callers wore blue. One of his troopers from the old days in the United States Cavalry came with a basket of food saying that as long as he had a cent, his old colonel would not go hungry. Lee explained that he wanted for nothing, but seeing the disappointment in the soldier's face said he would take the food and send it to a hospital where the sick could enjoy it. "Good-bye, Colonel! God bless ye!" the Union soldier cried, and embraced his old commander. More substantial offers than his were made. The representative of an insurance company came to proffer the Lee presidency of his concern, at a salary of $50,000 a year. Lee thanked him but said he must decline, as he was not familiar with such work. "But, General," the man said, "you will not be expected to do any work. What we wish is the use of your name."

"Do you not think," Lee replied, "that if my name is worth fifty thousand dollars a year, I ought to be very careful about taking care of it?" But there remained the question of what, at fifty-eight, he should do. A British nobleman wrote offering the lifetime use of an estate in England; he replied that he was very grateful, but could not think of accepting.

The photographer Mathew Brady came and asked if he could photograph the general in the uniform he had worn at Appomattox. He had been a friend of Winfield Scott's for years and had met Lee many times before the war, but Lee said, "It is utterly impossible, Mr. Brady." Brady persevered and got Mrs. Lee interested. Word was sent to Brady that he could come with his camera for an hour. There was very little conversation as the photographer made his pictures, Lee simply asking where he should stand or sit, and then complying.

Richmond was like some medieval city stricken by plague, with the people venturing out of their homes only at night. Sometimes in the evenings Lee went for a walk. The close confinement wearied him and made him restless, and in early June, two months after the surrender, he took Traveller and, alone, rode out into the countryside. He made for the Pamunkey River home of his relative Thomas Carter, 25 miles away, where unexpected and unannounced he arrived just as dinner was being served. He spent several days with Carter, the happiest time he had enjoyed in years. He talked about Mexico and people he and Carter knew. He said nothing about the war except when asked a direct question. In the family were two little girls of five and three and he followed them around talking to them and getting them to talk to him. Each morning before he got up they went into his room at his special request to pay him a visit. He liked to watch Traveller out on the lawns peacefully eating rich grass.

When he got back to Richmond it was to learn that a federal grand jury sitting in Norfolk had indicted him for treason. He wrote to Ulysses Grant saying that he had thought the members of the surrendered Army of Northern Virginia were by the terms of their surrender to be free from molestation. "I am ready to meet any charges that may be proffered against me, and do not wish to avoid trial," he told Grant, enclosing an application for amnesty addressed to President Johnson. Grant took the application and wrote, "Respectfully forwarded through the Secretary of War to the President, with the earnest recommendation that this application of General R. E. Lee for amnesty may be granted him." Johnson sent for Grant and asked of Lee and Jefferson Davis, "When can these men be tried?" To him they were aristocrats of the type he had always hated.

"Never," said Grant. "Never, unless they violate their paroles."

"I would like to know by what right a military commander interferes to protect an arch-traitor from the laws!"

"I have made certain terms with Lee," Grant said, "the best and only terms. I will resign the command of the Army rather than execute any order directing me to arrest Lee."

Nothing else was ever heard about the indictment.

In Lexington, Virginia, that summer, on August 4, the trustees of a tiny bankrupt college in the mountains met to name a new president for their institution. Washington College had four professors. Forty students were expected in the fall. Of no great national, or even statewide, reputation, the college was situated in a remote part of Virginia accessible only by mule-pulled canal boat or primitive stagecoach jolting its way over wretched twisting roads. The trustees discussed offering their presidency to various men, and then somebody said that he had heard from a lady friend of his that Miss Mary Lee, the general's daughter, had said that while the Southern people were ready to give her father anything he might need, no offer had yet been made by which he could earn a living for himself and his family.

The man was asked if he was nominating Robert E. Lee for the presidency of Washington College. He said he was not. Someone else remarked that it would be a great thing to have such a president. In a moment they had nominated and elected him. Then there was a long silence as the trustees reflected upon what they had done. Suddenly they felt that had acted rashly: "How could they announce to the world that they had elected to the presidency of a broken down college not only the greatest man in the South, but in many respects the greatest man in the world?"

But the deed was done. They decided to go ahead and inform Lee, not through the mail, but by one of their number. They asked Judge John Brockenbrough, the rector, to go to Lee. He said that he could not possibly, for he now had on his best clothes and they were far too worn to wear while on such an errand. Another board member said that his son in the North had recently sent him a suit of broadcloth which he thought would fit Brockenbrough. The judge thanked him, but brought up the subject of travel money. He himself had none. Another trustee said a woman in town had recently sold some tobacco. Perhaps the college could borrow money from her. Judge Brockenbrough went off to Lee.

At first glance the job seemed ridiculous. If Lee wanted to assume the tasks of an educator, his friends and family said, he could certainly find himself a post with some great university. But little Washington College in Lexington, forty students? Lee did not see it that way. The work lent its own dignity, he said. If the college wanted him, he would go. This was the job that Providence had made available to him. On September 18, a lone horseman four days on the road in an old Confederate uniform with buttons and insignia removed, rode into the main street of the mountain town and dismounted in front of the Central Hotel. Professor James White, late captain of the Army of Northern Virginia, happened to be passing by. He rushed up and said that General Lee must be the guest of his family. Lee demurred, saying it was late in the afternoon and he did not want suddenly to arrive and inconvenience people. White insisted. So Lee spent his first nights in Lexington with White's father-in-law and then while the college authorities worked to evict a stubborn rentor from the president's house, lived in one room of the hotel. Finally the rentor, a doctor, left.

"You know I am a poor hand and can do nothing without your advice," Lee wrote his daughter Agnes, telling her of his plans to fix up the residence for her occupancy and that of Mrs. Lee and the other two daughters.* He planted shrubs and roses and set out fruit trees. A few days after his arrival he was inaugurated as president of Washington College. The trustees had thought to send invitations far and wide, to have a band and girls in white bearing chaplets of flowers, songs of welcome, speeches, a holiday—but he vetoed all of that and took his oath of office in a ten-minute ceremony. Then he went to work. He was at once president, dean, director of college development, advisor to the faculty, registrar, purchasing agent and supervisor of grounds. He concerned himself with selecting kitchen utensils, and stovepipes for the dormitory rooms. His salary was $125 a month. His staff consisted of one secretary. It was hard for him, but he set himself to writing letters seeking financial aid for the school from men in the North. Cyrus McCormick, George Peabody, Henry Ward Beecher and Samuel Tilden, among others, responded generously.

The students shortly arrived, mature war veterans who had spent years in the Confederate army, and seventeen-year-olds who heard themselves addressed as "Mister" for the first time in their lives upon the occasion of their presentation to the president of their college. He asked each student his religious affiliation and then introduced him to the minister of the appropriate Lex-

*The second oldest daughter, Annie, had died during the war. She was twenty-three. The news of her passing was contained in a letter handed the general by Walter Taylor along with some official notifications. Lee scanned it, and then discussed the official matters. Taylor left the commander's tent, remembered something he had forgotten, and reentered without announcing himself. He found Lee crying. "Lee the man must give way to Lee the patriot and soldier. His army demanded his first thought and care; to his men, to their needs, he must first attend." Then, and only then, could he give himself up to his tears.

ington church. When classes got underway he checked the result of each test each student took, and those who did not do well found themselves trying to explain why to Robert E. Lee. One boy, knowing he had cut too many classes, prepared all kinds of explanations for his absences and in response to the president's gravely polite questions started piling on reasons—he had been sick, he had left his boots at the cobbler's—when Lee interrupted, "Stop, sir! One good reason is enough." The boy could not miss the twinkle in his eyes. Lee did not believe in forcing boys to do their duty, he told the faculty, but in trying to get them to see what was the correct fashion in which they should conduct themselves. The professors had to remind themselves this was a lifelong professional soldier.

In line with letting the students rule themselves as much as possible, he abolished the rigid compulsory curriculum in favor of an elective one, which at his urging included the first course in journalism ever given at an American college. He was tolerant of collegiate hijinks, telling one new student who asked for a copy of the rules, "Young gentleman, we have no printed rules. We have but one rule here, and it is that every student must be a gentleman."

He seemed almost too modest in displaying the power of his position and his fame at faculty meetings, the professors came to feel, for he never gave orders, but instead permitted a general sense of the group to determine the answer to any question. Only after he had greeted the president from his horse and then gone on did one professor realize that "I'm sorry your horse has sore feet" meant Lee would have preferred the animal to be kept on the roadway and not on a college lawn. He was that way with the students, gently telling a boy whose work was slowing up how happy he had been in the past to write the boy's mother with good news of her son's progress, and how he hoped to be able to write in the same vein again. To a boy who cut classes to go hunting he said, "Yesterday was such a pretty day, and you would kill the birds that enjoy the day so much. I don't think I would do so again." When he had to write parents detailing indifferent academic performance, he did so as tactfully as possible: "He does his Mathematics pretty well, but is neglecting his Latin and Greek," or "He is making good progress in the languages, but is deficient in his Mathematics and the sciences." He often said he did not want the young men to injure their health by overzealous studying—but he wanted them to come as close to doing so as possible.

So different was he from the image of the South's great warrior that one seventeen-year-old found him "in a certain way an effeminate man because he was so extremely kind, gentle, and considerate of everybody." Another student, told by the president that if he did not work harder he would certainly fail, permitted himself to say, "But, General, *you* were a failure" and got in return only, "Yes. But let us hope you will be more fortunate than I." When the Washington College students and faculty marched in joint proceedings with the personnel of the nearby Virginia Military Institute, it was noticeable how he deliberately did not keep step with the drumbeat, but simply strolled along.

When the president's house was ready for occupancy, Mrs. Lee and her daughters came. The war had been cruel to Mary Lee. Her son Rooney was attempting to bring back her burned-out White House plantation on the peninsula, her son Rob was trying to do the same with her Romancoke Plantation, but Arlington was gone to be the center of a vast United States government cemetery. Graveskeepers and caretakers lived there. All her life she had avoided leaving Arlington, spending years on end there while her husband served his lonely tours of duty elsewhere. Now she came, an all but total invalid, by mule-drawn canal boat to a remote mountain town and a modest home. He showed her the pickles, preserves and brandied peaches the ladies of Lexington had put in the storeroom; but when she saw some of the rugs from Arlington that a cousin had stored during the long years since she had last seen her home, she broke down.

To her the Radicals of the North were "cowards and base men." The country allowing "such scum to rule them must fast be going to destruction. Oh, God, how long?"

Such thoughts did not come into her husband's mind. Nor did, apparently, any opinions on the war or the Yankees. He devoted himself to his duties, which were to see that the college functioned efficiently. "You know our friend is accustomed to make his prayers too long," he said of a minister who conducted morning chapel exercises. "He prays for the Jews, the Turks, the heathen, the Chinese, and everybody else, and makes his prayers run into the regular hour for our college recitations." He appealed to a faculty member, "Would it be wrong for me to suggest that he confine his morning prayers to us poor sinners at the college, and pray for the Turks, the Jews, the Chinese, and the other heathen, some other time?"

He spent much time with his daughters. Mary, thirty years old in 1865, was good looking, arrogant, sharp-tongued—remindful in personality very much of her mother. Agnes, twenty-four, was intelligent but somber, saddened forever by Annie's death. They had been very close. Mildred, nineteen, was her father's pet. "Where is my little Miss Mildred?" he would call when he came into the house at the end of the day. "She is my light-bearer," he said, "the house is never dark when she is in it." Spoiled and immature, she read romantic novels despite his injunctions that she should not do so. He loved her perhaps best of all, and she worshipped him; but with a dreadful premonition of what her life was to be, what she was to become, she wrote a friend upon arrival in Lexington: "The number of old maids here appalls me. My fate was decided the first moment I put my foot on the shore. Lucy, do you know what starvation of the heart and mind is? I suffer and am dumb." She could add immediately, "You ought to see the beautiful new black silk dress I've got, all trimmed with steely beads," but she had seen her future all too clearly. None of the Lee daughters ever married. It was obvious their father did not wish them to do so. The possibility never appeared to enter into his thoughts for the future, for he spoke of having them with him always. They would take care of him and of Mrs. Lee, make them clothing and collect the eggs from the chicken coop. But it was altogether different with the three sons, and he was forever asking young women to marry them—"You see, there is no Mrs. R. E. Lee, Jr. Cannot you persuade some of those pretty girls in Baltimore to take compassion on a poor bachelor?"

As in the entire South impoverished by the war and already sunk in nostalgia for the past, he was regarded in Lexington as a demigod, a knight, the realized King Arthur. "Mama, I can never remember," one of the town's little girls said to her mother, "was General Lee in the Old Testament or the New Testament?" Another stopped him in the street to complain of her even smaller sister's reluctance to do as she was told and go home, and he swept the child up on the saddle in front of him and took her himself. When the older girl's mother reprimanded her for bothering General Lee, the little girl explained, "I couldn't make Fan go home, and I thought *he* could do anything."

When in college assemblies his war record was extolled, he stared into space and, one faculty member thought, behaved as though the activities of the Man in the Moon were under discussion. Afternoons, almost always alone, he went for long rides on Traveller. Aside from Mildred, or very occasionally one of the professors, he did not care to have company on his excursions. For a couple of hours every day he went into the mountains around Lexington, doffing his hat to everyone he met, saying a few words to the farmers along the way. What he thought, what he remembered on those quiet rides, he never said. He read absolutely nothing about the late conflict, and when the Austro-Prussian War was fought in 1866 he took no interest in it. The contest for securing a place in history had already begun among other Confederate commanders who for thirty years and more into the future would fight their old battles once again through their memoirs and articles in *The Confederate Veteran* or *The Cen-*

tury disputing who had been at fault at Gettysburg, or to whom belonged the chief credit for success on happier fields. But Lee said nothing.

When his daughters were away from Lexington he wrote them cheery letters: "Our feline companions are flourishing. Young Baxter is growing in gracefulness and favour, and gives cat-like evidences of future worth. He is strictly aristocratic in appearance and conduct. Tom, surnamed 'The Nipper,' from the manner in which he slaughters our enemies, the rats and mice, is admired for his gravity and sobriety, as well as for his strict attentions to the pursuits of his race. They both feel your absence sorely. All send united love, and all wish for your return. Be careful of your health, and do not eat more than half the plum-pudding Cousin Eleanor has prepared for Xmas. Think always of your father, who loves you dearly." But in none of his letters to anyone did he discuss the war. Lexington was so out of the way and difficult of access—"Whichever route you select, you will wish you had taken the other," he wrote—that few of those who had known him in the war saw him. When they did, they were universally shocked at his appearance. Before, he had been the lighthouse in the storm, with the light of battle in his eyes, but now the cause was dead and he had taken off his armor and he was old—old.

19

President

"THE RESPONSIBILITIES of the position I feel, but accept them without fear," Grant said. He turned to Julia. "And now, my dear, I hope you're satisfied." She was. They shook hands and, President and First Lady, went to the inaugural ball, she in white satin and point lace with pearl and diamond ornaments. He had announced that he would not ride in the same carriage with, nor even speak to, his out-going predecessor, and so Andrew Johnson had not been at the Capitol at noon on March 4, 1869, to see the ceremonies. Grant, in plain civilian dress and wearing yellow gloves, drove down Pennsylvania Avenue with John Rawlins at his side. He sat as immobile as if encased in a suit of armor— "as modest, diffident, and shy as ever," wrote Emily Edson Briggs—while watching Vice-President Schuyler Colfax sworn in, and then gave his inaugural address in a thin voice hardly heard beyond the first row of listeners.

As with the writing of the speech, he had consulted with

no one on the selection of his Cabinet members. Their names astounded the world—and many of those named. Adolph Borie of Philadelphia, a very rich man who had contributed more than $50,000 toward buying and furnishing Grant's house in his home city, was riding on a train when he read in a newspaper that he was the new Navy Department chief. He had spent considerable time with Grant before the inauguration and Grant had never said anything about it. He knew nothing of naval affairs. To the post of Secretary of State Grant named his congressman, Elihu Washburne, a personage previously unconnected with foreign affairs and not looked upon as being smoothly diplomatic. But it was explained that Washburne had no intention of serving in the post. He wanted and would be given the ministership to France, but felt having been Secretary of State would give him prestige in Paris. He served less than a week and then Grant sent the Senate the name of Hamilton Fish, a one-time congressman, senator, and governor of New York as Washburne's replacement. Fish had been out of politics for years and had no interest in the post. He at once telegraphed his refusal, but Grant sent Orville Babcock to see him and say that it would be appreciated if he at least tried out the job. If he didn't like it after, say, half a year, he could give it up.

To the Treasury was named the vastly rich New York merchant Alexander T. Stewart, prominent in giving the Grants gifts. Much of the new First Lady's clothing came from his emporium, the largest in the country. There was a law forbidding men engaged in commercial enterprises to hold the Treasury; Grant asked, in vain as it turned out, that the law be set aside for Stewart. Rawlins got the War Department. The other four Cabinet men were of no great distinction. Nor were the host of other political appointees who poured into Washington and spread out all over the country, some two dozen of them being relatives of the President and his wife. The sole questions asked on any federal civil service examination ought to be, said the New York *World*, "Were you a contributor to either of Grant's three houses?" and "Are you connected by blood or marriage with General

Grant?" All the Dents and Grants getting foreign ministerships
(a Presidential brother-in-law to Denmark), collectorships of customs, nominations to West Point, postmasterships, jobs as state
bank examiners, etc., people said, indicated that the new President had gotten in the family way immediately upon taking the
oath of office.

Grant himself looked upon his election (to further which he
had not said a word in public, holding that he did not need to
give the voters advice and that they would elect him if they
thought it best) as a promotion from his status as four-star general. He had no great cause to serve, no personal involvement
with any issue. With all the familiar men of his staff, Generals
Badeau, Porter, Babcock, Ingalls, Dent, he moved into the White
House where, as with the reign of Louis Philippe, the theme of
his Presidency might have been: *Enrich yourselves*. "One had seemed
to know him so well, and really knew so little," reflected Henry
Adams, realizing his previous thoughts of Grant were absurd,
laughable. United with the world in great expectations, Adams
had only to learn the names of the Cabinet members to know
how total his misconceptions were. "A great soldier might be a
baby politician," said a senator to Adams, but Adams saw Grant
not as a child in the hands of those who at once set out to make
money, but rather as a primitive throwback to an earlier era.
"He had no right to exist. He should have been extinct for ages."
Grant, Adams decided, made the idea of evolution ridiculous.
The evolution from President Washington to President Grant
ought to suggest to Darwinists that America was reverting to the
Stone Age. "He was archaic and should have lived in a cave and
worn skins."

But Adams had been away from America for years, serving
as his father's aide during the elder Adams' service as minister
to England. Perhaps he did not see his own country clearly.
What he took for an immediate nationwide wave of cynicism
about Grant and about American society was instead, perhaps,
the sudden push forward of an industrial giant that had not
known itself or its strength before the war that welded it together

and made it ready to build great enterprises and make the Gilded
Age. The mission that had given birth to the Republican Party
was accomplished; the Slave Power was dead. Its wealth, once
controlled by Southern planters, was now in the hands of railroad
entrepreneurs, corporation officials, bank presidents, gold corner
specialists, speculators and men on the make, and they were out
for more money and more power. They were crude. They used
spittoons. Their women, observed Emily Edson Briggs, were
not born to culture, refinement and dignity grown from within.
The woman of the man who bought and sold legislatures and
sent his agents to gee and haw so as to tell the beasts which way
to turn, all she owned was new. "She, herself, is new." She
moved in Washington in glare, glitter and pomp remindful of
the Arabian Nights. From the North's great victory had come
bonnets decorated with aigrettes of diamonds, flutters of lace and
silk, room corners adorned with potted bushes and trees, rising
railroad shares, gold stickpins and rings and such a display of
wealth and splendor as to make the writer E. F. Ellet think of
a carnival. The writer Mary Clemmer Ames found the young
girls of the "newly enriched" to be hard and old, blasé, brazen
of manner. The dew of their innocence was gone forever, like
that, perhaps, of the country. In the world in which they and
their parents moved, the courtesan and the stockjobber gained
quick acceptance. Bank notes covered everything.

And in the midst of this stood Ulysses and Julia Grant, she
elaborately coiffed and gowned for her Tuesday afternoon Blue
Room receptions through which a river of humanity poured,
over velvet carpet and past satin damask and rare hothouse flowers, to be greeted and announced and then herded along by the
shining brass-buttoned officers of the President's staff; he with
a far-off look in his eyes, Mrs. Briggs observed, and with his
nostrils rising and sinking like the gills of a fish out of water.

He gave good dinners, Mrs. Briggs thought, but then, as
"no man during the existence of the republic has ever been the
recipient of so many costly gifts," it behooved him to be generous
in return. On the State Dining Room's center table was a con-

struction of gilt and looking glass, several feet long and perhaps 2 feet wide. There were splashing perfumed fountains, mountains of flowers in the receptacles and vases, gleaming mirrors and great chandeliers. The women were in jewels and gowns and the men in black swallow-tailed coats and white gloves and ties. Mrs. Lincoln had given a hand to the staff in her day, helping out; and President Johnson's daughter, Martha Patterson, his official hostess, had checked to see that the milkpans were clean and sweet, just as women in wayside cottages did, but now paid government employees did everything as they produced meals of up to thirty courses. Six wineglasses of different sizes and a small bouquet of flowers were in front of each guest. An "ambrosial soup said to be a little smoother than peacock's brains, but not quite so exquisitely flavored as a dish of nightingale's tongues" was followed by French croquette of meat. The third course might be fillet of beef flanked by potatoes the size of a walnut, with mushrooms to keep them company. Next, "luscious leg of partridge." The rice pudding dessert Mrs. Briggs found herself quite unable to describe. Then came peaches, pears, quinces, confectionery, nuts, ice cream, coffee and chocolate. It was all paid for out of the President's private purse, at a cost of up to $1,500 per dinner. After the hours of dining were over the President and First Lady received briefly under a life-size portrait of the family, and then the guests left and the Grants retired to the state bedrooms. There the walls were hung with purple and gold and furnished with rosewood and crimson satin. The ceiling was profusely frescoed and hung with a vast chandelier; the bedstead, high and massive, was carved and canopied with damask curtains from a gilded hoop near the ceiling.

"Is that you, Ulyss?" Julia asked in the morning when he tapped to see if she had completed her toilette.

"Breakfast is ready," he said.

"I will be there in a few minutes, General." She was always late. He waited patiently. They went down arm in arm and then he saw her back to her sitting room where they chatted before he got to his desk at ten. In a long linen duster he worked until three, minus time out for lunch, and then went to his stables and the carriage house where he had his horses and his racing buggy, a landau, a barouche, a light road wagon, a regulation buggy and a phaeton. The rich meals surrounded by ices formed into temples, towers, minarets and pagodas soon made his face puffy and added some fifty pounds to his frame, and he gave up riding in favor of driving.

Within six months of his inauguration his administration was in trouble and he himself perhaps even more so. His spinster sister, Virginia, getting on to forty, had in recent days married one Abel Rathbone Corbin, a not very young and not very savory lawyer, speculator and lobbyist. On visits to New York the President stayed with his sister and new brother-in-law, where hardly by happenstance he was thrown into frequent contact with certain financiers who cultivated Corbin. ("I am right behind the throne," Corbin told them.) Foremost among these moneymen were the coldly sinister Jay Gould, who cared for nothing but money, and the flamboyant Jim Fisk, who in addition to money cared for actresses. Gould had the President for a cruise on his yacht; Fisk had him to the theater he owned. The two men decided to corner the market on the gold supply of the United States. To do so and then hold the price of their acquisitions at a high level, they had to be assured that government holdings would not be offered for sale. Corbin assured them that he would influence Grant not to permit federal sales. All through the summer of 1869 the conspirators bought. It was entirely in line with Gould's way of doing business that he should buy for General Daniel Butterfield, who had organized the raising of the funds for the purchase of Grant's Washington home and was now the Treasury agent in charge at New York, $1\frac{1}{2}$ million worth of gold. He also bought half a million for General Horace Porter. (Butterfield kept his, Porter refused to do so. Other men of the staff were not so finicky.)

Wherever Grant went he seemed to find Gould and Fisk urging that no government gold be sold. He took a cruise on Fisk's yacht, the owner in blue uniform with gilded cap band, three silver stars on his coat sleeves, a diamond breastpin gleaming and a covey of aides similarly bestarred and bestriped alongside, including a selection of the lady friends of "the Admiral," as Fisk liked to be called when at sea. (When he marched with the New York militia outfit whose gaudy uniforms he had supplied, he styled himself as "Colonel.") Eventually Grant became annoyed and complained to Corbin that his friends always seemed to want something. But the price of the conspirators' vast holdings steadily rose.

In September, Gould went too far, ordering Corbin to write a letter to the President urging him not to permit the sale of government gold under any circumstances. In fact, Gould told Secretary of the Treasury George Boutwell, appointed in favor of the banished merchant-nominee Stewart, it would be a good idea for the government to buy gold. That was too much. Grant had Julia write a letter to his sister saying that if, as seemed to him not impossible, Gould was speculating in gold, she had better have her husband Corbin disassociate himself from the financier. Gould realized his pipeline to Grant was gone and began secretly selling through intermediaries the millions of dollars of gold he had accumulated. He did not choose to reveal this to Fisk, who enthusiastically bought. On September 24, 1869, "Black Friday," the selling and buying reached a frenzy never approached before. Fisk raced around yelling buy orders and screaming that he was the Napoleon of Wall Street, while alone in his office, tearing up bits of paper, no gesture or word showing his feelings or plans, Gould sold. In the midst of the hubbub of wildness and unearthly shrieking of orders, a telegram from Washington announced that Secretary of the Treasury Boutwell had ordered the selling of government gold. The market shot downward and brokers literally went crazy on the floor of the Gold Exchange, one yelling "Shoot me! Shoot me!" until he was led away.

The day's activities ruined hundreds of speculating firms and thousands of individuals, among whose number Fisk's name did not appear. After calling Corbin a "damned old scoundrel," he decided in complicity with Gould to repudiate all his purchases. The greatest loser was the President of the United States, of whom it was whispered that his wife had profited in the debacle, which she had not, and that half his staff had likewise made money, which they had. It saddened people to see the hero of Appomattox consort with such persons as Gould, who was known as "the meanest man born since the beginning of the Christian era," and the mountebank Fisk, who was shot to death some years later by a rival for the favors of one of his doxies.

The Black Friday episode was of a piece with many other such incidents of those years. The city of Washington was spruced up marvelously—grassed circles with center fountains or statues replacing great swatches of mud, lines of trees planted along newly paved avenues—but it was done to the accompaniment of charges of gigantic graft. A contract was let for the erection of a government-paid tombstone over the grave of every fallen Union soldier, but the bidding was rigged after money changed hands. Moth repellent, useless, was foisted off on the Army after certain people had been contacted. Orville Babcock went down to the Caribbean nation of San Domingo and, styling himself Aide-de-Camp to the President of the United States, an office not in existence, contracted with a bandit-politician of doubtful position to annex the country. Charges that the millions Babcock offered in the name of the United States would be equally divided between bandits and White House aides were immediately voiced on the floor of the Senate, and the newspapers almost universally termed the whole thing a swindle, a corrupt job, a monster job. Like Ulysses of old, so the papers said, Grant stopped up his ears and sent United States Navy warships to back up the clique trying to sell San Domingo. Rufus Ingalls said the idea offered great opportunities, including the instant solution to the race problem: All the freed slaves would be settled there.

Entirely unconsulted, completely bypassed in the highly questionable negotiations, a flabbergasted Secretary of State Fish said he would resign, but Grant prevailed upon him not to do so, partly on the basis that the First Lady needed Mrs. Fish.

Her dignity and high social standing lent a tone to the White House otherwise lacking. For years afterwards, Grant worked at getting the United States to buy San Domingo, long after it was obvious that no one save a small White House coterie wanted annexation.

Fish was not the only man who early on offered his resignation, or had it demanded. Those of other Cabinet members were accepted or asked for in the most casual fashion, and replacements came and went with regularity. When sending an order of dismissal, the President offered no explanations, simply informing the official in question that his resignation was desired. It was all very haphazard and in line with no visible program that the President had in mind, for he had no program. He took an interest for a time in civil service reform but dropped the matter when it met with opposition from the no-nonsense new men of the Senate interested only in patronage and place-giving to their cronies. His appointments to the Supreme Court were made casually and with little apparent concern.

Sympathetic to the Indians, he said he would follow what he called a "peace policy," but it was only sporadically adhered to by officers who said and believed that the only good Indian was a dead one. The endless cheating of the tribes by government agents went on as it always had. He made Ely Parker, the Iroquois who had written down the terms of surrender, Commissioner of Indian Affairs, but he was forced out amid charges of corruption. When John Rawlins died of the consumption that had dogged him for years, the new War Secretary, General William Belknap, lived in grand style on proceeds of the sale of post traderships to men who had virtual licenses to rob Indians and frontier soldiers alike with monopoly stores charging inflated prices. Traderships were gold mines. "When he come he bring everything in little bag, when he go it take two steamships to carry away his things," a popular story depicted a tribal chieftain as saying of the typical trader. Several such were sharing their profits with the Secretary of War, whose wife made the arrangements. When the wife died, Secretary Belknap married her sister, and the second Mrs. Belknap continued her sister-predecessor's collections from the corrupt agents. She and her husband entertained brilliantly at the house previously the property of Lincoln and Johnson's Secretary of State William Seward.

A large portion of the federal government's income came from the levying of whiskey taxes on bottles leaving the distilleries, but the whole process was shot through with fraud by falsified invoices, manufactured internal revenue stamps and the bribery of government agents assigned to check shipments. It never seemed to occur to Grant to wonder how or why General John McDonald, an old army friend made collector of customs at St. Louis, managed on a $3,000-a-year salary to present Orville Babcock with diamonds and $1,000 bills and the services of a woman known as "the Sylph." It was only late in the day that he learned of Babcock's dealings, but early on he failed to ask himself how collector McDonald managed to contribute horses and a carriage and a harness with gold fitting to the White House stables. The answer was, of course, that McDonald was carefully milking distillers as a functionary of what was called "the Whiskey Ring" while letting it be known that the President was in on everything. That discouraged any honest distiller from taking action against McDonald. But it was not true.

All around Grant men who had been with him in the war— good soldiers, then—were filling their pockets from banking rings and railroad rings that wanted government decisions in their favor, iron and coal rings, money-grabbing combinations of every name and sort—but the President's hands were clean. He took presents but not bribes and he did it innocently, trusting everyone who had been his friend. Within two years of his inauguration the best men of his administration had left Washington, and, said Representative James A. Garfield, "Political vermin infest the government and keep it in a perpetual state of lousiness." When Zachariah Chandler of Michigan, who long ago in Detroit had been sued by the young Captain Sam Grant for not keeping his sidewalk free of snow and ice—the two of them laughed about it now—became Secretary of the Interior, the

Springfield *Republican* said of him that he was typical of the President's men: "Very rich, very coarse, very fond of pleasure, a thorough materialist in fiber and life, a very Grantish selection." The soldier's rule, his critics said, amounted to "Caesarism."

The country cared—but not very much. The cornerstone for the State, War and Navy Building* was laid. It was a vast and ornate structure that with other grandiose constructions replete with turrets, bays, buttresses, trefoils, filials, traceries and crenellated roofs and windows filled with diamond-lighted sash and edged with bits of colored glass, with vaulted ceilings of heavy and ornately carved dark wood and marble, came to be known architecturally as "Late General Grant." The President's annual vacation began with the graduation ceremonies at the United States Military Academy where his son Fred, saying, "No damned nigger will ever graduate from West Point," readily partook in the hazing of the first black cadet. Then the President went on to the fashionable watering place of Long Branch in New Jersey where he drove, chatted, played cards and billiards, always with rich men.

The children were growing up, Fred to graduate from West Point and be assigned, at Julia's strong urging, as an aide to Grant's successor as chief of the Army for a tour abroad. It amused Sherman when the Europeans, apparently thinking they were dealing with the crown prince of America, paid their homages first to the newly commissioned second lieutenant and only afterwards to the four-star general.† Nellie Grant, held on far too loose a leash in the eyes of those who looked for their lessons in comportment to an earlier era, for she was permitted when in her early teens to dance at White House cotillions until dawn, also went to Europe and was received as a reigning princess. Neither parent raised any objection nor had any reservations regarding the elaborate receptions given their children, one born in the residence of his maternal grandfather because his father

---

*Now the Old Executive Office Building, seat of the Vice-President's staff.
†Sheridan succeeded to the Lieutenant Generalcy of the Army, devastating Meade, who felt the position should have been his.

did not have a home suitable for the lying-in, the second born in the wretched homemade cabin her father titled "Hardscrabble."

Initially Julia had kept Nellie on a short string, telling a teacher who detained the girl after school that the teacher had done right to treat her as she had, for her pupil was "only plain, simple Nellie Grant, subject to the same rules which govern all the scholars," but that gave out. Julia had never been a beauty, "fair, fat and forty," the newspaper woman Emily Edson Briggs put it before relenting to say, "General Grant thinks her beautiful, and as he is the highest authority in the nation, this question is settled. Now let the country hold its peace."* Nellie was far more graceful and her opportunities unlimited. It was a shame she misused them, and made a terrible marriage. On the boat back from her European trip she made the acquaintance of one Algernon Sartoris, the son of a former opera singer named Adelaide Kemble. Adelaide was a sister of the famed actress Fanny Kemble, who forty years before had seemed to at least one young officer at Fortress Monroe—Lieutenant Robert E. Lee—to be just about the most beautiful woman he had ever seen. Sartoris was a swine. He married Nellie Grant in a White House wedding which her father observed with unwiped tears running down his cheeks before going to her room and throwing himself face down upon her bed. Then the bridegroom took the bride to his English home where, a drunk and a profligate, he made her life a misery. Julia could sympathize with her only daughter, and fully countenance and perhaps even counsel the divorce, for that was a family matter, her province. Of her husband's political doings she knew nothing. It was enough for her that she dressed wonderfully and lived in a mansion with her husband and children around her, and her father too, old "Colonel" Dent still an un-

---

*"I don't want to have your eyes fooled with," Grant had said when she considered an eye operation to remedy the squint that resulted from her strabismus condition. "They are all right as they are. They are the same eyes I looked into when I fell in love with you. I have felt and seen that expression in them through all the years since. I should miss the way you have always looked. So, if you don't mind, please let's keep your dear eyes just as they are."

reconstructed rebel cursing the damn Yankees and amusing the officers of the President's staff. (Because of the "Colonel's" presence, the President's father declined to stay at the White House overnight, preferring to lodge in an inexpensive nearby hotel. The President's mother never once came to Washington in her life.)

Devoting his time almost exclusively to finding posts for the spoilsmen and political hangers-on, his henchmen who for the moment had stolen the life and meaning of the Republican Party and turned it into a scramble for place and power and nothing more, the President seemed to the deposed Indian Affairs Commissioner, Ely Parker, to have taken "unto himself of false and strange Gods who at last ruined him utterly." It was Julia who had been the primary malignant influence, Parker decided, "her worship of wealth and wealthy men." It was Washington that was to blame, said William T. Sherman, writing that the place had been the destruction of Grant's children and forming in his own mind his later classic rejection of political power.* With the persistence that had been his salvation as a soldier but was his undoing as a President, Grant kept on as he had begun. He discharged the minister to England, John Lothrop Motley, on the grounds that in addition to wearing a monocle and parting his hair in the middle he was a friend of the idealistic Senator Charles Sumner, who had always opposed the San Domingo take-over and now was on the Senate floor referring to the President as "self-seeking . . . indolent . . . neglectful of his duties." In Motley's place Grant appointed one Robert Schenck, whose sole distinction appeared to be that he had written a definitive book on the game of poker and who, once arrived in London, occupied himself with selling shares in a gold mine out west. The word "Grantism" came to be understood as meaning the moral degradation of politics.

In 1872 the Republicans named the President again as their candidate. A whole wing of the party refused to accept the verdict

---

*"If nominated I will not run, if elected I will not serve."

and split away to nominate the editor Horace Greeley as a Liberal
Republican to whom Democrats might also rally. Grant's 1868
opponent, Horatio Seymour of New York, had not been a strong
candidate, but Greeley, an eccentric vegetarian and spiritualist
who, in Grant's eyes, physically resembled the Man in the Moon
wearing glasses, was even weaker, a truly hopeless choice whose
nomination was in the eyes of Henry Adams a complete ab-
surdity, beyond explanation. Yet the total of the vote that returned Grant to office a second time was less than the amount
that elected him the first time.

Even earlier, Henry Adams remembered, "every intelligent
man about the Government prepared to go." No one any longer
expected anything of the President—save for his henchmen using
him to make money. His coterie cared nothing for him, William
Sherman said, and would "gladly sacrifice him" if it served their
ends. Detesting all politicians, Sherman tried to speak to Grant
about what was going on all around him, but Grant would not
listen. "He seems to be unconscious that he is losing the confidence of some of the best men of our country," Sherman told
his brother, Senator John Sherman of Ohio. "The wreck of
General Grant's fame," said *The Nation*, "is a national misfortune.
That fame was a national possession, and it was the best people
of the country, those whom he is now repudiating or refusing
to rely on, who built it up."

But he was beyond changing by then, wholly the creature
of men who told him all criticism was basely inspired by political
motives. The Congress voted itself and the President pay raises
to take effect retroactively, and so his salary went from $25,000
a year to $50,000, and on the floor of the House of Represen-
tatives a congressman openly sold shares below their real price
in a railroad building enterprise totally dependent upon favorable
Congressional backing. Both the "back-pay grab" and the Crédit
Mobilier railroad scandal were laid at Grant's door, though he
had little to do with the first and nothing at all to do with the
second. It was Grantism that was responsible, people said, and
it was Grantism that explained how Secretary of the Navy George

Robeson, entering office with a net worth of $20,000, managed in his years of office, on a salary of $8,000 a year, to make bank deposits of more than $300,000.

Some of the clouds of scandal that descended upon him he could not ignore. On the day that Lee surrendered Orville Babcock had said that his possession of the pencil with which Lee receipted Grant's last note constituted his sole valuable trophy from the war. But in the years that followed, the White House years, Babcock, charming, kind, tasteful, beloved of Grant and Mrs. Grant, let no opportunity for gain escape his attention. His finger was in every pie. In St. Louis, the excesses of the Whiskey Ring with its $1,000 bills and the Sylph could no longer be hidden, and a grand jury started handing down indictments, including one with Babcock's name on it. His answer was to present a deposition by the President of the United States made in the White House before the Chief Justice of the Supreme Court. It stated that Grant had always had great confidence in the integrity of his aide and friend since Vicksburg days and had never known him to have anything to do with questions involving whiskey taxes. The President and savior of the Union had spoken, the man who had driven the rebels from the Rapidan to Appomattox, and Babcock was acquitted. He went back to Washington, spent an hour alone with the President and left the White House never to return. In later years Grant's friend George W. Childs asked Grant what had most distressed him in political life and received the reply, "To be deceived by those I trusted." Childs wrote: *He had a great many distresses.*

Babcock's replacement as aide to the President was young Ulysses S. Grant, Jr., "Buck" to the family. At breakfast one day a White House servant came to Buck and said, "The President requests your presence in the Red Drawing Room, Mr. Ulysses, at once, sir." Buck went in to find his father with a pale and distraught-looking Secretary of War Belknap. "Mr. President," Belknap said hoarsely, "I come to tender you my resignation. Accept it at once. For God's sake, do not hesitate!" Handsome, of an illustrious military family, a brave soldier during the war but entirely corrupted afterwards, Belknap had learned that one of the post traders who for years had been giving a portion of his profits to the two Mrs. Belknaps was now talking to a Senate committee. Grant had Buck write out an acceptance for the resignation and Belknap wrung his hand and said, "Thank you, you are always kind." He then rushed out, almost passing as he went Senators Morrill of Vermont and Morton of Indiana, who had come to tell the President that the Senate would that day vote impeachment proceedings against the Secretary. But he was no longer the Secretary, and so the whole matter was moot, and he got off scot-free.

That afternoon Grant sat for an artist who was doing his portrait. Representative James Garfield asked him if the artist had seen anything strange in his expression, considering the events of the morning, and the President seemed surprised by the question. He had felt no emotion, he told Garfield, who wondered if this indicated greatness or stupidity. By then Garfield found no reason to disagree when Schuyler Colfax's replacement as Vice-President, Henry Wilson, told him that Ulysses Grant was a millstone around the neck of the Republican Party. The Congress took to sniping at Grant, voting that his salary should be returned to the $25,000 a year he had received before the back-pay grab raised it to $50,000. He vetoed the measure. Senators and representatives nastily demanded justification for his lengthy vacations, in answer to which he compiled a list of the time off enjoyed by his predecessors back to George Washington.

It was all political, his cronies told him, everything; and so when George Custer, always idealistic—though headstrong— spoke freely to the Senate of the corruption ex-Secretary Belknap had fostered, and through which the President's brother Orvil had profited, the President turned against him and refused to see him when he called at the White House. Custer sat in an anteroom sending in appeals through Rufus Ingalls, who had to say he could not be received and, even worse, would not be permitted to lead his Seventh Regiment in a great summer drive aimed at ending the Indian menace in the West forever. Custer left Washington without orders and went to St. Louis to appeal frantically to Phil Sheridan for the right to be with his troops, and then to Fort Abraham Lincoln near Bismarck, Dakota Territory, and then to the Little Big Horn where, desperate to make a brilliant showing, he fatally pushed his men on without making any kind of a reconnaissance. The result of that action was learned of by the world at the height of the 1876 celebration of the 100th anniversary of the Declaration of Independence. It was the last full year of the Grant administration, and the President sent to Congress a last, strange message, a farewell address, in which he sadly said that he had come to his high office without political experience, having never even voted but once in his life, that he had made mistakes, that he wished he had done better. That he had meant well. His presidency was accounted to have been the most lamentable in history, and the judgment was continued and confirmed by later generations. Perhaps his failures were preordained by the temper of the times, the ruthlessness, corruption, brutal materialism and self-seeking that may have been a reaction to the mass impulse of idealism that had made and won the war. Ulysses Grant was not the only soldier to lose his way when the new epoch demanded new approaches beyond the soldier's code. And it seemed to those about him that nothing meant much after the drama of the brief April days of 1865 was played out. Only yesterday, then, the Army of Northern Virginia had held the long lines of the Confederacy, seemingly as secure as they had been for so many years; and then in so little a time he was walking up the steps of the McLean house. *I met you once before, General Lee, while we were serving in Mexico . . . Yes, I know I met you on that occasion.*

Grant was created, Horace Porter said later, for great things. In ordinary things he was an ordinary man. "He was made for great things, not little." The great soldier, the great instinctive soldier, who knew nothing of military history but knew how to beat Lee and end the war, considered the Presidency a sinecure, an honorary position of no great drama. It had little meaning to

him—as indeed it had but limited meaning to most Americans
of the period. Hayes came, and Garfield and Arthur, and their
impact on their times was not overly great, no greater than that
of Pierce or Buchanan before them; and the city where they
served was a sleepy deserted place when Congress was not in
session. The glitter of arms and the flutter of banners, the faces
of soldiers lit up in the glare of burning wagons, the flourish of
sabers—*Farewell the plumed troop, and the big wars. . . . Farewell
the neighing steed, and the shrill trump, the spirit-stirring drum, the
ear-piercing fife, the royal banner, and all quality, pride, pomp and
circumstance of glorious war*, Othello said, and many a Yank and
many a reb understood him—after that, what were bills to be
signed and Congressional maneuvering and trying to convince
senators? He tried. "I like Grant," wrote James Russell Lowell
when Grant had been one year into his first term, "and was
struck with the pathos of his face; a puzzled pathos, as of a man
with a problem before him of which he does not understand the
terms."

Later the historian James Schouler remembered the first
time he saw General Ulysses Grant, in uniform, at Army headquarters in Washington. Never before or after, Schouler wrote,
had he felt for any human being such a mingled feeling of awe,
gratitude and admiration. Then the soldier took off his uniform.
"Somehow Grant, the general, as first beheld in military dress,
appeared to me quite a different person from Grant the President,
rigged out at a ball in white tie and regulation black suit, or
when seen standing alone in early dusk at the White House gate,
with glossy top hat, smoking a fragrant cigar."

20

"The Very Oldest Man
You Have Ever Seen"

WASHINGTON COLLEGE'S STUDENT BODY grew from 40 to more than 400, and courses in chemistry, metallurgy, architecture, astronomy, mechanical and civil engineering and the study of modern languages were set up. The faculty got used to having the president of the college come into a classroom and sit down in the back to listen while the students recited. He was proud of the new dining hall, the library, the planetarium, the new chapel. Students came from all over the South and also from Massachussetts, New Jersey, Pennsylvania, Kansas, California. The Prussian consul in New Orleans sent his sons.

"I much enjoy the charms of civil life," Lee said, "and find too late that I have wasted the best years of my existence." He had made the greatest mistake of his life, he said, when he went to West Point.

But of course what he had been as a soldier determined the manner in which he was treated. At the White Sulphur Springs resort* 500 diners rose to their feet and stood silently when he came in to take his place at table. Later he sat with a group of young girls, and, indicating some Northern visitors whose number included the wartime governor of Pennsylvania, asked if anybody had made their acquaintance. No one had. It was in their minds that the Yankees were sneering at their new poverty and makeshift dresses. "I shall now introduce myself," he said, "and shall be glad to present any of you who shall accompany me." None of the girls got up. Finally Christina Bond of Baltimore said, "I will go, General Lee, under your orders."

"Not under my orders, but it will gratify me deeply to have your assistance." They crossed the room to where the Northerners were, he telling her of how it pained him to see resentment and bitterness in the people of the South. It was sinful to hate.

"But, General Lee," she asked, "did you never feel resentment to the North?"

"I believe I may say, looking into my own heart, and speaking as in the presence of God, that I have never known one moment of bitterness or resentment." They went to the Northerners and sat with them. "Well, General Lee," one of the Southern girls said to him later, "they say General Grant is coming next week, what will you do then?"

General Grant was not coming and no one had ever said he was, and the other girls realized Lee was being baited, but he said, "If General Grant comes, I shall welcome him to my home, show him all courtesy which is due one gentleman from another, and try to do everything in my power to make his stay here comfortable." Once when a faculty member spoke disparagingly of the President of the United States, the president of Washington College said, "Sir, if you ever again presume to speak disrespectfully of General Grant in my presence, either you or I will sever his connection with this university."

It was one of the few times he displayed any passion during those years. When a student came into his office chewing tobacco,

*Now Greenbrier.

was told to get rid of it, and came back with the cud still in his mouth, Lee wrote on a piece of paper, showed it to the student and told him it would be put on the bulletin board in ten minutes: "Mr.——— is hereby dismissed from Washington College for disrespect to the president." He did not raise his voice. He did not threaten. He seemed the image of a teacher, grown old.

One day he said to his nephew George Taylor Lee, a student, "A sweet young friend of ours, in church last night, seemed to be very uneasy and troubled about something, and I have been thinking of advising my young lady friends to wear pins in the shoulders of their dresses, points up."

The boy saw what was coming but asked innocently, "Why, sir? What was troubling her?"

"She was intently watching a young gentleman's head which, seemingly, was about to rest itself on her shoulder, and she was pushing herself as far back in the corner of the pew as she could."

"And the pins."

"Yes, the pins in their dresses would, when the gentleman's head fell on a shoulder, cause him to awaken to the realities about him."

Young George laughed and admitted he had been awfully sleepy in church the previous night. No long afterwards he saw Lee sitting at services with his eyes closed for what seemed quite a lengthy period. "Uncle Robert," he said, "I think I saw an old gentleman last Sunday night in church who sat with his eyes closed for some time, although his head did not threaten to lay itself on the shoulder of the lady sitting by him."

Lee grinned hugely. "Did you? Well, you must recollect that old people are allowed to cogitate sometimes with their eyes closed." In later years George always thought of his uncle not as the great soldier but as the kindly old gentleman rather grave with most people but always cheerful in the family circle. Reserved, of course, but neither cold nor distant. Was he lonely? George didn't know. "Did anyone really know him? I doubt if any person ever did know him altogether."

At the president's house, nights, men came to see the daughters—students to visit Mildred and Agnes, professors from the college and Virginia Military Institute to visit Mary. Just before ten, Lee would go into the outer parlor where the girls and their guests were chatting or singing at the piano. That was the signal for the gentlemen to make their good nights. If one failed to take the hint, Lee would sit by his side and look at him. His final weapon was to get up and start closing the window shutters. (One young man, told by friends that Lee had expressed a high opinion of him, said it was because he was always out of the house before ten o'clock.) None of the callers ever became serious suitors. The fact was not entirely explained by the war's losses, which had so stripped the South of its youth, nor by possible awe on the part of any young man who thought to pay court to a daughter of Robert E. Lee. "Experience will teach you," Lee wrote Mildred, "that notwithstanding all appearances to the contrary, you will never receive such a love as is felt for you by your father and mother. That lives through absences, difficulties, and time. Your own feelings will teach you how it should be returned and appreciated." When Agnes went to Baltimore for a friend's nuptials, Lee wrote, "I hope that this is the last wedding that you will attend."

He planned instruction in the new art of photography, a summer school, and worked to set up courses on business, the management of banks, insurance and joint stock companies, railroads and telegraphs. He made plans for a school of agriculture and a demonstration farm at the college. But walking was becoming increasingly difficult for him and he found Traveller's trot difficult to sustain. Always weary and often short of breath, he looked twenty years older than he was. The doctors treated him for rheumatism, lumbago, sciatica. It was his heart. The symptoms had begun showing themselves during the war.

He ignored his physical situation as best he could, sitting on the vestry of Lexington's Grace Episcopal Church and often going to the market for groceries. He showed no disinclination to carry a basket on his arm, although even on the rainiest days he disdained to use an umbrella.* He was quite homey, in his way, but Lexingtonians gasped when Mrs. Lee interrupted him when he was speaking to say, "Robert, Herbert Preston has left his cap in the back parlor; will you go and get it for him?" It seemed a strange errand, Herbert's mother thought, for the former commander of the Army of Northern Virginia. Yet when the boy and his brother fell ill with croup Lee came on a stormy night to ask how the sick ones were. Told they were not allowed past the nursery threshold, he came the next night, in even worse weather, with presents: a basket of nuts for one little invalid, a picture of a dog for the other. Their mother's eyes were wet when she told people.

When the president of the college found that an Alabama student whose family had lost everything in the war was living with a farmer several miles out of Lexington who gave him food and lodging in exchange for help with the chores, he stopped by the boy's place and asked what he did with himself between classes, where he went. The boy explained that he traveled from classroom to classroom until he found an empty one where he could do his studying. "Now that is very inconvenient," Lee said. "I have a little office and always a good fire. You will not be disturbed in your studies if you will sit there, so come to my office tomorrow." The boy went and found Lee had placed a chair and table in the room for him, and so there he sat day after day. One day the boy, H. B. Fergusson, caught a cold and decided not to make the long trip from his lodgings into Lexington. The next day Lee came on Traveller. "He had missed me from his office and was afraid I was sick and so had come to see about me." In the summer Lee came again to find young Fergusson, unable to afford a trip back home, working for the farmer by separating the chaff and wheat from the straw. He was dirty and grimy. Lee spoke of the usefulness of farm work, but said he had something for the boy that might be more con-

*Both practices are taboo for the officer.

genial. It turned out to be a job teaching summer school. Fergusson grew up to be a United States congressman from New Mexico.

Each day, the president went to talk with the workmen who were building the new chapel. "Oh, Doctor," he said once in a broken voice to the minister who taught moral philosophy, "if I could only know that all of the young men in the college were good Christians, I should have nothing more to desire!" His eyes overflowed as he spoke. He had not cried at Gettysburg or at Appomattox.

In the spring of 1869 he was prevailed upon to go to Baltimore with a group of men seeking funds to put a railroad into Lexington, to stand with them on the floor of the Corn and Flour Exchange and there lobby the financiers for money. (He had tried to beg off, but the men insisted.) Thousands cheered him, and at church the next day he found lines of people extending down the street. (Back home in Lexington one of the girls criticized his headgear and he said, "You don't like this hat? Why, I have seen a whole cityful come out to admire it!") He had another call to pay during the Baltimore visit. Through an intermediary the President of the United States had asked that he visit the White House. He took the train from Baltimore to Washington and a carriage from the station to where Grant was. Across the Potomac he caught a glimpse of lost Arlington. It was May 1, 1869. Five years earlier on that date the Army of the Potomac had been preparing to break camp and go south to cross the Rapidan and meet the Army of Northern Virginia.

Grant stood up. They shook hands. Lee mentioned his trip to Baltimore was in connection with railroad construction and Grant essayed a mild jest: "You and I, General, have had more to do with destroying railroads than with building them." Lee did not smile. The others in the room withdrew, the Baltimore couple who were Lee's hosts, the aides to the President, and the victor and vanquished of The Wilderness, Spotsylvania, Cold Harbor, the Siege and Appomattox sat down together alone. Beyond telling people of his little joke that fell flat, Grant discussed their talk in no detail. Lee never referred to it, not even mentioning it in a letter to Mrs. Lee. For fifteen minutes they spoke together and then Lee arose. They shook hands. It had been a quarter of a century since the elegant colonel in Mexico told the scrubby captain that he should wear dress uniform when coming to headquarters. It was four years and three weeks since one had stood by the McLean house to watch the other ride away to tell his army that their war was over. Lee left.

At White Sulphur Springs ex-soldiers who had known him before turned away and wept to see him as he was. He stood, they said—the South said—for the concept that there is something higher than mere victory, something better than the belief that what succeeds is good. The North had won, they said, but where was the real glory in victory that brought the basest kind of corruption, the company town and tenement-row exploitation of immigrants more terrible than the excesses of slavery, the reduction of the great and generous soldier Ulysses Grant to the pawn of partisan spoilsmen? Opposed to that was a man whose material failure was a moral success, one who had lost, yet had saved his soul.

But he was old. The magnificent carriage was gone and the shoulders sagged. The slightest exercise brought pain to his chest. He was the symbol of all that was best in what had been lost to the South forever, the proof to his countrymen living through the troubled dream of Reconstruction that earthly success was not the criterion of merit nor the measure of greatness, and as that symbol he kept up appearances to the outside world. But at home he was silent and depressed. He began to speak of himself as an invalid. An invalid could not run Washington College. He said he would resign his position in the near future. The trustees told him that the president's house was his to occupy for the rest of his life and that his salary, raised now from $1,500 to $3,000 a year, would be remitted to Mrs. Lee so long as she lived. He replied that he could not permit such arrangements; all the college's buildings and funds should be devoted to educational matters.

In the spring of 1870 the faculty united to urge that he take a vacation. The professors put their suggestion in the form of a letter. Let him go south for a couple of months. Perhaps he would regain his health. He agreed to go, saying he would take Agnes—"or perhaps she will take me." On March 24, the students and faculty saw him off from the canal boat wharf. Agnes waved. He took off his hat. That night he had trouble sleeping on the boat, and the dust of the railroad into Richmond bothered him. He felt feverish. The two travelers left Virginia and crossed into North Carolina. In the half a decade since the end of the war he had left his native state only for the brief trip to Baltimore and Washington and to the resorts in what had become West Virginia.

He appeared to think of himself as an ordinary tourist concerned with schedules and accommodations, and as such a tourist, at ten o'clock at night on March 28, got off the train in Warrentown, near where his daughter Annie was buried. There he was spotted by an amazed local Confederate veteran who was at the station to meet his sister. It seemed impossible to Will White that this was actually happening, but he asked his former commander to come to his parents' home, and there the travelers spent the night. In the morning the ex-soldier's people lent them a carriage and gave Agnes an armful of white hyacinths to lay at Annie's grave. They went on by train toward Augusta, Georgia, but now the news of their coming went flying before them. At midnight in Raleigh the streets surrounding the station were jammed with people roaring, "Lee! Lee!" Neither Agnes nor her father raised the blinds by their berths. The train went on and even at tiny little wayside depots the right-of-way was lined with wagons carrying people who held up their babies and waved handkerchiefs in the air. It bewildered him. "Why should they care to see me?" he asked. "I am only a poor old Confederate."

The entire population of Salisbury gathered to welcome the train, a band blaring. Charlotte was the same but a bigger crowd, a bigger band. They rolled into South Carolina. A holdiay had been declared at Columbia and stores and offices were closed. In a steady rain masses of Confederate veterans paraded to the station, trumpets and drums sounding. A long line of former officers stood on the platform, among their number former General E. Porter Alexander, who once had wondered if Lee was audacious, and who later commanded the artillery that shelled Cemetery Ridge at Gettysburg. The old man realized he would have to get out of the train, and went into the rain to receive bouquets and cheers and salutes and to lift his hat and then bow in response to the pleas that he make a speech and, finally, to sweep Alexander's little daughter up into his arms.

At Augusta, the Planter's Hotel, a line of people surged through an hours-long receiving line, wounded veterans mixing with little boys who, too young or shy to say their names, pushed forward cards upon which their fathers or mothers had written that the child's given names were Robert Edward Lee. Exhausted, weary and haggard, he had to greet thousands of men and women who wore their Sunday clothes for this moment. Cheers thundered through the air, rebel yells, serenades. Outside Savannah the train halted to permit a delegation of former officers to board, and in the city the largest crowd ever seen there waited. It took half an hour of determined pushing to get him to a nearby carriage. What had been meant to be a peaceful and relaxing search for better health was turning into a nightmarish triumphal tour. "I do not think traveling in this way procures me much quiet and repose," he wrote home. If he walked at more than the slowest pace, his chest pained him.

They took a steamer south and stopped at Cumberland Island off the Georgia coast to visit his father's grave. Agnes covered it with fresh flowers. They went on in the boat. "The pain in my chest, along the heart bone, is ever present when I walk or make any exertion." At Jacksonville so many people rushed on board their steamer that it was in danger of capsizing, and he had to walk out on the deck and be seen so that the throng would be satisfied and leave. They sailed along the Florida coast and sometimes at remote locations he was able to walk slowly along the shore in the sunshine. They went back to Savannah and took the train to Charleston. He had hoped to arrive there and leave unnoticed, but delegations of all kinds, military groups, bands, crowds, pursued him. Invitations poured in from all over asking that he visit. "Our kind people seem to think that I am running loose or have a roving commission to travel the country."

At Wilmington, North Carolina, his attempt to keep secret the time of his arrival failed and he was met by boys in uniform from a military academy, presenting arms. He issued a request that there be no more special demonstrations, but at Portsmouth, back in Virginia, thundering cannons greeted him and when he boarded the ferry to Norfolk it was to the accompaniment of candles and rockets shooting up into the air. He was on the very last reserves of his declining strength. From the far shore the United Fire Company's gun salutes shook the wharves. Only a narrow pathway through a mass of cheering people led to Christ Church the next day, and he almost had to force his way through, so weak that those close to him thought he might actually die there. He took a steamer up the James and visited with relatives along the river. He got to his son Rooney's place, where Mrs. Lee was waiting. "I do not like his complexion, and he still seems stiff," she wrote Mildred. They went back to Lexington.

"My child, I think that I am the very oldest man you have ever seen," he told a youthful admirer. The heat that summer bothered him terribly, and when he went to the mountain springs resorts there was no longer any question of riding there on Traveller—it had to be the stagecoach. In the fall Washington College's classes got underway. September 28 was rainy. He worked in his office during the morning, went home, ate and took a nap in his armchair, Agnes rubbing his hands as he fell asleep. In the afternoon he put on a cape to go to a meeting of the vestry of Grace Church. Mildred was playing the piano in the parlor. He kissed her and left. The church was cold and damp and he wore his cape throughout. The last item to be discussed was the salary of the minister. The total of pledges was $55 short of what was required. "I will give that sum," Lee said. The meeting adjourned and he walked up the college hill to the president's house.

Tea was on the table. "You have kept us waiting a long time," Mrs. Lee said. "What have you been doing?" He did not answer but stood silently at the head of the table. They waited for him to say grace, but he did not utter a sound. "Let me pour you a cup of tea, you look tired," she said. Again he did not answer, but slowly and deliberately he sat down and then straightened himself in the chair. His wife saw in his face a look she had never seen there before. They sent for the doctors.

21

Mountains and Valleys

So RELUCTANT TO DEPART the White House that they stayed late into the afternoon of Rutherford B. Hayes' first day of office and made people wonder if they would ever go, ex-President and Mrs. Ulysses S. Grant really had nothing to do with themselves. To take up residence in the house that their little Galena in Illinois had given them—it seemed an inappropriate setting. They still had the gift house in Washington's "I" Street, but not the means to maintain it, for his income from the monies presented him after the war totaled only $6,000 a year. Others had made millions during his eight years as President, but he had saved very little. A banquet here, a reception there, and they decided to go tour the world. "As long as the money holds out," he said.

They departed, general and his lady, for he was thought of more as the ex-soldier than the ex-politician, on May 17, 1877. They had no fixed plans, no itinerary. By the time they had finished their trip two and a half years later, they had put Marco

Polo in the shade. Imperial Highness and peasant alike competed to do honor to Ulysses Grant. More people saw him than had beheld anyone else in history. Through him, America came of age. Before, it had been viewed as a remote frontier country of no world importance, but now it was seen as a vastly rich and determined nation capable of fighting a war whose length and breadth made European encounters look like skirmishes, and whose new millionaires rivaled King Midas. And here was its representative, the generalissimo of its armies and intimate of its rich men, a personage who by his own efforts had in Arabian Nights fashion come from nowhere to reach undreamable heights, all in a manner no European could possibly emulate, and no Oriental even comprehend.

The Grants had expected nothing when they arrived in England. Other ex-Presidents, Millard Fillmore and Martin Van Buren, had gone to Europe when their times in the White House had ended without exciting much notice. But at Liverpool there was a gigantic crowd. They had thought a few paid officials of the American government might be there to make them welcome, but instead there were hundreds of thousands of cheering Englishmen, bands, signs, banners, a Lord Mayor's speech comparing him to Hannibal. Amazed, they went to London and found themselves at dinners and balls and receptions offered by the Prince of Wales, the son of the Duke of Wellington, Lord Derby, Gladstone, Salisbury. Crowds jammed the streets wherever they went, they were given the freedom of the City of London, were received at Guildhall, the Queen had them overnight at Windsor Castle. An international sensation was created by twenty-year-old Jesse Grant's refusal to eat at the table of the Queen's Household. He would not dine with the help, he said, disdaining the explanation that the Household was composed of members of the nobility. Grant passively supported his son's stand, saying he guessed he'd feel the same way in his place. Courtiers scurried to Victoria and she decreed that Jesse might join his parents at her table. Britain's monarch had surrendered to Grant's son, trumpeted the papers at home.

The Duke of Devonshire had them to dinner at a table where sat fifty peers of the realm. Disraeli gave them what he termed a "colossal" meal. Bands thundered "Hail Columbia" and fireworks shot off into the skies wherever they went. In Belgium, Grant sat silently while Julia chatted with the King and then said to her husband, "Do you know Her Majesty is a fine whip? Yes, King Leopold tells me she sometimes drives four-in-hand." A German colonel came with letters from Bismarck and the army chief, von Moltke, the latter writing that he would of course meet General Grant with all military honors. The envoy was astonished to learn that no war-like pageantry was desired, just a trip for relaxation and pleasure. In France, Marshal-President MacMahon called him one of the three greatest soldiers in history—he did not say who the other two were, Grant noted—and M. Worth personally supervised the fitting of dresses for Julia. There were speeches and dinners hailing the general as a liberator and a man of forgiveness who had chosen not to give the rebels prison, the scaffold, the galley, Devil's Island or Siberia. Alsace greeted them with rigid Prussian soldiers in pickelhauben; Lake Maggiore yielded a vacationing Russian princess Jesse remembered as the most beautiful woman he had ever seen.

In Southern Germany, Wagner played his music for them; and Pompeii's authorities excavated a house for him, finding a loaf of bread wrapped in cloth. They wandered north to Scotland and the castle of the Duke of Argyll, bagpipes shrilling as they dined. The Duke of Sutherland's Great Hall was lined with stag heads mounted upon oak shields, each inscribed in gilt with the name of the sportsman who had secured the trophy. Grant declined to join their number. They decided upon a Mediterranean cruise and went to Palermo, passing through decorated streets, hearing the sound of innumerable bells, being greeted by besworded Italian officers and officials in uniforms glittering with decorations and gold braid, and finally boarding the U.S. Navy's *Vandalia* there. They sailed on Christmas Eve and went past that Stromboli whose sirens had so enchanted an earlier Ulysses. This time Penelope was along, Julia said.

Their trip was feeding upon itself, the news of it, the excitement. At Alexandria so much smoke rose from the shore cannons firing salutes to be returned gun for gun by the *Vandalia* that it almost appeared a naval engagement was taking place. The Khedive put at their disposal Cairo's Palace of Kassr-el-Noussa with its marble halls and servants appearing noiselessly when one clapped one's hands. From it they sallied forth into a panorama of mosques, palms, bazaars, monkeys and camels and beggars seen from their open carriage preceded by runners in white flowing garments who held up silver wands. On the Khedive's long, narrow flat-bottom river steamer hung with amber and turquoise satin they went for a three-week cruise up the Nile. The director of the national museum served as their guide and showed them the Abydos ruins where 4,500 years before the birth of Christ Menes, the first Egyptian king, ruled. Swathed in headdresses and wearing sun helmets, they rode through golden desert sands on donkeys rented from owners extolling their virtues while at the same time shrieking for baksheesh. Girls carrying water in jugs on their heads ran by the side of their mounts. Dust rose into the air from their caravan. They went to the colossal statues at Memnon, the Great Hall of Karnak.

After Jaffa and before Jerusalem they saw the brook where David found the stones with which he fought Goliath, and then they rode into the city, Grant riding the Pasha's favorite white Arab with trappings of solid gold. In New York, young Ulysses S. Grant, Jr., met a Wall Street wizard, Ferdinand Ward, who helped him invest his father's money, the profits gained enabling the travelers to continue their journey. The Sultan Abdul-Hamid was their host in Constantinople, and in Athens the Parthenon was specially illuminated for them by means of 1,000 Bengal fires lit one after the other so that each corner of the structure was bathed in a sea of light. In Italy they met King Umberto and had an audience with Pope Leo XIII, who blessed the diamond cross Julia wore, her husband's twenty-fifth anniversary gift. Then came Venice, where Grant was reported to have said it would be a nice place if they drained the streets. Museums

and cathedrals everywhere bored him, but he liked industrial
plants and railroad stations, and walking in the streets. Julia
happily spoke English to everybody and as happily assumed they
understood her, believing, Minister to Spain James Russell Lowell said, "the language of Shakespeare and Milton as something
universally applicable that had triumphed over Babel."

They went on to Milan, Amsterdam, and dinner with the
German Crown Prince and Princess in Berlin. Grant strolled
from the hotel to Bismarck's palace, astonishing the guards who
had looked for a coach with postillions, threw the stub of his
cigar in the street, and had a long talk with the Prince-Chancellor.
Julia's hand was kissed and complimented on the return call.
Copenhagen was dinner with the Danish monarchs at the Castle
of Elsinore, and a look at the brook where Ophelia died; then
came Stockholm, with every prominent point in the harbor and
every island filled with American flags. They went to Russia and
Julia told the Russian Crown Princess she brought love from
that royalty's mother, the Queen of Denmark. St. Petersburg's
fountains were played for them and were magnificent; the Winter
Palace had halls 30 feet wide with superb vases mounted on
stands 7 feet high. On the Tsar's yacht they sailed through
saluting squadrons of the Imperial Russian Navy. They went to
Moscow, then Warsaw, and then Vienna for dinner at Schön-
brunn with Francis Joseph—Elizabeth was off hunting in Ire-
land.

In Spain there was a dinner with Alfonso XII in captain-
general's uniform, then a brilliant reception by the King and
Queen of Portugal, His Majesty telling them of his translations
of Shakespeare into Portuguese and presenting a copy of the
translated *Hamlet*. Cordova, Seville, banquets, receptions, jammed
streets, signs bursting into flame: WELCOME, GENERAL GRANT. The
Alhambra, he, bored, saying, "Come on, or I will leave you and
shut the door after me." A priest unlocked a closet with iron
doors and took out the silver jewel box in which Queen Isabella
had kept her gems, the ones said to have been pawned to finance
Columbus' trip. "It looks very new," Grant whispered. "He was

skeptical about a great deal he saw abroad," Julia remembered.

Valencia, Barcelona, Paris and Tiffany's, where he bought Julia a Christmas present of a jeweled butterfly with diamond wings, ruby eyes and body of glittering topaz. Cold weather was coming and so they went to Marseilles and sailed the length of the Mediterranean, after which they took a train to Suez with its flies, tiny narrow streets, exotic flowers and trees, strings of camels and mud houses. There the Pasha saw them off on the *Venetia* of the Peninsula and Oriental Line. With brilliant sunsets and great hovering moon at night, and long days on straw chairs under the awning extended the length and breadth of the ship, they made Bombay. British troops presented arms as they debarked, bands played and a carriage of state with outriders took them to the Governor's residence.

Dozens of servants in turbans and gowns saw to their every wish there, and they went to the caves of Elephanta with carvings of gigantic figures of the gods. After magnificent state dinners they went to Jubbulpore, officers and ladies in full dress seeing them off, regimental colors drooping in salute. They rode elephants, saw a river running through marble rocks, went to Allahabad as guards of honor in tigerskins turned out, saw the Taj Mahal, stayed at the home of the Resident. Garlanded in flowers they toured shrines, saw temples and beggars, sacred gardens. Their son Fred came over to join them and go pigsticking and tiger hunting. The Viceroy welcomed them to his Calcutta palace, which was three times the size of the White House, and so did the Maharajah of Jeypore, the Maharajah of Johore, the Maharajah of Tongore. When they left Lucknow a long line of elephants raised their trunks and held them up as gun after gun went off, heard from their departing train as finally a dull thumping far away.

Policemen standing 10 feet apart, a mile of them, saw them from train to palace and palace to train; they met with Indian princes gorgeously attired and wearing jewels beyond value; they went through avenues of manicured private parks ablaze with lights—thousands of tapers in glass cups—up marble staircases to immense rooms to stand on balconies and hear masses of people playing trumpets, horns, drums, and see them wave fans as mountains of fireworks went off into the skies. The East expected to behold warrior and generalissimo and, as they thought, ex-King of America, in High Victorian military finery of feathers and plumes or in potentate's ceremonial robes, and instead saw a short, plainly dressed man grown chubby from the White House dinners and the feasts of the tour, always with a cigar in his mouth. No one knew exactly what to make of him or his stubby wife. They did not know what to make of America. "You know," said the son and heir of the last Emperor of Delhi, Tamerlane's direct descendant, "General Grant don't speak English. I was told that he only talked American Indian. I can speak English, but, I am sorry to say, I cannot speak American Indian." Prince Kung, Regent of the Chinese Empire, asked Fred Grant if he had children, and learning that he had one and that she was a girl, said, "What a pity."

They went to Burma and up the Irrawaddy, to Penang, Malacca, to Singapore where cannons boomed in the harbor and American flags rose to the tops of hundreds of masts. On the pier were evergreens entwined around great wooden arches of welcome. Easter Sunday they spent in the home of His Royal Highness Prince Somdetch Chowfa Bhanurangie-Scoanwongs of Bangkok, whose servants flocked about bowing almost to the ground. The palace of the King of Siam, set in grounds encompassing as much space as a good-sized city, had doors of mother-of-pearl inlaid in ebony, with solid gold images of Buddha set under canopies of gold, surrounded by more images with the god's fingers holding diamonds, emeralds, rubies. The floors were made of blocks of brass. The King paraded his elephants, their howdahs filled with armed men of war. They went on to French Cochin-China and at Saigon stayed with the Governor in heat so fearful that Julia was unable to sleep. In Hong Kong, British officials and esteemed opium merchants met them. They went up the Canton River into China, forts on the shore firing salutes. Hundreds of differently colored flags floated from the lances of the fortresses' garrisons. Coolies at Shampeen, the foreign settlement of Canton, carried them ashore, and in the morning they awoke to the sound of river junks firing salutes and setting off deafening firecrackers. Carried in chairs high in the air, each traveler alone in a pagoda-like conveyance closed in by glass windows and shaded by bamboo matting blinds, they called upon the Viceroy of Canton. For more than an hour they were carted along, up one street, down the other, through crowds packed as far as the eye could see, the people entirely silent and immobile. When someone from the pressure of the throng was pushed past a designated line, a policeman's lash instantly came down on the interloper's back. Hundreds of soldiers were lined up in front of the Viceroy's palace and a band ground its way through what seemed to be *Lohengrin* to Dr. John M. Keating, one of several friends who joined the Grants on and off during their trip.

Carried in—more dead than alive, Keating remembered—to Lin Kwan Yu, the Viceroy, they talked through an interpreter in a room whose walls were tapestried in silk. In the next room were hundreds of mandarins and their attendants. Tea was served and some sweetmeats for which the visitors awkwardly used their silver-mounted ivory chopsticks. Then came the whole sedan-chair trip in reverse, salutes, soldiers, the crowds, the 3-mile swaying journey. The next day the Viceroy returned the visit, preceded by horsemen, then two men carrying enormous gongs struck in unison at each step, then a double file of carriers with banners giving the titles of the Viceroy, then an armed guard with huge shields and murderous swords, then other men with spears and flags. The Viceroy was carried in, Grant offering tea and sweatmeats. The weather "having been carefully and thoroughly discussed," the Viceroy departed. That evening they were carried in the fashion they had come to think of as usual back to the palace to be offered a meal of eighty-six courses, fish, roasted peach kernels and watermelon seeds, pork, dainty morsels of bird, soup, more soup, pigeons' eggs—they made a pass at forty-six courses and took their leave.

Macao was next, then a departure from Amoy that Keating found indescribable for the tumult of the salutes fired from the rocky cliffs—it was like the war—then the Formosa Channel and Shanghai, where it was impossible that one additional person could be added to the crowd on the wharves. Ships of all nations flew flags, showed buntings. They went to the theater and the audience rose and the actors bowed. They were seated in the best seats, just by the orchestra whose gongs and drums deafened them. They understood nothing of the play and could not talk because of the orchestra. A scream would have seemed a whisper in that noise, Keating thought.

They went to Japan where, on July 4, 1879, the Mikado received the touring couple, Julia in mauve silk gown by Worth, demitrain, trimmed with Brussels lace, with a hat of clustered flowers and lace. It was an event of the highest importance in the history of the Japanese nation. Like all his predecessors, the Emperor Mutsuhito was accustomed to having his ministers give their reports and opinions to him while on their hands or knees or flat on their faces. Never had a Japanese Imperial Majesty addressed anybody in the world on anything remotely approaching an equal basis. But for Ulysses Grant he stepped forward and offered his hand, in so constrained and awkward a manner that it was obvious he was doing it for the first time. They sailed for San Francisco on the *City of Tokyo*, Japanese warships escorting them far out to sea. They landed and began a slow progression back to the East coast, stopping here and there. "Julia, that is the field where I planted my potatoes," he said in Oregon. On December 16, 1879, they reached the Philadelphia they had left May 17, 1877.

Even before winning election President Hayes had said he would not seek a second term, and so the Republican nomination was open. Away from America, a being depicted as continually consorting with kings and god-emperors, Grant's flaws as President had been if not forgotten then at least pushed out of mind. Those who had been his political controllers in the past preferred him away garnering headlines on triumphal foreign tours, and so he went off to Cuba and Mexico, another leg of that great journey of receptions, crowds, dinners. At the Republican Convention that summer Senator Roscoe Conkling of New York nominated him for a third term, saying, "When asked what state he hails from, our reply shall be, He hails from Appomattox, and its famous apple tree."*

Grant received 304 votes on the first ballot, 370 being needed for the nomination. The delegates went through vote after vote for days, but his total did not rise. Julia begged him to go on the floor of the convention, saying he would stampede the people, but he said he would rather cut off his right hand than beg. "Oh, Ulyss," she said, "how unwise, what mistaken chivalry. For heaven's sake, go, go tonight." He would not. They chose James Garfield. Grant's political career was over. He was still relatively young, fifty-eight—Bismarck had told him he had expected a much older man—but, as before the world tour, he had no place to go and nothing to do. Some rich men in New York and elsewhere took up a subscription to buy him a house and give him an income, and raised sufficient funds for the purchase of a townhouse at 3 East 66th Street and some railroad bonds.

There remained the question of a job, an endeavor, something to do. His son Ulysses, Jr., "Buck," was going into a brokerage partnership with Ferdinand Ward, the Wall Street man who had offered good tips on investments, and Grant decided to join the firm. Buck put up $100,000 supplied by his wealthy father-in-law, Senator James B. Chaffee of Colorado, and Grant put up a like amount. Ward contributed $200,000 in securities. They set up offices in the building at the corner of Wall Street and Broadway, and from the start things went well. The

---

*"The famous apple tree" was the one under which Lee waited to hear from Grant on the last day at Appomattox. The source of American legend, it became transformed into the place where, before echelons of troops lined up in parade-ground order, with parks of artillery and squadrons of cavalry in the background, Lee formally offered his sword to Grant, who magnanimously refused it. A whole railway carload of trinkets, charms and keepsakes were marketed as coming from the tree, said the reporter Sylvanus Cadwallader.

son of a minister from Geneseo in upstate New York, suave, polite, Ward ran everything. Within a short time he was alloting Buck and Grant salaries of some $3,000 a month each. Grant went to the office each day, smoked, signed some papers, talked with friends who came by to give the firm capital for investment. One old Army associate deposited $50,000 with Grant & Ward, came back from a European tour and stopped by to ask of his money's progress. Ward said he did not know offhand but would look at the records. He came back to Grant and the friend in a few minutes to say that the man's total was now a quarter of million dollars, which he could of course withdraw if he so wished. "Set that hen again," the man said. All of Grant's relatives put in their money—his widowed sister, his young nieces. Ward multiplied it, multiplied it again. They ought to think about helping friends buy houses and giving them regular allowances, Grant told Julia. There was no need to worry about leaving a large estate for the children—"Ward is making us all rich, them as well as ourselves." His partner, he said, was the finest financial mind America had produced since Alexander Hamilton.

He played cards, went to Long Branch, devoted himself to his grandchildren. "Your father and mother have come to pay us a visit," he wrote Fred's daughter, "and we are very sorry they didn't bring you. They brought me instead the beautiful picture you made me for my birthday, and I hasten to thank my big pet for all the trouble she took to give her grandfather such a fine surprise. Grandpa hung the picture up where he can see it all the time." She remembered him in later years as always talking to her seriously and taking her for buggy rides behind a fast horse, she standing up between his knees. He taught her how to count and to make a cat's cradle. Her father, Fred, quit the Army and went to live in a suburban New Jersey house nicely furnished from Grant & Ward profits, and she and her parents were often with her grandparents at Long Branch. She remembered Grant with George Pullman, George W. Childs and A. J. Drexel, all very rich men. He was almost of their type now, for his worth was in the vicinity of $2½ million, he told members of the family—and others. It was undignified of him to talk about money all the time, William T. Sherman thought, and to glory in spending his time solely with rich men who, Sherman also thought, would have given their all to have won even one of Grant's great victories during the war. It was bewildering, Phil Sheridan said, to hear his old chief talk of nothing else but business and money while never mentioning one thing about the Army or the war. But Grant kept up his money talk. He turned his income from the gift railroad bonds over to Ward, sold his Washington house for $65,000 and gave it to Ward, borrowed $45,000 on his New York house and gave it to Ward.

On Sunday, May 4, 1884, Ward called at Grant's home. The city chamberlain of New York was going to make a large withdrawal from the Marine Bank in Brooklyn, he said, and the result would be to put the bank into a temporary embarrassment. Grant & Ward, he said, had $650,000 on deposit at the Marine Bank, and it would be unpleasant if the bank failed and the deposit was lost. Therefore he felt it best to shore up the bank. He, Ward, would raise $150,000 to deposit. Would General Grant undertake to do the same? Grant went down Fifth Avenue to the mansion of William Henry Vanderbilt,* which took up the entire space between Fifty-first and Fifty-second streets. For the Marine Bank he cared nothing at all, Vanderbilt told him, and for the firm of Grant & Ward little more. "But I'll lend you the money personally. To you—General Grant—I'm making this loan, and not to the firm." Grant took the check and endorsed it over to Ward, who was waiting back at Sixty-sixth Street.

Two days later, Tuesday, Grant came into the offices of the firm and found his son coatless and with a frantic look on his face. "How's it, Buck?" he asked.

"Grant & Ward have failed," Buck replied. "Ward has fled." Unable to open the office safe where the securities were kept, Buck had the door taken off. The safe was empty. Neither the

---

*Of "The public be damned" fame.

Marine Bank nor any other bank contained a cent of Grant &
Ward money. Everything had been a colossal swindle. Ward had
lied, forged, run a pyramid scheme to pay off Peter while stealing
from Paul. Even the securities he had originally put up to match
the Grants' investment were fraudulent. Grant & Ward had
obligations of more than $15 million, and assets of less than
$100,000, among which was not included the money lent by
William Henry Vanderbilt. Ward had decamped with it.

Grant went into his office and sat down, his hands clutching
the arms of his chair. Late in the afternoon the firm's cashier
broke away from the people outside shouting for money they
had entrusted to Grant & Ward and looked in on the general.
He was sitting holding the arms of the chair. "How is it that
man has deceived us all in this manner?" Grant asked. The
cashier had no answer. "I don't see how I can trust any human
being again," Grant said. Silently the cashier withdrew. Grant's
head was buried in his hands.

Julia had some $130 in the house, and he had $80 in his
wallet. There was nothing else. To make things worse, railroads
were going through a difficult period, and the payments on the
gift railroad bonds were suspended. Fred immediately rented out
his New Jersey house, sold his horses and carriage and went
with his family to live with his parents, hitching a ride to the
railroad station with the village grocer. Orders placed for food,
cigars and wine for delivery to summer homes were cancelled.
Soon checks written the previous week started coming back,
bounced by the banks. Grant's financial situation was what it
had been back in the days before the war, with the additional
humiliation that the whole world knew. In Lansingburgh, near
Albany, New York, one Charles Wood, whom Grant had never
heard of, sent a check for $1,000, a loan, he said, given in con-
sideration of "services ending in April, 1865." They lived on
that plus a check for the same amount left on the parlor table
by Matías Romero, the Mexican minister to the United States.

There remained the matter of the $150,000 owed to William

Henry Vanderbilt. The financier indicated that the matter could be let go, but to Grant it was a question of personal honor. He could not make good the debts of Grant & Ward, but this debt of Ulysses S. Grant he could. He made over the deed of his house to Vanderbilt, and, as a dray waited outside, Buck and Fred packed up to add to the deed everything of value that their father owned: ornaments from hats worn at Belmont and Fort Donelson, shoulder straps from uniforms of Vicksburg and Petersburg days, a gold model of the McLean house table, a pen used in writing orders, canes and swords, forty medals of gold, silver, bronze, an onyx cabinet given by the people of Puebla, Mexico, a portrait of General Scott, vases from Yokohama, an elephant tusk given by the King of Siam, the menu of a Paris dinner inscribed on silver, gold cigar cases, the silver trowel used for laying the cornerstone of New York's Museum of Natural History, his warrant as cadet at West Point and commissions from brevet second lieutenant to four-star General of the Army.

Ward would be tried and sent to jail for almost ten years, as would the head of the Marine Bank, who abetted his thievery, but that would not pay any bills for Grant. For years people had opportuned him to write his memoirs of the war, but he had always declined, saying he was no writer and didn't need the money in any case. He would leave notes behind, he said, and his children could do a book, if they so decided. But now the situation was different, and when the editors of *The Century* magazine said they would give him $500 apiece for four articles, he set to work.

That summer he wrote of Shiloh. What came out was dry, like an official battle report. The magazine people hinted that something more personal was needed, and he redid the piece, adding details, telling what he had done and thought about, back then, in the rain on the slopes above Pittsburg Landing along the Tennessee, twenty-two years earlier. He worked on articles about his other fights of long ago. He used the money from the magazine articles to pay back Charles Wood, the complete stranger who had sent $1,000.

That fall, after giving a reading in New York's Chickering Hall, the author Mark Twain fell into conversation with Richard Gilder, editor of *The Century*. Gilder described how anxious Grant was to do the articles and how happy he had been to get the series of $500 checks and how he was now thinking of doing a full-fledged book for *The Century*'s publishing house. Twain was always ready to believe the worst of publishers—an honored place in heaven was assured anybody who could manage to cheat one of that breed, he said—and to him the payment of $500 an article to Ulysses S. Grant was not only "the monumental injustice of the Nineteenth century, but of all centuries." Ten thousand would have been trivial, and even $20,000 inadequate.

In the morning, Twain hustled to Grant's house. He asked if it was true that Grant was going to do a book *The Century* would publish. Grant said a rough contract had been drawn up, and read it aloud. Twain "didn't know whether to cry or laugh." The terms, he felt, would have been quite reasonable for "any unknown Comanche Indian whose book they had reason to believe might sell three thousand or four thousand or five thousand copies." But Ulysses S. Grant? Twain was in the publishing business himself now, and would soon be bringing out *Huckleberry Finn*, and he told Grant *The Century* offer was absurd. Under its terms Grant was hoping to make perhaps $30,000, if all went well. That was the amount Sherman had realized from the sale of his memoirs. Twain said the Grant memoirs should consist of two volumes and that he, Twain, would offer an advance of $50,000 plus the hope of royalties. Grant said he could not accept so substantial a down payment when there was no certainty Twain's firm would ever make it back. They settled the down payment at $20,000. At the signing of the contract Grant's lawyer, Frederick Seward, son of the wartime Secretary of State, took a Twain associate aside and said the Grant family was waiting at home for some money. They did not "have a penny in the house." The associate at once wrote a check and Seward gave it to a messenger boy.

And so began *Personal Memoirs of U. S. Grant*, the story of his hate for his father's tanning business, his inept horse-trading experience where everyone laughed at him because he told the seller his father had told him to offer $20 and if the offer wan't accepted to offer $25, West Point and his hopes the place would be abolished so he could escape, Mexico and then Belmont and Shiloh and The Wilderness and all the days of 1861–1865, and finally Appomattox and Lee: "In my rough traveling suit, the uniform of a private with the straps of a lieutenant general, I must have contrasted very strangely with a man so handsomely dressed, six foot high* and of faultless form." Sitting at a table with a pen and paper the silent man found his voice, and what he wrote was acclaimed upon its publication as a great American autobiography, a judgment time has not changed.

One day at Long Branch he bit into a peach and felt an excruciating pain at the base of his tongue. It was so sharp a pang that Julia wondered if an insect concealed in the peach had bitten him. He thought it was a throat cold, but the feeling hung on. A Philadelphia doctor who was visiting Grant's friend George W. Childs, the publisher of the Philadelphia *Public Ledger*, was asked to examine the throat. He told Grant he should see his own doctor at once. Grant dallied away some weeks, hoping the pain would go away, and then on October 22, 1884, went to his physician. The same day he was sent to the offices of a throat specialist, Dr. John Hancock Douglas.

Douglas took one look and knew what the eventual outcome would be. Something must have shown in his face, for Grant asked, "Is it cancer?"

"The disease is serious, epithelial† in character, and sometimes capable of being cured."

From then on Grant went to Douglas' office every day, riding streetcars and using transfers to save on fares. The doctor worked at trying to reduce a lump that despite his efforts went from the size of a pea to that of a plum. He painted on a solution

---

*He was five feet ten.
†A euphemism of the time for the word cancer.

of hydrochlorate of cocaine to alleviate the pain. To operate was out of the question. The inflammation crept over the palate. Winter came. Grant worked on his book. Fred helped, looking up dates and maps. Adam Badeau of his wartime staff, a professional writer, came and helped.

He gave up cigars, writing friends that it had not been as difficult to do as he imagined. "For a day or two I felt as though I would like to smoke, but after that I never thought of it." The lump grew. He had trouble getting liquids past it and Douglas applied iodoform. In mid-February the ulceration began to increase rapidly. To spare him a trip, Douglas came to the house for the treatments. In late February the patient had frightful pains in one ear; his cancer was spreading. Into early March he suffered nausea, headaches, sleeplessness. His throat was an angry scarlet. It was agony to drink anything—"If you could imagine what molten lead would be like going down your throat," he told George W. Childs, "this is what I feel whan I am swallowing."

The illness could not be kept from the newspapers and their stories soon said what was the truth. GRANT IS DYING, headlined the New York *World* on March 1. *The New York Times*: SINKING INTO THE GRAVE. GENERAL GRANT'S FRIENDS GIVE UP HOPE. DYING SLOWLY FROM CANCER. WORKING CALMLY ON HIS BOOK IN SPITE OF PAIN. The *Sun*: GENERAL GRANT MORTALLY ILL. HIS DISEASE A CANCER FROM WHICH HE CANNOT RECOVER.

Day and night reporters had questions for Douglas and George F. Shrady, a second doctor called in on the case. The physicians were horrified at being asked to talk about a patient, but the reporters explained that Ulysses Grant was the patient not of the doctors but of the entire nation. They laid siege to 3 East 66th Street. Frank Mack of the Associated Press learned that a home a few doors away had a telephone, and conceived the idea of asking the house's butler to fasten a cord around his ankle when he went to bed at night, the other end to dangle out the window. Mack could then wake him by yanking the cord and have swift access to a telephone to report the general's death.

"Seriously, are you in earnest with this suggestion?" asked the home's owner.

"Dead earnest, sir!"

"Is my butler willing to do this jackanapes thing?"

"I trust he may be induced to help us." The arrangement was made. Other reporters prepared skyrockets to shoot off from atop a house in the block, a signal to another house farther downtown from which a final rocket would go up to be seen in Printing House Square where the Extras announcing the death were already set in type. One reporter seduced a housemaid across the street so that he could look from her upstairs window into the Grant home.

The reporters spent their time lounging on the low wall that enclosed Central Park across from the house. They called themselves "the Fifty Million Club" after the number of people hanging on the outcome of the story they were covering. A Cleveland paper denounced them for outraging decency by ghoulishly waiting for the man to die; an Albany paper said they were only doing their duty. They set up a telegraph and messenger office on Madison Avenue between Sixty-fifth and Sixty-sixth streets. The deathwatch was becoming institutionalized, reporters present and alert twenty-four hours a day, jumping off the park wall whenever lights went on at night, as they did on April 1 when a clergyman was sent for. Dr. Douglas wept as the Reverend John Phillip Newman baptized the unconscious Grant. Shrady said they ought to be doing something of a medical nature, but Douglas said, "You can see the condition—he's dying now."

"The preacher is busy and the doctors ought to be busy too," Shrady replied.

"It would be a torment without avail."

"I say, Douglas, something must be done! If this man dies here now, what can we say to the medical world? That for ten minutes at the last, half an hour so far as I know, we stood idly and stared at a dying man?"

"But what would you do?"

"Something, anything—a hypodermic of brandy first!" They

gave him one. His breathing, very weak, improved. He did not die. He worked on his book. The Reverend Mr. Newman went about saying he had been the humble instrument of Divine Providence and attributing spiritual thoughts and words to Grant that Mark Twain declared the general would not have uttered alive or dead. To his family Grant said that if it made Newman feel better to sprinkle him with water he had no objection. His sickness and the attention paid to it was without precedence in the history of the world. Every day he read the papers with the descriptions of his impending death and then went back to his work. He wrote of a bullet hitting the scabbard of his sword at Shiloh, a young Southern woman crying when on her porch he received a dispatch telling that Lee was being pushed over the North Anna River. The twentieth anniversary of Appomattox came, April 9, 1885.

Every day people stood silently in front of 3 East 66th Street, sometimes for hours. The reporters felt something in the air: an allegiance to the haggard man inside who was trying to finish his book before he surrendered to an enemy unbeatable. On Decoration Day* the band of the Seventh Regiment came and played, and a window shade went up to reveal a stooped and shrunken figure in a dark dressing gown, wearing a black skullcap. The face was gray and drawn by suffering. The colonel of the Seventh raised his sword in salute and Grant lifted his hand in return. In the street the people saw how white and thin it was. A murmur like a groan came from the crowd. There was no cheer, no other sound. The reporter Frank Mack thought to himself that the people might have been inspired by the Seventh's blaring band and rattling drums to shout themselves hoarse, but that this was more impressive, more moving. It told of much more. Grant smiled a thin, weak smile. Men took off their hats. Parents held up their children to see him. He slowly waved and withdrew from the window.

When he lay down, nights, saliva from the growing bulge

---

*Now generally called Memorial Day.

flowed back down his throat and choked him, so he slept sitting up in a leather armchair. He lived on beef and mutton broth mixed with milk and eggs, an agony to drink. The doctors gave him morphine, they used potassium permanganate and borax on his throat, Majendie by hypodermic needle. Sometimes sputum from the terrible lump threw him into coughing fits that brought hemorrhages of blood to pour from his mouth. Nothing of the agony he was undergoing showed in his face when he was awake. When he dozed off it was different.

He worked on his book, dictating to a stenographer from Twain's publishing company for several hours mornings and afternoons, sometimes getting out as much as 10,000 words a day. It was difficult for the doctors to get a view of the growth in his throat, for he could no longer completely open his mouth, but its progress could be seen in the bulge it was making in his neck. They tried sodium bromide to help him sleep, and when that did not work switched to chloral. His arms and legs were pitted with the marks of their needles. On occasion the drugs affected his thinking. Once he rose and clutched his throat and, hollow-eyed, said to Fred, "The cannon did it." But usually he was clear in his mind, clearer perhaps than he had been in the days since the war when it seemed to people that he had no focus and no real place.

Sherman came one day when Grant sat voiceless and un-moving, and away from her husband Julia said she could not stand the sad look that sometimes came to his face to accompany his deep silence. Sherman tried to cheer her up by talking about how the general had always been a quiet man and how back at City Point, twenty years ago, that spring, Grant had sat silently while he, Sherman, marched up and down spewing cigar ashes everywhere as he talked and planned and cursed the rebels. She liked Sherman, always had. The years since the war had made him a cheery aging man much in demand as an afterdinner speaker, always lively and ready to kiss the women and girls, still an avid theatergoer, terming all actors and actresses "my children." But of course he could cheer her up only so much. Sometimes she seemed almost in a daze, oblivious to the grandchildren warned not to make too much noise, and to the reporters about whose stories she often complained, able to think only of that Lieutenant Sam of long ago who now sat with a warmed scarf around his head to stem the dreadful pain in his ear and throat. He was holding off death with one hand, his people said, as he wrote with the other of his and Julia's early days together and those that followed, of Spotsylvania and Cold Harbor and Petersburg, of charge and countercharge, infantry and cavalry. For twenty years he had said nothing of the war, but now he brought it all back to life so that something could be left behind for her and for the children and grandchildren. The newspaper stories dwindled down to a few paragraphs each day in the back pages, for there was nothing new to say but that General Grant was dying and that dying he worked on his book.

22

"When Kings or Heroes Die"

ROBERT LEE never arose from the bed they put him into the evening he returned from the church vestry meeting, September 28, 1870. Fifteen minutes after he sank into his chair, unable to speak, the doctors arrived. There was little they could do. For two days he slept almost continually. Then he seemed to be getting better, and ate with some appetite. He spoke clearly although with effort. Mrs. Lee and the girls sat by him, holding his hands and wiping the perspiration off them.

His symptoms, the doctors thought, resembled those of a concussion of the brain without the attendant swoon—the debility, somewhat impaired consciousness, tendency to doze. Any improvement he showed, they saw, was not likely to be a lasting one. And, they thought, he did not wish it to be. "You must make haste and get well; Traveller has been standing so long in the stable that he needs exercise," one of them said to the patient, who slowly shook his head and closed his eyes. When the girls offered him medicine he turned it aside, saying, "It is of no use." Mrs. Lee talked of the future, "when Robert gets well," but in her heart she knew that time would never come. The look she had seen in his face, never seen before, when he sat down unable to speak, had been of resignation. Acceptance. It was time. "I saw he had taken leave of earth," she said afterwards.

For two weeks he lay in bed. For several days in that period there were tremendous rains, and, in the nights, an aurora borealis. A Lexington woman showed what W. E. Aytoun had said in his "Edinburgh After Flodden":

> All night long the northern streamers
> Shot across the trembling sky:
> Fearful lights, that never beckon
> Save when kings or heroes die.

On October 10 his pulse speeded up and he breathed with great rapidity. In the evening he was seized by spells of shivering. The next day he wandered back into the past, into the war, giving orders and hearing the guns sound again. Once long ago Stonewall Jackson had in his own last delirium called for Ambrose Powell Hill: "Order A. P. Hill to prepare for action!" Then he had died, and Hill had died too, on the morning that the lines broke at Petersburg. His courier, Tucker, on Hill's gray horse, had attached himself to Lee and with Lee had gone to the McLean house, riding ahead with a white flag. "Tell Hill he *must* come up!" Lee cried on his bed.

That night Mrs. Lee in her wheelchair sat holding his hand. Dawn came. Nine o'clock, October 12, 1870, Lexington, Virginia. He was sixty-three. The funeral would be stark, all military display entirely absent, no flags, just the college students and the VMI people going behind the coffin. And Traveller, of course. And the townspeople who knew him as the civilian who had been president of their local college longer than he had been a general. There would be virtually no people from outside Lexington because of the rains, which produced the area's greatest flooding of the century.

A little before 9:15, just before the end, he roused himself for a moment. "Strike the tent," he said.

23

Surrender

On June 16, 1885, Ulysses Grant, in a Prince Albert much too large for his shrunken frame, with a white silk bandage around his neck and purple and white bedroom slippers on his feet, shuffled slowly through Grand Central Station on his way toward William Henry Vanderbilt's private car attached to a train heading for Saratoga Springs. "My God! Is that the general?" gasped a spectator.

The leather chair in which he had slept sitting up for months had been put in Vanderbilt's car. Grant sank into it. His head fell back. New York City's hot weather had become unendurable for him and Anthony Joseph Drexel had offered the use of his cottage atop Mount McGregor, on the grounds of the enormous Balmoral Hotel. After slowly and in silence touring the rooms of his house from which had been taken all the wonderful things of the trip around the world, and the things from the war, the sick man took a carriage to the station. At nine in the morning the train started north through the tunnels under the city. Dust and smoke came into the car and his people closed the windows and hung up a curtain to deflect the air, but he almost suffocated. Not until they reached the pure air coming off the Hudson on Spuyten Duyvil was he able to breathe in even the harsh fashion that had become normal for him.

Frank Mack of the Associated Press was in the car with numerous heavy manila envelopes weighted with lead sheets into which he put details of the trip; at selected points he threw them out of the moving train. Associates on the platforms telegraphed his stories to A.P. headquarters in New York for transmission to the country and world. Silent, sitting before the broad double window at the center of the car, Grant seemed only half-conscious, and said nothing when Julia pointed to West Point's buildings across the river. Then he smiled slightly. Mack was disappointed. He had hoped for something dramatic but instead had to write only that the general had passed the Academy with many silent reminiscences but no spoken word. He showed little apparent fatigue, Mack scribbled. Grant whispered, "Do you put that off at the next station? I'd like to see it." Mack handed it over and Grant changed "little apparent fatigue" to "there was little fatigue." At the next station an A.P. employee stood waving a white handkerchief up and down, and Mack sailed the manila envelope at him as the train went by, getting a flash of him diving for it. Grant looked up with pleased interest and gave a nod that, Mack thought, meant, "He got it; I saw him."

They went through Poughkeepsie, Rhinecliff, Hudson, Albany. Once at a bend in the river the train halted briefly. A flagman's shanty was directly below the window at which Grant sat. The flagman looked up into his eyes. The flagman waved his arm. There was no hand. "Thank God I see you alive, General Grant," the flagman cried. The train started to move. "I lost that with you at The Wilderness, and I'd give the other one to see you well!" Grant's lips immediately tightened, his hand went up quickly and he took off his hat to the flagman. Mack looked at Julia and saw her lips trembling. Dr. Douglas cried.

Just north of Saratoga he stepped from Vanderbilt's car into one that would carry him the 12 miles to Mount McGregor. A Grand Army of the Republic detachment waited. He saluted. At the mountaintop he attempted to walk to the Drexel cottage, but it was impossible. A rattan wheeled chair took him up. He slept ten hours, awoke, sat motionless on the veranda. The cottage was two stories high, 1,000 feet above sea level. The porch faced eastward toward Vermont's Green Mountains.

At the end of the afternoon he got up and, head bent to ease the pain in his throat, shoulders stooped, took an unsteady walk for a few minutes. The reporter Mack saw a haggard face in which bravery mixed with a look that spoke of surprise, hopelessness and pain. Mack cursed at the general's servant, Harrison Tyrell, for not offering physical aid, but Tyrell explained that was the general's wish. Grant toiled on a few more steps to a bench upon which he dropped exhausted, hands gripping a cane between his knees. He bent his head, and his cheek and then his chin rested on his clasped hands holding the cane, his eyes staring at a large rock nearby.

For some time it had become increasingly difficult for him to speak—the cancer was digging its claws into his vocal cords—and the next morning he wrote out a long note for Douglas. *Doctor: Since coming to this beautiful climate and getting a complete rest, I have watched my pains and compared them with those of the past few weeks. I can feel plainly that my system is preparing for dissolution in three ways: One by hemorrhage, one by strangulation, and the third by exhaustion. There cannot be a hope of going far beyond this time.* He wrote that if the doctor felt other physicians must be called in he would understand, but that he dreaded it, knowing their examinations meant additional suffering. From then on he communicated almost entirely by penciled notes, for it was next to impossible for him to speak. He sat on the porch wearing a woolen cap with a long peak, a plaid shawl on his knees, and on a pad of paper he wrote his book with a little white stylus pen.

Crowds came from the hotel to see him writing on his porch, and a guard was posted to keep them at a distance. Ladies bowed and children sang; when he could, he took off his hat or waved. Sometimes old friends were received for a few minutes. Simon Bolivar Buckner came, friend from the days of the Twelve in One society back at West Point, enemy from Fort Donelson. . . . "I propose to move immediately upon your works. Unconditional surrender." They sat together, Buckner speaking and Grant answering with written notes. At the end Buckner rose and bent over the figure in the chair. They held each other's hands. "Grant," the dying man's visitor said. "Buckner," he whispered back. At the hotel later, Mrs. Buckner said she wished she could have the written notes. One of Grant's people was applied to, and they were collected and put into her hand. *I will have to be careful about my writing. I see every person I give a piece of paper to puts it in his pocket. Some day they will be coming up against my English.*

Unable to sleep for more than an hour at a time in the chair he occupied twenty-four hours a day, he hawked his throat constantly for the mucus pouring out of the ruptured glands. Douglas gave him four and five shots of morphine a day, in the arms, the legs, the chest. He painted cocaine onto the frightful lump in his throat to dull the pain. He irrigated the ulcerating mass with a syringe. *I notice that your little girls and Julie* get along very happily together. With their swing, their lawn tennis (croquet) and nice shade, they seem very happy.* Sometimes Julie and her little brother were brought to him for a moment, their mother or Aunt Nellie returned from England saying, "Grandpapa isn't quite so well, dear," always to receive a smile and a nod. Their father Fred was hardly out of the sickroom for a moment at a time, sleeping fully clothed in a bed by the patient's leather chair. Julie in later life remembered someone saying, "The book is killing him!" and someone else replying, "No, the book is keeping him alive; without it he would already be dead." Her younger brother retained no memory of the moment when his grandfather wrote a letter to a future President of the United States asking his admittance

---

*His son Fred's daughter, later Princess Cantacuzene.

to West Point when he came of age. By doing so, he wrote the future President, "you gratify the wishes of U. S. Grant." Sherman was with him and he asked Sherman to endorse the request, which was done with a note to the future President, saying gracefully that really additional words were wholly superfluous. In 1901 President McKinley honored the request for the boy.*

Grant would throw up, feel weak, gasp for breath, sometimes wander in his thoughts. *I cannot help repeating two advertisements of the B&O Railroad when I am half awake. There may be no such advertisements but I keep dreaming of them all the same.* Yet he kept at the book. The galley proofs of the first volume came, and he spent hours going over them, penciling in corrections and additions. When for a brief period he was able to sleep, he awoke covered with perspiration. Sometimes the painted-on cocaine was able to still the pain, sometimes not. *If I live long enough, I shall become a sort of specialist in the use of certain medicines, if not in the treatment of disease. It seems that man's destiny in this world is quite as much a mystery as it is likely to be in the next. I never thought of acquiring rank in the profession I was educated for, yet it came, with two grades higher prefixed to the ranks of general officers for me.† I certainly never had either ambition or taste for a political life; yet I was twice President of the United States. I now have written a book. I have already too many trades to be proficient in any.*

He had his book. It was finished a month after arrival at Mount McGregor. It would sell twice as well as Mark Twain's *Huckleberry Finn*, and Twain would have the pleasure of handing Julia a larger royalty check than any previously written. Hundreds of thousands of dollars would come to her from this work to which he had given his last strength. *There was never one more willing to go than I am. I know most people have first one, and then another thing to fix up, and never quite get quite through. There is nothing more I should like to do now, and therefore I am not likely to be more ready to go than at this moment.* On the afternoon of July

*Later Major General Ulysses S. Grant III.
†Lieutenant General and General of the Army.

20 he asked if he might be taken in the wheelchair to a wooden gazebo mountain overlook, and his servant Harrison Tyrell and Fred pushed him to it. At one point the chair could not be moved with him in it, and so he had to get up and walk three steps and pick his way through a coal pile. When he got back to the cottage he was pale and faint. The next day was beastly hot, the temperature reaching eighty-five degrees. Fits of hiccuping took him. He tried to drink liquids to halt the spasms, but choked trying to get them down. Sitting in his chair he was too weak to hold his cane. It fell from his hand. Fred's wife came out on the balcony and called to Julie and her brother, "Quick, papa wants you to come and see dear grandpapa." They went in. Julia was crying silently and dampening his brow with cologne. His eyes were closed. "Kiss grandpapa." Julie could not reach his face as he lay back in the chair and so she bent and kissed the wasted hand. "We must go now," Fred's wife whispered.

In the evening he indicated for the first time in many months that he wanted to be out of the chair and in a bed. During the night Douglas gave him brandy to try and steady the flickering pulse. The children arose in the morning and, warned to make no noise, went with their nurse to the Balmoral Hotel. A little while later at breakfast a waiter said, "It is all finished over there at the cottage." Grant had died at eight, drifted away. There were no real last words. FINAL BATTLE IS OVER. SURRENDER! THE GREAT COMMANDER YIELDS, read the headlines of the country's papers, black-bordered. He was sixty-three.

Little Julie wandered away from the sound of her grandmother's sobbing and went to make a wreath; she knew one made them for dead people. There were no flowers in the woods, so she made one of oak leaves and went into the cottage to seek her father. She couldn't find him. In the cottage was a coffin. She had never seen one before. Two strangers were there. They asked what she wanted and she said, "I've brought grandpapa a wreath; I thought my papa was here." One of the men hesitated and said, "Sure, Miss, and your papa is just after going up to snatch a little sleep, and I wouldn't disturb him if I was you. Suppose you give me the wreath to lay on the general. It's a mighty fine wreath; and I think there's no harm in your coming in to help me yourself." She looked at her grandfather under the glass cover. When Fred saw the wreath he said he would have it varnished so that it would keep, and then it would be buried with grandpapa. "I know he would like to keep it with him always." Despite the carloads of flowers arriving on every train, her wreath was the only thing that rode on the casket as it went down Mount McGregor and to an open railway carriage that had a top supported by columns but no sides to block the view of the hundreds of thousands of people standing by the tracks south.

A bell sounded from the rumbling black-draped engine slowly pulling the single open car; bells answered from churches. The locomotive and car were given the right of way over any train coming from or going to New York City. Men stood uncovered by the tracks as the car went slowly past, women fluttered mourning scarves, bands played dirges and bugles wailed. People put pennies on the tracks to be crushed and taken home and handed down as trophies that had touched the wheels of the funeral train of Ulysses S. Grant. Work was suspended in the river villages through which went the slow black train tolling its bell, and boats with black flags stood in the Hudson. Barely moving through the cities, his body went past pictures of him, veterans on crutches, shrouded flags at half mast. Even in open fields people held up draped flags, some of them used twenty years previous to honor Abraham Lincoln's last journey, back to Illinois. Past Tarrytown and Nyack and Yonkers there was a solid mass of people. Slowly the train entered the rail tunnel under New York City, preceded ten minutes earlier by a pilot engine swathed in heavy black cloth and the dead man's name in gilt, and a flag.

The engine and single car slowly rolled into Grand Central. Men of the Seventy-first Regiment, wearing mourning bands, took the coffin outside to a catafalque in absolute silence. Twelve black horses wearing black fly nets stood in the traces. Before them was a gigantic formation of mounted police, hundreds of cavalrymen and General Winfield Scott Hancock—still superb, if older—in cocked hat, gold buttons, gilded braid and decorations. Black-draped muffled drums rolled and the procession started south, to City Hall and the lying-in-state. The Light Battery Band of Fort Hamilton directly behind General Hancock played Chopin's Funeral March. Soldiers marched with arms reversed. There were Navy officers and enlisted men with plumes on their helmets, Marines, National Guardsmen, six-horse guns and ammunition wagons, more bands, the Ninth Regiment, the Eleventh and the Twelfth. Drs. Shrady and Douglas rode in an open carriage with the Reverend Newman.

Then came the funeral car, its high plumes tossing in unison, men going in front with long poles to lift up electric wires the plumes might reach. Closed carriages followed with the family. Not Julia. She was still back at the cottage on Mount McGregor. Completely undone, she had draped her late husband's leather chair in black and collapsed. Then came the carriages of city dignitaries, more troops and a fife and drum corps. The procession went south to the tolling of all the city's church bells. Atop City Hall the statue of Justice held out a wreath of mourning.

It was seven in the evening and almost sunset when the first marchers got to their destination. The Twenty-second Regiment played the "Dead" March from "Saul." The troops in double lines formed a square in the plaza. In the perfect silence the only sound was that of the hooves of the black horses coming in. They halted. As the coffin went up the steps, two buglers of the Second Artillery sounded a wailing funeral call.

He lay in state. From all over the country people poured into New York, trains running in sections, the ferries over the Hudson jammed, the new Brooklyn Bridge black with people. More incoming passengers came to Grand Central than ever before in history. The elevated trains from Brooklyn carried more passengers than on any other day. Every hotel had cots in the halls. The President, the ex-Presidents, twenty state governors, ex-generals and ex-privates came. The funeral the next day was the most superb pageant military and civil in the history of the country. Saturday, August 8, 1885, dawned clear. More than fifty sidestreets near City Hall were filled with troops. Save for the line of march, New York seemed empty, even the summer resort of Coney Island.

Twenty-four horses in black drapery pulled the catafalque. Choral societies sang as the casket was born down City Hall's steps—the Pilgrim's chorus from "Tannhäuser." Along Broadway, in front of stands erected during the night, Grand Army of the Republic men, grizzled now with the war two decades in the past, stood on the west side of the street. They carried their worn old battle flags. Opposite, on the east side, stood their young and spruce successors in uniform carrying bright new banners. Every rooftop was jammed. Men clung to the telegraph poles.

The interment would be in the Clermont section of Manhattan, on Riverside Drive at 122nd Street, in a temporary vault of steel on a pedestal of marble on which 200 men had labored in nonstop shifts. Wherever he lay, he had told Fred, there must be a place for Julia. They had considered West Point, St. Louis, Galena, Washington—and had finally picked New York, where they had lived their last years. From City Hall at the extreme southern end of Manhattan the procession of tens of thousands moved toward the extreme north of the island. At the head of each of twenty-four horses pulling the funeral car marched a formally dressed groom, volunteers from a black church's congregation. The Old Guard marched in bearskin cap, white coat and blue trousers, their band playing "Nearer My God to Thee"; the Governor's Foot Guard of Hartford marched and also the City Guard of Atlanta and the Virginia State Troop. The Loyal Legion marched, and delegations from every Grand Army of the Republic post in America. They moved uptown through Broadway and Fifth Avenue to Seventy-second Street and then west to Riverside Drive. Hundreds of private boats were anchored in the Hudson, and a line of Navy men-of-war with sailors in mourning attire standing at attention save for those who sent salute volleys rolling over the water.

President Cleveland was in a six-horse. Behind him were

the equipages of ex-Presidents Hayes and Arthur, and those of the Supreme Court. The head of the column reached 122nd Street. Sheets of fire crashed from the ship's gun ports. Smoke wreathed up. Pennants danced in the riggings. In billows of gold lace and white plumes Hancock and his staff arrived, Marines with yellow epaulettes, a river of flat Navy caps and white leggings. The hills shook from the artillery salvos. The sun glinted from lines of shining bayonets. It was four-thirty. The march from City Hall had taken six hours.

The funeral car came up, and it seemed to those who were waiting that the air throbbed with dirges. The thunder of the guns and the beating of the drums ceased. The scores of marching bands were silent. The casket was taken from the car. A Grand Army of the Republic man stepped up to it. There was absolute silence save for the chomping of the horses.

"God of battles! Father of all! Amidst this mournful assemblage we seek Thee with whom there is no death!"

A bugler played a call. Ministers prayed. An Army trumpeter stepped to the side of the casket and sent the notes of Taps shivering through the air, and, across the casket from Buckner and old Joe Johnston and next to Sheridan, Sherman began to cry. The American flag on the casket was folded and handed to Fred Grant. Little Julie's wreath was put on. Into the temporary tomb was committed the body, shrunken in its illness, the undertaker said, to less than 100 pounds. The guns spoke again and the hundred of thousands of marchers and viewers left him.

24

Envoi

HE LIES IN A CRYPT below the college chapel whose building was of special interest to him in the last years of his life. He attended services there every morning, once it was finished. In the crypt are all of his relatives save Annie, whose grave he and Agnes visited on his last trip, in 1870. Agnes is in the crypt, and the two other spinster daughters, Rooney, Rob, Custis, Mrs. Lee, his mother, and even Light Horse Harry's remains brought from Cumberland Island off Georgia.

Above, behind the chapel's altar, is Valentine's statue of him at rest, a recumbent figure with hand on breast, in Confederate uniform. The chapel never seems empty. Washington and Lee—so now the college is called—holds symposia there. There are lectures and concerts. Musicians play the piano by the altar. There are always customers at the basement gift shop buying postcards or silver pins that bear the countenance of Robert E. Lee.

Grant lies in a monument 150 feet tall, of gray granite, with ten fluted Doric columns below a conical arch, with interior walls of marble block, with bronze doors 30 feet high. Julia is next to him. The vast tomb is magnificently placed on the promontory overlooking the Hudson that was his temporary resting place. President Harrison laid the cornerstone. President McKinley spoke at the dedication, five years to the day later. A million people watched 60,000 marchers go to the ceremonies, and ten warships from the North Atlantic Fleet stood out in the river along with warships from five other countries. Julia used to go to the tomb often before her own death. Once a woman embraced her as she came out. Julia drew back. "I am the wife of Jefferson Davis," the woman said. After that Julia often went there in company with Varina Davis.

There are flags, faded now, pictures. Above is the last of those phrases with which he strangely gripped people, written when accepting the first nomination for the Presidency. LET US HAVE PEACE, it says on Grant's Tomb.

It was all a long time ago. Once a soldier, R. J. Burdette, went back, years and years later, to where he stormed an enemy position. He took his wife. He remembered the column of fours, the yellow dust, a cavalry trooper galloping down the line with a dispatch in an envelope sheathed underneath his belt. He remembered hills, the blazing Southern sun, the heat, the battery wheels rumbling, rolls of musketry, fires in the trees, skirmishers ahead shooting—then the advance, cheering, the enemy fluttering a white flag and the colonel that night trying to write his wife that their son had died, sheets of paper around him on which he had tried to begin.

He could find the place stone blind, Burdette told his wife. But when he got there, nothing was left. There was grass, and violets. It was May. Children played on what he recalled as a hell-crater. Snow, rain, winds, sheep grazing on the spot, children, vines . . . it was all gone. So it is with the two soldiers and with their hosts. They had their time together, and then it was over. *And lo!* Burdette wrote. *While the soldier's memory yet held the day of its might and strength and terror, it was gone.*

BIBLIOGRAPHY

——. *Battles and Leaders of the Civil War*, four vols. New York: Century Company, 1884–87.

Adams, Charles Francis. *Richard Henry Dana*. Boston and New York: Houghton Mifflin, 1890.

Adams, Henry. *The Education of Henry Adams*. Boston: Houghton Mifflin, 1918.

Alexander, E. P. *Military Memoirs of a Confederate*. New York: Charles Scribner's Sons, 1907.

Allan, Elizabeth Preston. *The Life and Letters of Margaret Junkin Preston*. Cambridge, Mass.: Houghton Mifflin, 1903.

Ames, Mary Clemmer. *Ten Years in Washington*. Hartford, Conn.: Worthington, 1873.

Andrews, Marietta Minnigerode. *Scraps of Paper*. New York: E. P. Dutton, 1929.

Armstrong, William H. *Ely S. Parker*. Syracuse: Syracuse University Press, 1978.

Atkinson, C. F. *Grant's Campaigns of 1864 and 1865*. London: Hugh Rees, 1908.

371

Bates, D. H. *Lincoln in the Telegraph Office*. New York: The Century Company, 1907.

Bauer, K. Jack. *The Mexican War*. New York: Macmillan, 1974.

Bill, Alfred Hoyt. *Rehearsal for Conflict*. New York: Cooper Square Publishers, 1969.

Bond, Christina. *Memories of Robert E. Lee*. Baltimore: Norman, Remington, 1926.

Boyd, Thomas. *Light Horse Harry Lee*. New York: Charles Scribner's Sons, 1931.

Briggs, Emily Edson. *The Olivia Letters*. New York and Washington: Neale Publishing, 1906.

Brooks, Noah. *Washington in Lincoln's Time*. New York: Century, 1896.

Burdette, Robert J. *Drums of the 47th*. Indianapolis: Bobbs-Merrill, 1914.

Cadwallader, Sylvanus. *Three Years with Grant*. New York: Alfred A. Knopf, 1956.

Cantacuzene, Princess. *My Life Here and There*. New York: Charles Scribner's Sons, 1921.

Catton, Bruce. *U. S. Grant and the American Military Tradition*. Boston: Little, Brown, 1954.

Chamberlain, Joshua Lawrence. *The Passing of the Armies*. Dayton, Ohio: Morningside Bookshop Press, 1974.

Chesnut, Mary Boykin. *A Diary from Dixie*. New York: D. Appleton, 1905.

Chetlain, Augustus L. *Recollections of Seventy Years*. Galena, Ill.: Gazette Publishing, 1899.

Childs, George W. *Reflections*. Philadelphia: J. B. Lippincott, 1890.

Chittenden, L. E. *Recollections of President Lincoln and His Administration*. New York: Harper and Brothers, 1891.

Connelly, Thomas L. *The Marble Man: Robert E. Lee and His Image in American Society*. New York: Alfred A. Knopf, 1977.

Cooke, John Esten. *Hammer and Rapier*. New York: G. W. Dillingham, 1887.

————. *Robert E. Lee*. New York: D. Appleton, 1871.

Crook, William H. *Through Five Administrations*. New York: Harper and Brothers, 1910.

Cullen, Joseph P. *The Siege of Petersburg*. Eastern Acorn Press, 1981.

Custer, Elizabeth. *The Custer Story*. New York: Devin-Adair, 1950.

Dana, Charles A. and Wilson, J. H. *The Life of Ulysses S. Grant.* Springfield, Mass.: Gordon Bill, 1868.

Davis, Burke. *Jeb Stuart.* New York: Rinehart, 1957.

————. *To Appomattox.* New York: Popular Library, 1960.

DeLeon, T. C. *Four Years in Rebel Capitals.* Mobile, Ala.: Gossip Printing, 1892.

Dodge, Grenville. *Personal Recollections.* Council Bluffs, Iowa: Monarch Printing, 1914.

Dowdey, Clifford. *Lee.* Boston and Toronto: Little, Brown, 1965.

Ellet, E. F. *Court Circles of the Republic.* Philadelphia Publishing, n.d.

Elliott, Charles Winslow. *Winfield Scott.* New York: Macmillan, 1937.

Fishwick, Marshall. *Lee After the War.* New York: Dodd, Mead, 1963.

Flood, Charles Bracelen. *Lee—The Last Years.* Boston: Houghton Mifflin, 1981.

Freeman, Douglas Southall. *R. E. Lee,* four vols. New York: Charles Scribner's Sons, 1934–35.

————. *Lee of Virginia.* New York: Charles Scribner's Sons, 1958.

Fremantle, Lt. Col. A. J. *Three Months in the Southern States.* New York: John Bradburn, 1864.

French, Samuel G. *Two Wars.* Nashville, Tenn.: Confederate Veteran, 1901.

Fry, James B. *Military Miscellanies.* New York: Brentano's, 1889.

Fuller, J.F.C. *The Generalship of Ulysses S. Grant.* New York: Dodd, Mead, 1929.

Garland, Hamlin. *U. S. Grant.* New York: Doubleday and McClure, 1898.

Gerrish, Reverend Theodore. *Army Life.* Portland, Me.: Hoyt, Fogg and Donham, 1882.

Goodenough, Simon. *Tactical Genius in Battle.* Oxford: Phaidon Press, 1979.

Gordon, John B. *Reminiscences of the Civil War.* New York: Charles Scribner's Sons, 1904.

Grant, Jesse Root. *In the Days of My Father.* New York: Harper and Brothers, 1925.

Grant, Julia Dent. *Personal Memoirs.* New York: G. P. Putnam's Sons, 1975.

Grant, Ulysses S. *Personal Memoirs.* New York: Charles L. Webster, 1894 edition.

Hancock, A. R. *Reminiscences of Winfield Scott Hancock.* New York: Charles L. Webster, 1887.

Harrison, Mrs. Burton. *Recollections Grave and Gay*. New York: Charles Scribner's Sons, 1911.

Hebert, Walter H. *Fighting Joe Hooker*. Indianapolis and New York: Bobbs-Merrill, 1944.

Helm, Katherine. *Mary, Wife of Lincoln*. New York: Harper and Brothers, 1928.

Hendrick, Burton J. *The Lees of Virginia*. Boston: Little, Brown, 1935

Hesseltine, William B. *Ulysses S. Grant, Politician*. New York: Dodd, Mead, 1935.

Hitchcock, Ethan Allen. *Fifty Years in Camp and Field*. New York: G. P. Putnam's Sons, 1909.

Hopkins, Luther. *From Bull Run to Appomattox*. Baltimore: McGinley, 1915.

Jones, J. William. *Personal Reminiscences, Anecdotes, and Letters of General Robert E. Lee*. New York: D. Appleton, 1874.

Keating, John M. *With General Grant in the East*. Philadelphia: J. B. Lippincott, 1879.

Keckley, Elizabeth. *Behind the Scenes*. New York: G. W. Carleton, 1868.

Keyes, Erasmus D. *Fifty Years*. New York: Charles Scribner's Sons, 1884.

Lee, Fitzhugh. *General Lee*. New York: Fawcett Publications, 1961.

Lee, Robert E., Jr. *Recollections and Letters of General Robert E. Lee*. Garden City, N.Y.: Doubleday, Page, 1924.

Lee, Susan P. *Memoirs of William Nelson Pendleton*. Philadelphia: J. B. Lippincott, 1893.

Lewis, Lloyd. *Sherman, Fighting Prophet*. New York: Harcourt, Brace, 1932.

―――. *Captain Sam Grant*. Boston: Little, Brown, 1950.

Long, A. L. *Memoirs of Robert E. Lee*. New York, Philadelphia and Washington: J. M. Stoddart, 1887.

Longstreet, James. *From Manassas to Appomattox*. Philadelphia: J. B. Lippincott, 1896.

Lyman, Theodore. *Meade's Headquarters*. Boston: Atlantic Monthly Press, 1922.

McClellan, George B. *Own Story*. New York: Charles L. Webster, 1887.

McClure, Alexander K. *Abraham Lincoln and Men of War-Times*. Philadelphia: Times Publishing, 1892.

MacDonald, Rose. *Mrs. Robert E. Lee*. Boston: Ginn, 1939.

McFeely, William S. *Grant*. New York: W. W. Norton, 1981.

Mason, Emily V. *The Life of General Robert Edward Lee*. Baltimore: John Murphy, 1874.

Maurice, Major General Sir Frederick. *An Aide-de-Camp of Lee: The Papers of Colonel Charles Marshall*. Boston: Little, Brown, 1927.

Meade, George. *George G. Meade*, two vols. New York: Charles Scribner's Sons, 1913.

Meredith, Roy. *Mr. Lincoln's Camera Man*. New York: Charles Scribner's Sons, 1946.

Miles, Nelson A. *Personal Recollections*. Chicago and New York: Wener, 1896.

Nelson, Truman. *The Old Man: John Brown at Harper's Ferry*. New York: Holt, Rinehart and Winston, 1973.

O'Connor, Richard. *Sheridan the Inevitable*. Indianapolis and New York: Bobbs-Merrill, 1953.

Page, Thomas Nelson. *Robert E. Lee*. New York: Charles Scribner's Sons, 1911.

Patrick, Rembert W. *The Fall of Richmond*. Baton Rouge: Louisiana State University Press, 1960.

Perkins, J. R. *Trails, Rails and War: The Life of General G. G. Dodge*. Indianapolis: Bobbs-Merrill, 1929.

Pleasants, Henry. *The Tragedy of the Crater*. Eastern National Park and Monument Association, 1938.

Porter, Horace. *Campaigning with Grant*. Bloomington: Indiana University Press, 1961 (originally published 1897).

Post, James L. *Reminiscences*. St. Louis: J. L. Post, 1904.

Pryor, Mrs. Roger A. *Reminiscences of Peace and War*. New York: Macmillan, 1905.

Richardson, Albert D. *Personal History of Ulysses S. Grant*. Hartford, Conn.: American Publishing, 1868.

Riley, Franklin L. *General Robert E. Lee After Appomattox*. New York: Macmillan, 1922.

Rister, Carl Coke. *Robert E. Lee in Texas*. Norman: University of Oklahoma Press, 1946.

Ross, Ishbel. *The General's Wife*. New York: Dodd, Mead, 1959.

Roth, Margaret Brobst. *Well, Mary: Civil War Letters of a Wisconsin Volunteer*. Madison: University of Wisconsin Press, 1960.

Rusling, James F. *Men and Things I Saw in Civil War Days*. New York: Eaton and Mains, 1899.

Sanborn, Margaret. *Robert E. Lee*. Philadelphia and New York: J. B. Lippincott, 1966.

Sandburg, Carl. *Abraham Lincoln, The War Years*, four vols. New York: Harcourt, Brace, 1939.

Schaff, Morris. *The Battle of the Wilderness*. Boston and New York: Houghton Mifflin, 1910.

Schouler, James. *History of the Reconstruction Period*. New York: Dodd, Mead, 1913.

Seward, Frederick. *Reminiscences*. New York: G. P. Putnam's Sons, 1916.

Shanks, William. *Personal Recollections of Distinguished Generals*. New York: Harper and Brothers, 1866.

Smith, Gene. *The Impeachment and Trial of Andrew Johnson*. New York: William Morrow, 1977.

Stiles, Robert. *Four Years Under Marse Robert*. New York and Washington: Neale Publishing, 1910.

Stoddard, Henry Luther. *Horace Greeley*. New York: G. P. Putnam's Sons, 1946.

Tarbell, Ida M. *A Reporter for Lincoln*. New York: Macmillan, 1927.

Taylor, Walter. *Four Years with General Lee*. Bloomington: Indiana University Press, 1962 (originally published 1877).

———. *General Lee*. Norfolk, Va.: Nusbaum Book and News, 1906.

Townsend, Brevet Major General E. D. *Anecdotes of the Civil War*. New York: D. Appleton, 1884.

Townsend, George Alfred. *Campaigns of a Non-Combatant*. New York: Blelock, 1866.

Twain, Mark. *Autobiography*. New York: Harper and Brothers, 1924.

Von Borcke, Heros. *Memoirs*, two vols. New York: P. Smith, 1938.

Von Bort, Ph. *General Grant and the Jews*. National News, 1868.

Warch, Richard and Fanton, Jonathan. *John Brown*. Englewood Cliffs, N.J.: Prentice-Hall, 1973.

Wilkeson, Frank. *Recollections of a Private Soldier in the Army of the Potomac*. Freeport, N.Y.: Books for Libraries Press, 1972 (originally published 1886).

Williams, T. Harry. *Lincoln and His Generals*. New York: Alfred A. Knopf, 1952.

Wilson, David L. and Simon, John Y. *Ulysses S. Grant: Essays and Documents*. Carbondale and Edwardsville: Southern Illinois University Press, 1981.

Wilson, James Harrison. *The Life of John A. Rawlings*. Washington: Neale Publishing, 1916.

Wing, Henry. *When Lincoln Kissed Me*. New York: Eaton and Mains, 1913.

Wise, John S. *The End of an Era*. Boston and New York: Houghton Mifflin, 1900.

Woodward, W. E. *Meet General Grant*. New York: Horace Liveright, 1928.

Young, John Russell. *Around the World with General Grant*, two vols. New York: American News, 1879.

NOTES

I

page 1.—sprung from his mother's womb a soldier: General Charles Lee is quoted in Freeman, Vol. I, p. 2.

1.—"I am wedded to my sword": Hendrick, p. 336.

3.—"that bird is laughing at you": Sanborn, p. 38. Robert E. Lee told the story to many people. He was not present when Washington made his joke but presumably heard about it from his father or mother. It was his favorite story about his father.

3.—"in love with every sweet nymph": Boyd, p. 203.

4.—"you do not know what you are throwing away": Hendrick, p. 381, quotes a letter written by the husband of Maria's granddaughter, Samuel Appleton Storrow, Judge Advocate General of the United States Army.

4.—"I am right as to time": Ibid.

5.—The alleged sale of the horses and slave: Ibid., p. 389.

6.—"I trust, my dear Mr. Lee": Dowdey, p. 26.

7.—delivered of a dying woman: Sanborn, p. 3

7.—to say good-bye: The two cherubs can still be seen in the fireplace, as the author discovered when he got down on his hands and knees to peer upward.

8.—"You lie, young man": Boyd, p. 304.

8.—"Tell your aunt": Hendrick, p. 396.

9.—Then Robert came: Long, p. 22.

II

10.—Jesse's character and background: Woodward, p. 11ff.

11–12.—The naming of the infant: Richardson, p. 49.

12.—Hannah's character: Dana and Wilson, p. 24; Woodward, p. 13.

12.—trying to swing on their tails: Woodward, p. 13ff. Woodward wrote that he interviewed scores of people who knew Hannah Grant and that they agreed her emotional flatness was particularly noticeable when she dealt with her oldest son.

13.—refusal to say anything more violent: Dana and Wilson, p. 25.

13.—"Useless": Richardson, p. 69. For an authorized campaign biography written with the approval of a Presidential hopeful, Richardson's book is remarkably frank.

13.—The pony: Woodward, pp. 21–22.

13.—The horse trade: Ulysses S. Grant, pp. 22ff.

14.—"I would like to be a farmer": Garland, p. 21.

15.—The discussion about West Point: Ulysses S. Grant, p. 22

15.—"my own mother did not cry": Garland, p. 31.

15.—"I'm astonished": Richardson, p. 76.

16.—ill-fitted clothing and coarse shoes: Garland, p. 31.

16.—United States Grant, Uncle Sam Grant: Ibid., p. 42, quotes Sherman as saying, "I remember as plain as if it were yesterday."

17.—"that horse will kill you some day": Richardson, pp. 92–93.

18.—"Those ten weeks": Ulysses S. Grant, p. 28.

18.—The jumping exhibition: Fry, p. 292ff.

19.—"Soldier! Will you work?": Ulysses S. Grant, p. 30.

19.—The stable man: Ibid., pp. 30–31.

III

21.—He carried the keys: Mason, p. 22.

21.—what *was* it?: Andrews, p. 198.

22–23.—Details on Henry Lee: Dowdey, p. 39.

24.—"practice self-denial": Mason, p. 22.

25.—"How can I live without Robert?": Ibid., p. 23.

26.—eyes lingering on the door: Long, p. 26.

27.—Details on Mary Custis are found throughout MacDonald.

27.—Imperious and temperamental: Connelly, p. 7, calls her spoiled and unpleasant.

28.—Fruitcake on a sideboard: Freeman, *Lee of Virginia*, p. 21.

29.—"they would be rather stupid": Sanborn, p. 94.

29.—"I am a wanderer" and "can't consent to your remaining": MacDonald, p. 41.

30.—"Master Custis is the most darling boy": Freeman, Vol. I, p. 117.

30.—"I find it rather tiresome": MacDonald, pp. 75–76.

30.—"I don't know that I shall ever overcome": Dowdey, p. 60.

31.—"Sweet, innocent things": Freeman, Vol. I, p. 133.

31.—"Oh Mercy": Ibid., p. 113.

31.—"I am waiting": Ibid., p. 135.

32.—"Oh, she is a rare one": Ibid., p. 136. The letter was to Talcott.

32.—he feared to come home and find her bald: Dowdey, p. 62.

32.—"Spec has become so jealous": R. E. Lee, Jr., pp. 7–8.

33.—"No tickling, no stories!": Ibid., p. 10.

33.—"I am sure to be introduced to a new one": Freeman, Vol. I, p. 172.

33.—"I felt so elated": Freeman, Vol. I, p. 177. The letter was to his cousin Hill Carter.

IV

35.—The first time: Emma Dent Casey wrote a brief memoir of her brother-in-law; it is now in the Missouri Historical Society, St. Louis.

37.—"They're looking at us, Emmy": Casey memoir.

37.—The exchange with Captain Buchanan is described in Lewis, *Captain Sam Grant*, p. 108.

37.—"I understood the reason": Ulysses S. Grant, p. 34.

38.—she had dreamt: Julia D. Grant, p. 50.

38.—He asked her to cling to him: Garland, p. 63.

39.—The flocks of wild turkey: Ulysses S. Grant, p. 49

39.—sorry that he had ever gone to be a soldier. "I felt sorry that I had ever enlisted," Grant says, p. 58.

39.—Taylor's fearful responsibility: Ibid., p. 59.

39.—"You can have but little idea": The letter is in McFeely, p. 27.

39.—637 officers, 5,925 enlisted men: Bauer, p. 397.

40.—curiosity getting the best of his judgment; "lacking the moral courage": Ulysses S. Grant, p. 68.

40.—"Without you *dearest*": McFeely, p. 34.

41.—"And Lieutenant Grant": Lewis, *Captain Sam Grant*, p. 236.

42.—Fred Dent's experiences in the storming of Chapultepec: Ross, p. 41.

42.—The belfrey howitzer: Ulysses S. Grant, pp. 96–97.

42.—"just one": Ibid., p. 105.

43.—"I feel it is my duty": Page, p. 577. Grant told Dr. Fordyce Barker of the incident; Barker told Dr. William Polk, who told Page. Maurice has essentially the same story on p. 274.

44.—"We have bullied her": Sanborn, p. 158.

44.—"The best soldier in Christendom": Connelly, p. 194.

44.—"Without whose aid": Ibid., p. 194.

45.—"Friends" . . . "Officers": Hitchcock, p. 243.

45.—"It was terrible to think of the women and children": Fitzhugh Lee, p. 44.

45.—"Scott is lost!": Elliott, pp. 501–502.

46.—"again indefatigable": Fitzhugh Lee, p. 45.

46.—"That splendid city shall be ours!": Lewis, *Captain Sam Grant*, p. 225.

46.—"No! No! You're dreaming": Bauer, p. 292.

47.—"the greatest feat": Fitzhugh Lee, p. 48.

47.—"His campaign was unsurpassed": Bauer, p. 322.

48.—" 'The' engineer": Hitchcock, p. 277.

48.—wept with Joe Johnston: Long, p. 71.

48.—The meeting with the Mexican desperado: Freeman, Vol. I, pp. 285–86.

48.—"almost idolatrous" regard: Keyes, p. 206.

48.—$5 million a year: Ibid., p. 206.

48.—"Can't you cure poor Spec?": R. E. Lee, Jr., p. 8.

48.—It seemed to Lieutenant Raphael Semmes: Dowdey, p. 85.

48.—"I tell you": Cooke, *Robert E. Lee*, p. 512. Scott made the statement to William Preston, later a Confederate officer, who related it in a speech years later.

49.—"Where is my little boy?": R. E. Lee, Jr., p. 4.

49.—"golden epaulettes and all": Ibid., p. 11.

49.—"Just like that": William Mack Lee, a former slave of the Lee family, talked of his memories in an as-told-to article by James C. Young in the March 5, 1927 issue of *Collier's*. Besides being embarrassing, with William Mack Lee represented as remarking that darkies naturally love to steal, it is also inaccurate. (The ex-slave's clear memory of seeing General Lee offer his sword to General Grant, and the latter's refusal to accept it, a scene witnessed by no other person known to history, will serve as illustration of the article's grounding in firm fact.) Yet some of the details seem likely, and one or two are used in the body of this book. The ex-slave, described in the article as the only Negro ever to address the Virginia Legislature, was slated for depiction as holding Traveller's bridle in the Stone Mountain Memorial, Georgia.

49.—"I always knew that it was impossible": R. E. Lee, Jr., p. 9.

50.—"I might as well be a pile or a stone": Sanborn, p. 202.

50.—"My precious Annie": R. E. Lee, Jr., p. 14.

51.—"I wish boys would do what is right": Ibid., pp. 12–13.

51.—Cadet Whistler and the bridge: *New York Times*, April 25, 1982.

51.—"Don't you think": Freeman, Vol. I, p. 338.

51.—"Pa's delights": Sanborn, p. 219.

52.—"Why don't you wear your dresses longer?": Ibid., p. 206.

52.—"Who is *he*?": Ibid.

52.—The seven hens: Rister, p. 17.

53.—Katumse: Ibid., p. 21.

53.—"My rattlesnake": Ibid., p. 39.

54.—"My servants": Ibid., p. 81.

54.—"Their skill in cooking": Ibid., p. 113.

55.—"I almost dread him": MacDonald, pp. 125–26.

55–56.—Without alluding to himself or his wife: Hancock, p. 46. Mrs. Hancock remembered Lee telling her as a relatively junior officer, her husband Winfield Scott Hancock then being even lower in rank, "I consider it fatal to the future happiness of young married people, upon small provocation, to live apart, either for a short or long time. The result is invariably that they cease to be essential to each other." As a result of this advice, Mrs. Hancock dismissed thoughts of staying behind when her husband, later one of Lee's greatest opponents, went to distant California.

55–56.—Arlington matters: Freeman, Vol. I, p. 380ff.

VI

57.—She and the wife of another officer: Julia D. Grant, p. 68.

58.—inoffensive little chap: Garland, p. 113.

58.—Gore as a man, Grant as a boy: Richardson, p. 131. When years later the name of Ulysses S. Grant was second in renown only to that of Abraham Lincoln, the teacher-landlord, a Mr. W. A. Bacon, asked himself, so he told Richardson, "Grant, Grant; was not that a Lieutenant Grant who lived in my house with Captain Gore?"

59.—Delia Sheffield . . . saw him: McFeely, p. 47.

59.—"murder" for them: Lewis, p. 298.

59.—In Panama: McFeely, p. 47ff; Ulysses S. Grant, p. 116ff; Lewis, p. 300ff.

59.—Thirty-seven people died: Garland, p. 119.

60.—"My God, I've got the cholera": Lewis, *Captain Sam Grant*, p. 303.

61.—"Give my love to all at home": Ibid., p. 305.

61.—He had dreamt one night: McFeely, p. 50.

61–62.—Details on Grant's business ventures are in Garland, p. 123; in an article by John W. Emerson in the June 1897 edition of *Midland Monthly;* Richardson has material scattered throughout; McFeely covers the matter on p. 48ff and Lewis on p. 316ff.

62.—"I want to resign from the Army": Lewis, p. 315.

62.—"He seemed to be always sad": Ibid.

62.—McClellan's visit: Richardson, p. 145.

63.—"Does Ulys. walk yet?": Lewis, p. 320.

63.—His wages less than that of a cook: Ulysses S. Grant, p. 121.

63.—*"poverty, poverty":* McFeely, p. 53.

64.—"You do not know . . . I do nothing": Ibid., p. 52.

64.—On his drinking: That Grant drank prodigiously is an idea as fixed in history, McFeely accurately remarks, as that the Pilgrims ate turkey on Thanksgiving. In a paper considering the matter, prepared for delivery at the 1982 annual meeting of the organization of American Historians, Lyle W. Dorsett of the University of Denver concludes that Grant was an alcoholic of the binge type. All evidence indicates that Dorsett is correct.

64.—His membership in the Sons of Temperance: Lewis, p. 293ff.

64.—"If you soldiers would keep sober": Richardson, pp. 134–35.

65.—His problems with Buchanan: William C. Church, a military scholar and editor, corresponded at length with men who had known Grant during his Far West period. Their remembrances can be found in Church's Papers, Library of Congress.

66.—"Why, Grant": Garland, p. 128ff.

66.—Buckner's doings: Ibid., p. 129; Richardson, p. 149.

66.—"I never wished him to leave": Lewis, p. 338.

67.—West Point and the Army had ruined his son: Garland, p. 129.

67.—a very poor slave driver: "The Negroes did pretty much as they pleased," remarks Post, p. 35.

67.—"Is this my destiny?": Julia D. Grant, p. 78.

68.—A man with the air of an all-pervading bad luck: Garland, p. 137.

68.—The hat: Richardson, p. 153.

68.—"Good God": Lewis, p. 346.

69.—The broker gave him $22: The photo section of Hesseltine's book has a picture of the pawn ticket.

69.—"Old Ulysses S. Grant of the Fourth Infantry": Lewis, *Captain Sam Grant*, p. 347.

69.—His room in the Boggs house: Richardson, p. 159.

70.—A hardware store . . . Julia's father: Garland, p. 144.

71.—The meeting with Sherman: Lewis, *Sherman*, p. 97.

71.—Paralyzed at what he had come to: McFeely, p. 65.

71.—"He would have to take U.S. and his family home": Ross, p. 93.

71.—Two chairs under his arms: Garland, p. 148.

72.—It was the blue-caped coat . . . "I suppose people think it is strange": Ibid., p. 150.

72.—Not good at remembering the prices: Lewis, p. 377.

72.—"Mister, do you want to fight?": Jesse Root Grant, pp. 10–11.

VII

73.—Brown read in his Bible: Warch and Fanton, p. 1.

76.—Brown's follower sighted his rifle: Nelson, p. 146.

76.—"Aren't you old Osawatomie Brown?": Warch and Fenton, p. 64.

77.—"If you are uncomfortable": Davis, p. 13.

77.—"an honest conscientious old man": The future Mrs. George Pickett's father talked with Lee on a train shortly after the latter's capture of Brown. Mrs. Pickett recorded Lee's word in the December 1913 *Cosmopolitan*.

79.—"A divided heart": The letter was to Mrs. Anna Fitzhugh, Freeman, Vol. I, p. 411. Embarrassment? A divided heart? Coming from a man who all his life enjoyed the company of good-looking women? Who is married to a difficult woman increasingly invalided? But the page of history is blank on this matter. No proof of any romantic attachment on Lee's part has ever turned up.

79.—"My dear General": Freeman, Vol. I, p. 412.

80.—"How his spirit would be grieved": Fitzhugh Lee, p. 87.

80.—"I can anticipate": Ibid., pp. 420–21.

80.—"I am unable to realize": Ibid., pp. 421–22.

81.—"Any man who attempted by force": Chittenden, p. 38.

82.—"Old dotard!": Elliott, p. 692.

82.—"Who are these men?": Mrs. Caroline Darrow wrote of her talk with Lee in *Battles and Leaders*, Vol. I, p. 36.

82.—"it is reported that you concurred in Twiggs' surrender": Keyes, pp. 205–06.

82–83.—Scott was . . . strangely silent: Ibid., p. 206.

83.—" 'Where shall Virginia go?' ": Sandburg, Vol. I, p. 137.

84.—"If I could only mount a horse": Seward, pp. 167–68.

84.—"There is one officer": Ibid., p. 168.

84.—The dinner party with his relatives: Sanborn, p. 310.

86.—Blair offered the great answer: Long, p. 92; R. E. Lee, Jr., p. 27.

86.—"Since the Son of Man": Fitzhugh Lee, p. 89.

86.—"I could take no part in an invasion": Ibid., p. 88.

86.—"the greatest mistake of your life": Mason, p. 73.

86.—"Are you not well?": Helm, p. 185.

87.—"I must say": Freeman, Vol. I, p. 439.

88.—Attitudes of Rooney and Custis: Ibid., p. 442.

88.—"Slavery as an institution": Dowdey, p. 108.

89.—"I shall carry to the grave": R. E. Lee, Jr., pp. 24–25.

89.—"I have the honor": Ibid., p. 440.

VIII

90.—"I have been a Democrat all my life": Wilson, p. 48.

91.—"I think I ought to go into the service": Richardson, p. 179.

91.—got pine laths: Chetlain, p. 72.

92.—"very indifferently dressed": Lewis, *Captain Sam Grant*, p. 415.

93.—"The politicians have got everything here": Garland, p. 163.

93.—"Come to my office tomorrow": Woodward, p. 183.

93.—"I am tired of this work": Chetlain, p. 75.

93.—"A dead-beat military man": Garland, p. 164.

94.—The letter to the adjutant general: Grant reprints it on p. 143.

94.—The fruitless calls upon McClellan: Young, Vol. II, pp. 214–15.

95.—On the buffoonlike colonel: Garland, p. 166.

95.—"Just appoint him": Lewis, p. 426.

95.—" 'What a colonel!' ": Ibid., p. 427.

96.—"How-de-do, Colonel": Porter, p. 67.

96.—"The Quiet Man": Lewis, *Captain Sam Grant*, p. 428.

96.—"Don't talk to me about this Federal": Post, p. 94.

97.—"You can't fall out now": Lewis, p. 429.

97.—"Men, go to your quarters": Ibid., p. 430.

97.—The march against Colonel Harris: Ulysses S. Grant, pp. 148–49.

IX

99.—"Friend Robertson": E. D. Townsend, p. 5.

100.—"My husband has wept tears of blood": Freeman, Vol. I, p. 442.

100.—"As I think both parties are wrong": Dowdey, p. 134.

100.—"I had to meet the question": R. E. Lee, Jr., pp. 25–26.

100.—"I am now a private citizen": Ibid., pp. 26–27.

101.—He tried to find a copy of the music: R. E. Lee, Jr., p. 36.

101.—"I hope we have seen the last of secession": Freeman, Vol. I, p. 465.

101.—"one of the proudest recollections of my life": Jones, p. 140.

102.—"Mr. President and gentlemen": His words are engraved on the pedestal of a statue of him that stands on the site where he said them.

102.—"I believe there is treachery here": Dowdey, p. 148.

102.—"At heart Robert E. Lee is against us": Chesnut, p. 63.

103.—"He looks so cold": Ibid., p. 94.

103.—"What is General Lee going to do?": Jones, pp. 409–10.

103.—"Oh, that you could command peace": Fitzhugh Lee, p. 96.

104.—"Soldiers of the Army of the West": Ibid., p. 116.

104.—"If anyone had told me that the next time": R. E. Lee, Jr., p. 39.

104.—The campaign in northwest Virginia: Fitzhugh Lee, p. 116ff.

105.—"Granny" Lee: Connelly, p. 16.

105.—"Evacuating" Lee: Ibid., p. 17.

106.—"If Lee is not a general": Freeman, Vol. I, p. 607.

106.—where his father lay: Long writes of the visit, pp. 22–23.

106.—"Not at all cheering": Fitzhugh Lee, p. 132.

X

107.—"My standing": Ulysses S. Grant, p. 150.

108.—made good his debts: Post, p. 127.

108.—"Who would have dreamed": Woodward, p. 213.

108.—"cursed and went on": McFeely, p. 84.

108.—Rawlins' hatred of liquor: Wilson, p. 25.

109.—"Go, boys": Garland, p. 158.

109.—Method was to put all papers in his pockets: Woodward, p. 208.

109.—exotic Hungarian and German uniforms: Williams, p. 36.

110.—"I have come among you": McFeely, p. 91.

110.—The battle of Belmont: Ulysses S. Grant, pp. 161–67; Dana and Wilson, p. 51.

112.—On Halleck: Fuller (p. 76) remarks: "A cautious, witless pedant. A type to be met with in every war."

112.—"my plans were preposterous": Ulysses S. Grant, p. 170.

113.—Crushed the papers in his hand: Lew Wallace, *Battles and Leaders*, Vol. I, p. 422.

114.—In St. Louis: Post, p. 92; the railroad man's thoughts are in Cadwallader, p. 350.

115.—Halleck's complaints: Conger, pp. 205ff.

116.—Rawlins replied: Wilson, p. 68.

117.—The money owed Longstreet: Undated newspaper clipping, Grant Family Papers, Library of Congress.

117.—Background of McClellan: He all too accurately describes himself in his book, of which it was said that it defamed him more than his worst enemies. Rusling speaks of him, p. 36ff; James Harrison Wilson's unpublished study of him can be read in the Wilson Papers, Library of Congress.

117.—"The people call upon me": McClellan, p. 85.

118.—"It may be": Ibid., p. 173.

119.—"By direction": Halleck's correspondences, as indicated above, are to be found in every Grant biography.

119–120.—Shiloh description: Ulysses S. Grant, p. 195, and in all books on the Civil War.

120.—he was mad: Lewis, *Sherman*, p. 201.

120.—he would kill himself: Ibid., p. 204.

122.—"I can't spare this man": McClure, p. 179.

XI

124.—"Isn't he a rare bird?": Williams, p. 45.

124.—Rascals . . . hounds . . . fools: McClellan's book and his letters to his wife therein teem with such characterizations of his superiors.

124.—"No one but McClellan": Sandburg, Vol. I, p. 474.

125.—"in defiance of Scripture": Ibid., p. 490.

125.—"Richmond *must* be defended": Dowdey, p. 202.

127.—Gray also was the horse he rode: Laura Spencer Portor [sic] and Charles Marshall Graves wrote the story of the horse's life in the January 1908 *Ladies' Home Journal*.

128–129.—"Mystery is the secret of success": Mason, p. 103.

129.—"We are here fortifying our lines": Alexander, pp. 110–11.

130.—"Stop, stop!": Freeman, Vol. II, p. 153.

131.—a trifle disheveled: Dowdey, p. 231.

131.—"Those are A. P. Hill's men": Ibid., p. 232.

131.—"Who is all this army?": Harrison, pp. 72–73. Mrs. Harrison's future husband was an aide to President Davis.

131.—"I am glad to see you": Freeman, Vol. II, p. 153.

132.—He remembered always: R. E. Lee, Jr., pp. 73–74.

132.—Not a muscle quivered: Stiles, p. 98.

132.—"We've got him": Ibid., p. 99.

133.—Mrs. Lee's note: Freeman, Vol. II, p. 264.

134.—The suffering of his men haunted him: The letters will be found in McClellan's book.

134.—Kearney said . . . Hooker volunteered: Sandburg, Vol. I, pp. 495–98.

135.—Pope was tall, impressive: G. A. Townsend, p. 221.

136.—Pope's trousers: French, p. 11.

136.—Pope's pronouncements: Sandburg, Vol. I, pp. 515ff.

136.—"miscreant Pope": Freeman, Vol. II, p. 264.

137.—one arm held straight out: "A strange habit," Long remarks, p. 264.

138.—"How close?": George Taylor Lee, the son of Robert E. Lee's brother Charles Carter Lee, was told of the extreme tension by General R. F. Hoke. He wrote of Hoke's words in the *South Atlantic Quarterly*, July 1927.

138.—"I observe": Ibid.

138.—"What are you doing here": Freeman, Vol. II, pp. 339–40.

140.—the sight and sound was magnificent: von Borcke, Vol. I, p. 185.

141.—"I hate to part with McClellan": Davis, *Jeb Stuart*, p. 248.

142.—"Oh, those men!": Williams, p. 208.

143.—"It is well that war is so terrible": Fitz Lee, p. 283.

XII

145.—So that Grant would not overhear: James Harrison Wilson, p. 92.

145.—if his opinion was desired: "I was little more than an observer," Grant writes on p. 224: "My position was embarrassing."

145.—no more influence than a lame mule: Keyes, p. 216.

145.—The conversation about leaving: Lewis, *Sherman*, pp. 235–36.

147.—an order barring all Jews: discussed in Von Bort's pamphlet-length book, in McFeely, pp. 123–24; and in Wilson, p. 96.

147.—Major General J.F.C. Fuller discusses the Vicksburg campaign in his *Decisive Battles of the U.S.A.* (New York: Harper and Brothers, 1942), Chapter VIII, as does Goodenough, p. 93ff.

148.—how their chief's mind worked: Henry Adams quotes Badeau on p. 268.

149.—Julia gave him mustard footbaths: Ross, p. 138.

150.—"foolish, drunken, stupid Grant": Woodward, p. 292.

150.—Objections of his officers: Fuller, *Decisive Battles*, p. 260.

152.—"I want to congratulate you": Lewis, *Sherman*, p. 274.

152.—Grant got drunk: Cadwallader, p. 103ff.

153.—"Dear General": Wilson, p. 128.

XIII

154.—"the Beautiful Captain": Shanks, p. 191.

155.—"I was at Bull Run the other day": Shanks, p. 182.

155.—"Swing him before sundown": Ibid., p. 76.

155.—"Only those generals": Ibid., p. 79

155.—"If you get to Richmond, General—": Sandburg, Vol. II, p. 86.

156.—Now "Mr. F. J. Hooker": R. E. Lee, Jr., p. 93.

156.—"barroom and brothel": Hebert, p. 180.

157.—"What a cruel thing is war": R. E. Lee, Jr., pp. 88–89.

157.—"Captain, what do you young men mean?": Freeman, Vol. II, p. 507.

159.—"It's all right, Couch": *Battles and Leaders*, Vol. III, p. 161.

161.—*in the full realization of all that soldiers dream of:* Maurice, pp. 172–73.

163.—"My God!": Brooks, p. 61.

164.—"If he is there tomorrow": Longstreet, pp. 358–59.

164.—"Look at Pharaoh's army": Sandburg, Vol. II, p. 339.

165.—"where have you been?": Davis, *Jeb Stuart*, p. 334.

165.—Details on Pickett's charge can be found in all histories of the war.

166.—"All will come right in the end.": Fremantle, p. 268.

167.—"this has been a hard day": Imboden wrote of the conversation in *Galaxy* for April 1871.

168.—"Oh, I don't know": Rusling, p. 16.

XIV

169.—"Retain your side arms": S. H. Beckwith, Grant's Telegrapher in Wilson and Simon, pp. 82–83.

170.—"I knew you at sight!": Wilson, p. 163.

170.—"the only man that can whip the rebs every time": Roth, pp. 21–22.

170.—they had expected a swaggering magnifico: Porter, p. 14.

171.—"That's damned ungenerous": Shanks, p. 154.

171.—"All we needed was a leader!": Dana and Wilson, p. 149.

171.—Lee's letter of resignation and Davis' reply: Long, pp. 496–97.

172.—The meeting with Johnson is described in Dodge, p. 139 and in Perkins, pp. 143–45.

172.—The night out: Dodge, pp. 139–41 and Perkins, pp. 144–45.

173.—"My father's table": Fred Grant wrote of his experiences in *Outlook*, 1898, pp. 533ff.

174.—Brady's talk with Grant at the station: Meredith, p. 162.

174.—Parlor A: Chittenden, p. 318.

175.—Word spread: Fred Grant described the scene in a speech to the Illinois Commandery of the Loyal Legion of the United States in January 1910; the speech was published in pamphlet form.

175.—"It was the only real mob I ever saw": Brooks, p. 135.

176.—"anybody will not do!": Stoddard, p. 217.

176.—Sheets of glass poured down: Meredith, p. 162.

178.—"Bobby Lee" . . . "Jeffy D": Bates, p. 205.

XV

180.—Signs of Lee's temper: Noted in Taylor, *Four Years*, p. 77, and by Charles Venable in *Battles and Leaders*, Vol. IV, p. 240.

180.—"You wait and see": Ranson wrote of his experiences in *Harper's Monthly* for February 1911.

180.—not safe to breathe normally about him: The future President Woodrow Wilson spoke of his reaction in a 1909 speech printed in 1924 by the University of North Carolina Press.

181.—it took God to make a man like Marse Robert: Freeman, Vol. III, p. 245.

181.—Wolseley's views: Found in *Macmillan's*, March 1887.

182.—"Not at all": Ross, pp. 161–62.

XVI

185.—"There was nothing marked in his appearance": C. F. Adams, pp. 271–72.

185.—"There is a habit": Wilson, pp. 426–27.

187.—"Leave things as they are": Wilkeson, p. 41.

187.—"I never maneuver": Cooke, *Hammer and Rapier*, p. 228.

187.—"We have got to whip them": Taylor, *Four Years*, p. 207.

187.—"We might have him to breakfast": Brooks, p. 264.

188.—"Is Imperial Caesar about": Dana and Wilson, p. 422.

188.—"I will agree to be there in about four days": Porter, pp. 43–44.

189.—Little pop-pops: Hopkins, p. 145.

189.—Eighteen-year-old farm boy: Schaff, p. 127.

189.—it seemed as if Warren had never had a greater surprise: Ibid., p. 126.

190.—Grant's breakfast and apparel are described by Porter, p. 41ff.

190.—His whittling, incessant that day, was only rarely taken up ever again.

192.—Schaff describes his thoughts on commanding the Army of the Potomac, p. 203ff.

193.—Wing tells of his adventures in his pamphlet-length book.

194.—"That man will fight us every day": Years later Longstreet told Porter what he had said; Porter quotes him, p. 47.

194.—"My God, General McGowan": Alexander, p. 503.

196.—the pot would be full in an instant: Wilkeson, p. 72.

196.—gloves were intatters: Porter, p. 65.

196.—"This is a crisis": Ibid., p. 69.

197.—"I am heartily tired": Ibid., p. 70.

197.—Wilkeson wrote in his book that he heard it fifty times: p. 79.

197.—"I don't believe it": Shanks, p. 103.

197.—the sound of muffled sobs: Wilson, p. 216. The two officers were Rawlins and Theodore Bowers, Rawlins' trusted aide. Schaff also reports that he heard sobs, p. 327.

197.—"Unpleasant thoughts ran riot": Cadwallader relates his thoughts and his talk with Grant, pp. 181–83.

198.—"In deep suspense": Hitchcock, p. 462.

199.—"a filthy young man: Wing relates his experiences in his pamphlet-book. They are amplified in Tarbell's short biography of Wing.

200.—"General Grant is not going to retreat": Gordon, p. 268.

200.—"Tonight Lee will be retreating south": Lyman, p. 102.

201.—a triumphal procession: Porter, p. 79.

201.—the supreme moment in the life: Sherman told his opinion to Porter, adding that he had written Grant that if Wellington could have heard of the move he "would have jumped out of his boots." Porter, p. 291.

202.—Taylor and Venable's thoughts: Taylor, *General Lee,* p. 238.

202.—"the brains of the two foemen": Gordon, pp. 269–70.

202.—"Well may you order us to move on": Freeman, Vol. II, p. 347.

203.—"Pooh, men": General Martin McMahon writes in *Battles and Leaders,* Vol. IV, p. 175, that Sedgwick repeated the elephant remark several times.

203.—"Is he really dead?": Porter, p. 90.

204.—"We shall never forget that particular sound": Briggs, p. 10.

205.—"Did he say that?": O'Connor, p. 161.

206.—"I can scarcely think of him without weeping": Gordon, p. 273.

207.—The conversation with General Johnson: Described by Porter, pp. 104–05.

207.—to conceal his emotion: Lyman, p. 111.

207.—"you shall not lead my men in a charge!": Gordon, p. 279.

208.—"without a parallel": Ibid., p. 284.

208.—a parson brought to read the funeral services: Schaff, p. 298.

208.—"just a scratch of the pen?": Richardson, p. 404.

209.—the wagons: Chittenden, pp. 251–52.

209.—"the most eloquent address": Page, p. 389.

211.—"to spot almost at the very instant": Gordon, p. 297.

211.—I wish they were all dead": Mason, pp. 322–23.

212.—"Why did you not do as Jackson would have done?": Dowdey, p. 463.

213.—"We must strike them a blow": Venable wrote of the conversation in Vol. XIV, Southern Historical Society Papers.

214.—The talk with the old woman: Porter, pp. 147–51.

215.—"What does this conduct mean?": Ibid., pp. 164–65.

215.—"too feeble to move about": Ibid., p. 167.

216.—"a fighting general": Wilkeson, p. 88.

216.—"as expressionless as a pine board": Ibid., p. 124.

216.—"a cripple or a corpse": Lewis, *Sherman,* pp. 394–95.

217.—"This exhibition of tailoring": Porter, p. 174.

217.—"if he breaks your line?": Ibid., p. 180.

218.—"I think Grant has had his eyes opened": Meade, Vol. II, p. 201.

219.—"Grant is beating his head against a wall . . . pretty tired of it": Taylor, *Four Years,* pp. 207–08.

219.—"it will become a siege": Jones, p. 40.

220.—"My troops do not charge": Richardson, p. 418.

221.—"The city is ours!": Wilkeson, p. 159.

221.—"Petersburg at that hour": Cullen, p. 9.

222.—"What are you thinking about, Baldy?": Shanks, p. 107.

222.—"The rage of the enlisted men": Cullen, p. 12.

223.—"his place was here": James Harrison Wilson, p. 243.

225.—"This army is nearly demoralized": Dowdey, p. 496.

225.—"A deadly calm": Brooks, p. 157.

226.—"Now, Mr. Secretary": Ross, p. 171.

226.—"He is a butcher": Keckley, pp. 133–34.

226.—"We could blow that damned fort": Pleasants, p. 32.

227.—Explosion and subsequent events: Ibid., p. 75ff.

227.—"If you are the general you claim to be": Cadwallader, pp. 214–15.

227.—"Nine-tenths of our bleeding, bankrupt, almost dying country": Lewis, *Sherman*, pp. 394–95.

228.—"I have seen your dispatch": Porter, p. 279.

228.—"Does General Grant smoke?": Cadwallader, p. 231.

229.—" 'Father, we have sinned!' ": Cooke, p. 287.

229.—"I grieve with you at the death of your gallant son": Freeman, Vol. III, p. 514.

230.—"Who are those people out there?": Ibid., Vol. III, p. 480.

230.—"I have never looked into such eyes as his": Ibid., Vol. III, p. 525.

230.—Sherman's view: Lewis, *Sherman*, p. 644.

230.—the question did not concern him: Jones, p. 143.

231.—a brigadier of cavalry's star: Jones, p. 148. Lee customarily wore a colonel's uniform.

231.—"Why, of course, my dear child": Harrison, p. 150.

231.—"There have been times in my life": Cadwallader, p. 351.

231.—"do you expect to take that yellow dog of yours into Richmond?": French, p. 17.

231.—it was sublime, heroic: Gerrish, p. 209.

231.—Christmas Eve: Cadwallader, pp. 279–80.

232.—"This, then, is my turkey?": *Harper's Magazine*, Vol. 122, p. 333.

232.—"If the soldiers get it": Dowdey, p. 517.

233.—"To them he represented cause, country and all": R. E. Lee, Jr., quotes Marshall on p. 138.

233.—"You should have seen Uncle Robert's dinner today": Pryor, p. 331.

233.—"when I reached my headquarters": Ibid., p. 336.

234.—"you know my weaknesses": Porter, p. 283.

235.—"General" . . . "Mr. Grant" . . . "Ulyss" . . . "Dudy" . . . "Victor": Ibid., p. 284.

235.—His bathing habits: Porter, p. 126; Woodward, p. 26.

235.—felt a ruthlessness: Keyes, p. 222.

236.—more forceful than the violent actions of another: Jesse Root Grant, p. 197.

236.—Only once had his father spanked him: Ibid., p. 18.

236.—"Yes, that's Rufus": Mrs Pickett wrote in the June 1914 *Cosmopolitan*.

236.—"But, you know . . . Blood-blood": Ibid.

236–237.—On John and Hetty Pegram: Harrison, pp. 202–03. Mrs. Harrison was Hetty Pegram's cousin and close friend.

237.—"The warmest instincts": Jones, p. 145.

238.—THERE IS A TRUE GLORY: Ibid., p. 145.

238.—Ord said to Longstreet: Longstreet, pp. 581–86.

238.—"How enchanting": Julia D. Grant, p. 141.

239.—a look of painful depression: Gordon, p. 385ff.

240.—clump through one round: Porter, p. 393.

240.—One . . . was "Yankee Doodle": Childs, p. 110.

241.—Mrs. Lincoln's doings: Largely taken from the accounts of Porter and Badeau and Captain Barnes of *The Bat*, are described in Sandburg, Vol. IV, p. 147ff.

242.—suggestions . . . to end the siege: Porter, pp. 372–73.

243.—"good deal of terror in cold steel": Ibid., p. 424.

243.—"I was afraid, every morning": Ulysses S. Grant, p. 592.

244.—"Lee was an active force": Young, Vol. II, p. 303.

244.—kissed her again and again: Porter, p. 425.

244.—"your luck is my luck": Richardson, p. 459.

245.—"You, only, General": Pryor, p. 337.

245.—"I tell you": Porter, p. 429.

245.—"I want you men to understand": Chamberlain, p. 144.

246.—"Go right over there": Porter, p. 439.

246.—"April fool!": Ibid., p. 442.

247.—"Let 'em come on!": Cooke, p. 293.

248.—from the 44th and following psalms: G. A. Townsend, p. 347ff.

248.—a look of rage: John Esten Cooke wrote in Appleton's Journal, Jan. 9, 1875.

248.—stamped it into the mud: Dowdey, p. 514.

249.—Taylor told of his marriage in *Four Years*, pp. 209–10, and *General Lee*, p. 277.

249–251.—Details on Richmond are found throughout Patrick.

251.—the most ridiculous moment of his life: Cadwallader, p. 310.

251.—"I have got my army safe out of its breastworks": Cooke, *Robert E. Lee*, p. 451.

251.—"Do you know that man?": Smith, p. 67.

252.—A fit of weeping took her: Julia D. Grant, p. 151.

252.—"Keep your command together": Long, p. 415.

253.—"Did those people surprise your command?": Davis, *To Appomattox*, p. 170.

253.—a picture of Lee: Patrick, p. 33.

254.—"Lee *is* in a bad fix": Richardson, p. 472.

254.—"Tomatoes are very good": Davis, *To Appomattox*, p. 221.

255.—"My God!": For many years Longstreet's description of this event was accepted. The recent discovery of a letter from William Mahone to Longstreet shows Mahone was the source of the story, and I have used Mahone's wording, which is slightly different from Longstreet's published version. The letter can be found in *Civil War Times Illustrated*, Jan. 1971.

255.—"Lee should surrender now": Davis, *To Appomattox*, p. 242.

255.—"General Lee! Uncle Robert!": Cooke, p. 300.

256.—"I hardly think it is necessary": Wise, p. 416ff.

256.—"my son" made him feel as if he would have gladly died: Ibid., p. 430.

258.—"play 'Now You'll Remember Me' ": Julia D. Grant, p. 151.

258.—"This is the end": Wise, pp. 433–35.

260.—"In blood and flames and torture": Ibid., p. 454.

260.—"Be prudent, stranger": Miles, pp. 39–41.

260.—had never seen such marching: Gerrish, p. 251.

261.—"I trust it has not come to that!": Susan P. Lee, p. 402.

261.—"I would answer no such letter": Davis, *To Appomattox*, p. 280.

262.—"He did not propose to surrender!": Cadwallader, pp. 317–19.

262.—"I will strike that man a blow in the morning!" Ranson wrote of the overheard conversation in *Harper's Monthly* for February 1911.

263.—"The race is not to them that's got": Maurice, pp. 259–60.

263.—"The best thing that could happen to me today": Porter, pp. 462–64.

264.—With the others he stacked his rifle: Gerrish, p. 254ff.

265.—"to a frazzle": Long, p. 421.

265.—"There is nothing left me to do": Ibid., p. 421.

266.—"You had better read it aloud": Cadwallader, pp. 321–23.

266.—"Oh, General": Long, p. 422.

266.—"How easily I could be rid of this": Mason, p. 404.

267.—"I have probably to be Grant's prisoner": Susan P. Lee, p. 404.

267.—a mysterious quality of great silence: Cooke, *Hammer and Rapier*, p. 324.

267.—his only valuable trophy of the war: Cadwallader, p. 324.

268.—"Maybe my house will do": Maurice, p. 269.

268.—a strange sense of some presence invisible . . . "Anthing like that would have been too little": Chamberlain, p. 246.

270.—The surrender: It does not seem practical to the author that he give a citation for each sentence spoken or move made during the proceedings at the McLean house, surely one of the most written-about moments in history. Among the observers recording impressions that differ only in slight fashion, and agree on all important points, are Porter, Marshall, Sheridan, Badeau, and Parker. Grant's description in his book is thin, but he talked about the proceedings at length with Richardson, who printed what he had said. It is interesting that in his book Jesse Root Grant says (p. 29) that he never heard his father refer to the surrender in later years. Lee made little mention of the matter, saying only that Grant's actions merited the highest praise. The publications and exhibits at Appomattox Courthouse National Park are very helpful.

273.—four months before his birth at the Tonawanda reservation near Buffalo: Armstrong, p. 14.

275.—Custer jumped on his horse: Custer, p. 159.

276.—"Ingalls, . . . do you remember?": Porter, p. 489.

276.—Rage seized him: Davis, *To Appomattox*, p. 345.

278.—"Don't you know me?": The meeting has been described by several writers, R. E. Lee, Jr. being one, on p. 154.

279.—"I would not distress these people": Julia D. Grant, p. 153.

279.—1,000 freed slaves sang: Sandburg, Vol. IV, p. 219.

280.—The cabinet meeting: Ibid., p. 265–66.

280.—would not spend an evening in the company of the woman: Ross, p. 188ff.

281.—the last musket stacked: Chamberlain, p. 261ff.

281.—"Well, old fellows": Gerrish, p. 262.

281.—Bingham's experiences are described by A. K. McKelway in *Harper's Weekly*, April 15, 1916.

282.—"Polly, come with me to Richmond": Flood, p. 36.

282.—"There was no excitement, no harrahing": DeLeon, p. 367.

XVII

283.—a well-stocked wine cellar: Cadwallader, pp. 119–20.

284.—did not have a single book dealing with military matters: Coolidge, p. 383.

284.—"you've become a great man, haven't you?": Woodward, p. 14.

284.—"I will make you a speech": Julia D. Grant, p. 164.

285.—The struggle between Johnson and the Radical Republicans: Details throughout Smith.

286.—"As quick as I'd talk politics": Hesseltine, p. 106.

286.—"The man who dwells behind a mask": Briggs, p. 45.

287.—"Traitor! Liar!": Smith, pp. 180–81.

288.—Barnes said he would take his pulse: Ibid., p. 182.

288.—"it would not be convenient for me": Ibid., p. 186.

290.—Grant as Secretary of War: Ibid., p. 213ff.

291.—His resignation: Ibid., p. 221ff.

292.—Talk with Henderson: Ibid., p. 245.

XVIII

294.—how gentle Fitz Lee was: Weitzel's aide, Thomas Thatcher Graves, wrote of his visit to Lee's house in *Battles and Leaders*, Vol. IV, p. 728.

295.—"I followed you for four years": Riley, pp. 52–53. Mildred Lee told the story to a Washington College student, who told it to Riley when, in the 'teens of the present century, Riley contacted then-mature men who had been students during Lee's presidency of their college and asked for reminiscences of him.

295.—"Good-bye, Colonel!": R. E. Lee, Jr., pp. 158–59.

296.—"you will not be expected to do any work": Page, pp. 647–48.

296.—"It is utterly impossible": Meredith, pp. 195–96.

296.—two little girls . . . He liked to watch Traveller: R. E. Lee., Jr., pp. 166–67.

297.—"I am ready to meet any charges": Jones, p. 201.

297.—"When can these men be tried?": Garland, p. 332.

297.—The meeting of the trustees: Described in Riley, pp. 2–3.

298.—General Lee must be the guest of his family: R. E. Lee, Jr., p. 183.

299.—"You know I am a poor hand": Ibid., p. 193.

299.—"Mister" for the first time in their lives: Riley, p. 139.

299.—"Lee the man must give way to Lee the patriot": Taylor, *Four Years*, p. 76.

300.—One good reason is enough": R. E. Lee, Jr., p. 332.

300.—"we have no printed rules": Former Washington College student John B. Collyar wrote of Lee's remark to Collyar's brother, also a Washington College student, in the *Confederate Veteran* for 1893, p. 265.

301.—"I'm sorry your horse has sore feet": The story is told in varying ways: Riley, p. 21 and Dowdey, p. 670 agree on essentials.

301.—"Yesterday was such a pretty day": Riley, p. 110.

301.—"He does his Mathematics pretty well": Jones, p. 130.

301.—Not injure health by overzealous studying: Ibid., p. 129.

301.—"in a certain way an effeminate man": Riley, p. 43.

301.—"*you* were a failure": Fishwick, p. 178.

301.—did not step with the drumbeat: Riley, p. 35.

302.—cowards and base men . . . such scum": MacDonald, p. 231.

302.—our friend is accustomed to make his prayers too long": Jones, pp. 426–27.

302.—Where is my little Miss Mildred": Flood, p. 130.

302.—"The number of old maids here appalls me": Dowdey, p. 670.

303.—"take compassion on a poor bachelor": R. E. Lee, Jr., p. 309.

303.—"the Old Testament or the New Testament": T. Harry Williams, *Journal of Southern History*, February 1955.

303.—"I thought *he* could do anything": R. E. Lee, Jr., pp. 266–67.

303.—activities of the Man in the Moon: Riley, p. 82.

304.—"Our feline companions": R. E. Lee, Jr., p. 248.

XIX

305.—"The responsibilities of the position I feel": Hesseltine, p. 143.

305.—"I hope you're satisfied": Ross, p. 204.

305.—"as modest, diffident, and shy": Briggs, p. 86.

306.—"Were you a contributor": Hesseltine, p. 154.

306.—"one had seemed to know him so well": Henry Adams, p. 266ff.

308.—"She, herself, is new": Ames, p. 261.

308.—hard and old: Ibid., p. 254.

308.—Like the gills of a fish out of water: Briggs, p. 169.

308.—"no man during the existence of the republic": Ibid., p. 201.

309.—"ambrosial soup": Ibid., p. 204ff.

309.—walls were hung with purple and gold: Ames, p. 174.

309.—"Breakfast is ready": Crook, p. 179.

310.—"I am right behind the throne": Henry Adams in *The Westminister Review*, October, 1870.

311.—"damned old scoundrel": Ibid.

305–322.—Details on Grant's Presidency can be found throughout Schouler.

312.—a swindle, a corrupt job, a monster job: The Grant Family Scrapbook, Grant Papers, Library of Congress, contain newspaper clippings using these terms.

313.—Parker forced out amid charges of corruption. He was probably innocent. His life is detailed by Armstrong.

313.—"When he come he bring everything in little bag": Armstrong, p. 140.

313–314.—On Belknap: Robert C. Prickett wrote on him in *North Dakota History*, January, 1950.

314.—"the Sylph": Hesseltine, p. 381ff.

314.—"Political vermin infest[ed] the government": Hesseltine, p. 218.

315.—"Very rich, very coarse": Updated clipping, Grant Papers.

315.—"No damned nigger": McFeely, p. 376.

316.—"plain, simple Nellie Grant": Briggs, pp. 355–56.

316.—"Fair, fat and forty": Ibid., p. 169.

316.—"General Grant thinks her beautiful": Ibid., p. 258.

316.—Face down upon her bed: Crook, p. 186.

317.—"false and strange gods": Armstrong, p. 173.

317.—"self-seeking . . . indolent . . . neglectful": Hesseltine, p. 276.

318.—"Every intelligent man": Henry Adams, p. 277.

318.—"gladly sacrifice him": Lewis, *Sherman*, p. 606.

318.—"The wreck of General Grant's fame": Schouler, p. 202.

319.—*He had a great many distresses:* Childs, p. 84.

320.—a millstone around the neck of the Republican party: Hesseltine, p. 373.

322.—"I like Grant": Schouler, pp. 145–46.

XX

324.—"I much enjoy the charms of civil life": Jones, p. 118.

324.—"I shall now introduce myself": Bond, p. 31ff.

324.—"General Grant is coming next week": Ibid., p. 39.

324.—"If you ever again presume": Flood, p. 188.

325.—"dismissed from Washington College": Fishwick, p. 140.

325.—"A sweet young friend of ours": George Taylor Lee wrote of his uncle in the *South Atlantic Quarterly* for July 1927.

326.—"Experience will teach you": R. E. Lee, Jr., p. 248.

326.—"I hope that this is the last wedding": Flood, p. 130.

327.—"Left his cap in the back parlor": Allan, p. 216.

327.—a basket of nuts, a picture of a dog: Ibid., p. 221.

327.—"Now that is very inconvenient": A. K. McKelway, *Harper's Weekly*, April 15, 1916.

328.—"Oh, Doctor": Jones, p. 441.

328.—"You don't like this hat?": R. E. Lee, Jr., p. 348.

328.—The meeting with Grant: Freeman, Vol. IV, p. 520, sums up all available information, remarking how much one might have wished for "something colorful, something dramatic." Unfortunately, it wasn't that way.

330.—A vacation: Details are largely from R. E. Lee, Jr., p. 379ff, who got his information from his sister Agnes, the only person accompanying their father for the duration of the trip, and from letters written home by the travelers. Freeman, Vol. IV, p. 444ff, also covers the trip.

330.—It seemed impossible to Will White: Flood, p. 233.

331.—At Augusta: It was here that the son of a local Presbyterian minister had the opportunity to stare into Lee's face. Woodrow Wilson was then thirteen years of age and generally addressed as "Tommy."

332.—"I think that I am the very oldest man": Bond, p. 51.

333.—"I will give that sum": Jones, p. 448.

333.—"Let me pour you a cup of tea": Mrs. Lee wrote a description of her husband's last illness in a letter to a friend, R. H. Chilton. It is reprinted in *Virginia Magazine of History and Biography*, January 1927.

XXI

By far the greater part of this chapter is extracted from John Russell Young's monumental work on Grant's trip. A reporter for the New York *Herald*, he filed tens of thousands of words during the journey and then put it all together in his book. Other sources are noted below.

336.—"do you know Her Majesty is a fine whip?": Julia D. Grant, p. 210.

336.—Penelope was along: Ibid., p. 219.

338.—"I will leave you alone and shut the door": Ibid., p. 259.

340.—"General Grant don't speak English": Keating, p. 116.

341.—they were carted along: Keating makes much of this, p. 176ff.

343.—"Oh, Ulyss, . . . how unwise": Julia D. Grant, p. 321.

344.—"Set that hen again": Twain, p. 47.

344.—"Ward is making them all rich": Julia D. Grant, p. 327.

344.—"Your father and mother have come": Cantacuzene, p. 30.

345.—It was undignified of him: Lewis, *Sherman*, p. 639. Sherman felt Grant was putting his war fame "into a banking venture as part of its capital."

345.—It was bewildering: Philadelphia *Ledger*, April 4, 1885.

345.—"I'll lend you the money personally": Woodward, p. 487.

346.—"I don't see how I can trust any human being again": Woodward, p. 489.

346.—hitching a ride to the railroad station: Cantacuzene, p. 24.

347.—ornaments from hats worn at Belmont . . . commissions from brevet second lieutenant: Frank Mack, who covered the story for the Associated Press, wrote of his remembrances in the *Saturday Evening Post*, February 12, 1910.

348.—"the monumental injustice of the Nineteenth century": Twain, p. 32.

348.—"any unknown Comanche Indian": Ibid., p. 35.

348–349.—"have a penny in the house": Ibid., p. 41.

349.—"In my rough traveling suit": Ulysses S. Grant, p. 630.

349.—"The disease is serious, epithelial in character": Douglas wrote a description of his treatment of Grant. Several hundred pages long, it is in the Douglas Papers, Library of Congress.

350.—"For a day or two": Childs, p. 113.

350.—"If you could imagine what molten lead would be like": Ibid.

351.—"are you in earnest with this suggestion?": Mack, *Saturday Evening Post*.

351.—"You can see the condition": Ibid.

352.—would not have uttered alive or dead: Twain, p. 70.

353.—Morphine, potassium permanganate, etc.: Douglas Papers.

353.—Sherman's visit: Cantacuzene, p. 39.

XXII

355.—"You must make haste and get well": Jones, p. 449.

356.—"I saw he had taken leave of earth": Mrs. Lee's letter, *Virginia Magazine of History and Biography*, January 1927.

356.—"Tell Hill he *must* come up!": Ibid.

357.—"Strike the tent": Jones, p. 450.

XXIII

358.—"My God! Is that the general?": John Hancock Douglas in the *New York Commerical*, June 16, 1885.

359.—"Do you put that off": Mack, op. cit.

359.—"Thank God I see you alive!": Ibid.

360.—*Since coming to this beautiful climate:* Douglas Papers.

361.—"Grant" . . . "Buckner": Julia D. Grant, p. 330.

362.—*I notice that your little girls and Julie get along very happily:* Douglas Papers.

362.—"you gratify the wishes of U. S. Grant": Cantacuzene, p. 162.

361.—"Grandpapa isn't quite so well, dear": Ibid., p. 51.

361.—"The book is killing him!": Ibid., p. 47.

362.—*I cannot help repeating two advertisements:* Douglas Papers.

362.—Hundreds of thousands of dollars: Some $450,000, actually.

363.—"Quick, papa wants you": Cantacuzene, p. 52.

363.—"I've brought grandpa a wreath": Ibid., p. 55

364.—The funeral train is described in dozens of newspaper clippings in the Grant Family Scrapbook, Library of Congress.

365.—The lying-in-state and funeral are detailed in clippings in the Grant Family Scrapbook.

XXIV

368.—The chapel never seems empty: Author's observations on a recent trip.

369.—The vast tomb is magnificently placed: Author's observations.

369.—"I am the wife of Jefferson Davis": Perkins, p. 322.

369.—He remembered the column of fours . . . *And lo!:* Burdette, p. 197ff.

INDEX

Gene Smith is the author of the best-selling *When the Cheering Stopped: The Last Years of Woodrow Wilson*, which was a Main Selection of Book-of-the-Month Club, and *The Shattered Dream: Herbert Hoover and the Great Depression*. A well-known writer, he also breeds race horses and lives in upstate New York with his wife and daughter.